one hundred and one things to do.

BIS Publishers
Herengracht 370-372
1016 CH Amsterdam
Postbus 323
1000 AH Amsterdam
The Netherlands
T +31 (0)20 5247560
F +31 (0)20 5247557
bis@bispublishers.nl
www.bispublishers.nl

ISBN 978-90-6369-144-8

do please read by Tyler Whisnand/KesselsKramer
Edited by Erik Kessels/KesselsKramer
Designed by Krista Rozema/KesselsKramer

Printed and bound in Singapore

one hundred and one things to do.

do is the ever-changing brand that depends on what you do. inside this book you will find 101 ideas, inspirations, projects and initiatives all within the involving brand mentality of do.
do is an initiative of communications agency kesselskramer.

by kesselskramer
BIS Publishers

one hundred and one things to do.

do please read.

Over the past 101 years, like it or not, brands have become a significant part of our lives. Perhaps the most meaningful way to define a brand has come by judging the type of relationship it forms with people. Probably the most successful, likable and enduring brands, in fact, behave like people. They are alive and open to suggestion and respond to current events, ideas and trends. Many brands, however, tend to behave selfishly and unresponsively. They prefer to talk only about themselves and how great they are.

It seems that the more interesting brands allow an entry into their purpose, their ideas and their philosophy. They ask for input and even collaboration.

Nowadays, we all have different notions of what brands are. To some, brands are just corporate logos that appear on advertisements. Others see brands as entire worlds that have limitless possibilities. Still others find brands just a fact of life and not of particular conscious interest.

In general, brands have some kind of value but their cache and worth are often hard to measure. Several systems have been tried, including polls, ratings, extensive research and the ever-popular Nielsen data. But brand relationships can be quite spontaneous. Perhaps the key component of value is in people's perception of a brand's behavior and worth. Brands have personalities ranging from the dull to the exciting, from mundane to innovative. Some brands are reliable. Some are risky. Some are steady and never change. Some are young. Some are intellectual. Some are rare. Some exist for 5 seconds. Some go on forever. Some are all of the above.

At the moment, the number of brands in modern society is growing at an ever-increasing rate. Just try registering a domain name on the Internet. It seems there are brands for everything. There are brands for mobile [1] phones and networks, getting rid of hemorrhoids, driving a car, drinking coffee, working out, sunbathing, electronics, food, cooking food, television channels, televisions, television programs, sports, Internet and even schools. A brand is anything that can be expressed. Even your own name can be viewed as a brand.

[1] do mobile
When you're in your car you're mobile and want to get somewhere. Traffic jams make this difficult. But now thanks to designer Cynthia Hathaway, you can do something positive when you're jammed. Just call a new mobile number and have a jar of jam made. It's Jam Jam. The jar label will have your GPS location, your time of call, and your license plate number. Jam Jam will be available at gas stations and toll booths as a product made by those who did something sweet with their jam time. (Page 41)

This could mean an overall devaluation in the real meaning of what we expect from a brand. If there are so many, perhaps their worth is disposable.

Traditionally, brands attempt to satisfy a person's need or want in a particular area. But this is changing. Now a brand can provide any number of things. It can design clothing but also publish a magazine, open a lounge or a bar or even a small theater for marketing purposes. A brand isn't just limited to its own expertise anymore but can apply its identity to several relevant items to complete what marketing specialists call an overall brand experience. More and more, brands want to do it all for you. They will bend over backward to provide you with their services and products, hoping to imbue people with their dedication, positive attitude and active nature. It's almost as if a person need not think anymore. A brand can do it all.

For example, a car brand will deliver your new automobile directly to your house or office. When your car needs servicing, the car brand will do its best to pick up the car wherever you are and deliver you a new one to test drive while your car is being serviced. Your car is more than a car, it's a way of life.

Similarly, a coffee brand will provide Internet connections in its branded café so you never have to leave. A dishwasher brand has a toll-free number to come rescue you when your kitchen floods. A carpet company cleans your carpet when you are on holiday.

Brands work hard to earn the trust of their consumers. In a way, that is the ultimate level for a brand: to be trusted. But do you trust yourself?

People have come to expect full service and therefore the relationship has become similar to a servant who does everything for them without hassle or barrier. An innovation, therefore, is not an interesting thought on the world but rather an extra call center or extra way to earn [2] airline miles. An evolution in the relationship is an added rewards program or an upgrade to a gold card instead of an interesting insight or chance for personal improvement. This is where brands depart from their human characteristics. Instead of being intuitive, they have become programmed to obey. In the end, the relationship can be rather empty.

[2] do earn
Looking for profit in as many ways as possible? Now you can earn money as you type. Just use the do earn typeface as developed by designer Martí Guixé. Each letter in the typeface has room for sponsorship. Now every sentence you write has a value that you can sell to whichever brand you feel is worthy of your prose. (Page 42)

What can this brand do for me? is a popular unconscious attitude amongst people who have grown accustomed to the total-service world. Brands may indeed spoil us with their subservient and often patronizing sensibilities. It appears that we seldom do anything for ourselves when it comes to these relationships, and perhaps this is a missed opportunity for both sides.

Inspiring and lasting relationships tend to be focused on challenging people. They respond. They think for themselves and demand something from the consumer's intelligence and creativity. For example, a brand of athletic shoes might challenge people to be active or pensive on the subject of racism or an issue of current importance. A clothing brand may decide that it's more interesting to discover and share what is really happening in the news rather than merely show its product in the typically fantasy-like medium of advertising. A car brand may encourage people to drive safely and offer safety tips and lessons along with its automobile.

In this way brands such as Nike, Benetton and Volvo might be brands that have the chance to mean more to people. These are the brands that endure and go beyond just their physical presence. Their idea, their personality, exists throughout each element of its being from its communication to the day-to-day operations.

Marketing experts have invented all kinds of new names to group this type of brand and explain how they earn trust and repeat purchase. But what is most differentiating about these brands is simply that they behave in a more human manner. They have the potential to dream, be honest, doubt and be open for two-way dialogue even if they don't always do so.

The mission and values of the The Body Shop, for example, have influenced the thinking of other companies. They concentrate on their products while also focusing on their vision, mission and philosophy. They share and explore what their company thinks about global issues. They explain where they stand on important subjects such as immigration, fair trade or the environment. Brand directors increasingly point to a vision statement and bounce every action of the brand's expression off its ideals. The concept of a philosophy has opened doors to other possibilities beyond the factory and store shelf. Just like people, brands can concern themselves with what they believe in terms of social responsibility and their impact on communities or individuals other than themselves.

With the foundation of a strong philosophy, brands can diversify. No longer are brands restricted solely to the products they have produced in the past. It's difficult, but some brands have managed to stick [3] their name on items where they have never been seen. This flexibility is well represented by Virgin. No matter what Virgin does, whether it is music or an airline or a soda, the philosophy of the Virgin brand is front and center. Therefore, the idea of Virgin can be applied to a wide range of products and industries. At Virgin, they just do everything the Virgin way.

But still, just like any brand, Virgin likes to do it all for its customers.

To go a step further, a new type of brand was developed and experimented with at communications agency KesselsKramer. It continues on its mission to inspire and challenge people today. It's a brand that remains incomplete. It requires the active involvement of people. Without participation, this brand is nothing. It requires people to take action and actually do something. This brand will never do it all for the consumer. It seeks to treat people with respect and demand the use of their brains and creativity.

For this brand, the consumer is a participant. The brand is called do.

The ever-changing brand that depends on what you do.

Normally, a brand is something created by its products. A product takes on some kind of identity or perception based on its purpose, function, success and reliability. The product becomes recognizable by its name and over time builds up a specific awareness in the public's mind.

First there is a motorcar built by Ford. The motorcar exists for several years and creates a perception for what a particular type of motorcar a Ford is and therefore what kind of company Ford is. In this way, the product is always first.

3) do stick
Valery Koshlyakov repaints masterpieces using various types of sticky tape. Next time you see a roll of silver duct tape, why not seize the opportunity to do stick a Raphael, Monet or Jackson Pollock? (Page 43)

The brand and its meaning come later.

With do, however, the brand philosophy was established first.

For this reason, the do philosophy can spread across many different mediums, products, industries and specialties. In the case of Ford, it would be difficult to produce anything that wasn't tied directly to a motorcar. The Ford brand is about cars. A Ford soda might sound strange. Ford software might be passed over in favor of Adobe.

But with the freedom of establishing a brand philosophy first, do can be anything, any product, service or idea, as long it is tied to that vision. do can create a line of clothing, software, home furnishings or even a motorcar as long is it in line with the do brand. This process, with the philosophy of do, is seemingly limitless as long as it fits with the do philosophy and its system of values.

So, what is do's brand philosophy? It's not very complicated (well, it might be).

do does not exist, nor can it function without the active participation of the consumer. A do consumer is not really a consumer at all, but someone who does something with do.

Therefore, do is always a two-way or multi-way interaction brand. In this way, do demands something. With do, people can't just expect to be passive.

No, do will not let people get away with just being serviced out the wazoo. The philosophy stems from the fact that there are enough brands that do everything. Instead, do is about taking part in the creation of something new and personal. do can adapt and change endlessly while still holding true to its philosophy. do takes on the personality of those who participate. In the end, the success of do is as much the responsibility of the consumer as it is that of the brand. It's an invitation to transform.

do is a relationship, an equal responsibility between brand and individual.

Quite traditionally do begins with a logo, the do logo.[4] A fingerprint forms the shape of the "o." This evokes the sentiment of a hands-on brand, a personal and human brand that requires a person's direct touch. The use of a copyright symbol next to the fingerprint is intended to show that individuals can also own do for themselves by taking part in do. The interaction that must occur with do makes its ownership universal and personal at the same time. do is a brand that listens and reacts rather than acting blindly.

do is yours and mine, together.

Perhaps a good analogy for do comes from the study of architecture. The meaning of architecture is not merely in the physical existence of a building but also in the way people experience and use the building. This is true of do. do's existence is only part of the story. How people use, create, interact, build, mold, shape, question, push, co-create, hit, swing, challenge or design do is its true meaning. The experience of do is unique every time but always in keeping with the brand's philosophy.

do's real value is not measured by money. It's measured by the value of the ideas, participations and collaborations. This may have a social ring to it, and that's intentional. do is interested in human potential in a positive way. do takes responsibility and also gives responsibility.

do's philosophy aims to treat people with respect for who they are and also for what they can do.

The do house style[5] immediately sets this precedence. Directly on the business cards,[6] letterhead[7] and envelopes[8] there are suggestions for what can be done with them beyond their first purpose. A do business card can be used to clean one's teeth[9] or can be placed within the spokes of a bicycle wheel. A do business card, or any business card for that matter, has more than one use. do envelopes can be used to hold clothes pins or worn as a brassiere or transformed into a watering can for plants. Letterhead can be used to decorate a pastry, as a child's bib or a mask. The images are just possibilities meant to show more possibilities. From the beginning of contact with do, these materials serve to quickly set the tone of do.

4) do logo
(Page 44)

5) do house style
(Page 45)
6) do business cards
(Page 46)
7) do letterhead
(Page 47)
8) do envelopes
(Page 48-49)

9) do teeth
Everybody is bored of eating the same food every day. So, enter Anthony Burril and his idea for do teeth, an imagined product that would enable everyone to extend their palette of culinary experience. do teeth asks people to remove their existing natural teeth and replace them with do teeth. These new teeth cut easily through most metals, wood, and many plastics. Burril imagines the nutritional benefits of "non-organic" food products as boundless. For example, a diet rich in concrete will give one a deeper feeling of solidity and connection to the ground. But take warning: do teeth must only be used in conjunction with do stomach and do intestines. (Page 50-51)

Also, by way of introduction, the do notepad,[10] a small scribble pad, provides an explanation of do's philosophy printed along its first pages. The notepad is meant to begin a dialogue with people. And inspire them to participate in do. The hope for do is always for the brand to evoke its brand mentality every time it appears. This is intended to build the mentality of do in as many relevant places as possible.

One of the first public actions of do was in the Spring of 1996. It is called "do a story."[11] This is in the form of an editorial and was commissioned by the new media magazine ROS. As electronic media rapidly develops, the effects of interactivity are of constant interest, especially when they are applied to brands. do was a dutiful match for ROS and would make appearances in two successive issues of the magazine.

In the first issue, do a story appears with a sheet of word stickers and an open story line. Readers are invited to fill in and write their own stories using the stickers provided. Additionally, do clearly explains its intention as a brand that has a strong mentality requiring collaboration in the making of different projects, products or services. do could be a software or a limited edition line of clothing. This time do is a story and readers are invited to be the authors and send their new and unique stories to do.

A handful of opportune authors demonstrated an interest in collaborating with this new type of brand. In the next issue of ROS, do provided a small book of
selected do stories[12] which was found bundled in the magazine. The editorial is one of the first initiatives of do and made clear that the mentality needed more explanation and exploration. The next step clearly was to write out the possibilities of do in more detail while enlisting some brains in different disciplines to collaborate in the brand's establishment.

Within the book, do 84,[13] do further explains its mentality with the help of interested and talented people in the fields of marketing, communication, strategy and design. do 84 stands as the first brand guide for do and contains 84 pages of ideas, thinking, concepts, dreams, possibilities, invitations and opportunities for people, brands, thinkers and, more specifically, do.

A brand is just like a person.

Most brands behave like a very boring person.

They only talk about themselves, not once, but every time we see them.

After a while, we don't want to talk to this person anymore.

Cause we know their story. We know their message.[14)]

We know how good they are.

We switch off. Thanks very much. Have a nice day.

We start to look for other people who will tell us something new.

A person who is also interested in what we say and think.

A person who has a personality.

A person who responds to emotions, thoughts and ideas.

This is the beginning of a relationship.

This is where a brand like do comes in.

Page 6, do 84

14) do message
Need to leave a short but important message somewhere? do it with a convenient collection of sand that comes in a little pocket-size bag courtesy of Gabriele Pezzini. Simply spread out the sand on a level surface and write your brief note. It's sure to get noticed. (Page 60-61)

While there are other brands that make a relationship important, very few, if any, brands make their whole existence only about a relationship. do depends entirely on relationships. And not just relationships with people. do is also interested in relationships with other brands and other companies or initiatives. do is always an invitation to participate and collaborate.

OK, if brands are just like humans, why do brands not talk more with other brands? Are brands scared of each other?
Can they only talk with each other when there's some money to earn??!?
Or can they actually do stuff together?
Marketing experts call it a joint venture. Or brand transfer.
Or a joint promotion.

Why don't we call it a chat. Or the bump. Or an affair.
Do likes to meet other brands.

do Swatch, do Budweiser, do Yahoo, do Saba, do Tango, do The New York Times, do The Body Shop, do Puma, do Coca-Cola, do Andre the Giant, do Shampoo Planet, do Volkswagen, do Mambo, do PepsiCo, do Schweppes, do Diesel, do Montis, do Nokia, do Ikea, do NetObjects, do Siemens, do

Spa, do Issey Miyake, do MSN, do Google, do Nickelodeon, do HMV, do Absolut, do CKone, do Olympus, do Universal and do whatever your brand you are...

Brands should have more sex with each other.

Page 5, do 84

Directly in the pages of do 84, do asks to collaborate with other brands. Because of the brand's flexibility, do also sees the capability to make a select line of products with existing brands.

Some examples include a line of Levi's with an e-mail address inside a pocket that connects the wearer with another Levi's wearer in a different part of the world: do Levi's.

15) do screw
5.5 designers from France provides people with fittings for basic cutlery that can be screwed onto and into everyday items for use at mealtime. do screw into your TV remote for TV dinners or when in France, try a piece of baguette. (Page 62-67)

An assembly of hardware that glows in the dark and can screw[15] into any piece of household furniture is a handy way of re-landscaping your house for evenings. This is called do Home Depot.

A niche run of bottles of water that include a global tracking device for water drinkers to stay in touch with their bottle[16] wherever it goes and whoever has it at a given moment: do Evian.

16) do bottle
86 the onions offers a solution for the excessive amounts of plastic bottles in the world. Their do bottle is an urban garden grenade, a Molotov cocktail of love, that includes soil, fertilizer, and seeds inside a biodegradable, corn-plastic bottle that can be filled with water and hurled into urban areas that require beautification and more nature. (Page 68)

A selection of sneakers that come in multiple colors and designs for exchanging components with friends or strangers who also wear these special sneakers in an effort to share shoes around the world: do Puma.

A new type of MP3 player that includes a digital rock band or jazz group inside that owners must manage, direct, consult, write new songs with and handle their concert tours in different cities and towns: do Sony.

do's interest in applying its concept to an existing brand and its products provides an opportunity for a brand refreshment. A company or initiative that seems stodgy or lacking excitement can contact do for a new project. do can customize, redirect, inspire and breathe new life into different facets of a brand that everyone has grown tired of or expects great things from in the department of innovation and experimentation. do's freedom can be a type of brand application.

In do 84. do also challenges marketing and product managers to question given formats.

Managers all go to the same kind of schools. They read the same kind of books. They learn about the product cycle. They study brand equity and the 4Ps plus[17]*1. They experience the Unique Selling Proposition. They discover all manner of management advice, tips, failures and successes. But do wonders in which classroom or boardroom did they leave their subjective instincts? Their creativity and dreams? do is a brand that can infuse their categories with turnaround thinking and ideas. do would like to help marketing and product managers get a life again.*

Page 30, do 84

[17] do plus
Designers FAT from London add a series of components that can be rearranged and used for a variety of purposes from the mundane to the ultimate. (Page 69-71)

Amen.
The first mighty institution that had an impact on society was religion, whose brand was god(s). Then there came along government, whose brand was Nixon. And now there is business, whose brand is defined everyday. Let's look.

A lot of businesses today see that "value-led" marketing makes a difference in brand relationships with consumers and therefore the bottom line. A guy concerned about homelessness is more apt to buy a brand of jeans that gives a % of earnings to a shelter than a brand that doesn't.

It's all part of business – giving a little back to the society that has helped it be successful.

But what often happens is that these companies do this rather ad hoc. They simply add on green action to their brand image. "Brand Plus." For every washing machine we make, we'll plant a pine tree. This is nice, at least it's a step in the right direction. But maybe businesses can take on a bigger role.

Instead of just adding on a social element to their marketing strategy, maybe businesses should look at how they operate as a whole, all the way through. Instead of being "value-led" they could be "value-based." In facets of its overall running, a business might find ways that help or give back to society. Maybe it's a part of their mission statement.

Maybe it's a new way of manufacturing plastic that sets up a direct supply line from plastic recycling bins. A full-value-based business from start to finish maximizes a brand's social responsibility. This is the role business has as the mightiest institution in today's world.

What's your company doing in the social responsibility department? What's your company's gospel? Ten commandments? Fables? Teachings? Are you writing them? Are you involved?

Page 65, do 84

do 84 is the first in an ongoing series of do brand manuals. Usually brands write their manual internally, but do involved many people in the process. The thoughts and definitions in do 84 reflect the dynamic qualities of do.

Using a brand's strategy externally is now something used by other brands. Being open about the purpose and intention of a brand can lead to more trust and understanding with consumers. Brands have even placed their mission directly on their products. One interesting case is the cosmetics brand, philosophy™. On every bottle and jar of philosophy™, the brand writes its thoughts and philosophies on beauty, being unique and about life in general. Behaving in this manner opens the window[18] between brand and consumer.

18) do window
Nienke Schachtschabel suggests friendly neighborliness by connecting your own window to one of your neighbor's. This is done by stringing threads or even attaching a rope ladder for making a gesture toward the community. (Page 72)

Similarly, Ben & Jerry's ice cream offers informational stories about what the company is doing to be responsible to the environment (Hey, we know it belongs mostly to Unilever now, but there's still hope). Consumers can read on each ice cream package about the brand's commitment to social responsibility. This courage and confidence may not be right for every brand but it is a new facet of brand behavior that is important for do. After all, do's brand mentality is its most valuable product.

Here are some other passages from do 84.

Know How.

On two opposite sides of global manufacturing practice, we have a company that makes cars and a company that makes ice cream. Although one has four wheels and the other is eaten, both are products that come from companies that have built themselves as brands. However, these brands differ ever so slightly in how their company thinks and how their products are made.

The point of difference concerns our lungs and our planet's lungs to be precise. You see, the car company, we won't name them (Mitsubishi), purchases and trades timber extensively around the world. In fact they are one of the worst corporate destroyers of the world's forests. They buy from countries such as Malaysia, Borneo, The Philippines, Indonesia, Chile, Canada and Brazil. No one at Mitsubishi seems to mind that the rainforests are shrinking rapidly and it's mostly due to massive clear-cutting for timber.

On the other side you have an ice cream company – we won't name them either (Ben & Jerry's) – that behaves in a different manner. They discovered that the rainforest could be just as profitable to its inhabitants if it were used for harvest instead of clear-cutting. Together with a group called Cultural Survival, this Vermont ice cream company began purchasing Brazilian nuts for a new flavor of ice cream with nuts harvested in the rainforest. The whole philosophy stems from the idea that with a profitable, living rainforest there is less incentive to destroy it.

These are just two very different company and brand philosophies in action. Now the purchasing of a car or the purchasing of an ice cream either helps to cut down forest or helps to grow forest. Simple. So, next time you find yourself in the market for a car, you might just ask a few questions, or you might just want to go for an ice cream and buy a bicycle.

Page 82, do 84

do admire

It's argued that the next minor evolutionary step for humans is to lose all our hair. It makes sense. What do we need it for? It used to keep us warm, but now we've replaced its function in life with central heating and double glazing. So the next bald guy you see walking down the street, shake his hand or give him an admiring look. He's more advanced than you.

Page 68, do 84

Do we really need that latest product invitation in the candy bar segment?

Page 68, do 84

do suicide.
Don't do it. Game shows can't last forever.

Page 22, do 84

The meaning of words.

St. Lucas is an art and design school for students aged 15-20 in Boxtel, the Netherlands. Students who attend St. Lucas are interested in finding creativity and learning how to use their own talents in the diverse areas of art and concept making. St. Lucas also offers its students courses in the English language, and the professors also wanted to handle this part of the curriculum in a creative way. The school invited do to hold a workshop for learning English in a new way.

In the summer of 1997, do held a week-long seminar and course focusing on English and the meaning of English words. Posters with hundreds of different words including: laser beam, Frisbee, cry, lawn chair, lounge, hole, smell, ocean, screen, velvet, large, expand, heat, sweater, fuzzy, magic, solo, war, famous, ice, above, astound, distance, playground,[19] expert and bubble were hung all around the school. The posters gave just a hint of what the project for the week would be for the students.

In the beginning stages, the concept of do was explained and covered (in English). The concept of the brand was discussed until there was a good understanding of do's proposition.

19) do playground
Edge Ltd. in China encourages the repurposing of basic red-white and blue bags to create new objects for a children's playground. Simply stuff the bags with soft material and set up a play date at a moment's notice. (Page 73)

Then a trolley cart arrived carrying 200 white, empty-paged books with the do logo stamped on the cover. A hush grew across the eager, young student artists. What was this? A library in search of a home?

A huge pile of white bricks stood at the front of the class. Within each book was a different single word on the title[20] page together with do. The do + word combination took the form a creative brief for the students to follow and answer. So all the words that previously appeared on the posters were now in the books together with do. The books were do laser beam, do Frisbee, do cry, do lawn chair, do lounge, do hole, do smell, do ocean, do screen, do velvet, do large, do expand, do heat, do sweater, do fuzzy, do magic, do solo, do war, do famous, do ice, do above, do astound, do distance, do expert and so forth.

20) do title
Take charge of the naming process with do title, designer Helmut Smits's answer to a more democratic and creative system of self-titling. A blank book cover can be used to title any book, while a medal made with coins and found ribbon can instantly pronounce anyone Lord, Lady or Superhero. (Page 74)

The students were given two days to fill in their particular do book[21] in a way that answered their new term or do brief. They had to find a creative idea within the meaning of these English words. This was not only a lesson in language, but also a lesson in how to think differently about the meaning and interpretation of words.

21) do book
(Page 75-77)

The results were diverse, interesting, disappointing, surprising, delightful and inspiring. For "do lounge" a student turned her do book into a velvet chair. "do search"[22] had a viewfinder hole to the back of the book. For "do expand," a do book was increased in proportion. "do flood"[23] found a do book flooded with typed pages. "do cry" contained a trapped onion. "do famous" contained a glamorous picture frame and all the equipment and tips for being famous. "do fizzle"[24] had delicate textural carvings into the book. "do connect"[25] attached the pages of the book together with a running story.

22) do search
(Page 78-79)
23) do flood
(Page 80-81)

24) do fizzle
(Page 82-83)
25) do connect
(Page 84-85)

The collection of completed do books was exhibited in Amsterdam at Art Book as a fulfillment of the seminar. The English courses at St. Lucas with do had incorporated different facets befitting a group of young creative thinkers. There were word meanings explored in a do way with collaboration on a creative project, as well as an exhibition with which to critique and analyze the results. Since teaching and learning have a danger of placing students mostly on the passive, receiving end, do took a more involved approach.

The lessons from do were not only applicable to learning a new language, but also relevant for other courses of the student's study, work and thinking at St. Lucas.

Many companies and brands hold workshops and seminars at schools or conferences. This is an interesting way to learn more all the way around. But for do, the workshop is always a time to test the theories of do and discover new collaborators and throw a meteorite[26] into normal behavior. That's why each and any time do holds a gathering, the audience is always invited to participate in a way that makes their brains sweat.

A wacky future brand.

"The do mentality is the punk rock do-it-yourself attitude, a rejection of passive consumption in favor of playfulness and interactivity."

Naomi Klein, The Financial Times, May 29, 2001.

After introducing do with do 84 and discussing the brand's initial hopes and dreams, it was time to dig in and further explain the potential of do. The investigation into do's breadth of inspiration is a continual process.

What followed is perhaps the most thorough book on do and its mentality, do future.[27]

Within the pages of this follow-up to do 84, do future explores many new thoughts for brands, marketing, product design, communication, interactivity, responsibility, consumer behavior, corporate ethics, product life cycles and issues of connectivity. do also seeks to establish a personal tone. do is aware and is a social brand; a brand that sets itself the task of questioning companies that behave irresponsibly. Instead, do would always try to act responsibly. This sentiment would be mutual in do's need for having multiple involvement and collaboration. Again, do is always about qualitative reward.[28]

do future
Once: Agriculture

26) do meteorite
Gabriele Pezzini suggests a new way to use a bottle of water at the beach to unearth your own meteorite. Make a pile of sand, pour water, insert your finger into the Earth, pour more water, and repeat. When you clean around the newly formed object, you can lift up a piece of extraterrestrial matter to astound your friends and any unsuspecting lifeguards. (Page 86)

27) do future
(Page 87-89)

28) do reward
Claude Closky offers his creative commercial suggestion for what to do with one hundred and one things to do. (Page 90-91)

Not so long ago: Industry
Now: Information
Tomorrow: Creativity
After that: Agriculture

Page 2025, do future

At the time of do Future's publication, the marketing world was fascinated by the innovative work of trend forecasters. Studies conducted by trend watchers and people who could zoom out from society and even make predictions on the future needs of consumers were heavily in demand. While do did not operate itself directly on the insights provided by trend forecasting, do and its thinkers began considering the power of trends in the creation of brands. Looking at the small and interesting trends could be interesting for do instead of generalizing and projecting data.

Could a brand initiate and identify its own trends?

A brand could certainly try to put itself in the right place at the right time. But what struck do as interesting was that while most brands and their products were trying to adapt to trends, there were very few brands that initiated trends. Why couldn't a brand start a new way of thinking? Were brands only supposed to wait and see what happened and then react? Certainly a brand could be more proactive by opening people's minds to new thinking not just in their local lives but in the lives of people living around the world. If a brand seeks to be relevant, if a brand desires to have i pact, shouldn't the brand have a global perspective? Why can't a brand have a dialogue with its consumers, its collaborators and its participants?

A sizeable part of do future is a project called do insight.[29] This intense field study of trends investigated the behavior of over 600 teenagers in different parts of the planet. By going to the source of new trends and changes in behavior, do observed the effects of society and daily life and the arrival of new movements where both brands and products might add, involve or have impact.

do insight covers a wide spectrum of the latest youth trends from Sound Collage™ to Brand All™.

29) do insight
(Page 92-95)

Following are some of do insight's learnings:

Have you tried Headphoning™? This happens when two or more people meet who are listening to personal audio players. The listeners plug their headphones into one another's players to hear (or audio greet) each other's music. It's a musical way of saying hello and introducing oneself. This is very popular in Bombay, Kyoto, Los Angeles and Brooklyn.

Word™ identifies rampant cases of magazine addiction and its effects on blanking out the mind with unreal worlds and over promises. Addicts have been treated by implementing meaningful messages in certain magazines. Some have even begun printing edible magazines to aid in the health crisis created by readers who seldom take time away from reading magazines to eat.

Another trend is TVanxiety™ which has struck predominately in the United States. Although no products have been created to combat the effects of this anxiety, several new media forms have been introduced. TVanxiety™ is the worry TV viewers experience when they are not watching TV. They have this overwhelming anxiety that they are missing something incredibly important on TV. The anxiety also occurs when viewers are changing channels during a commercial break. While flipping through the channels, they forget what they are watching and end up watching something else. For this reason, viewers never actually watch anything to completion and their lives and imaginations fill up with unfulfilled and rather meaningless stories.

However, there are stories in these wild channel-flippings, and new shows have been created on top of other shows by combining several. TVanxiety™ sufferers have created new shows that are a type of TV collage mixing different segments of TV programming. It's a much freer medium combining sitcom with documentary, made-for-TV movie, pay-per-view, game show, reality show and news broadcast to invent one new episode. Also known as TVZ, these episodes are created by viewers burning them on DVD or recording them with video cameras.

Brands are picking up on a new market invented by kids in parts of Japan. It's called MobileVending™ and it's the result of lack of a proper mealtime. Kids today are carrying large amounts of food around in backpacks that are now specially designed. Some even have refrigerators. The food is not necessarily for personal consumption. It's for sale. A kind of black market has popped up around schools with kids selling everything from cold soup, snacks to microwaveable meals. Microwaves are now part of a new bike messenger bag that has extra compartments for battery packs. Kids are turning themselves into mobile marts.

Also in Japan is a recurring crime that fuels an industry. HairMugging™ is the act of hair theft. It usually occurs on subways and buses where a victim is idly riding without paying attention. The most popular victims have red or blond hair. The snipped prize is then sold to wig-makers for rave parties. Other eager patrons are those anxious to have full-length beards without all the hassle of growing them the selves. Underground stores offer instant hair for a new baby.[30] Color and quality may vary. New technology is being developed to trademark certain types of hair and hair alarms have been developed by several discrete manufacturers.

Another product and trend is FearBeer™. This is a result of a highly developed beverage market. Kids don't want their drinks to be too specific. They want a drink that can do it all. They want a super strong beer that includes vitamins, weird chemicals, inoculations, flu remedies, energy,[31] caffeine and, of course, alcohol. FearBeer™ has opened up a wide variety of product innovations. There are AnythingCanHappenKits that include tents, medical supplies and GPS tracking beacons. There are also new kinds of jelly beans that absorb the active ingredients in FearBeer and allow the beer to work harder and longer. Also called FearBeans™, these jelly beans enhance the already mystical effects of FearBeer™.

Sports marketers are also getting into the act. You see, the usual sports are just not exciting enough, not even the so-called extreme sports. So, enter the BYO Sport™. It's a sport that is different at any given moment and incorporates all kinds of different elements in the making of a new game.

30) do baby
The next time you find yourself at the grocery store or market with your baby and heavy bags of shopping, balance yourself out with do baby. This simple (and strong) bag needs you to make openings for your child's legs and makes an impromptu counterbalance to heavy loads. As always, handle with care. (Page 96)

31) do energy
Frank Tjepkema offers an efficient and playful idea for the giant wind machines that communities often find unsightly. By adding a roller coaster to the structures, people can now take a spin up and down and around while creating energy for their homes. (Page 97)

In Chicago it's Rave Squash. It's not a game between two people. It's just you, a racket and thousands of squash balls. The idea is to see who can hit the most balls for the longest time while listening to intensely loud rave music. Players are wearing eyeglasses by Pony, sneakers by Converse and using rackets by Spalding. In Vancouver there's another game that includes BMX biking, tennis rackets and tennis balls. It's called BikeBall and nobody understands it as the rules change constantly. Kids are wearing Prada for this one and Polo shirts. Shoes are made out of old hockey skates without the blades. Don't ask us why. And, they often play against a new friend or a new neighbor.[32]

do future

The idea for seeking out these trends is twofold. First, there is a definitive interest by do in the creative and innovative ideas that occur naturally in the worlds of youth today. The second is the idea that a brand can also pinpoint its own trends. Why couldn't a new behavioral idea or opportunity for imagination be discovered with intuition?

The do insight research initiative in do future provides a rich resource for product and brand innovations. It also demonstrates do's curiosity. A brand doesn't have to adapt to large trends, it can be more selective and celebrate the more quirky habits of ever-surprising youth. do can observe and make comment.

do Future remains a central feature at do lectures, presentations, discussion panels and do workshops. It has been reprinted and updated three times. Subsequent copies are marked with corrections and edits and fresh thoughts on subjects that may have come to fruition. do Future also was an invitation for collaborators and brands. The idea of "brand sex" – do working with existing brands – is still a major do proposition. do could be a hard-working solution for brands who are having difficulty speaking to a more creative audience. Attracting this type of audience traditionally has never been easy.[33]

do Future continues to open the door to discussions and has peaked the curiosity of journalists. do was the subject of a documentary about brands

32) do neighbor
Daphne Koenen has designed an idea that will introduce neighbors to each other again. do neighbor is a two-handled bag that needs to be operated by two people for the successful toting of goods from market to home. (Page 98-99)

33) do easy
Jurgen Bey believes that cleaning is an undervalued activity that can be used for more purposes than just the obvious. It's easy. With do easy, a person can make cleaning into a new hobby and technique for creating pleasurable things. By providing various deflated shapes and forms, just use your vacuum cleaner to acquire the filler. This easy way of making sculptures, toys and objects gives new life to the beauty hiding in the carpets of the world. (Page 100-101)

undertaken by the VPRO, the Dutch documentary film company. In their film, the VPRO investigated companies that take a different approach. The film includes interviews with trend guru Ted Polhemus, the skateboard brand Girl & Chocolate and do. The awareness for do has also spread to magazines whose interest had been sparked by the very simple proposition of consumer involvement as well as the lack of concrete[34] products. do insight and its discoveries have also been discussed in issues of Campaign, BLVD and i-D magazines. Remember to check do publishing[35] for more books by and about do to keep handy on your shelf[36] or in your back pocket.

do a basic item.

do is a brand that is left unfinished by definition. The completion of any product or idea from do is left up to those who do. A project that shows this multiplicity of participation in do is the do shirt.[37] The do shirt is no normal T-shirt. It is a shirt that's 400 times too big for any ordinary person. The do shirt is meant to be more than an item of apparel. It is an action. Along with the do shirt come suggestions for how to wear and use the do shirt. do makes the request that a do shirt wearer use the do shirt in an unusual and unique manner and photograph it in action. The photographs are to be sent to do for an online archive, an exhibition and T-shirt inspiration.

The suggestions give some examples of different do shirt uses. There is do picnic[38] where the do shirt is laid out on the ground for a spontaneous lunch moment. There is do escape:[39] a linking of giant do shirts to escape from a tall building or institution. do dine[40] is a do shirt tablecloth. do marry[41] is a do shirt wedding dress. do hang-glide is a do hang-glider made out of the do shirt (please try under proper supervision). do wrap[42] is a suggestion for a headscarf. do with a three year-old kid wearing the do shirt while standing on a ladder is do transform.[43] do sleep[44] is the do shirt used as bed sheets. A mop with the do shirt attached is do clean.[45] Two frisky pairs of legs sticking out of a car is do affair.[46] A person in a wet[47] do shirt is do wet. All suggestions are photographed to illustrate the many possibilities of this super-big enormous shirt. Why not try do straight jacket[48] or do dress?[49] A do shirt can do it all.

34) do concrete
Live and build your own house with the basic architectural elements of foundation, stove, and chimney included in do concrete. Joost Grootens and Bart Guldemond challenge building regulators, architects, and mortgage suppliers to deal with the anarchy of the unfinished. With do concrete, inhabitants are invited to constantly build their house while they live in it. The ideal house is the never-finished house. Live and build, build and live. (Page 102-103)

35) do publishing
(Page 104)

36) do shelf
A technique for new bookshelf management. do shelf is a book that is placed under one side of a bookshelf to accommodate a shelf's new arrivals with the use of gravity. The tilt of the shelf makes small collections of books behave. (Page 105)

37) do shirt
(Page 106-107)

38) do picnic
(Page 108)
39) do escape
(Page 109)
40) do dine
(Page 110)
41) do marry
(Page 111)
42) do wrap
(Page 112)
43) do transform
(Page 113)
44) do sleep
(Page 114)
45) do clean
(Page 115)
46) do affair
(Page 116)
47) do wet
(Page 117)
48) do straight jacket
(Page 118)
49) do dress
(Page 119)

The April 1998 issue of Elle Magazine featured an editorial action with the do shirt. In the issue, the do shirt was shown and explained along with the many suggestions for doing. Readers could purchase a do shirt and then take part in the project by making photographs and sending them to do.

The do shirt is an example of how a basic item such as a T-shirt can be transformed by do into something more. A do shirt is, in the end, a shirt, an opportunity for involvement in do and a photography project that brings many different people together in one action. The do shirt shows that do can be a compelling and relevant brand that wishes to initiate new ways of thinking and interacting with brands or ideas.

do TV.

After making a basic T-shirt into a do project, it was time to turn do's attention to another basic, ubiquitous item: television. In the year 2000, a lot of attention was given to the current state of TV. There was a debate forming about the rise of the Internet and its impact on TV viewership. As a brand, do took it upon itself to wonder about the future of this box that sits in half the world's homes.

What would become of the boob tube?

do set out to hold a definitive discussion lab to analyze the current and future status of television with a variety of experts ranging from media gurus to advertising executives to marketing and brand directors. And as a forum, do turned to TV's supposed nemesis: the World Wide Web.

do TV would be an intensive and comprehensive discussion and dream session on the subject of television. On February 2, 2000 (02022000), do TV conducted a 24[50]-hour chat session online to cover a variety of subjects related to TV's past, present and future. Different "channels" on the do TV chat site were monitored to provide a platform for guests of all kinds. Experts joined in from all over the world on channels as diverse as the movie channel, the social channel, the future channel, the do channel, the world channel, the entertainmentchannel, the news channel and the brand channel. The chat

50) do 24
Photographer Hans Eijkelboom invites you to do take part in a photography project that examines your style decisions both past and current.
(Page 120-121)

began at 00:00:01 on February 2 and was monitored all over the world with additional computer access at the 2000 Rotterdam Film Festival.

Guest speakers, or chatters, included Maarten Reesink, a TV scientist from Amsterdam, Joshua Cooper Ramo, senior editor of Time Magazine, George Brugmans, editor-in-chief of DNW for VPRO Television, Jonathan Brunert, BBC, Lynne Carter, TV producer at Media TV Canada, Kim Wolf Tau, producer of the Cliffhanger Series, KesselsKramer and many journalists, film directors, writers, artists, marketers and TV personalities. The discussions ranged in topics from what's currently on TV, the reality craze, the slant of the news to what the possibilities would be as Interactivity combines with TV's usual formats. What are the opportunities for education, marketing and culture? What limitations does TV have? Will the TV just become part of a computer or home information system? These topics were addressed by an eager audience for 24 full hours.

Over 400,000 people visited the site. All together the chats took up about 8,100 pages of information.[51] The shortest living website was live for just one day and turned into a living, breathing, speaking and listening combination of sitcom, documentary, game show, news program, drama and thriller all wrapped into nine online channels at one location.

51) do information
For a wider point of view, step up into a new position and gather more knowledge and intelligence. Contact designers Stephanie Henzler and Henning Labuch for more information. (Page 122-123)

+ *hollywood has arrived.*
<*hollywood*> *hi hollywood!*
<*hollywood*> *not very social in here.*
<*hollywood*> *no.*
<*hollywood*> *maybe TV is a bit like talking to yourself.*
<*hollywood*> *yup.*
<*hollywood*> *no one can find you when you are into the TV.*
<*hollywood*> *you get lost.*
<*hollywood*> *within yourself?*
<*hollywood*> *no just along with something else.*
<*hollywood*> *the TV.*
<*hollywood*> *maybe the escape is the draw.*
<*hollywood*> *no thinking.*

<hollywood> I wonder if they've ever made a study of what happens to your brain on TV.

<hollywood> how low your signals go.

<hollywood> right.

<hollywood> what do you remember?

<hollywood> what can you recall?

<hollywood> what

<hollywood> what

<hollywood> what

<hollywood> just changing channels.

<hollywood> who

<hollywood> where

<hollywood> what

<hollywood> ?

<hollywood> ?

<hollywood> ?

<hollywood> bye.

<freud> hollywood, don't go...

- Hollywood just left.

<caligari> It is clear that people are no longer interested in shopping or watching TV as entertainment and no longer accumulating wealth as a sign of status. Let's reduce consumption and instead of a silly TV show, let's read a book. Or have a live chat. Let's play.[52] *Please Mr. Murdoch and Mr. Turner give us less. Do you agree???*

<JerrySpringer> Future of TV. Oprah Winfrey is starting her own TV channel. True? Ready for Oprah TV?

<spock> She already started her own magazine.

<Joshua> What about the all-women's network that's launching in the States this week? Does that make sense?

<spock> The women's network sounds pretty dangerous though.

<JerrySpringer> Is it scrambled for male viewers?

<Joshua> Great idea. A lamp[53] *going on.*

<spock> You would hear nothing But bleeps.

<spock> If you scrambled Oprah.

52) do play
More opportunities for play are recognized, pointed out, and dutifully equipped by Harmen de Hoop.
(Page 124-128)

53) do lamp
Used and cleaned food packaging are the core materials for Helmut Smits's line of home lighting apparatuses.
(Page 129)

Selections from the do TV[54] chats on the channels are printed in the do TV book.[55] Within this physical tome, the discussions can be reviewed with some of the most enlightening ideas are preserved.

<freud> Does TV bring us in contact with the real world?

<Johan> Well, many people experience "the real world" only through TV. Digital gun.[56] Digital fun.

<Hallo> It gives you that idea. Depends on the show and do people want to get in contact with that world perhaps it is TV that lets you hide from it.

<mcluhan> Increasingly TVG is almost the ONLY contact with the outside world for the elderly, disabled and sick: it is truly a "window on the world." And all that garbage on TV is no different, works no better than all the garbage in the so-called "real" world.

<Bill> So let's bring in a new topic. Is live-covered news better than normal-covered news?

<fluffy> depends on what's being covered.

<mcluhan> to me, it's not a matter of "better or worse." But TV is at its BEST when it is "live," because it's the ONE time no other medium can match/beat/ duplicate it. For insight into news, you better read the "Economist," but for late breaking news, NOTHING beats TV.

do TV

do TV is a way for do to demonstrate that a brand can be interested in topics, events and changes in the world around it. A brand, just like a person, cannot live completely in self-absorbed isolation. TV is a fountain[57] of information and entertainment created all over the place. And since do, as a brand, exists for the most part in communication, TV was an excellent subject to address. How TV will function is important to the way the world discovers new topics, cultures, geography and storytelling. If a person wants to know something about a given society, they need only watch a few hours of local television to get an idea. Television is the medium for us to celebrate our strengths and weaknesses. Here along the airwaves, we air our illnesses, our dreams, our hopes, our failures, our dramas and our points of view. Perhaps TV is a mirror as well as a window.

54) do TV
(Page 130-132)
55) do TV book
(Page 133-135)

56) do gun
No, don't worry, do doesn't like guns. But do sees that no matter how hard parents try to keep toy guns away, it is clear that children find a way of making them anyway. Despite their scary intention, these little sculptures are interesting to see for their inventiveness and playfulness. Wouldn't it be wonderful if all guns looked more like this and, of course, could not fire anything but imagination? (Page 136-141)

57) do fountain
Helmut Smits turns ordinary backyard swimming pools into a new pleasant and elegant waterfall experience. (Page 142)

58) do drum
*A sound solution for the
abundance of all those
empty food cans that have
a way of piling up in
your kitchen trash bin.
(Page 143)*

In any case, just when we think we've seen it all, along comes a new technology or realization such as Tivo or Digital Cable to further prove that there is an endless possibility for things to do with TV. Just when you think a program like Survivor or 24 has set the standard, along comes American Idol. Who knows what they will drum [58] up next?

Other brands also have taken a direct interest in the broader issues of today. Benetton is an example of a brand that continues to stay in touch with different events and situations in the world. Its magazine, COLORS, deals with themes from a different perspective several times a year. COLORS is a standalone magazine that investigates topics that are seldom covered in the mainstream media. The magazine adds a dimension to the brand and has helped position Benetton in a different category than the usual fashion house. Benetton could be viewed as a brand that has a conscience, a brand that is interested in what happens in the rest [59] of the world rather than just its own world.

59) do rest
*do please take some time to rest,
dream, and stare blankly into
space while thinking of something
else for awhile. (Page 143)*

60) do create
(Page 144-145)

do create. [60]

61) do hit
(Page 146)

Pick up a sledgehammer and feel the weight in your hands. Then walk to a large metal cube and begin smashing a dent into it. After a few swings you begin to sweat. Your hands begin to get sore. Blisters? After several swings the dents and the cube turn into a piece of furniture. This is do hit [61] a chair that you make yourself with the use of a sledgehammer and your own strength. do hit is one piece in an entire series of home furnishings found in the do create collection. do teamed up with Dutch design network Droog to create do's first complete range of products that required a bit more sweat and tears than the comfy, cushy, full-service sofas you can buy at Crate & Barrel or Restoration Hardware (what do you actually restore?). do hit is the creation of designer Marijn van der Poll.

do briefed these new collaborative do designers on the mentality of the brand and its intention to make products that were more than just one-way solutions for individual needs. Each product required some effort from the end-user in order to make the product function correctly. Jurgen Bey created chairs for do create that need adjustment and forethought before sitting down.

One chair, called do add #1 [62], has one leg shorter than the rest. A person wishing to sit in do add #1 must find something with which to balance the chair properly or they will topple over. Similarly, do add #2 [63] has an extra-long seat that sits atop two legs and requires a person to find someone or something to sit with to make the chair function.

Each do create product is left incomplete. The end-user, while suggested and directed by the designer, is nevertheless out of the designer's control. When purchased, and in some cases every time they are used, the do create products need something done to them in order to work. Martí Guixé designed a special tray of cups, saucers and plates that necessitate a person to cut them out for individual use. This product is called do eat. [64] Guixé also designed special tape with a pattern imitating that of a wooden picture frame for use with any picture a person chooses. The product is named do frame [65] and comes in a big fat roll for many, many uses.

"One can imagine the future shape of companies by stretching them until they are pure network. A company that was pure network would have the following traits: distributed, decentralized, collaborative and adaptive.

Kevin Kelly, "Out of Control"

Out of the control of the primary designer, a person jumps in the air and catches hold of do swing, [66] a lamp designed by Thomas Bernstrand. They shout out like Tarzan and go back and forth in the air in their imaginary jungle. In collaboration with an energetic person, a ceramic vase is cracked into a completely unique pattern as it lands forcefully against the wall. do break [67] by designers Frank Tjepkema and Peter van der Jagt is made of ceramic and industrial rubber to prevent any leakage and to ensure a special end-design as created by the owner.

Waiting for the snail mail is also made more immediate by do post, [68] designed by Dawn Finley. When a person inserts a letter into the box, a response pops out immediately. do post is an opportunity to spread opinion, take a poll or start the ultimate chain letter.

62) do add #1
(Page 147)

63) do add #2
(Page 148)

64) do eat
(Page 149)

65) do frame
(Page 150-151)

66) do swing
(Page 152)

67) do break
(Page 153)

68) do post
(Page 154-155)

do create was launched at the International Furniture Fair 2000 in Milan and received a lot of attention. Design Week in England wrote, "Dutch innovator Droog Design has joined with do, an umbrella 'brand,' also based in Amsterdam, that encompasses the work of several international designers, to create a show that encourages punters to create their own 'designs' or change what exists. It also encourages people to express emotions such as anger and joy through the way they react with the 'products.'" Wallpaper magazine claimed that do create "stole the show." The Independent on Sunday called do full of "smashing ideas."

69) do reincarnate
(Page 156-157)

Other items in the do create range include a way to reuse unwanted lamps and electrical appliances sentenced to the attic. Called do reincarnate,[69] the item provides a suspension system for a tired lamp to float above a table and thus have an afterlife. do cut [70] is a selection of materials that can be cut for different uses. A person equipped with an Xacto blade can create a stool, a vase, a lamp or even a hairband. Similarly do design #1 [71] and do design #2 [72] offer material branded by do that can be incorporated into any number of furnishings.

70) do cut
(Page 158-159)

71) do design #1
(Page 160)
72) do design #2
(Page 161)

Customization through participation was a principle the designers all understood. do scratch [73] is a light box that is covered by an opaque resin. To make it function, a person is asked to scratch in a unique design. do link [74] is a connection system that provides the top and bottom of a lamp with the ability to link objects of a person's own choosing in between. Connection is also the purpose of do connect [75] by designers Dinie Besems and Thomas Widdershoven. do connect can attach two disparate items to make them one.

73) do scratch
(Page 162-163)
74) do link
(Page 164)

75) do connect
(Page 165)

do create began touring stores, fairs and galleries. Significant displays and demonstrations took place at the Salone di Mobile,[76] Colette in Paris and the Kunsthal in Rotterdam. do create was also part of "Happening" at the Rocket Gallery in Tokyo. Subsequently, do create took part in the New York Furniture Fair and also held a demonstration at the Apartment in SoHo with a great deal of publicity and fanfare. Eventually, do create's novelty made the pages of The New York Times, The International Herald Tribune, i-D, Vogue Italy, Form Germany, Black+White Australia, Depeche Mode France, Design France, Abitare Italy and View on Color. It was also covered in an item by Naomi Klein for Channel 4 in the UK.

76) do salone di mobile
(Page 166-169)

It was important that each do create product also acted as communication for do as a brand. Each product in the collection followed the mentality of do closely and reinterpreted it into a piece for home furnishing. Jurgen Bey described his do add chairs as having "handicaps." The chairs' need for assistance serves to rethink the indulgence of service that consumers are used to. Why not ask a person to stop and consider their immediate surroundings with the task of finding a stack of magazines or a box or some suitable object to prop up their chair? See it as a chance to get to know you and your possessions better.

If we consider that the involvement in a brand such as do infuses creativity in all its collaborators from designer to end-user, we might also consider that the full-service world we live in might be stripping some people of their imaginations. If everyone does ever thing for you, what have you learned to do yourself? Perhaps one of the core lessons of do is that it is fun and challenging to do. It's also rewarding in many circumstances, both creatively and in terms of mental and physical inspiration, to do something for yourself within a collaboration. do create, as written in an article in Building Design, an architectural journal, transforms possibilities "from normal to lyrical."

The do create collection is available for sale online and through Amsterdam's largest department store, the Bijenkorf. It is now also a permanent part of the Central Museum in Utrecht. The line of products continues to gather attention to the potential of do. It also makes the do philosophy more tangible. do create is do in action.

Collaborating with do.

With the awareness of do in the design world, do was asked to take part in a design conference[77] at the Cooper Hewitt National Design Museum[78] in New York. For this, a new collaborative workshop was developed. During a week of intensive study, do challenged professionals in the design industry to think and do in a different way. It was here that the do together[79] workshop was given for the first time. The do together workshop uses do's multi-disciplined brand approach. Now, on top of a vision, manuals, communication and product design, do has entered the area of direct knowledge and inspiration.

77) do conference
Why not hold your own press conference to announce new plans or current ideas? Helmut Smits shows us how paint rollers and simple stands can be transfigured and repurposed for an official environment. (Page 170-171)

78) do cooper hewitt
(Page 172)
79) do together
(Page 173)

The brand and its meaning can also help others create a new idea for their work, their company, their brands or their projects. The workshop is an intense collaboration that doesn't let participants get stuck in their usual habits. Instead it bumps them around to work on several different ideas at once. In the end, everyone in the workshop works together toward solutions.

80) do size
Normal scales are a guilt trip gauged in kilograms. do size is a set of scales that has a more positive effect on your well-being. Based on a roulette system, you step on, the wheel spins, and chance takes over. Each denomination is a healthy or life-changing task such as: give up meat for a week, run around the park, quit TV, or have sex all night. Everyone wins on the do size scales.
(Page 174-175)

The workshop consists of 3-7 giant workbooks that are roughly A0 in size.[80] Each workbook contains a proposal or challenge with room inside to work out strategic thinking, name generation, market insights, brand collaboration and creative execution. The workshop is flexible in its length. It can be held for a few hours or over the period of a few days. The fundamental instrument next to do in the workshop is that at certain points in the exercise, participants are asked to exchange books and begin working on another challenge in whatever stage it may have reached. About five people work in a team with 3-7 people working together. At the end of the session, everyone must present their ideas back to the workshop. Since everyone has worked on all the ideas, the discussion and findings are usually a group effort with no one getting left behind.

The do together workshop continues to be taught at art schools, company headquarters, design academies and architectural institutes. do together has worked with companies and marketing departments including the Hema department store, Calvin Klein fragrances and the Fila sports brand. Some interesting and interested institutions who have participated include Benetton's

81) do fabrica
(Page 176-177)
82) do romania
(Page 178-179)

Fabrica[81] Institute and the Rhode Island School of Design. do together even challenged the advertising community in Bucharest, Romania[82] with a two-day session.

83) do value
(Page 180-181)

While some ideas that result from the workshop are merely inspirational, there are always a selection of concepts that are chosen for further work. The collaboration in the workshop has the value[83] of building team spirit and is helpful for people working in different departments or areas of companies and brands to feel a part of the working process.

With the doors wide open to do for collaboration, ideas continue to push back and forth across the airwaves. Whether through the Internet or conferences or e-mail or in workshops, concepts for do are always offering inspiration and insight and seeking the collaboration of those who find do an opportunity to transform and make their own. ·

do share [84) is one such experiment from do in the form of an editorial. do looked at the idea of sharing and dividing and finding an equal income level for everyone on the planet.

84) do share
(Page 182-185)

If, for example, the world gross national product in a given year is nearly US$ 29.2 trillion and we were to divide that evenly amongst the planet's six billion inhabitants, everyone would get US$ 4,890 a year to live on.

Of course, do is not taking into consideration the cost of living in each country, the number of children per household or the problems that would arise in performing such an experiment.

do is simply putting out the question: "What if the poor got richer, the rich became poorer and everyone became more equal?" How would this change your life? How would it change everyone else's?

By imagining this, perhaps you can see just how good you have it or how your life could be improved if everyone shared a little bit of the wealth.

In January 2002, Dutch Magazine published an issue in collaboration with the International Committee of the Red Cross. do found individuals and families from 13 countries who actually make the equivalent of US$ 4,890 a year.

In cases where there were more than one member per household, do divided the total yearly income to equal approximately US$ 4,890, or GNP per do share. We then compared this to the real GNP per capita in each country. What followed was a series of photographs that brought to life those who live on this income in several different countries of the world with the purpose of showing the differences in scale due to differences in equality and their effects on living situations.

do's philosophy always demands that do poses questions and makes suggestions that can initiate discussion. do is about knowledge and information and consideration. do can be a social reminder, a curious investigator, a tester of ways and means, a critic, a fan, as well as an interested reflector of daily events.

do spread out.

Sometimes do is a furniture collection, a book, a twenty-four hour event or a performance. do's philosophy continues to take on new experiences and joint projects all the time with the hope of continually spreading out, breathing and including and giving back.

85) dosurf.com
(Page 186)

As an online manifestation of do, dosurf.com [85] is not the usual website crammed with details. dosurf.com is just the beginning and more a source for requesting information and collaboration. Those who log on must request a particular story from do to be mailed to their e-mail. The formality of requesting information about do is the first step in participation. dosurf.com forms a new union [86] with those who visit because there are barely any details about do on the actual site. The future of working with do exists in their in-boxes burning holes in their desktop screens.

86) do union
Don't distress over a broken cup or plate anymore. Save it for more. Accidents do happen. When you have a good collection of shards, mend them together in different designs. Turn embarrassment into pride with your very own line of home furnishings that no one could possibly duplicate. (Page 187)

do is also in development with a TV program that is more interactive (do it yourself) and more open. A live TV program. A toy [87] for the TV.

87) do toy
You are now on the board of directors of do. Welcome. Whatever you do depends on you. (Page 188-189)

The question is: What if a person could choose what they want to watch?

do select would be similar in format to another TV channel, The Box, but not nearly as pastiche or repetitive. There is no preset play list influenced by record labels. Instead do select uses its success to let people choose their own version of art or television environment. This provides a wide variety of subject matter constantly changing on screen.

do select would have a list of six thousand artworks that people can call in to select and view live on TV for a select amount of time. They can also go to the teletext number for the program during and before the show to see what artwork they can select for viewing. In this way, as viewers watch and select the program, all of us get an idea of what people want to see.

Some of the art people can select might range through the following possibilities:

An artwork by Picasso.
An artwork by Dalí.
A sculpture by Rodin.
A famous goal by Pele.
A segment of pornography.
A segment of a music video.
A person screaming for 20 seconds.
A tree in a park.
A warm sweater being knitted.
A selection of cakes revolving in a café refrigerated unit.
A kid singing the national anthem.
An hour of rain.

do select would ask viewers to suggest as well as select instead of just melting away into the cushions of their sofas and recliner chairs.

Another do action is do change. do change[88] was an editorial in SOON magazine. Within four pages, do set out to knock readers off their usual habits.

88) do change
(Page 190-193)

do change
It seems we're running out of things to invent, so that we're regurgitating ideas and making complexities obsolete. What we should really be thinking about is that most of the products we have around us seem to work quite nicely, thanks very much. Affecting any real change and finding the things no one else has thought of before has to come from the everyday. That means waking up in a different way, doing your job in a way it has never been done before or with someone you've never considered working with before. Creating real change mostly involves small measures. What would happen if you decided to eat cereals in the evening instead of at breakfast?

do change goes on to provide a few examples of minor adjustments that could bring about real, temporary or significant change in people's lives.

At work, we could ask someone on the street for advice instead of our mentor or advisor. Swap[89] work space with our boss or employee. Leave our phone, diary, wallet and other pocket-bulgers at home. Open our shop/business when everyone else closes theirs.

89) do swap
Did you ever want to give a friend or relation a surprise present that would replace something old and tired they already have? Enter do swap, a new way to perform a present swap for an item already involved in a person's life. Simply place the replacement gift – a watch or a pair of shoes or a wish for that person to quit smoking – into the normal environment and attach a do swap announcement badge. The gift will be a spontaneous change to the familiar routine of those who are lucky to be swapped. (Page 194-197)

At home, we could answer the door naked the next time the doorbell rings. Have our evening meal on the stairs. Don't leave the house for a week. Turn off all the electricity. Sleep upside down. Use your living room window instead of the front door.

Anywhere, we could dress up as a magician for a day. Write notes instead of speaking. Leave strange post-it note messages on the street/ subway/ supermarket. Open our windows in a car wash. Don't avoid obstacles, walk into them. Repeat everyone's words. Change our name for different occasions. Wear a stripe [90] across our face.

90) do stripe
A ballpoint pen is an underused tool that can be used as a fashion accessory. Turn a plain white shirt into something more fun and decorative by striping it yourself with the pen color of your choice. (Page 198-199)

While the editorial, do change, was meant to inspire a little change in behavior, the overall message was that in a normal world, it is the normal person who lives quite comfortably. Therefore any progress is made by those who are not normal. Be unreasonable and put a little spin into the process.

Another spin is do asking people to take pictures with their hearts and not just their eyes.

91) do snapshot
(Page 200-201)

do snapshot [91] is a camera that is ready for production. It's a small, throwaway film camera that has one do feature: no view hole. Because of this, the do snapshot asks photographers to shoot with instinct instead of with their sight. Shoot with intuition. The result is photographs that are a complete surprise. Each roll of film will produce an alternate view of what transpired. do snapshot adds another dimension to holidays, special moments or everyday events. do likes to help people see things in a different way.

Here are a few more ways do continues to invite people to do things differently.

An alternative way of voting is do vote. [92] By providing a tick-box design and red pen, do vote is the chance for people to make their own political message with words or imagery. do remains happily neutral in this editorial project for a political race. [93] The objective is simply to include more people in the election process by providing tools to express themselves. But while the tools offer a start, it's up to the individual again to make their voice heard around the world.

92) do vote
(Page 202-203)

93) do race
(Page 204-205)

Speaking of world, have you heard of do fc? [94] While the world was going nuts for football at the World Cup in Japan in 2002, do created a special product that would tell a different story about football. do fc, or do football club, is a reminder to everyone that football is a simple game that can be played almost anywhere by almost anyone. It doesn't require wealthy sponsors, expensive equipment or fancy arenas. In fact, football is easy and to prove this, do fc provided a small kit to create your own football club. Called do fc, the kit contains rolls of thick tape that can be used for a variety of purposes. One roll has the pattern of a football that can be bunched up into a ball. Another roll can be used for lines on the pitch. There are rolls for names on shirts, fans and even silver tape for making a trophy or cup.

94) do fc
(Page 206-216)

do fc was exhibited, and played, at the Open Gallery in Tokyo, Japan during the World Cup in 2002. The games were played on a taped pitch using a taped ball and all the inexpensive equipment provided by do. It was just a pure way of saying that football can happen at any time and that we should never lose sight of this even in the shadow of heavily sponsored tournaments and events.

When do was invited to create an exhibition at the Rotterdam Photography Biennial, the concept of photography and its purpose were a central theme. Photography and the image culture we live in may erode how we look and remember. do remember [95] is a memory game that consists of photographed portraits of faces that are tightly cropped. What is plain to see when playing the game is that the faces all have a similar look. It's difficult to tell them apart.

95) do remember
(Page 217-220)

At the Biennial, do remember games were available for people to play in an exhibition space. Visitors were invited to play games at tables and challenge their memories. In this way, do made a comment on the way we see people nowadays. It seems that our visual culture has questioned our ability to see and remember faces that we see in our daily life. do remember makes us look closely again and find those unique features that make people singular and therefore memorable.

Oh, and by the way, do you remember the last plastic bag you were given with your shopping? More and more, plastic bags are piling up in our trash heaps, landfills and garbage dumps, contributing to the plastic portion of our ecosphere. In fact, some reports have stated that plastic fibers have been found in the membranes of certain sea life. In an attempt to breathe new life into people's plastic bag [96] collections, do a plastic bag is a way to reuse plastic bags of all kinds. Consisting of an instruction booklet and a pair of knitting needles, do a plastic bag provides a way for people to knit new designs of plastic bags for new and everyday purposes.

do always strives to raise certain questions about the possibilities of brands and their role in society. What can a consumer do in return? [97] do continues to wonder whether maybe, possibly, it's a great time for a do climb, [98] or a do warm, [99] or a do rain [100] or a do shout? [101] But that all depends on you.

Hey car companies, what happened to the electric car? do would like to meet you and discuss a way for electric power to meet human power. Transportation is not just about getting from point A to point B anymore. It's of global importance.

Well, do's here when you want to do something.

do forward.

The future of do is and always has been in the hands of those who do. do is interested in collaborating with other brands, designers, architects, product designers, scientists, writers, artists, company directors, thinkers, teachers, students, explorers and marketers (just to name a few). The strength of do, and its most fragile element, is its need for collaboration and multi-way action. You are now just as responsible for do as anyone is. Without you, do is over.

While times have changed dramatically since do's introduction in 1996, some key forces remain the same. A majority of brands still offer full-service while limiting spontaneity. Creative and insightful people remain hungry for different and challenging ideas, products and opportunities. And a brand called do continues to be ever-changing and depending on what you do. So, here are 101 things to do. We look forward to seeing and hearing from you and do.

Hey, just one last thought from do. do current: Did you know that the current generation can name more brand names than names of birds or flowers or trees? Just something to consider as a new member of do.

Greetings from do.

Credits

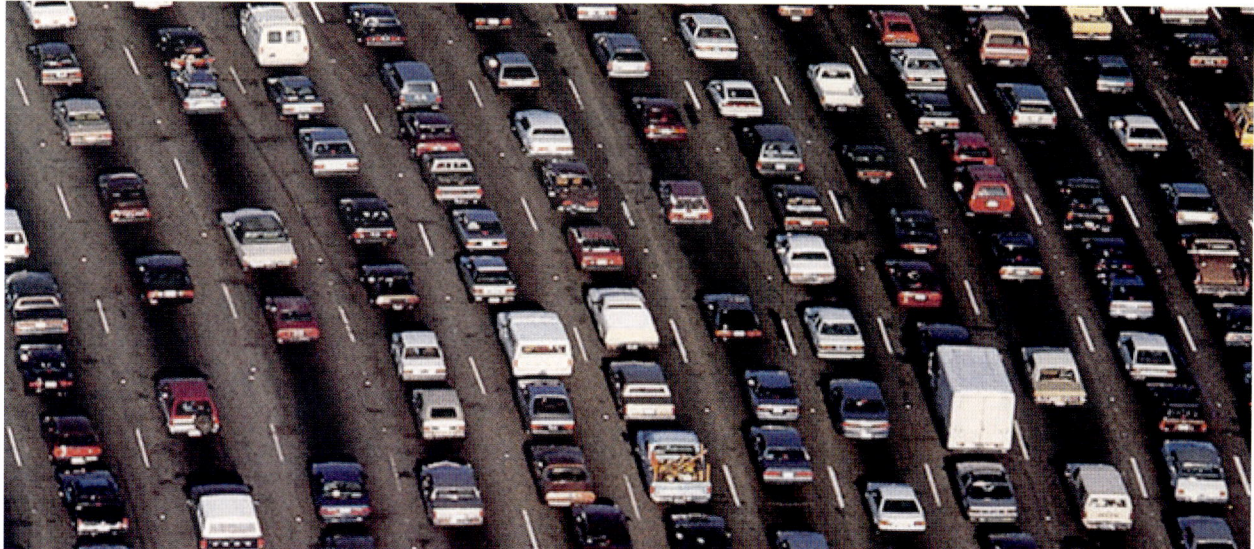

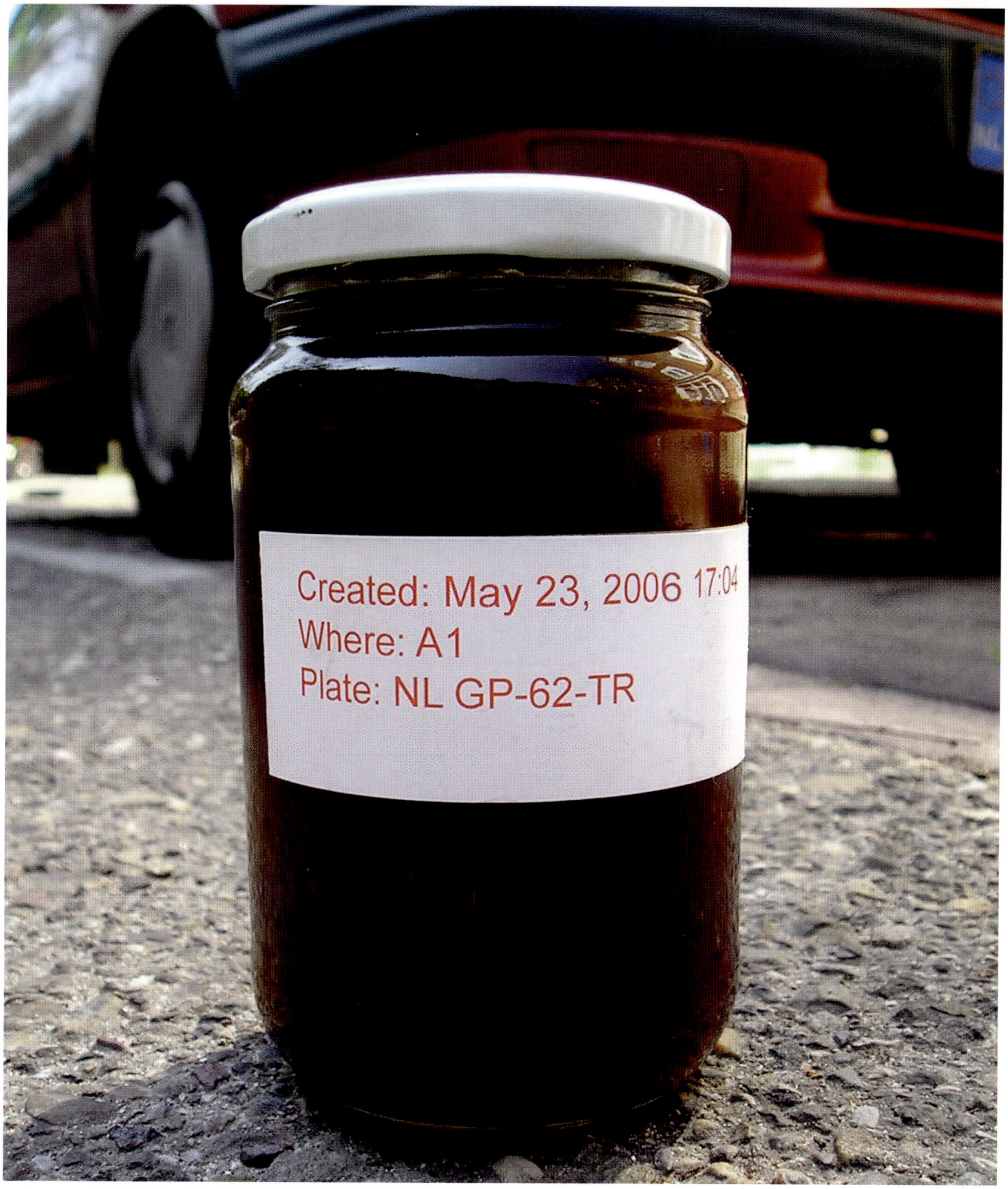

Created: May 23, 2006 17:04
Where: A1
Plate: NL GP-62-TR

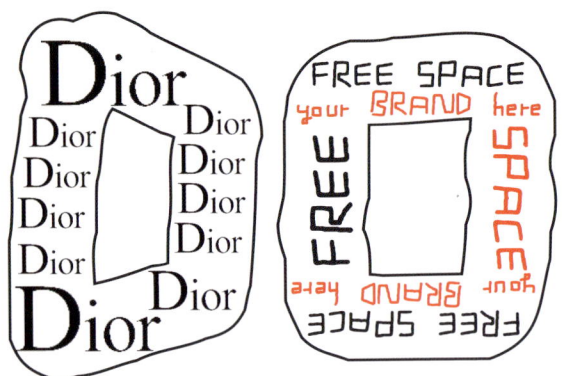
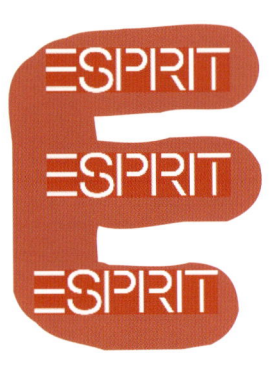
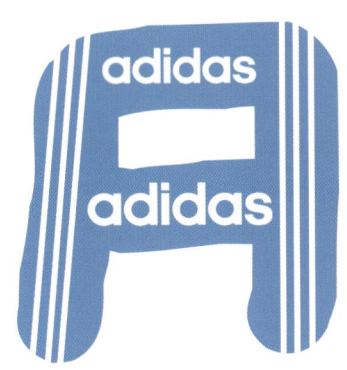
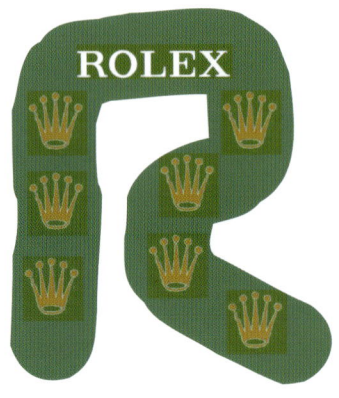
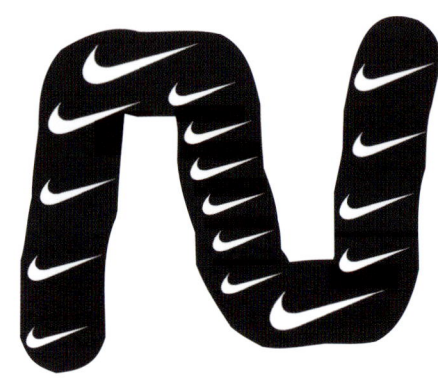

do earn Typo

Martí Guixé 2006

Instruction

1
Offer the letter space to brands

2
Use the typo

3
be payed per letter used

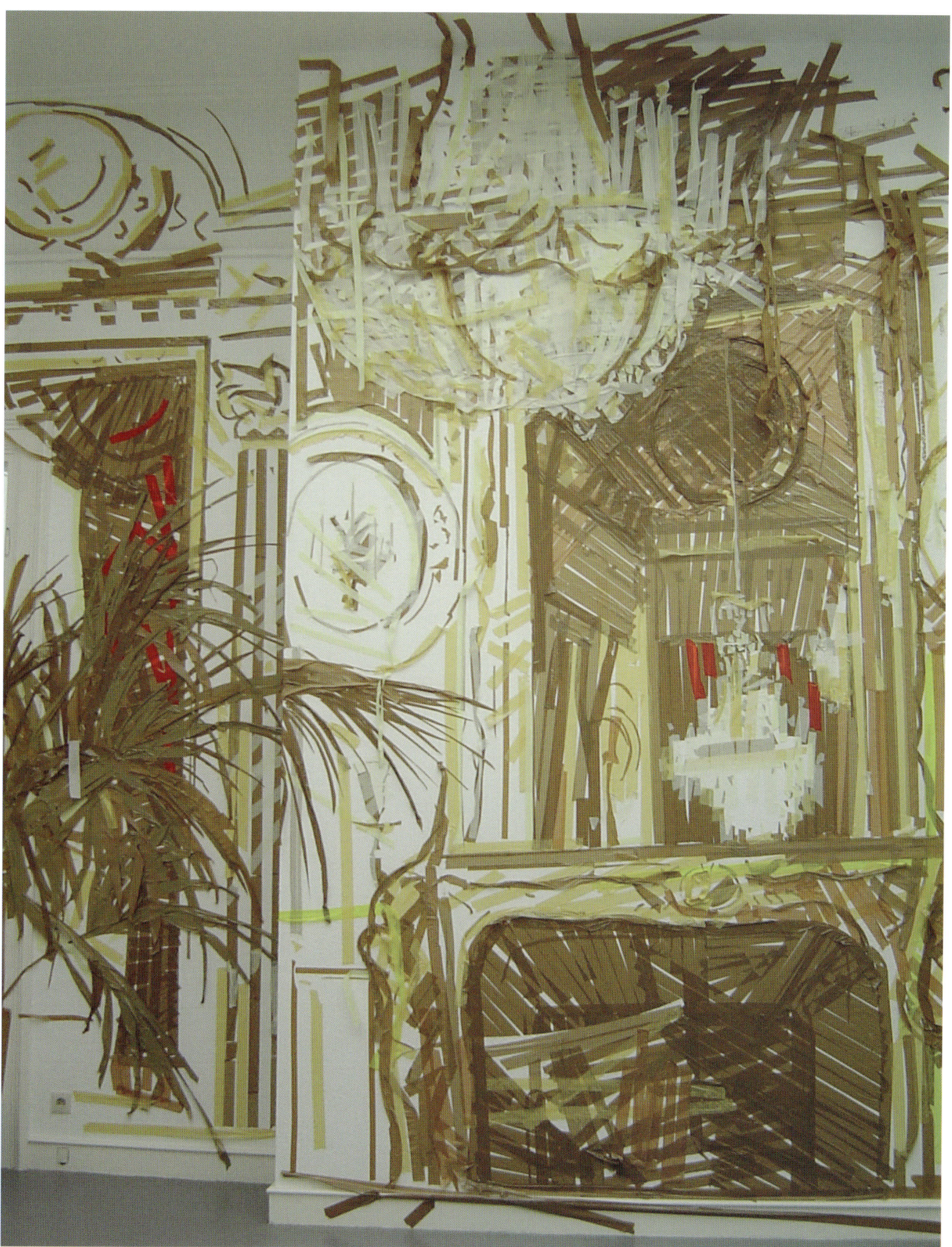

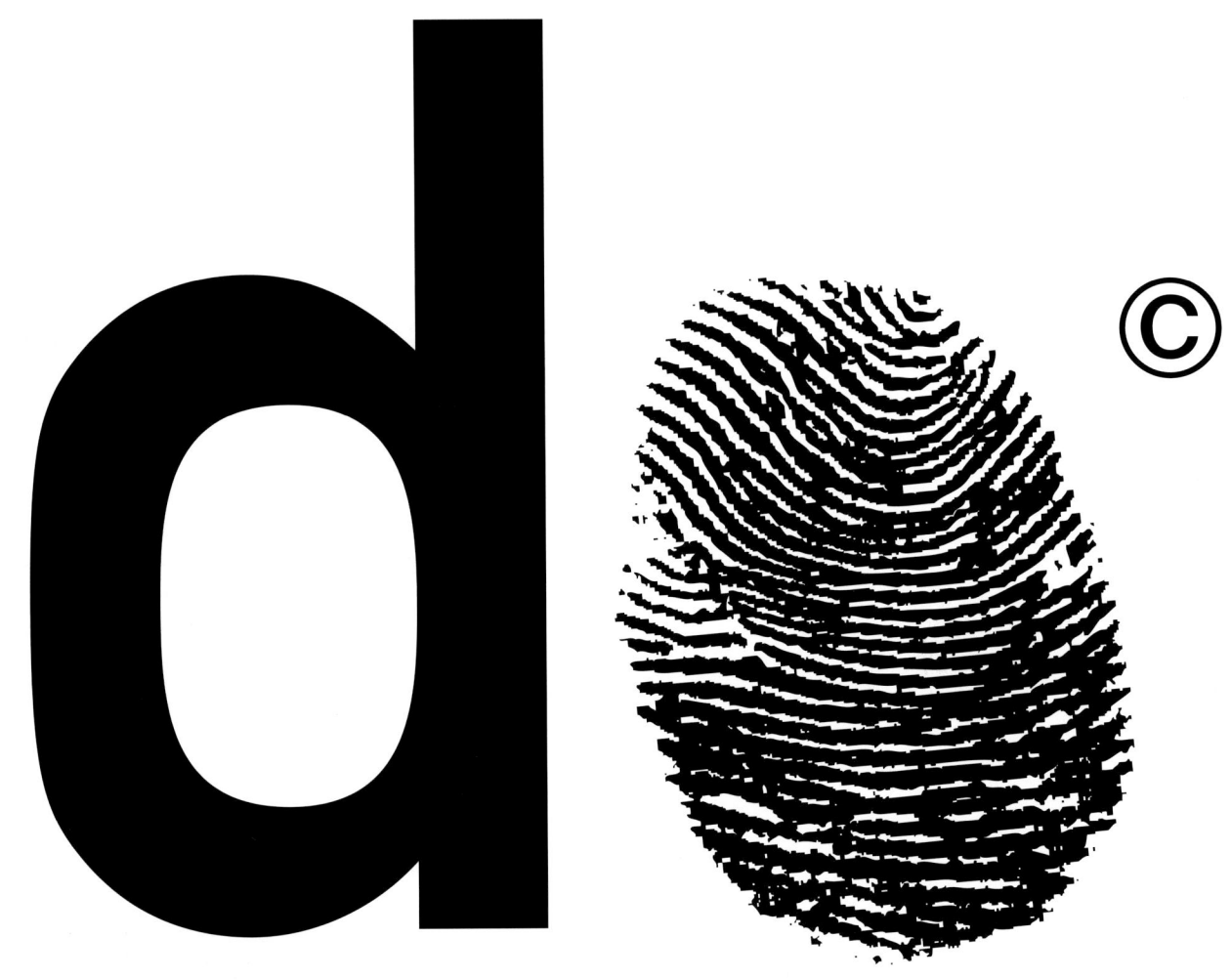

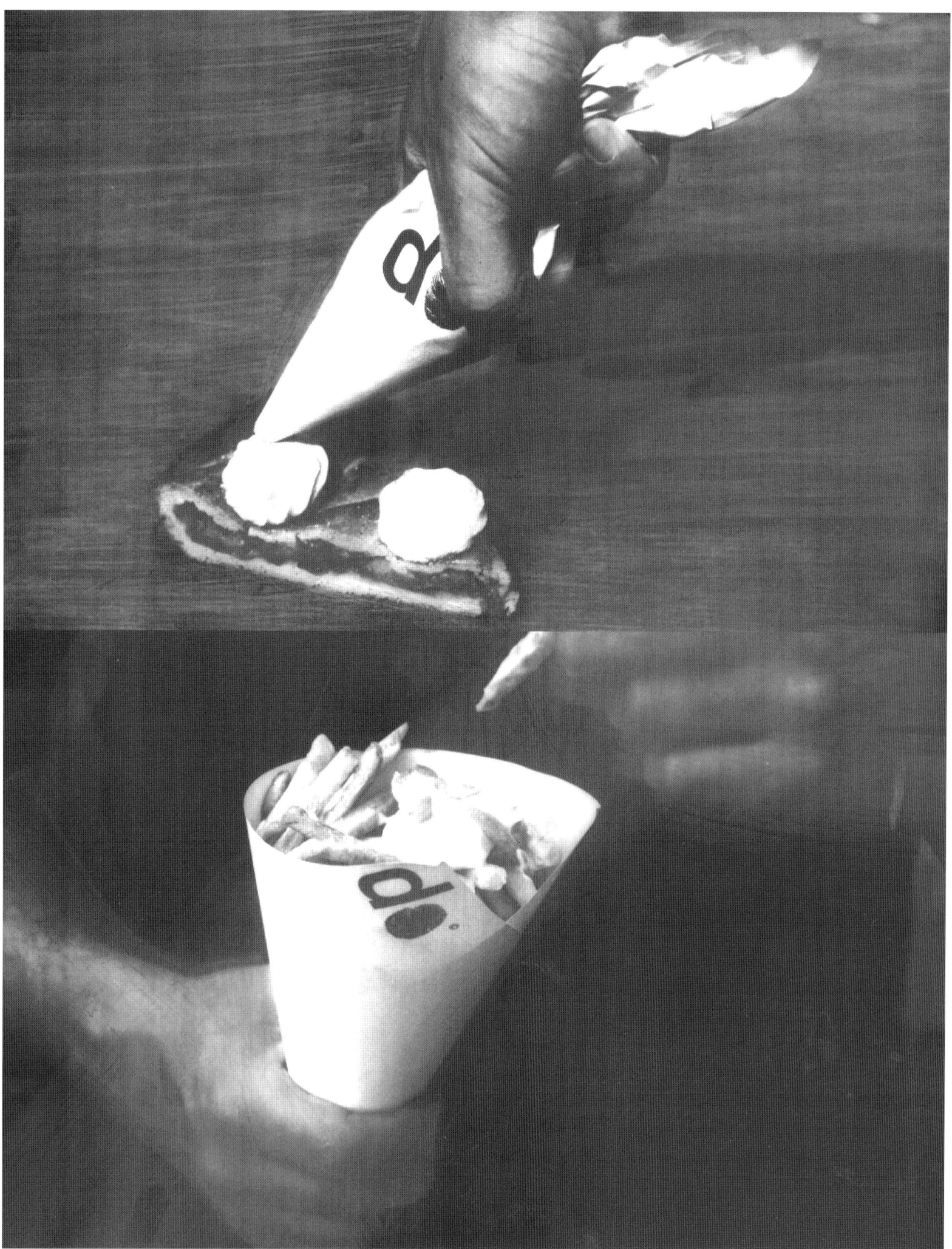

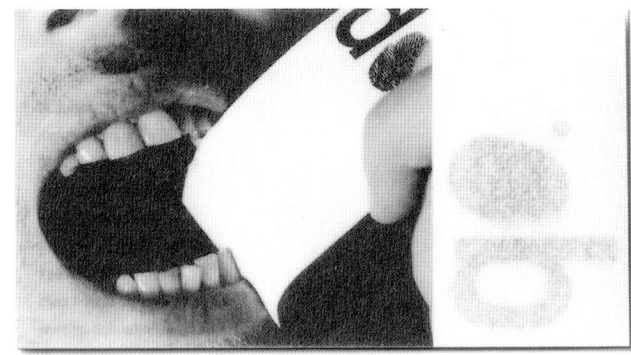

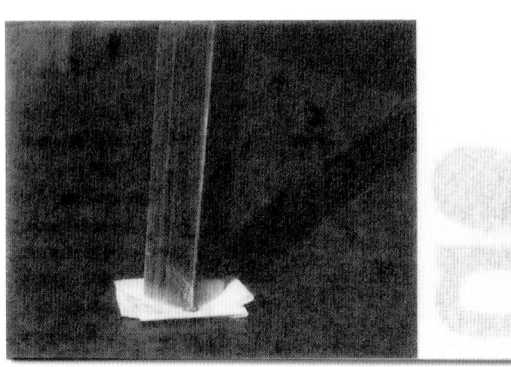

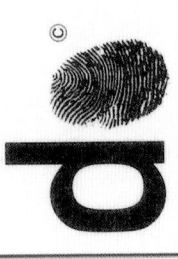 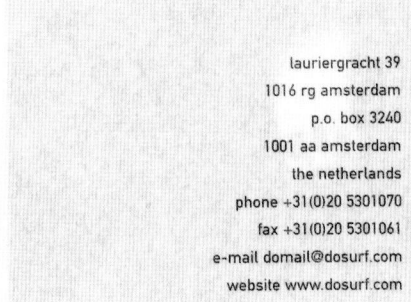

lauriergracht 39
1016 rg amsterdam
p.o. box 3240
1001 aa amsterdam
the netherlands
phone +31(0)20 5301070
fax +31(0)20 5301061
e-mail domail@dosurf.com
website www.dosurf.com

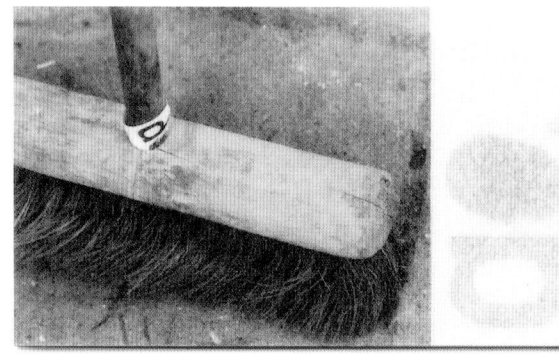

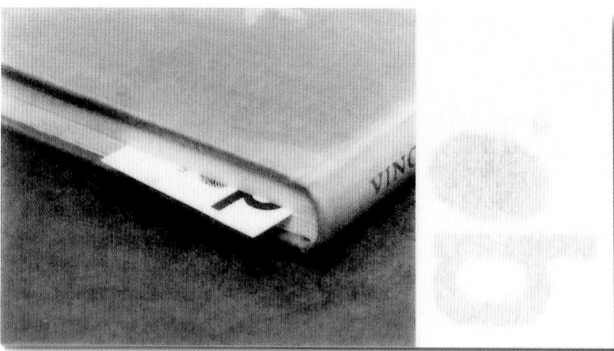

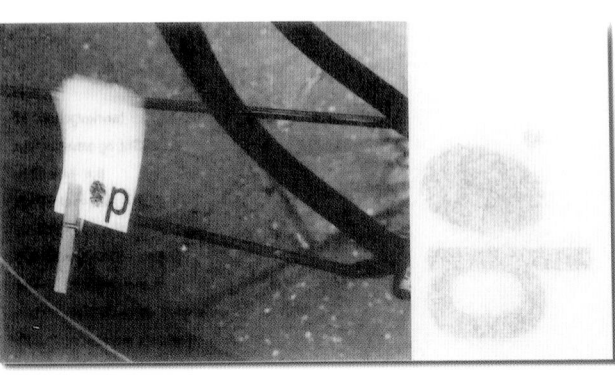

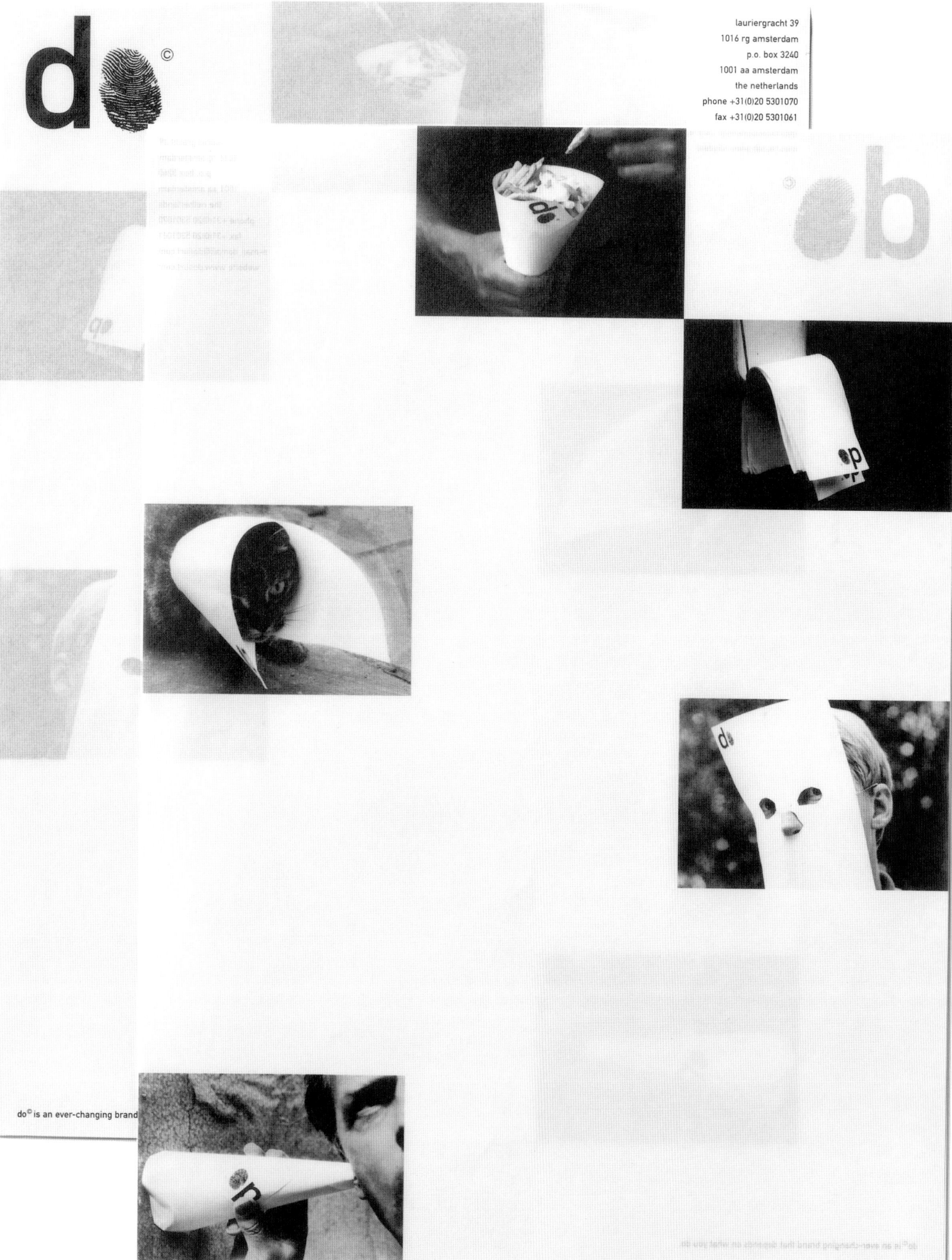

do©

lauriergracht 39
1016 rg amsterdam
p.o. box 3240
1001 aa amsterdam
the netherlands
phone +31(0)20 5301070
fax +31(0)20 5301061

do© is an ever-changing brand

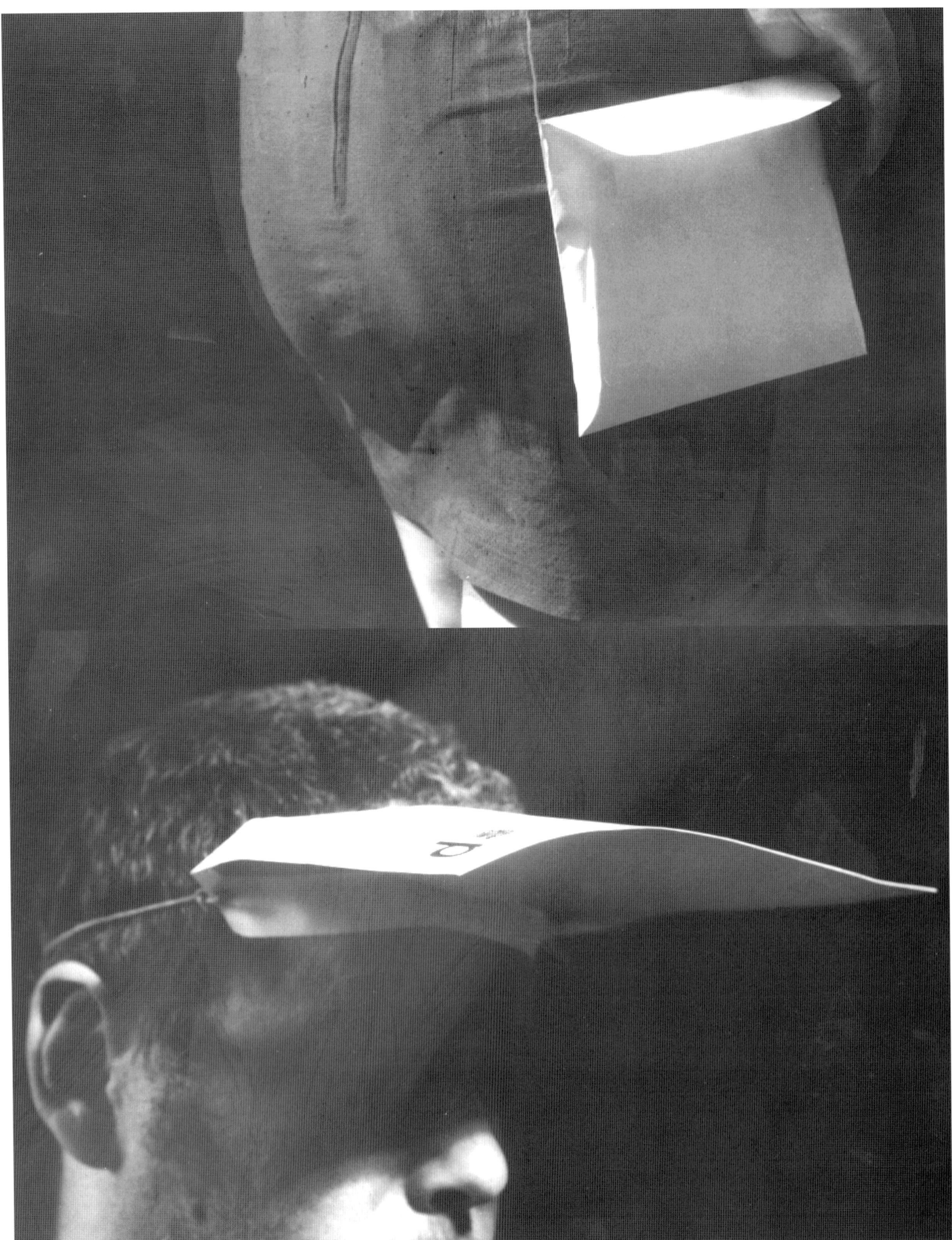

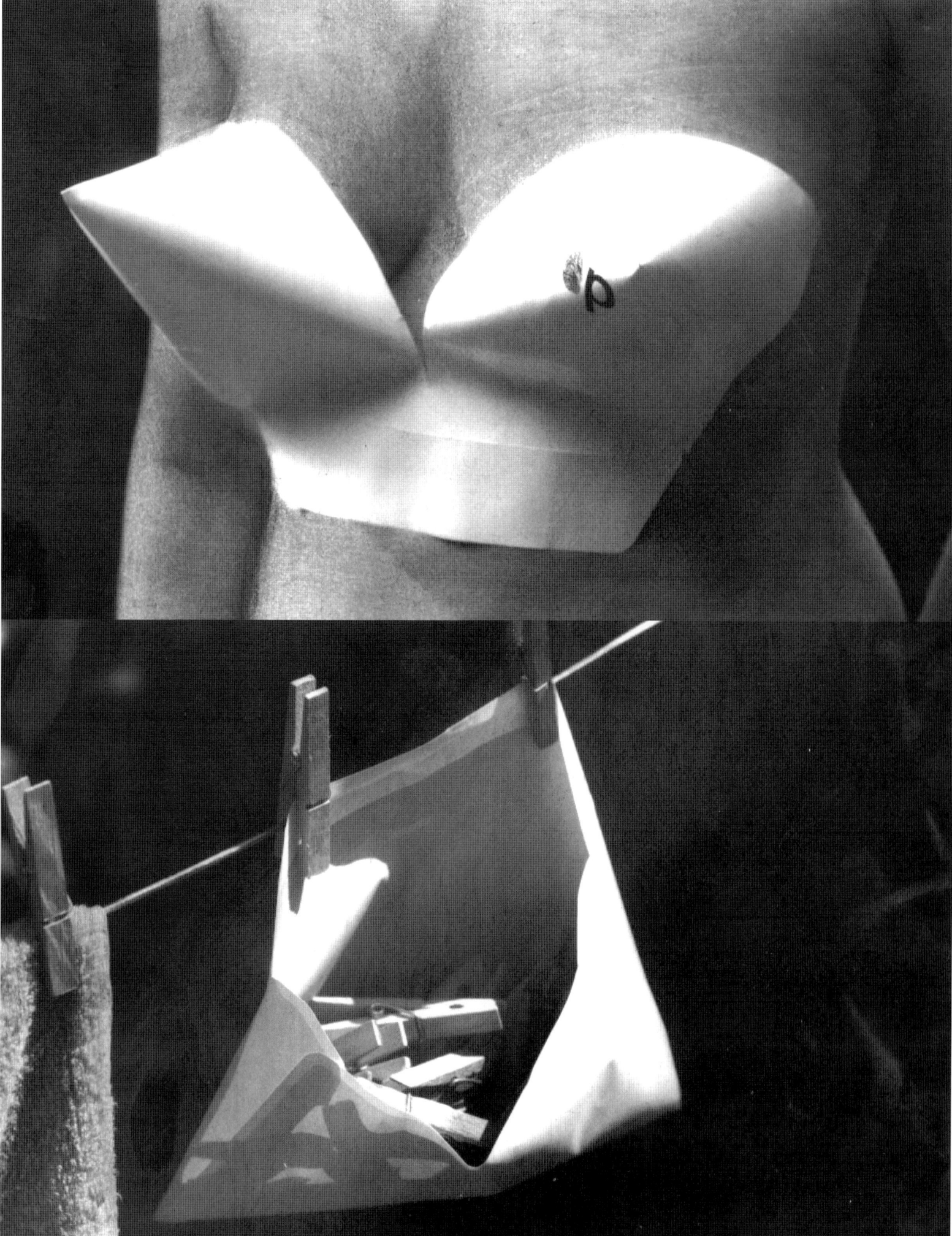

EAT IT ALL

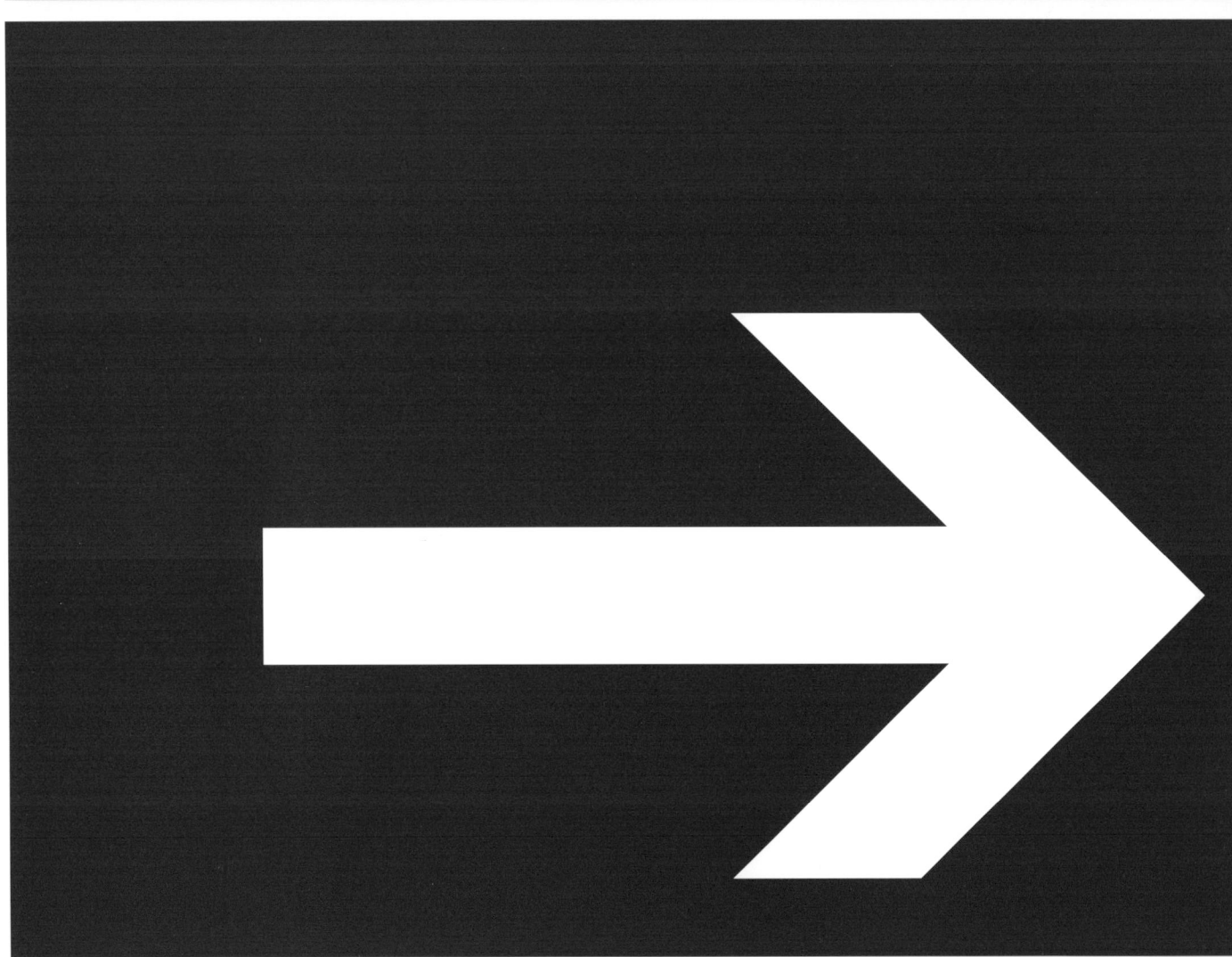

Food is boring, the limits of food are not endless, everybody is bored of eating the same kind of food every day. DoTEETH enables us all to extend the palette of culinary experience. By simply removing your existing natural teeth and replacing them with DoTEETH you can begin to explore a whole new world of pleasure. DoTEETH cut easily through most metals, wood, and many plastics. The nutritional benefits of 'non organic' food products are boundless, for example a diet rich in concrete will give you a deeper feeling of solidity and connection to the ground beneath your feet. So throw off the shackles of out dated and old fashioned food options with DoTEETH, your gateway to a happier tomorrow. Contact your local DoTEETH supplier for more information and to book a free 'no obligation' demonstration.

DoTEETH

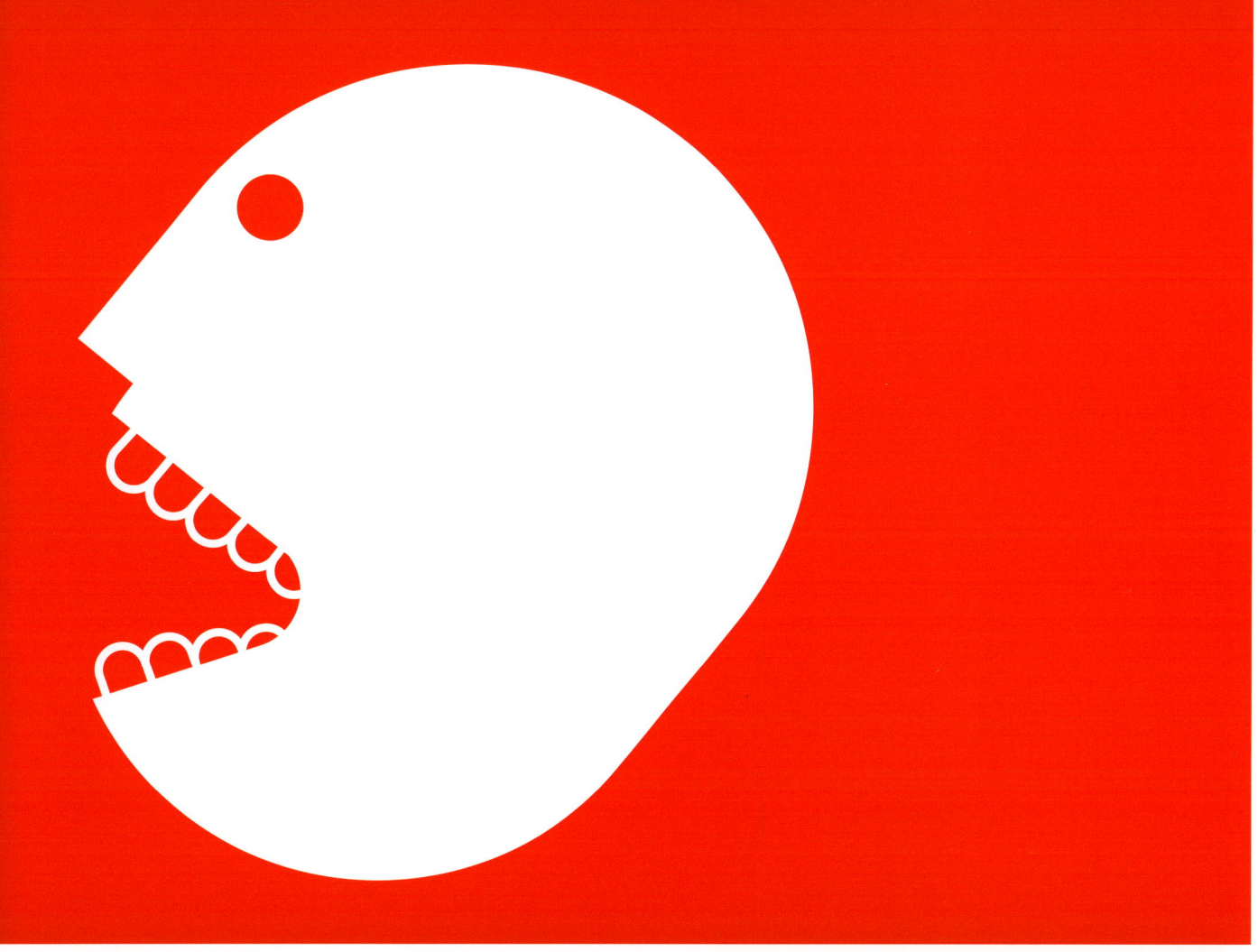

WARNING: DoTEETH must
only be used in conjunction with
'DoSTOMACH' and 'DoINTESTINES'.

Some modification of your home
may also be necessary.

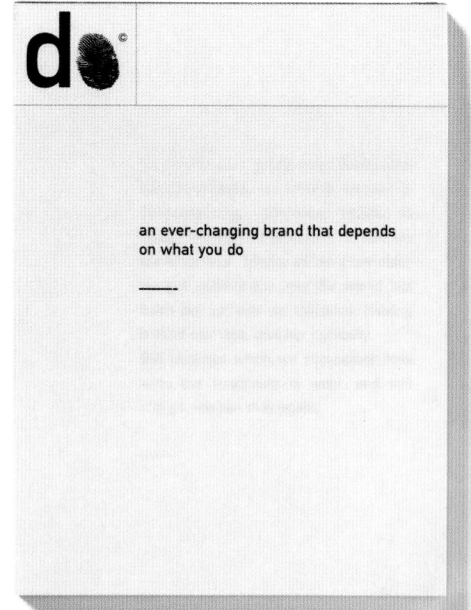

an ever-changing brand that depends
on what you do

——

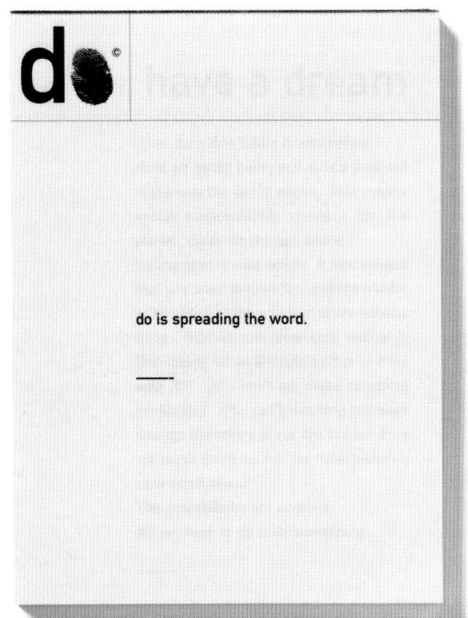

do is spreading the word.

——

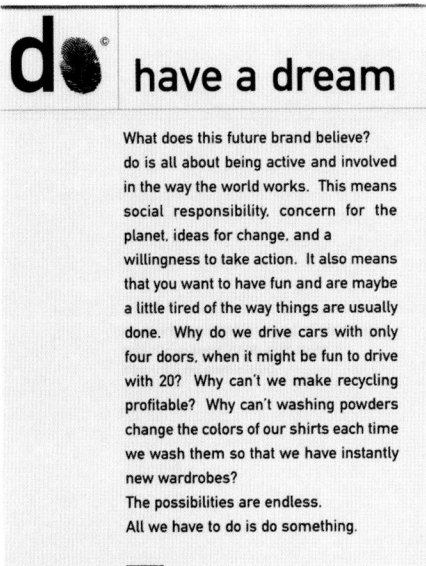

have a dream

What does this future brand believe?
do is all about being active and involved
in the way the world works. This means
social responsibility, concern for the
planet, ideas for change, and a
willingness to take action. It also means
that you want to have fun and are maybe
a little tired of the way things are usually
done. Why do we drive cars with only
four doors, when it might be fun to drive
with 20? Why can't we make recycling
profitable? Why can't washing powders
change the colors of our shirts each time
we wash them so that we have instantly
new wardrobes?
The possibilities are endless.
All we have to do is do something.

——

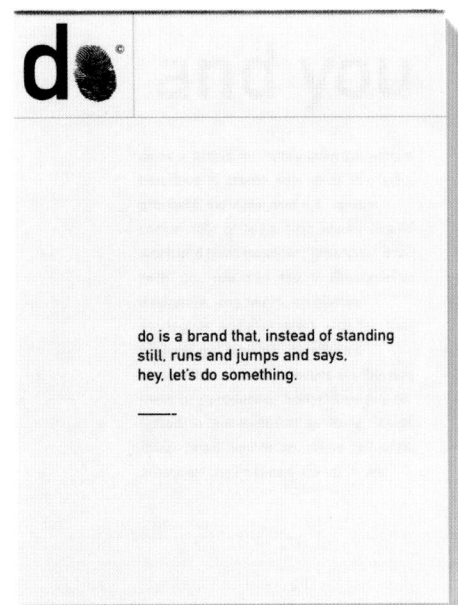

do is a brand that, instead of standing
still, runs and jumps and says,
hey, let's do something.

——

do

When we were young kids, punks and trouble-makers, we always wanted to do something. We never wanted to sleep. We didn't understand TV. And we were curious. Maybe as we grew older we got used to the way the world has been set up, and we adjusted, leaving behind our toys, and our curiosity. But perhaps when we remember how wide our imaginations went, and still can go, we can play again.

——

do

What we can do.
Somewhere in the future is a brand that you are creating. It is a brand that responds to your ideas, feelings, and thinking. It is a brand that is flexible enough to allow lots of people to be involved. This wacky, future brand is a way to make new and different products and services for people who like to think and do.

Hello from do.

——

do today

do doesn't have any products or services, just a dream. To communicate this dream, do is making all kinds of communication and actions.
This way, more people can find out about do. After people know what they can do with do, then products, projects and services will be added. This is a new way to begin a brand. Usually, a brand starts with a product and then builds a mentality. do is starting with a mentality and then building products. This will help do remain flexible and dynamic enough to create many different types of products. A brand that has an idea on everything from shoes to roofing tiles while behaving with the same personality.

——

do and you

do is a brand for many different people who love to create new ideas in media, products, services, and art. do is a community of folks who would like to work and think together. When you work with do, you can tap a resource of designers, engineers, architects, strategists and marketers who can help projects get realized. do offers a completely new perspective on the way ideas are produced. Sometimes you're linked to a net-maker in Nova Scotia. Other times you're an online resource. Whatever may happen, it's up to you.

——

do and other brands

do can also work with other brands. When working with other brands to make new products, services, and communication, do will change already existing formats. do might make a special edition or a new line of items for a brand with new elements involved. Maybe a few architects from Amsterdam would like to create a new shoe for a shoe brand, or a painter from Santa Fe has a great idea for scuba suits that glow. do is the brand to go to. A brand that dances with other brands. do can change, adapt and refresh other brands.

——

do

do values your input and suggestions. You are now a do brand doctor. Welcome.

——

do contact

If you have an idea, suggestion or concept for do, and want to work together to make it happen, or if you would like to be kept updated about do, please contact do.
do, P.O. Box 3240,
1001 AA Amsterdam,
The Netherlands.
domail@dosurf.com

——

do

Once upon a time in   a   asked a

him on a   to   so that when his

,and there would be a   and a

to   him with

arrived, and

and all the time after that th

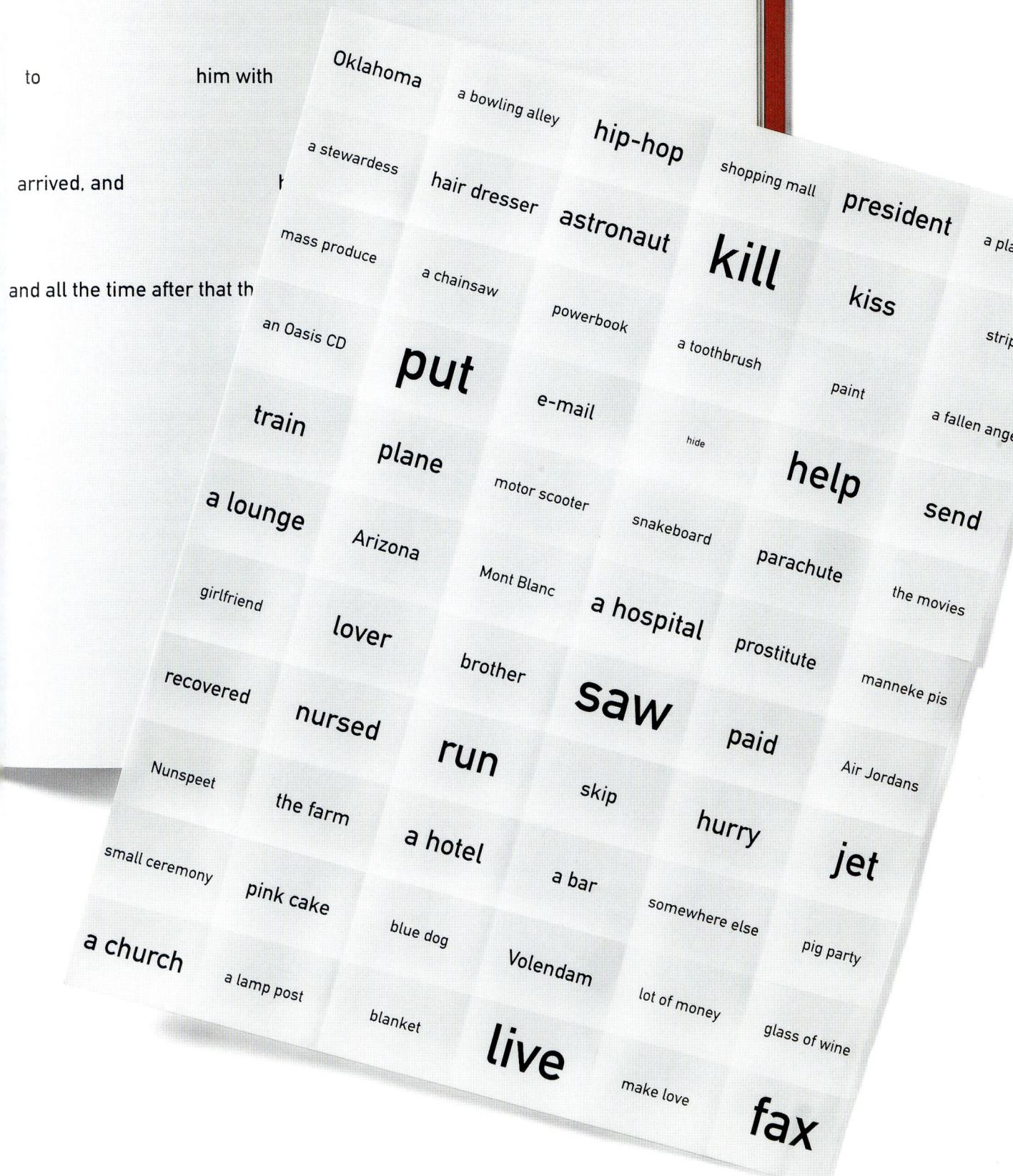

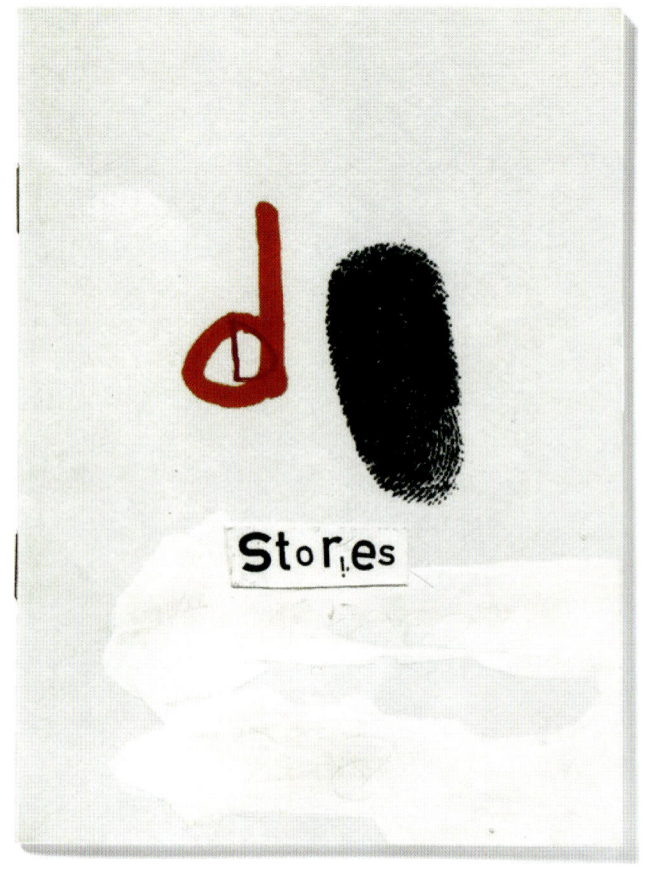

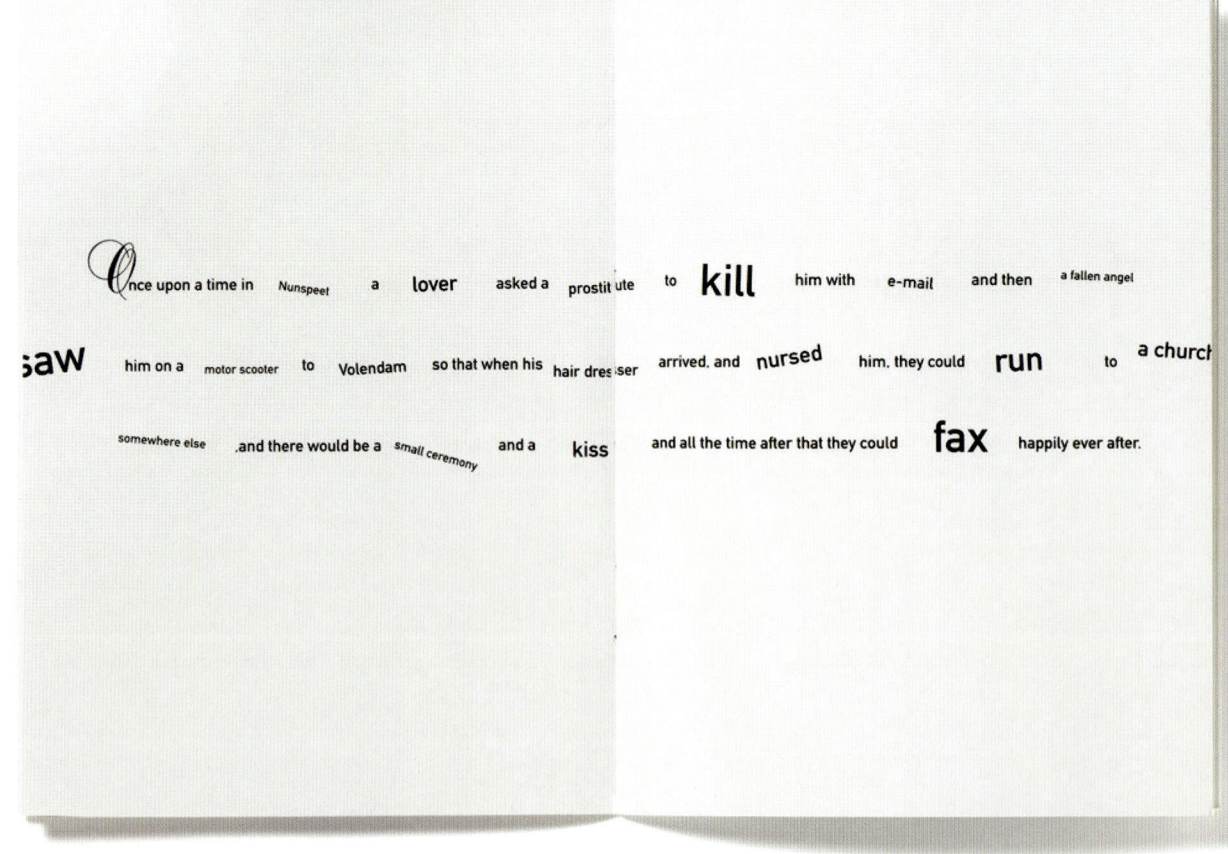

do asked people to compose

a story by inserting words into a basic story line.

Stories often twist and turn

depending on one word.

Words are important.

Words communicate.

Words tell others who we are, and how we feel.

So now, some stories from

some people.

do read.

Once upon a time in **a hospital** a brother asked a prostitute to mass produce him with pink cake and then hide him on a snakeboard to strip so that when his hair dresser arrived, and **paid** him, they could pig party to make love somewhere else .and there would be a chainsaw and a small ceremony and all the time after that they could **saw** happily ever after.

nursed by

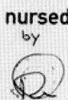

Once upon a time in Volendam a prostitute asked a a fallen angel to strip him with a stewardess and then hurry him on a train to Oklahoma so that when his lover arrived, and recovered him, they could make love to

empowering but not HUMAN enough?

manneke pis ,and there would be a small ceremony and a glass of wine and all the time after that they could **live** happily ever after.

a lamp post *—MORE positive?*

Once upon a time in a church a brother asked. a fallen angel to **fax** him with e-mail and then strip him on a train to Nunspeet so that when his girlfriend arrived, and **saw** him, they could hip-hop to an Oasis CD ,and there would be a small ceremony and a pig party and all the time after that they could **live** happily ever after.

send !

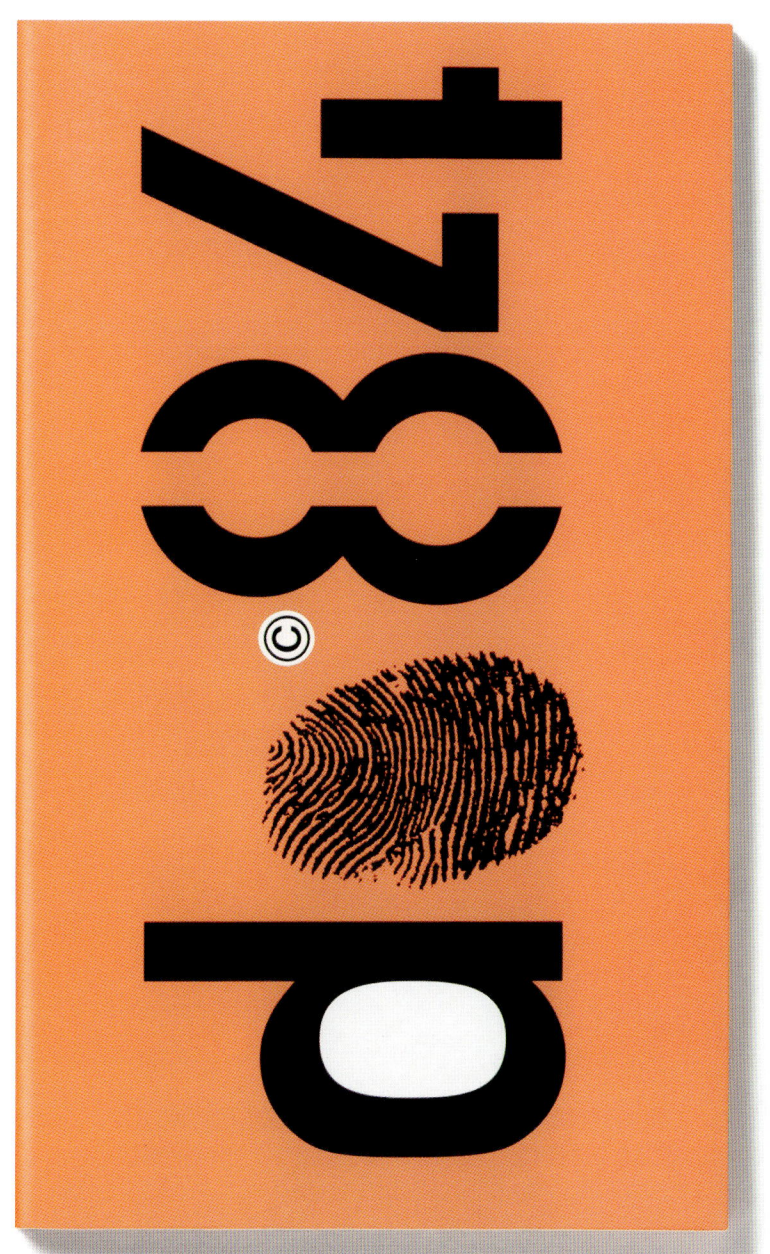

a book of 84 pages
of thoughts, strategies and
ideas about creating a
new brand.
with many different products
and services, a brand that
differs from the 6 billion other
brands existing today.
a brand that is not yet known.
a brand that is open to
interpretation by you.
a brand that is happening now.
a brand where you decide
what will happen next.
a brand called

ISBN 90-803927-1-5

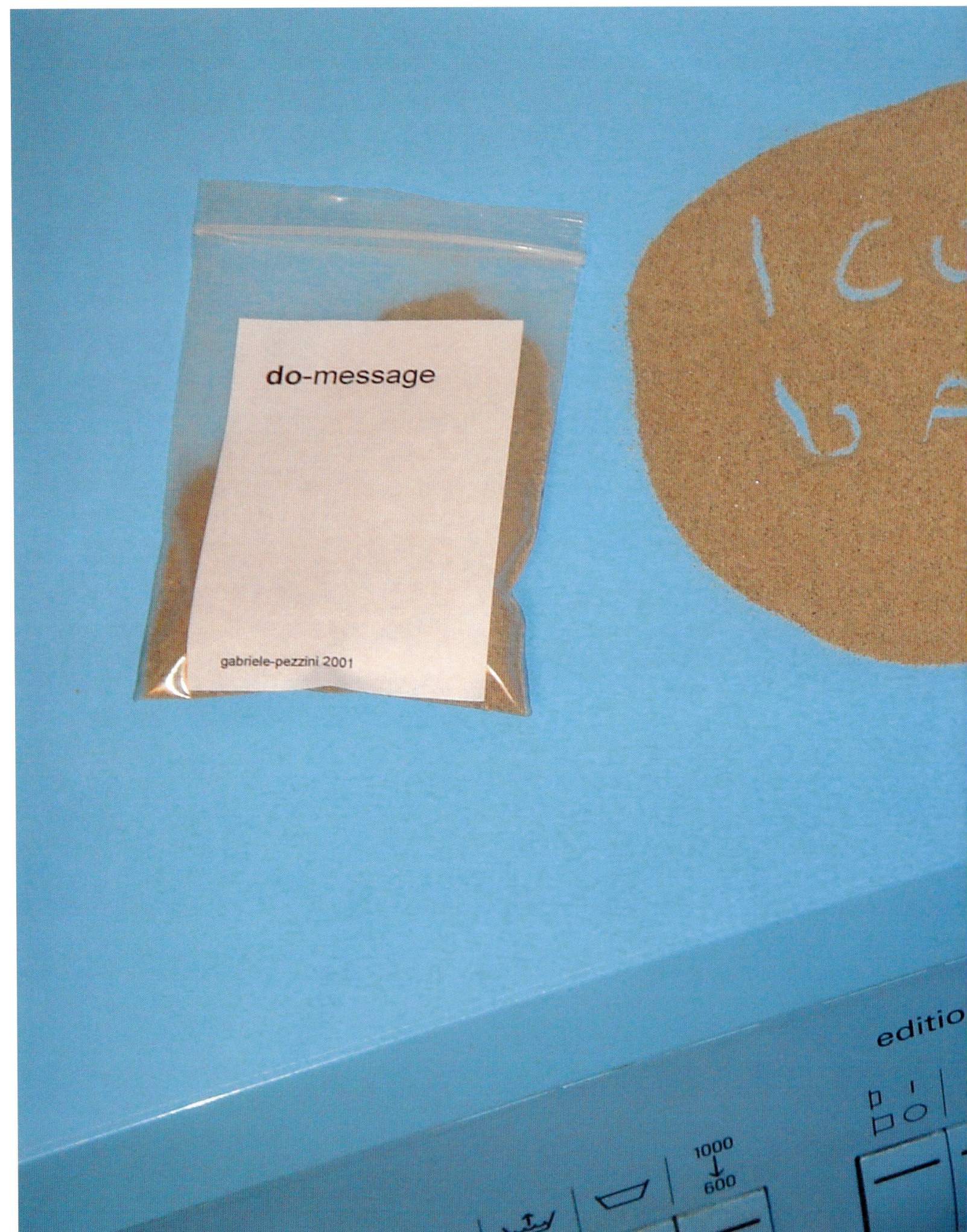

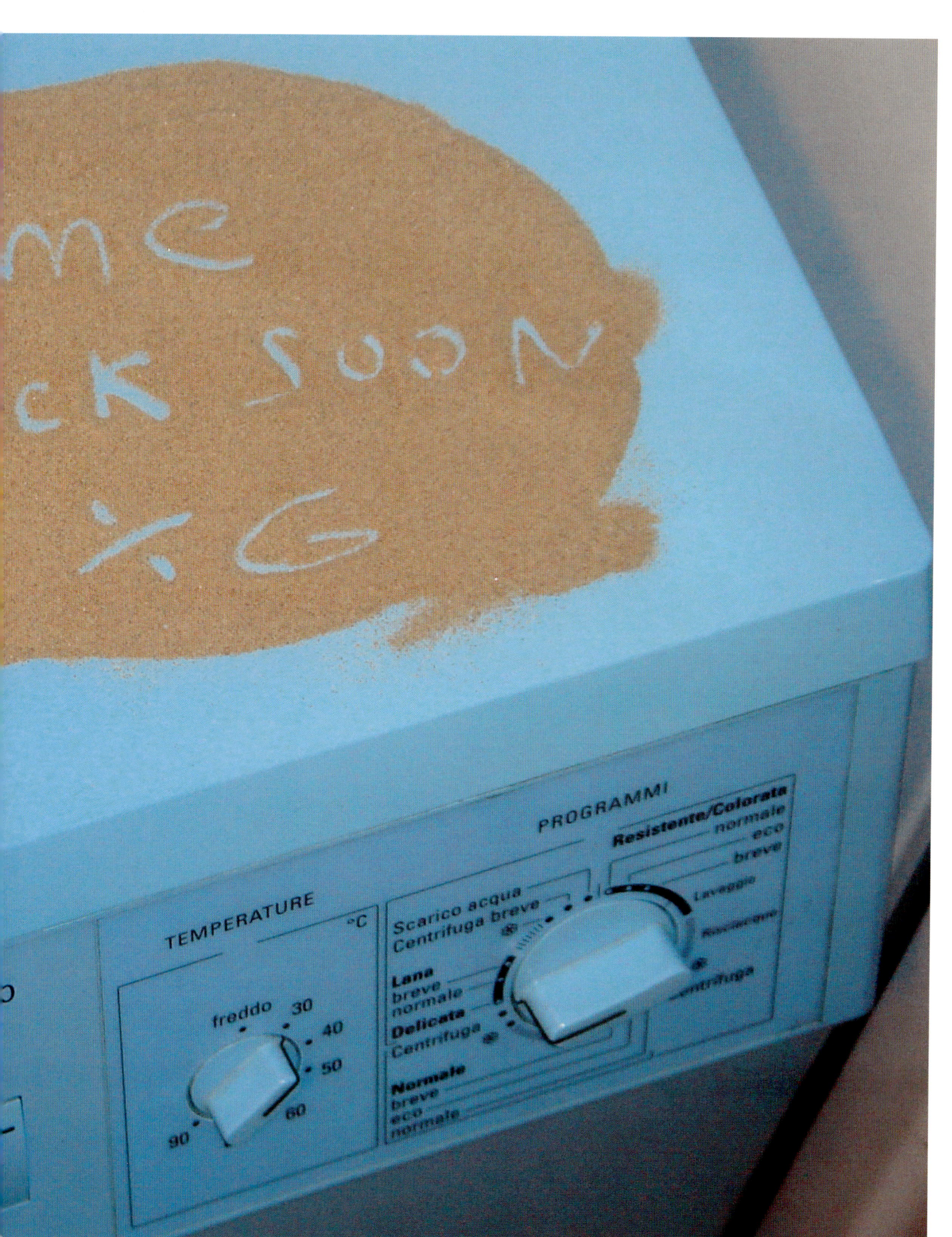

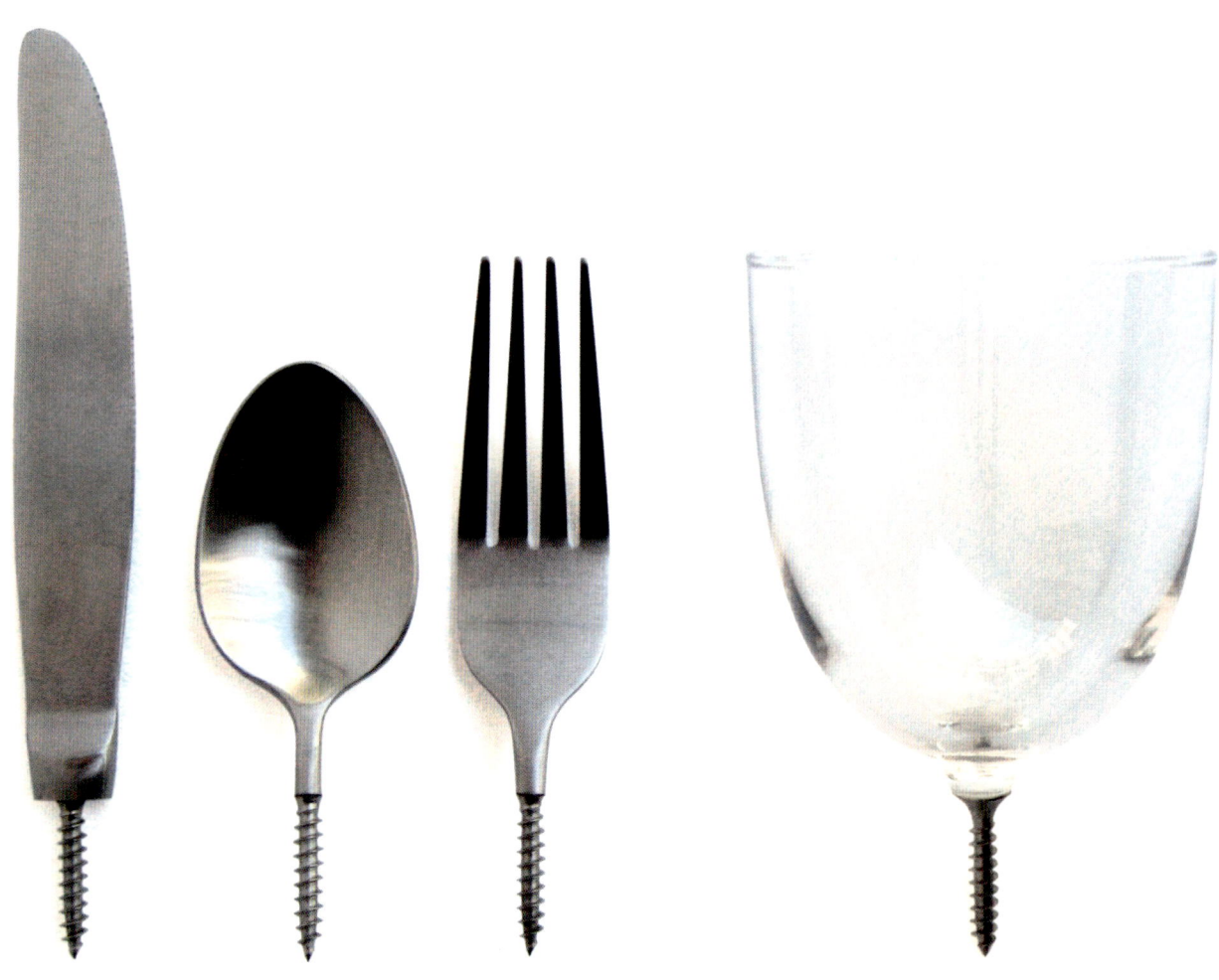

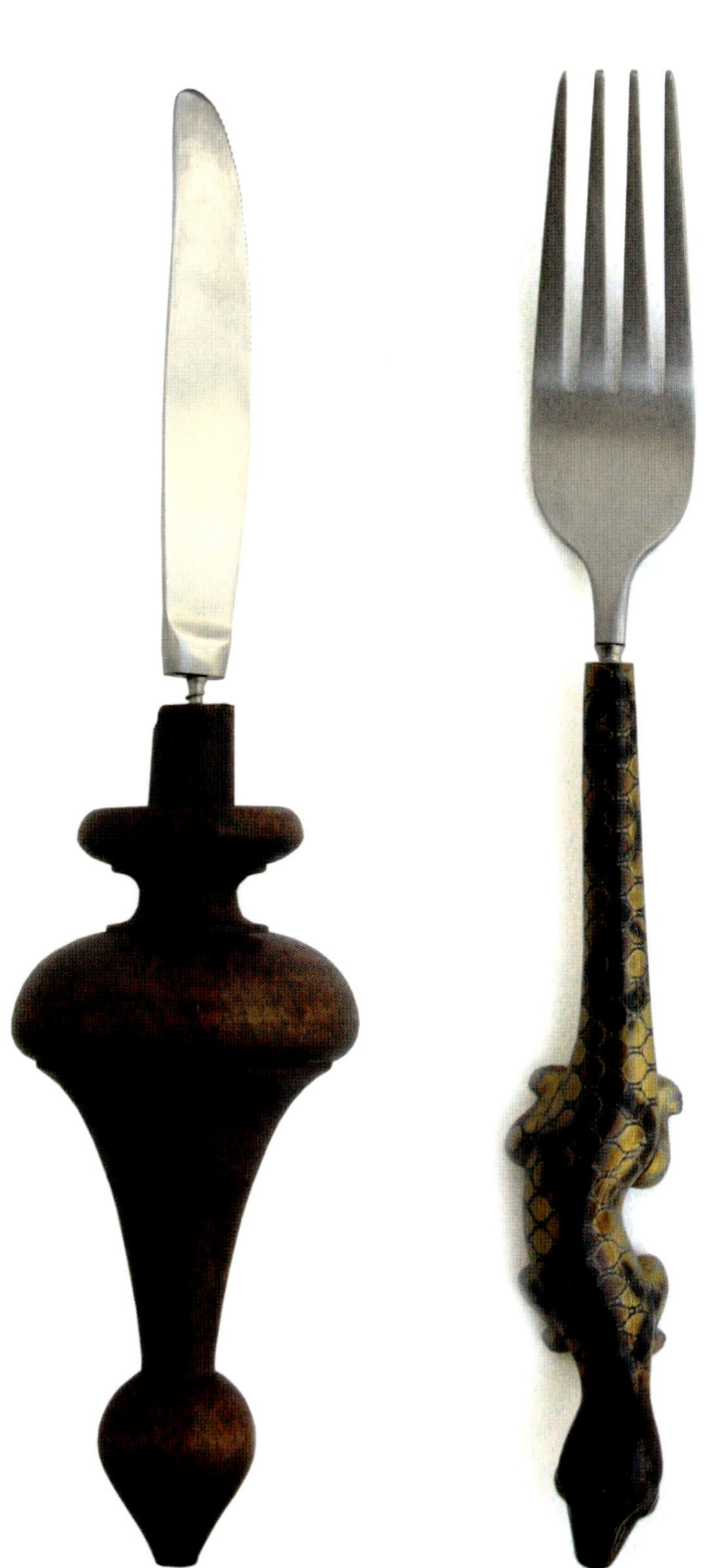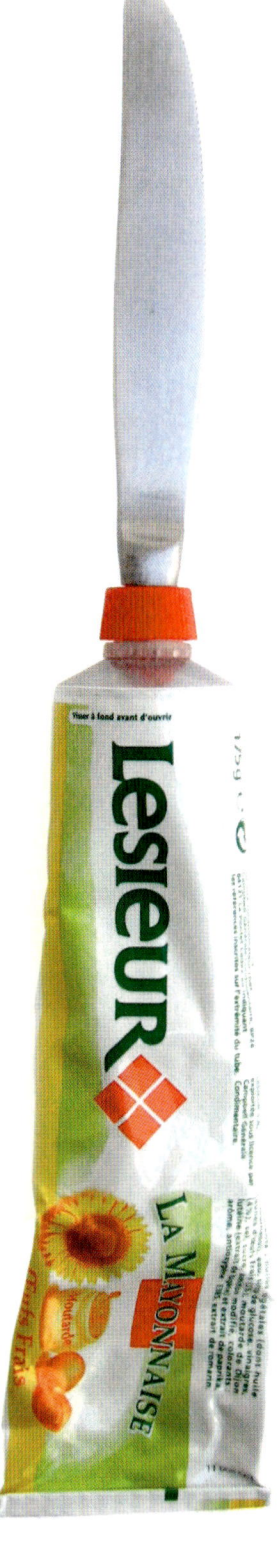

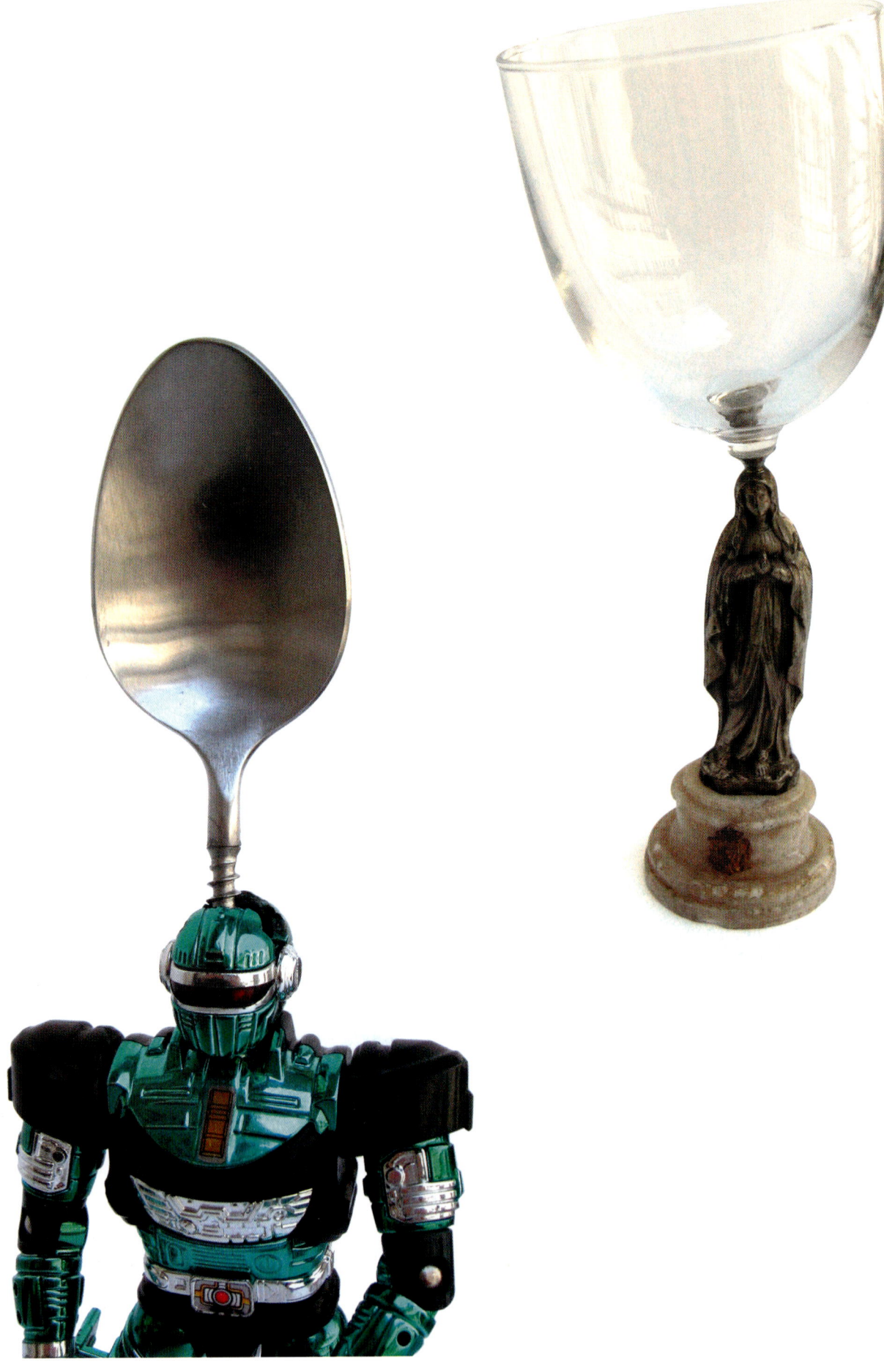

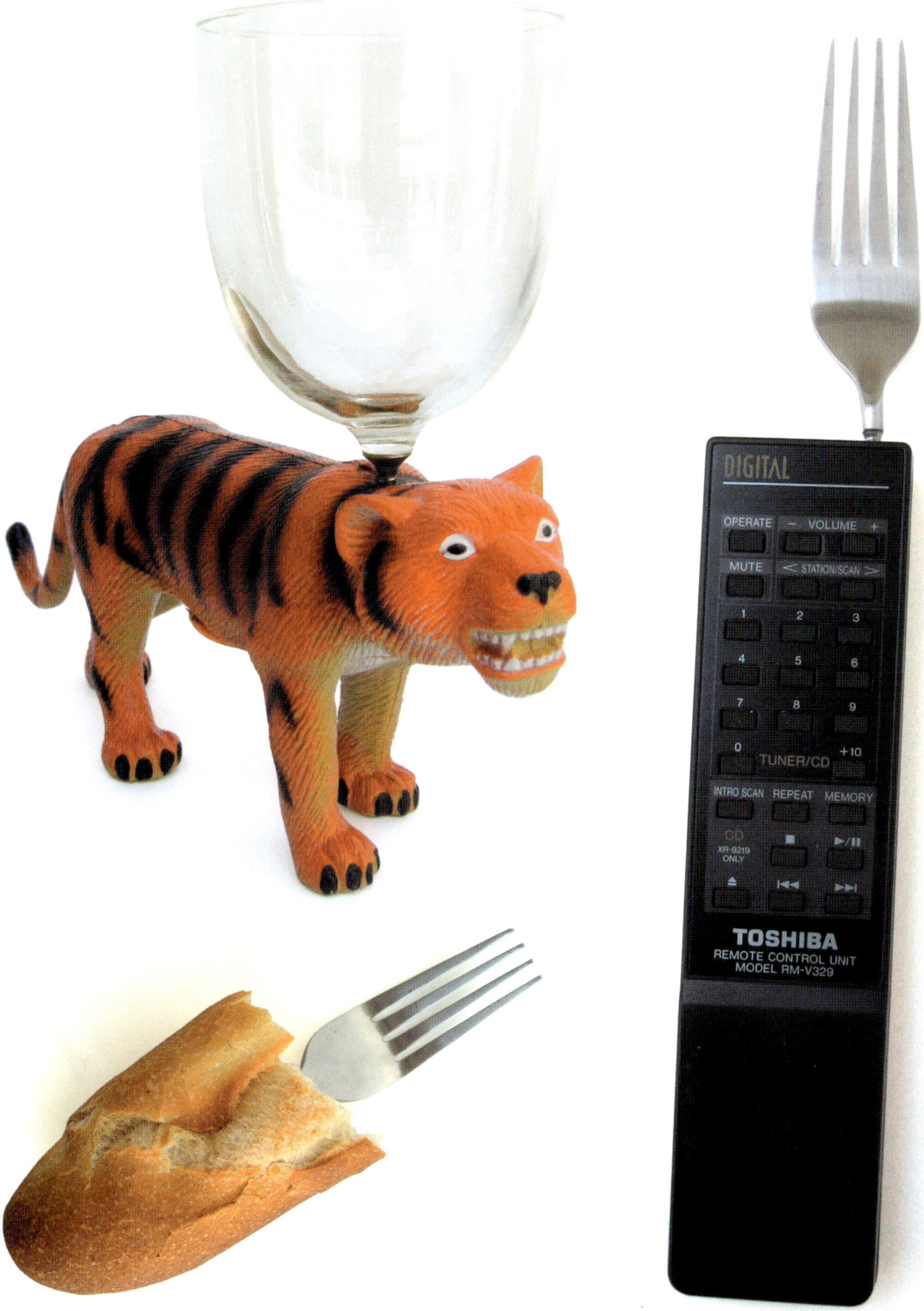

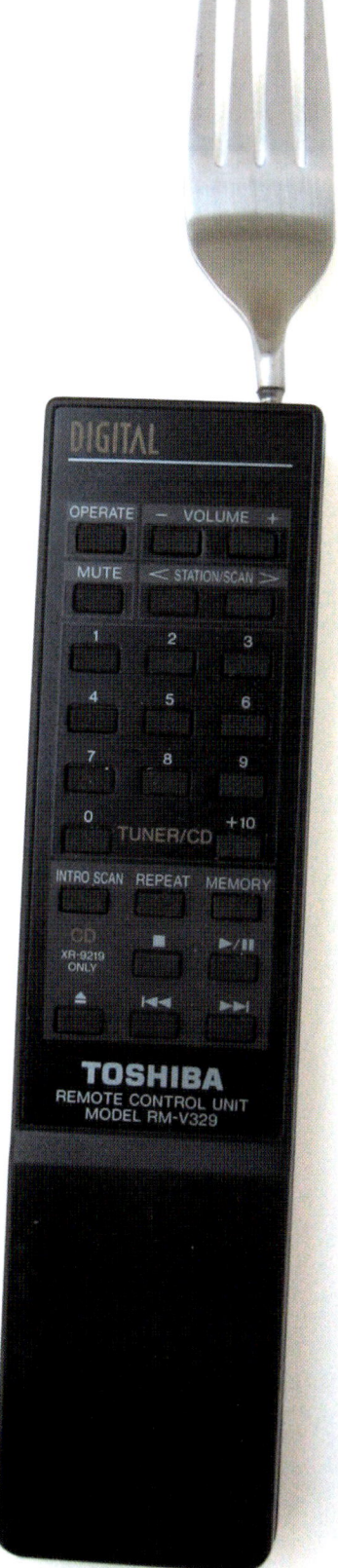

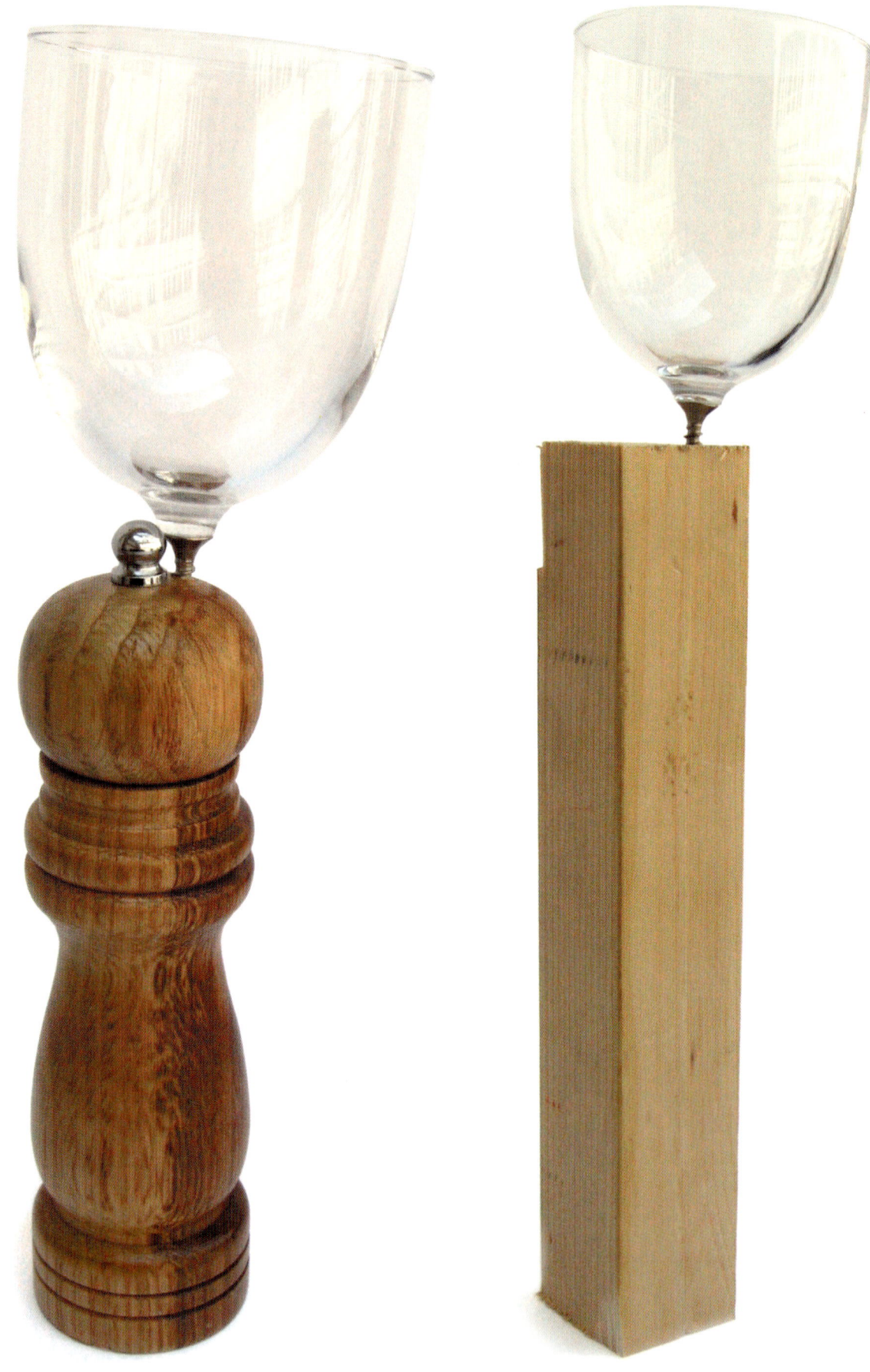

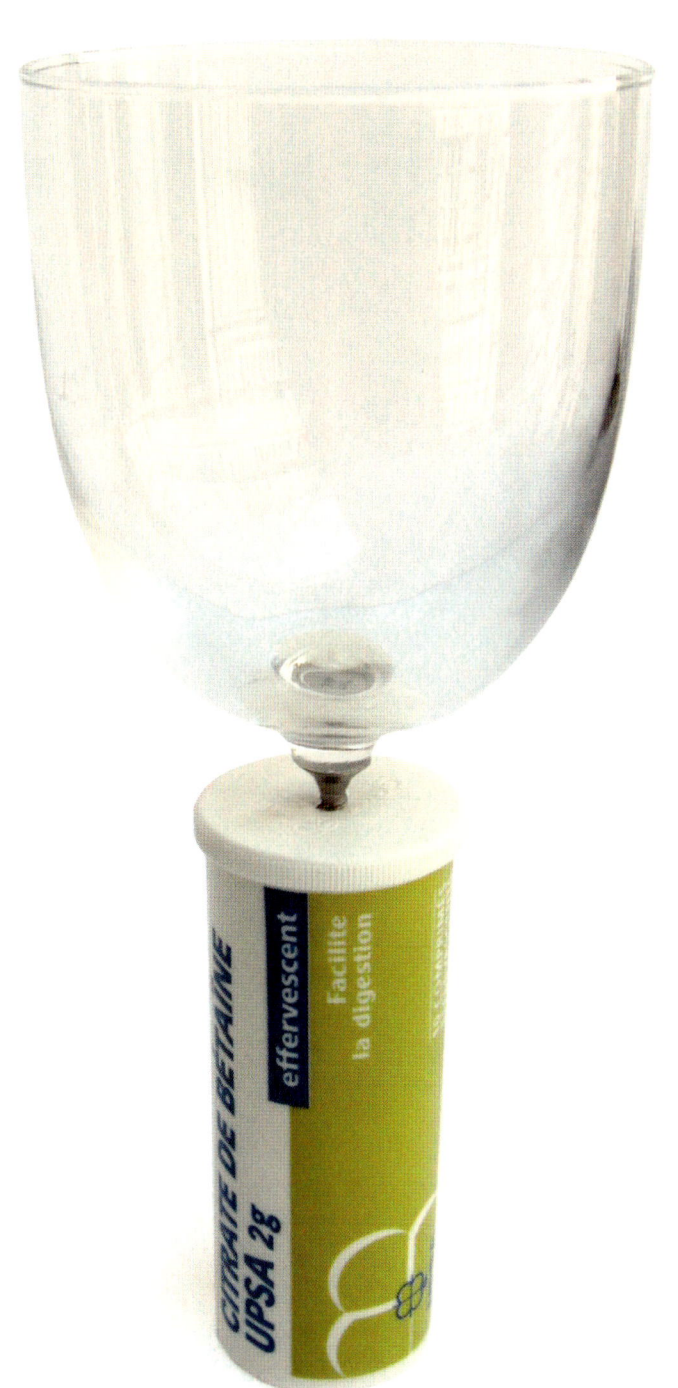
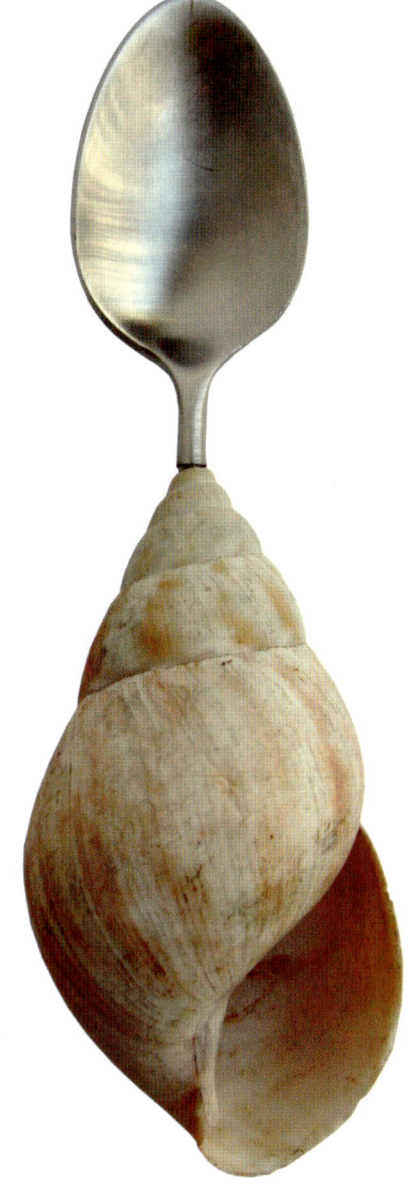

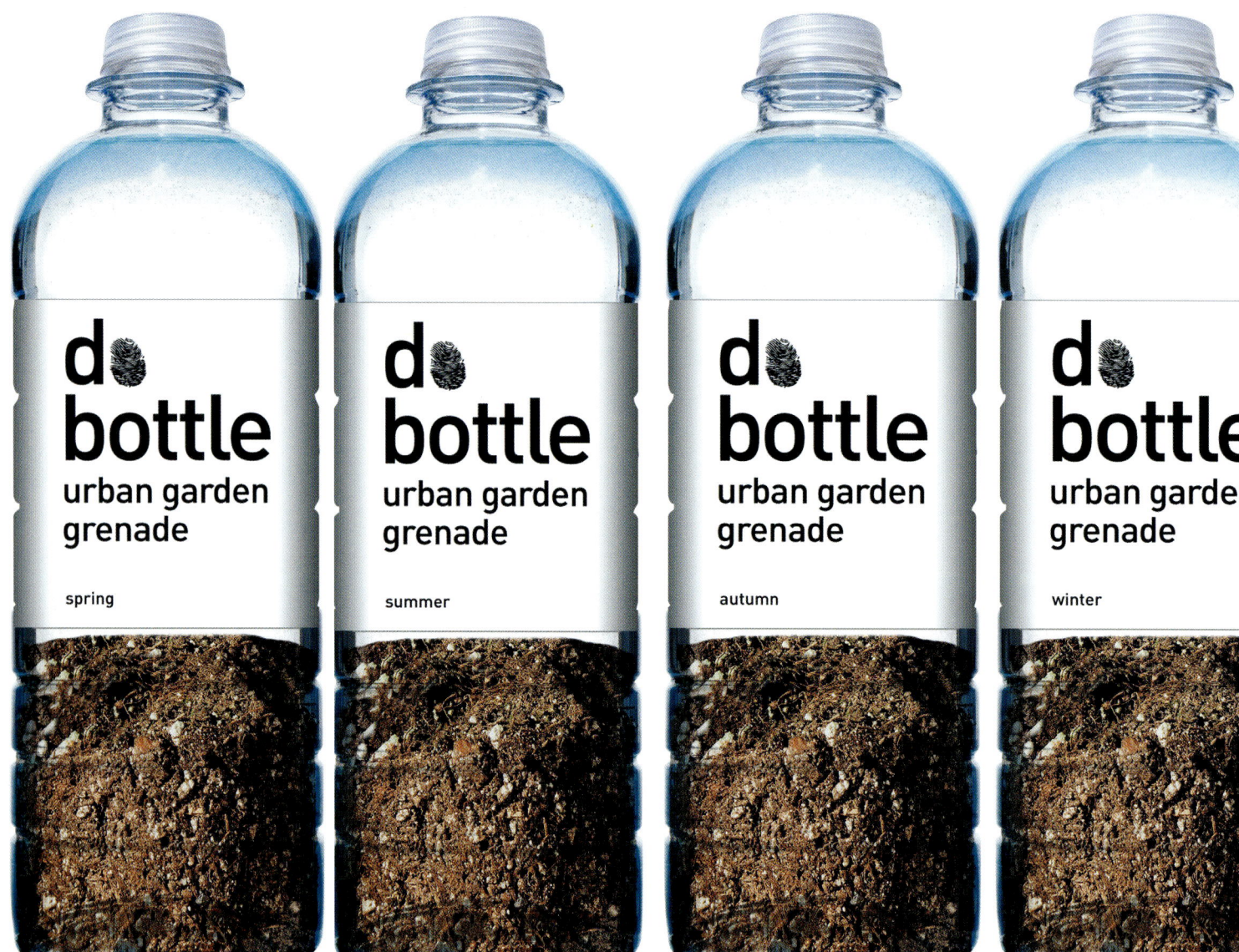

do bottle

urban garden grenade

spring

**instant karma.
just add water and throw.**

plastic bottles can take 450 years to degrade. that's a long time to be hanging out in a landfill. and in those 450 years, they create a lot of problems for our environment, like pollution and soil contamination.

but there's a better bottle. this bottle. it's made from corn and will decompose in a matter of weeks. fill it up with water, toss it somewhere in need of a little love and watch the gardens grow.

do bottle

urban garden grenade

spring

contains soil, fertilizer, peat moss, and seeds.

Do plus - componants. by fat

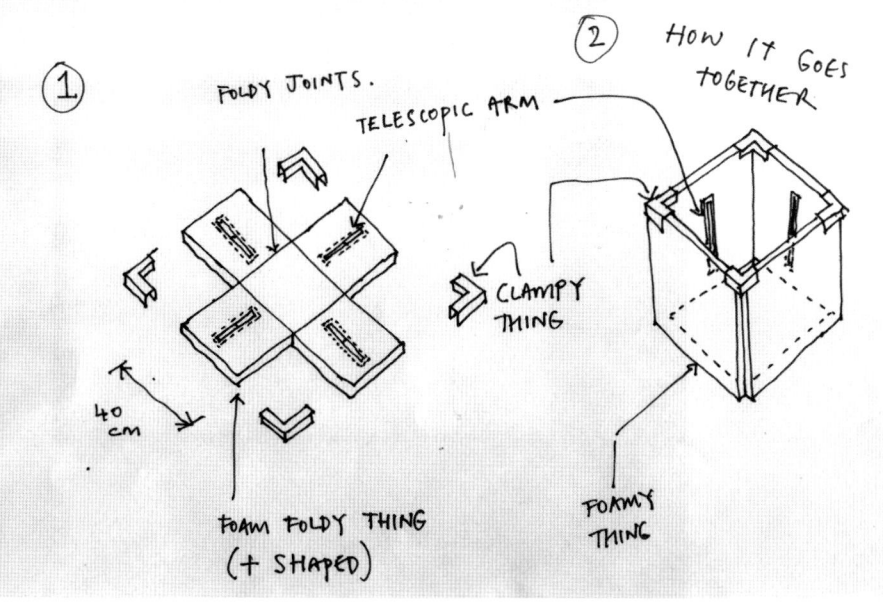

① FOLDY JOINTS.
TELESCOPIC ARM

40 cm

FOAM FOLDY THING
(+ SHAPED)

② HOW IT GOES TOGETHER

CLAMPY THING

FOAMY THING

③ HOW YOU YOUSE IT - YOU ADD THINGS TO IT TO MAKE NEW THINGS!

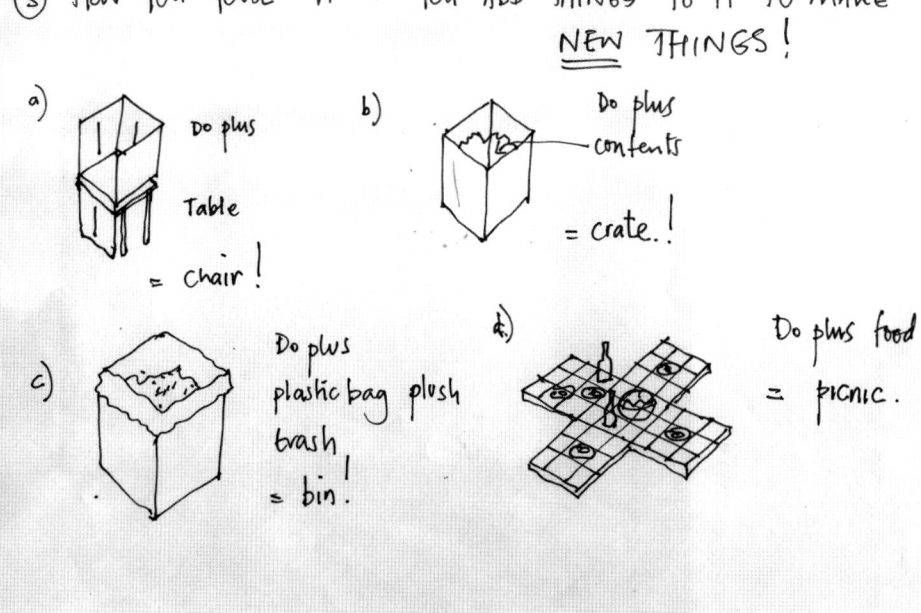

a) Do plus = Table = chair!

b) Do plus contents = crate.!

c) Do plus plastic bag plush trash = bin!

d) Do plus food = picnic.

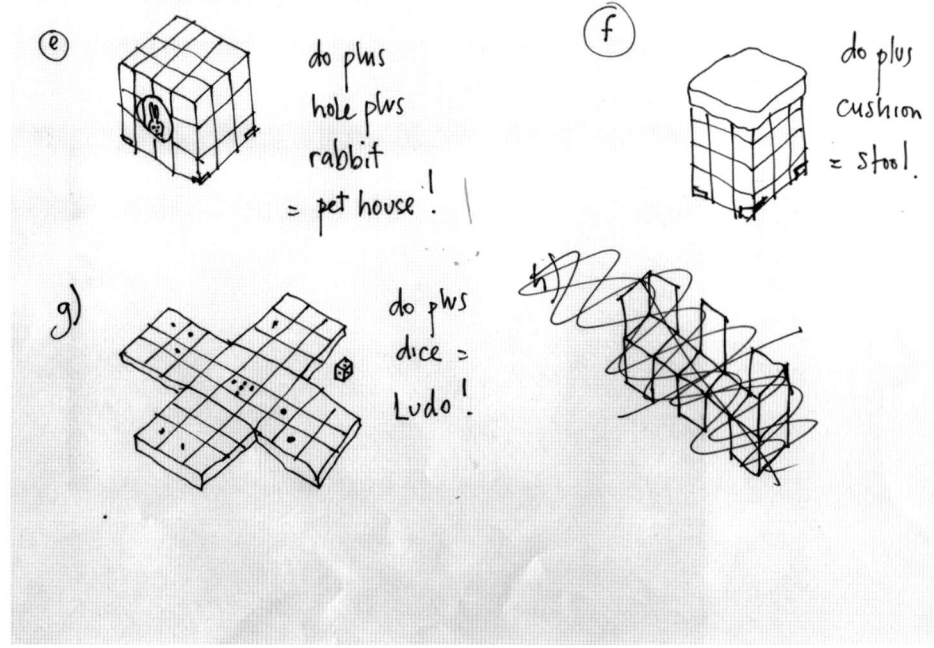

e) do plus hole plus rabbit = pet house!

f) do plus cushion = stool.

g) do plus dice = Ludo!

h)

do t

=

Sun

(j

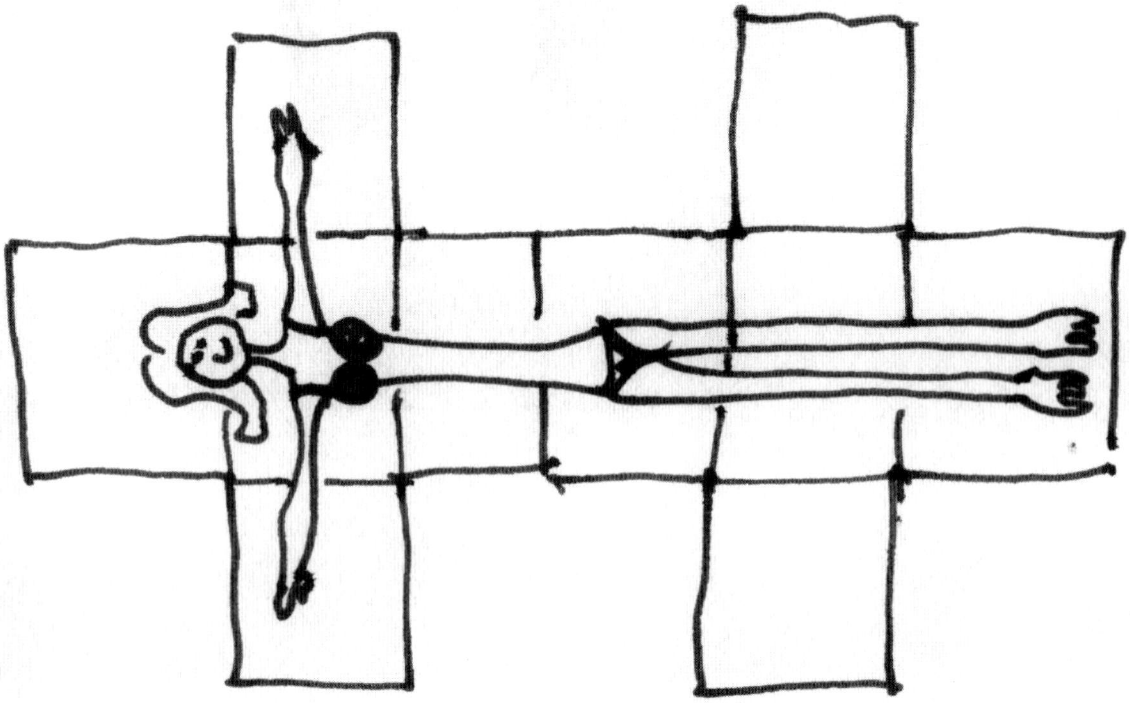

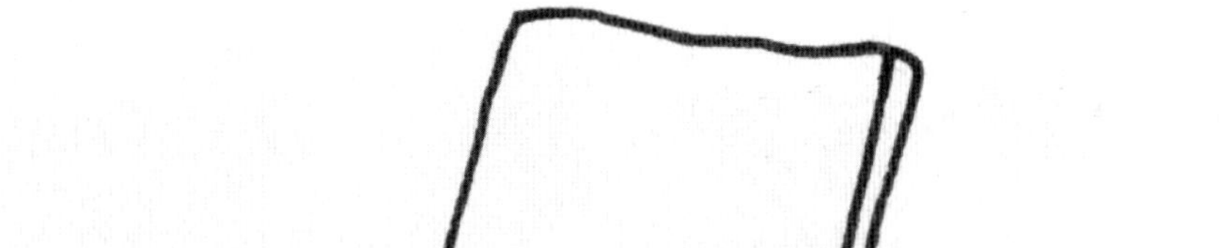

RIP
do

do

sto

sto

sti

ma

= gr

1)

do + do + do

= table !

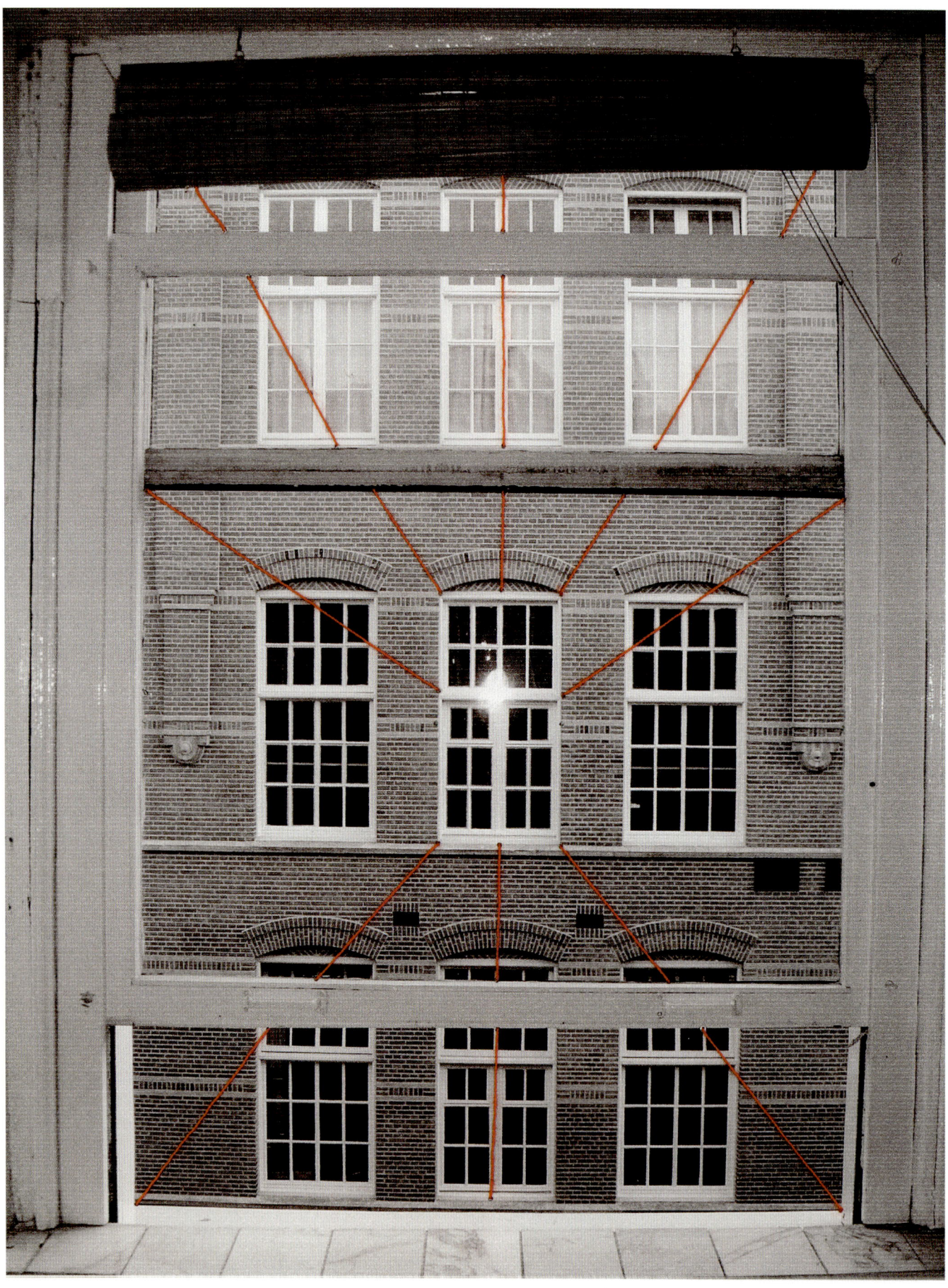

do connect your window to your
neighbour's

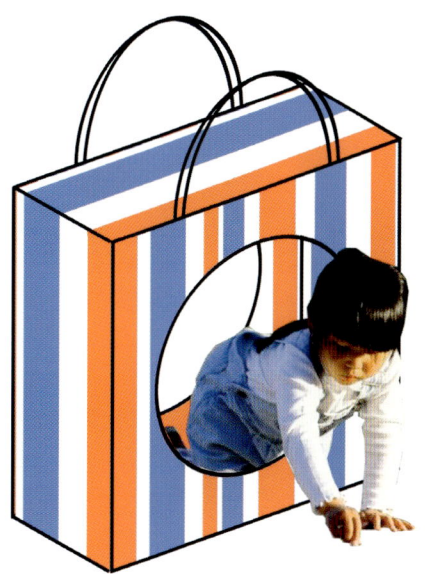

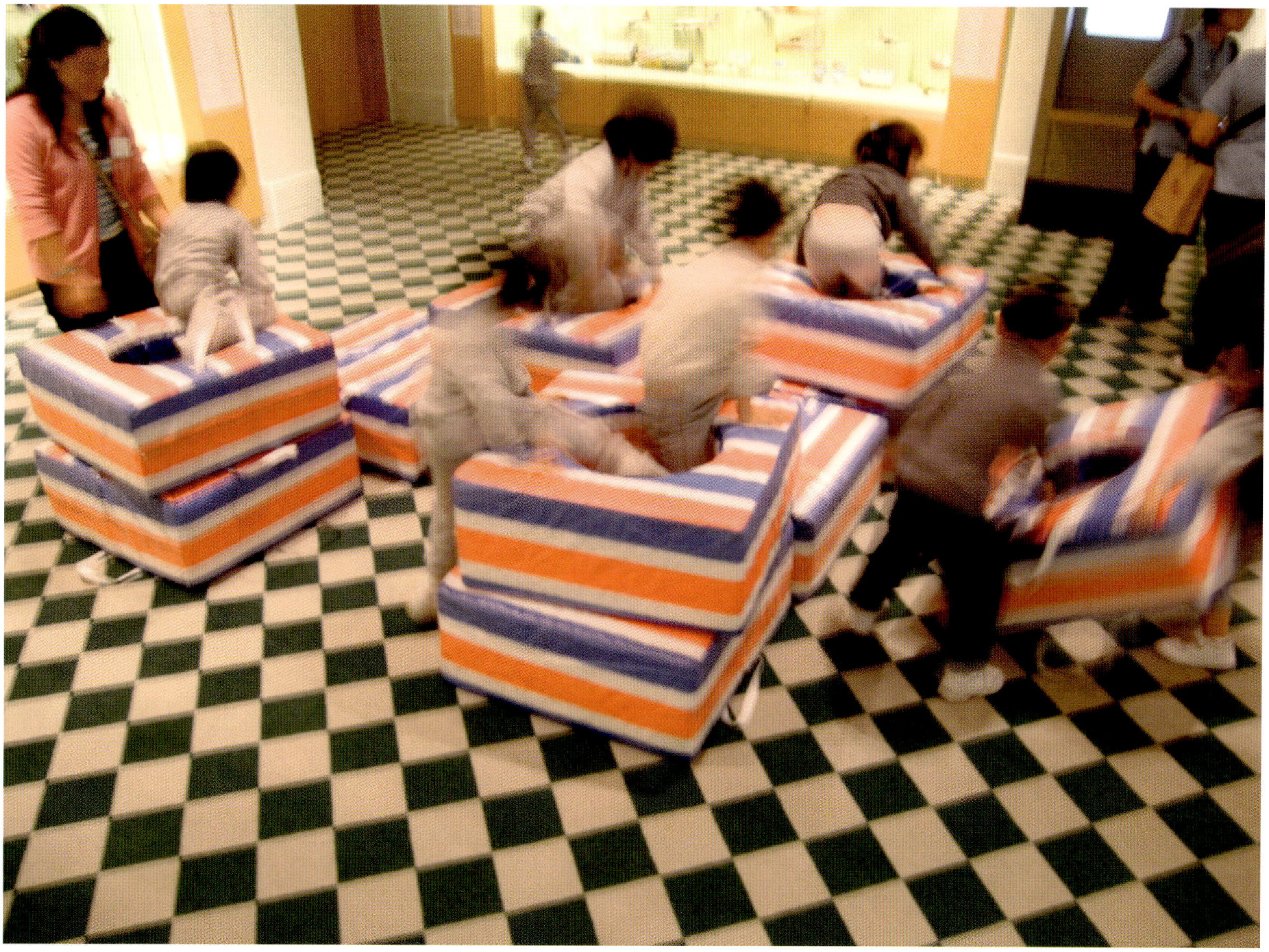

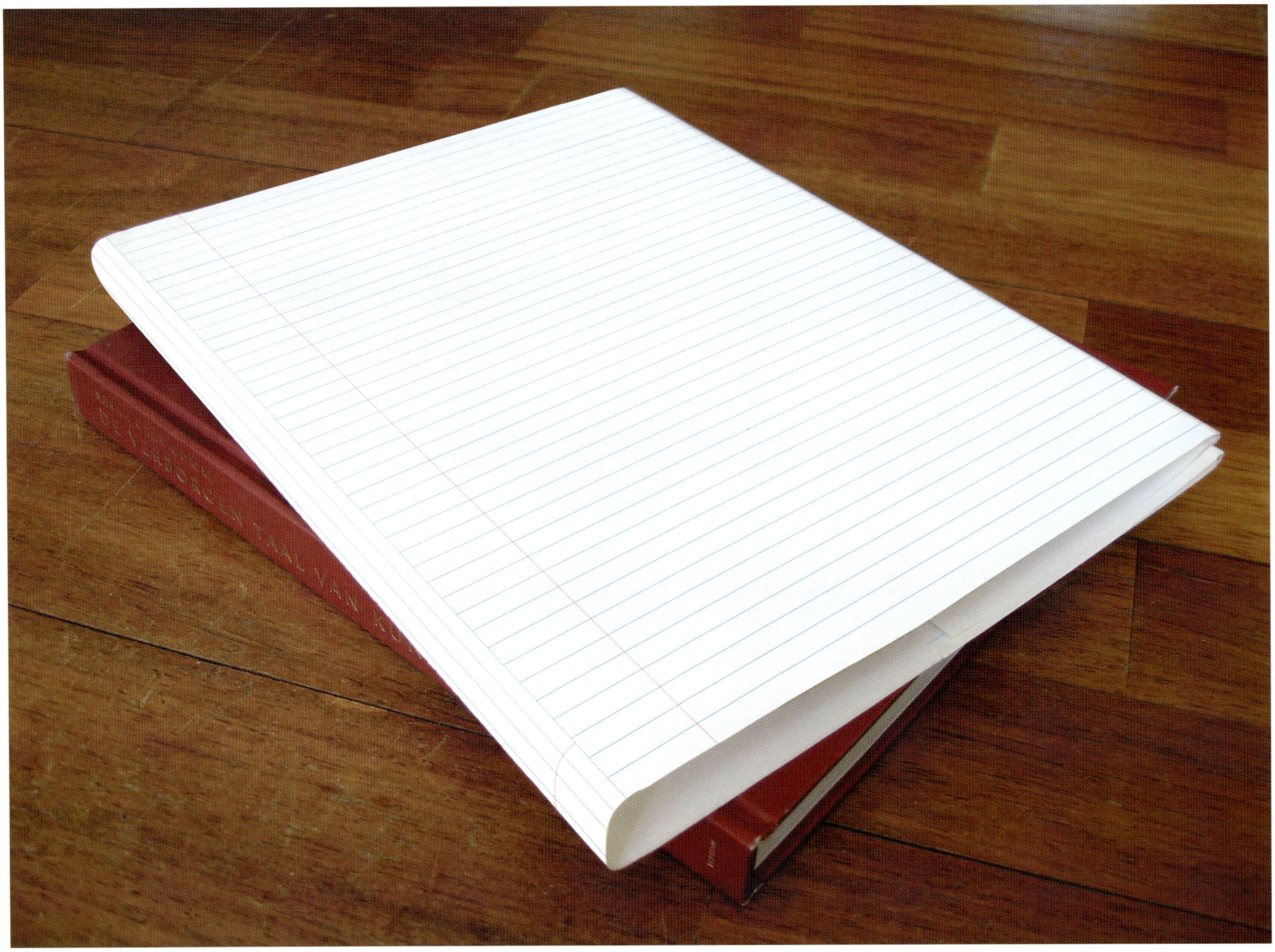

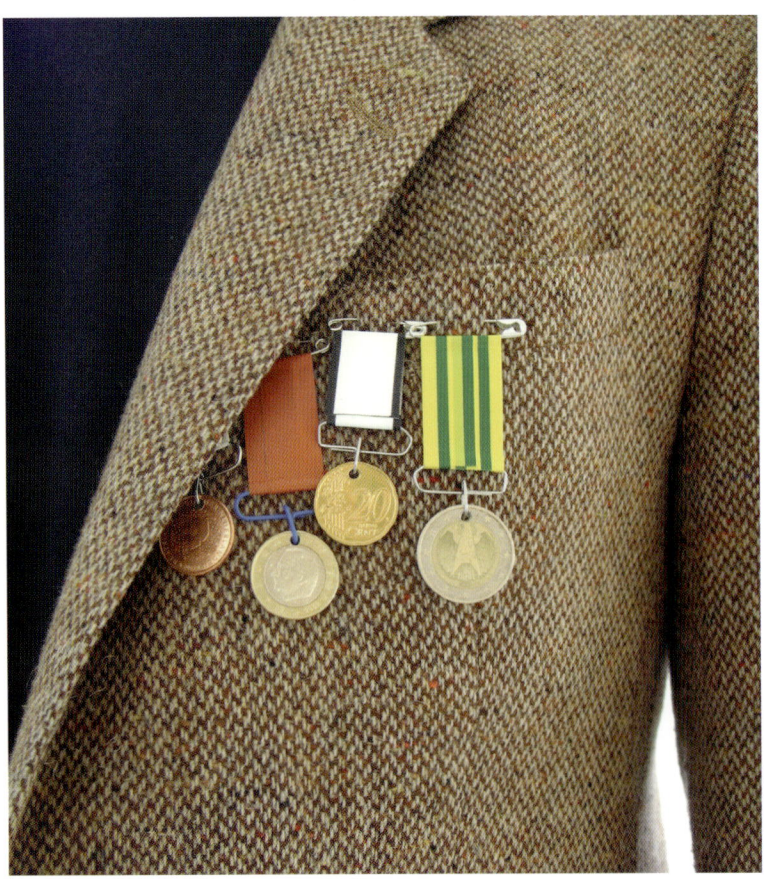

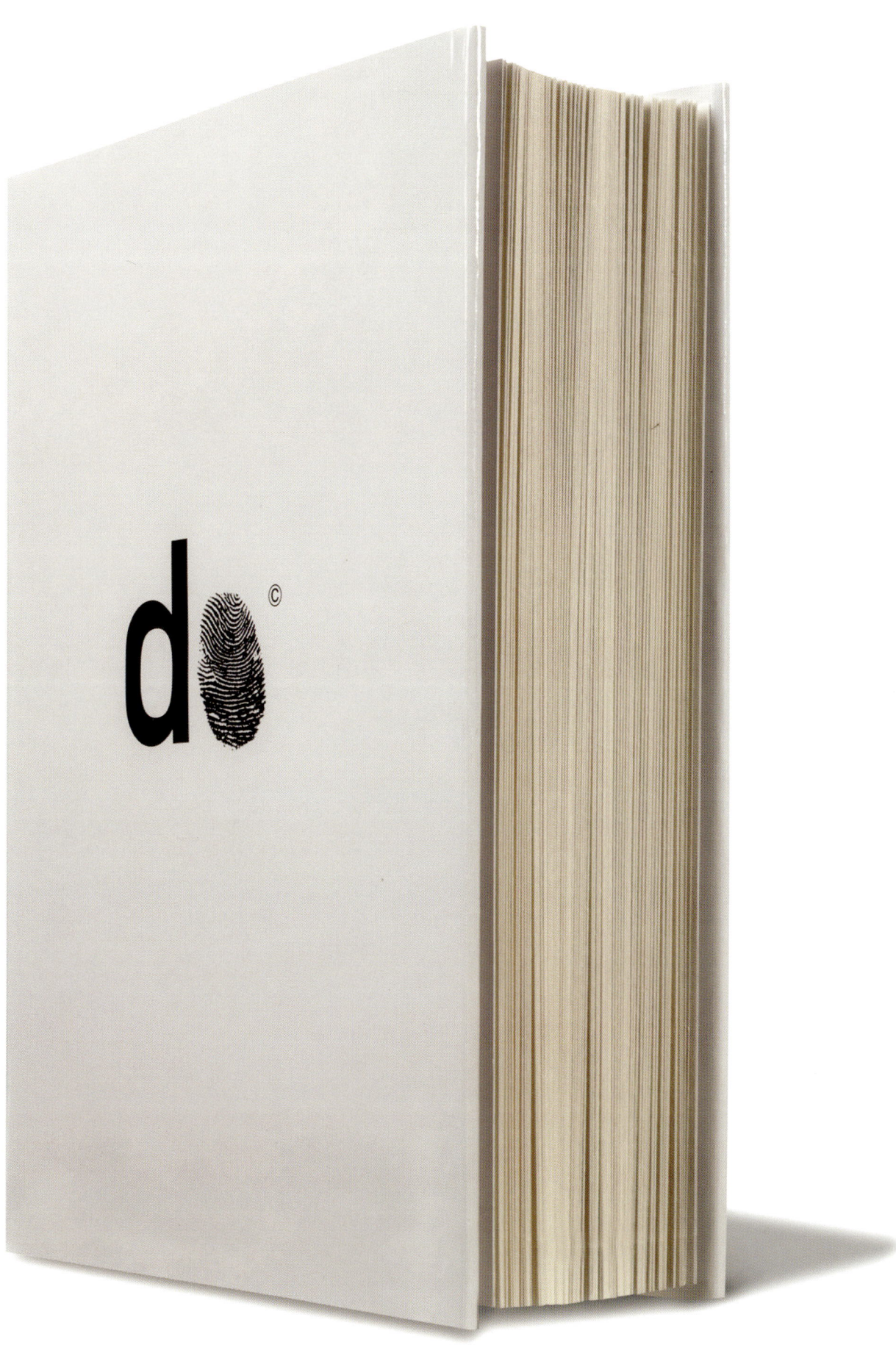

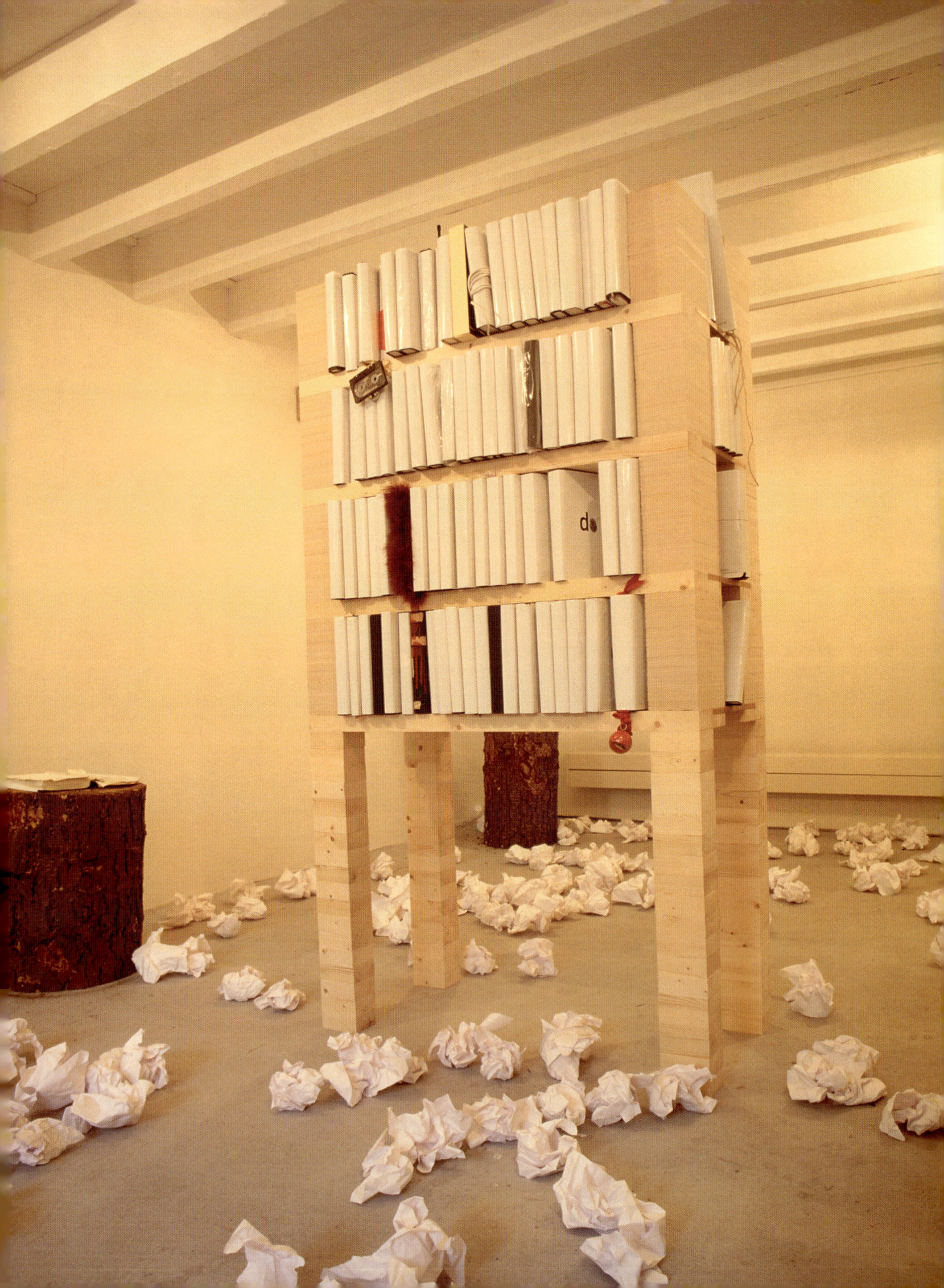

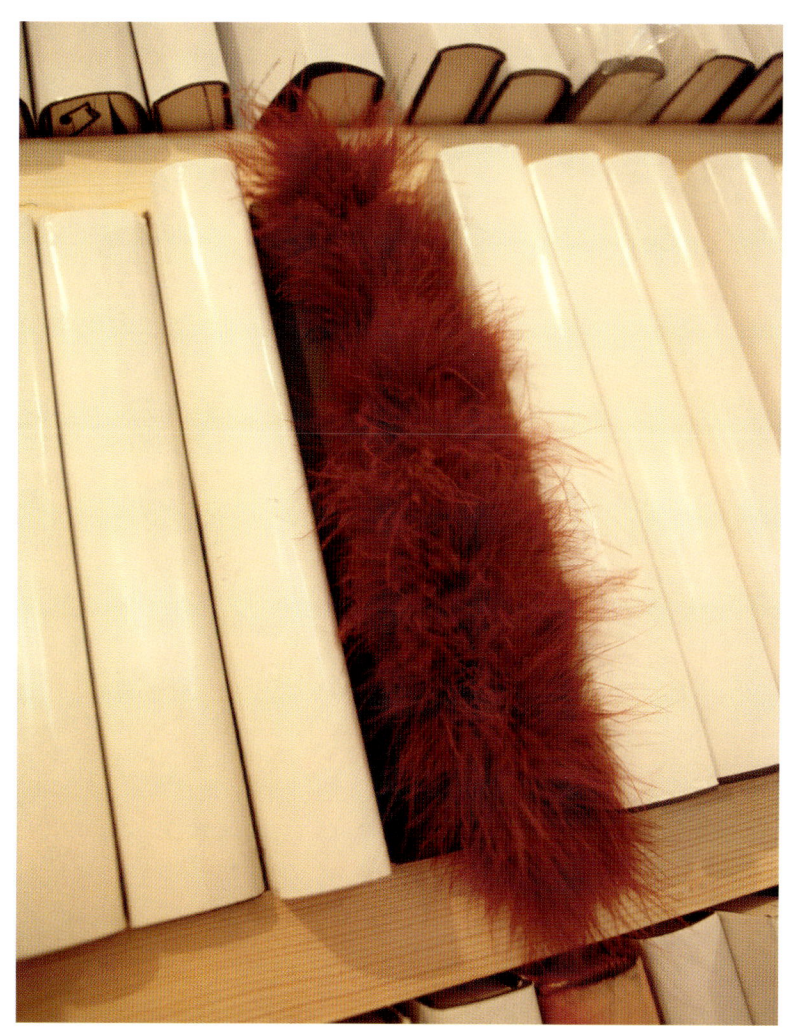

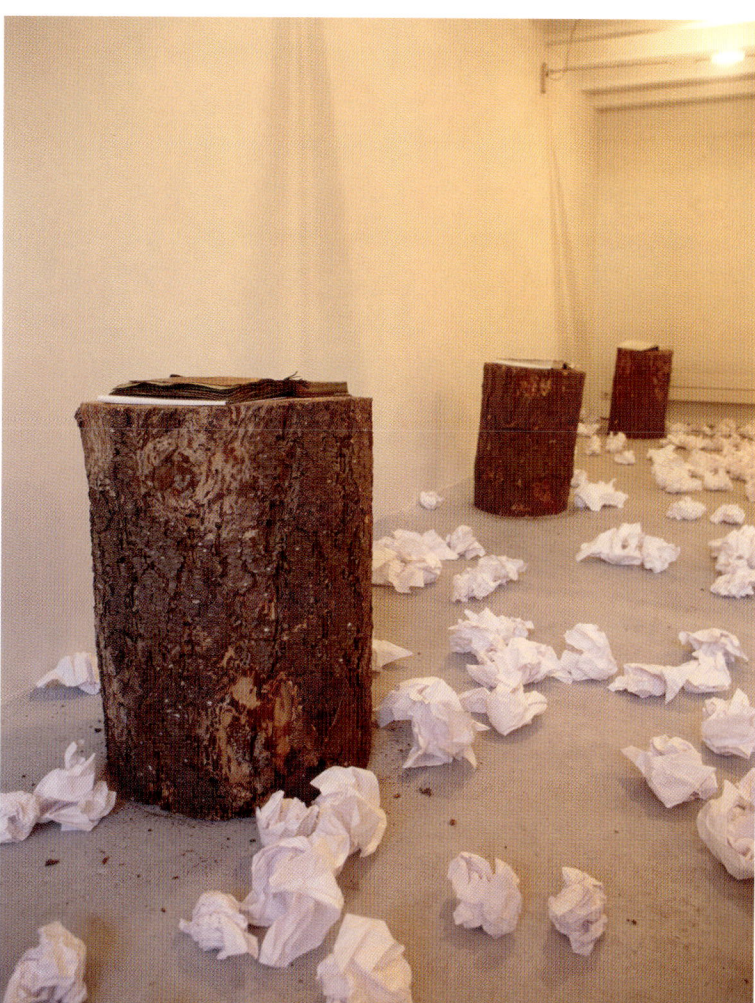

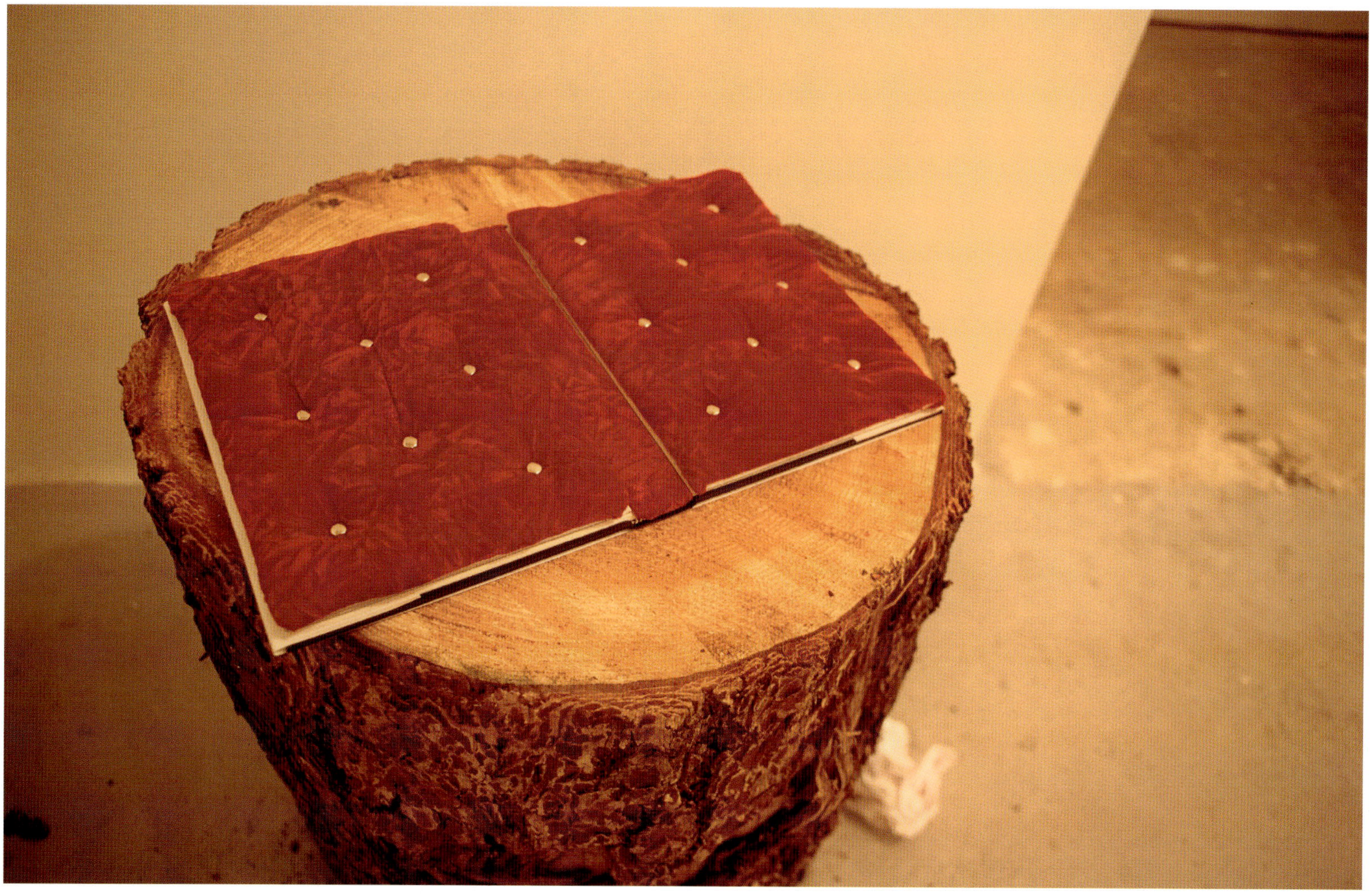

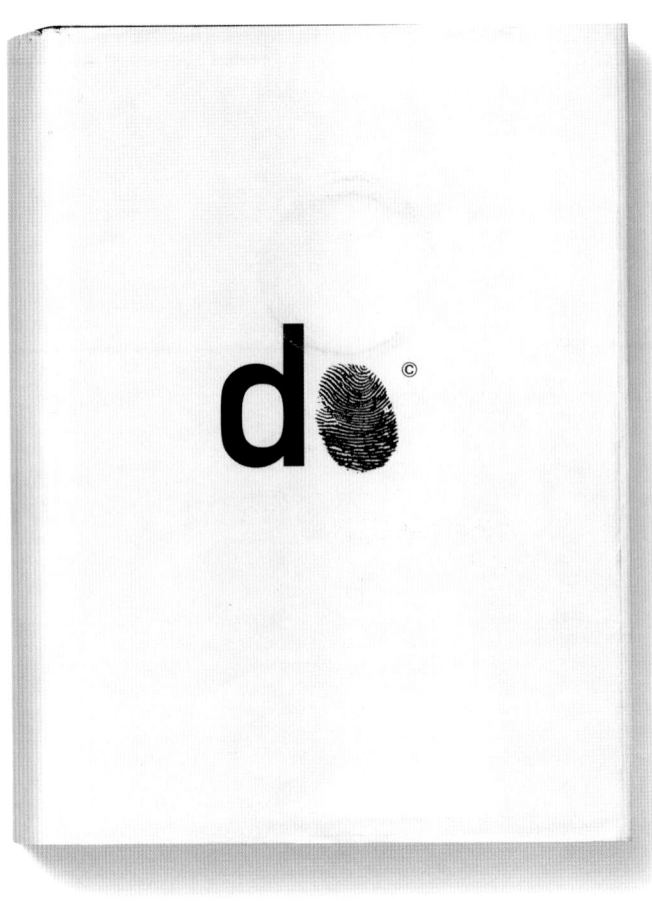

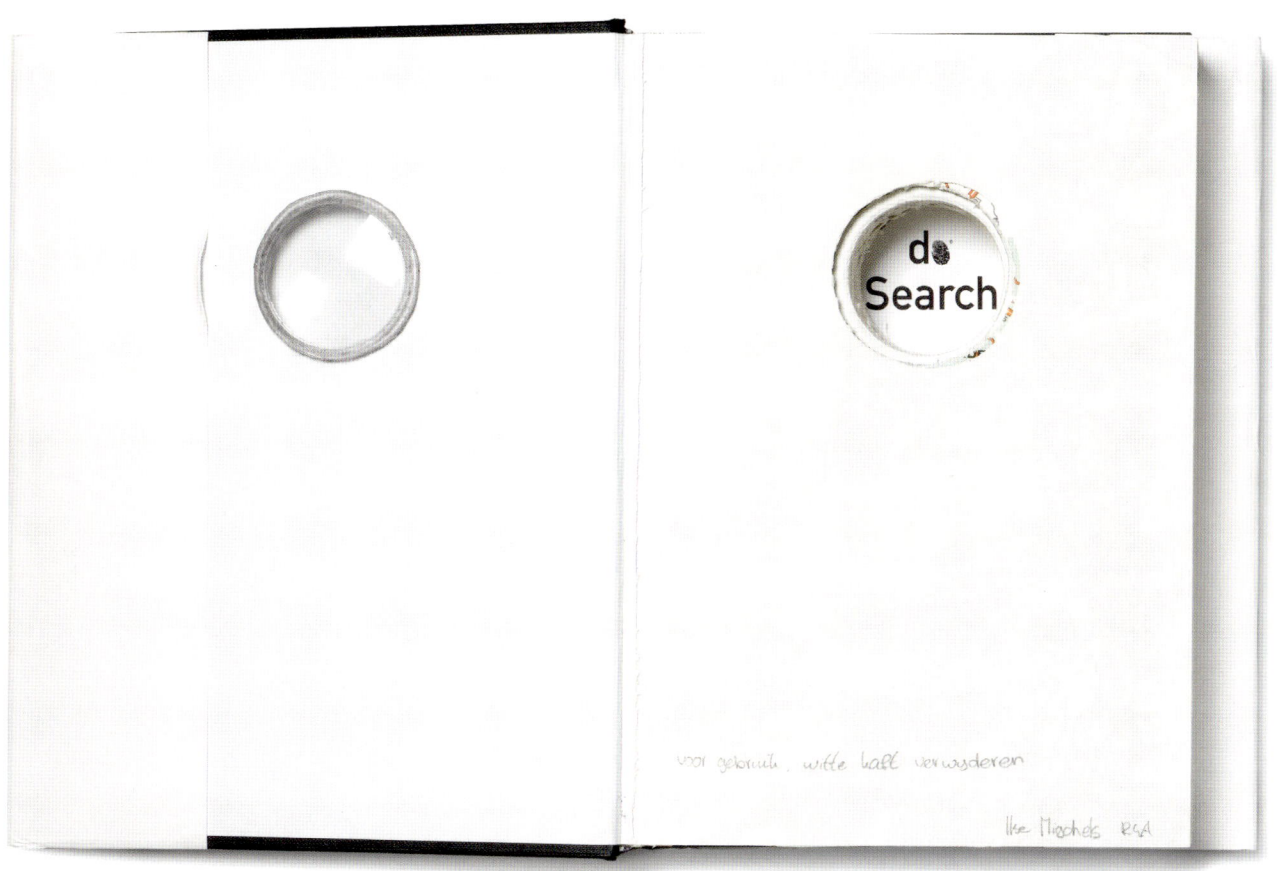

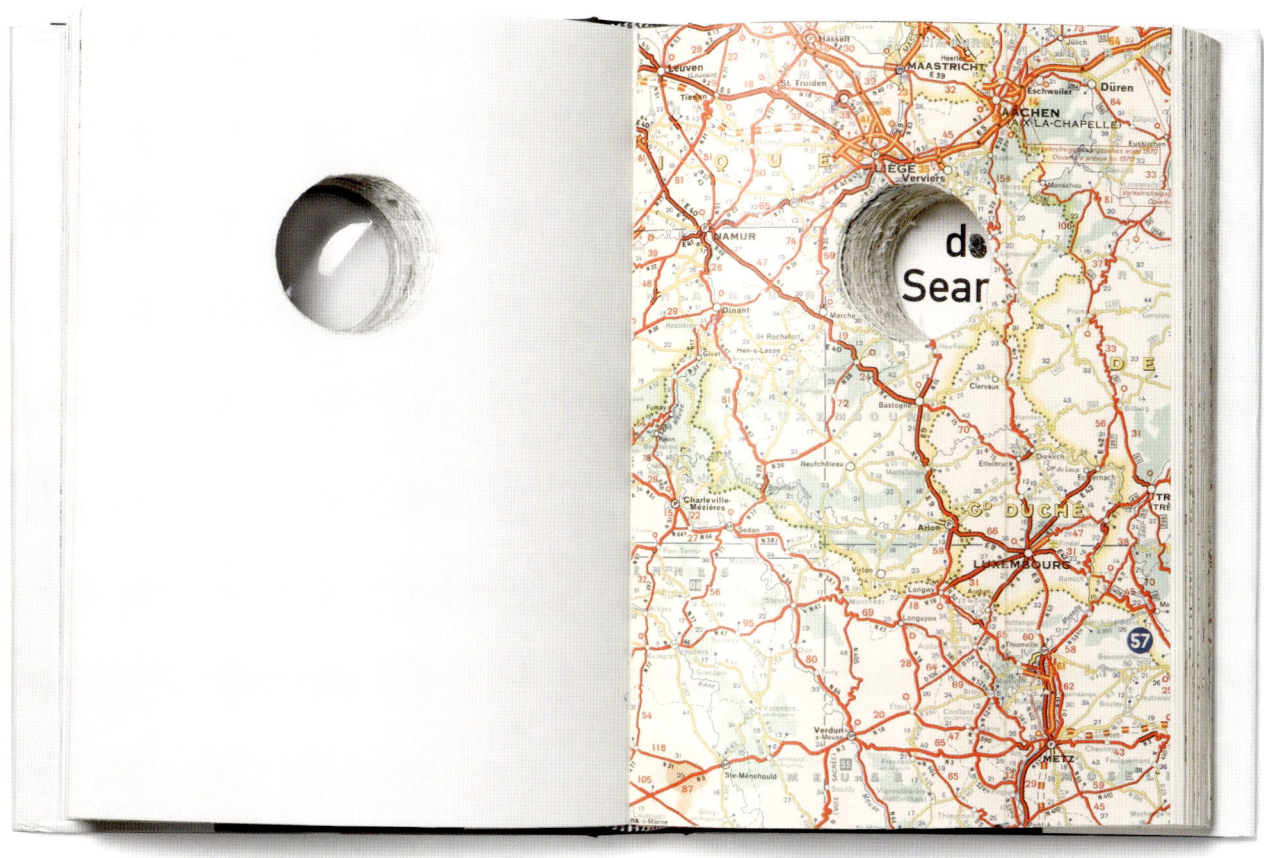

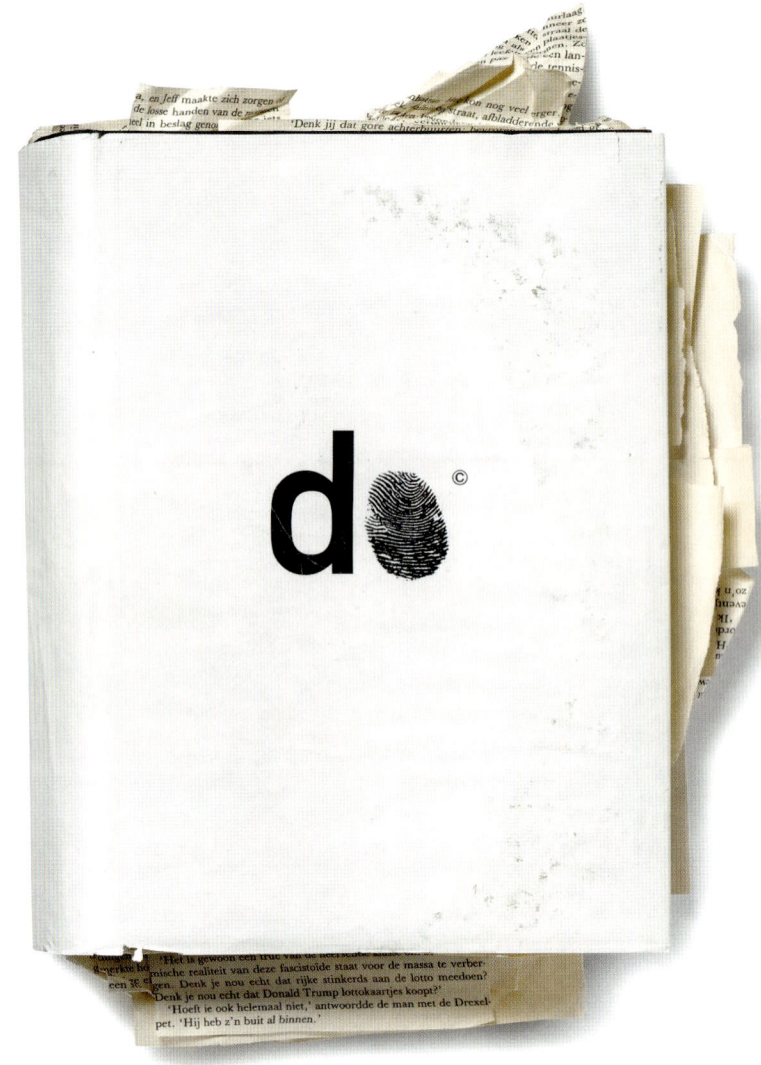

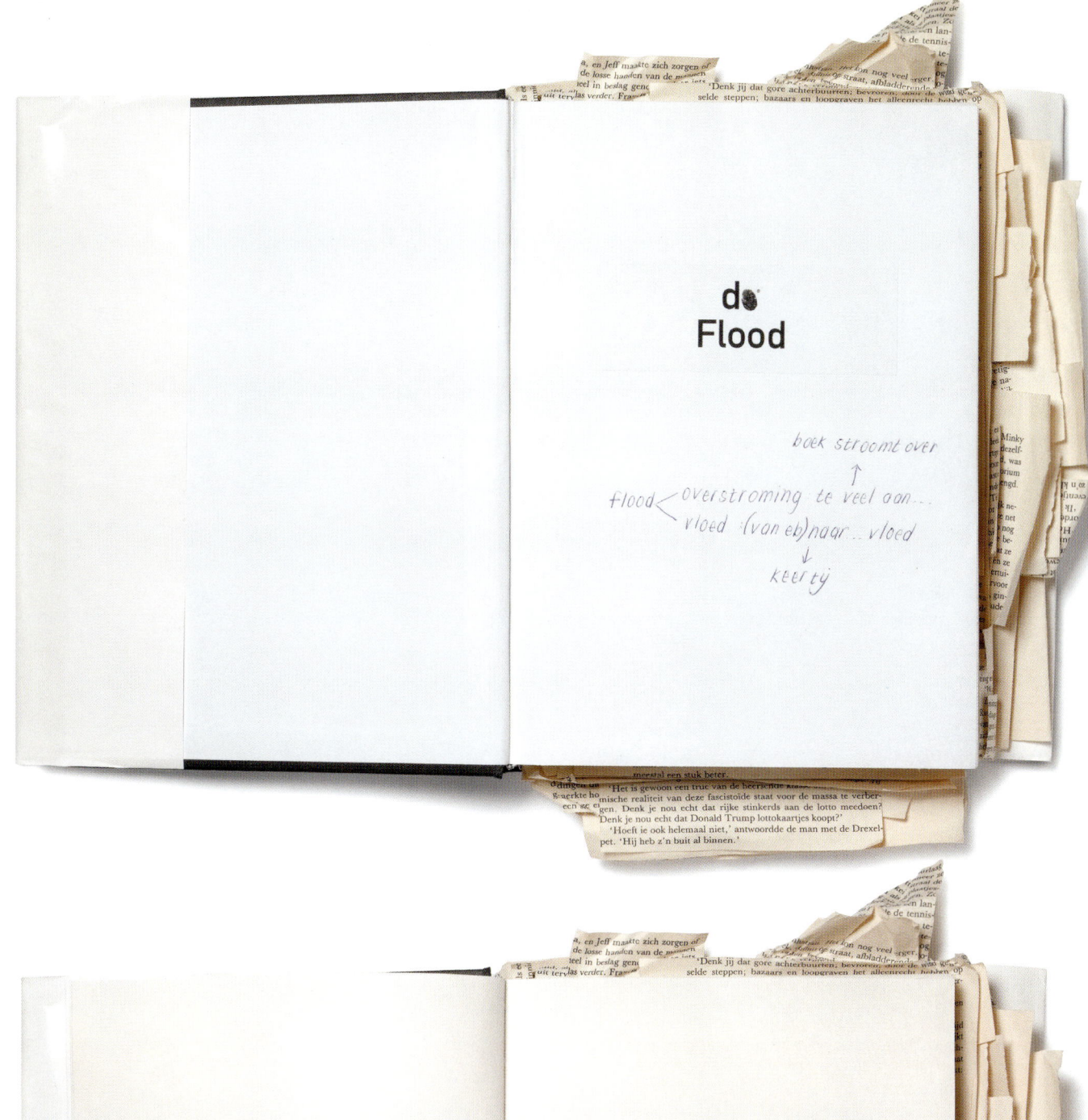

de
Flood

boek stroomt over
↑
flood < *overstroming: te veel aan...*
vloed: (van eb) naar... vloed
↓
keer tij

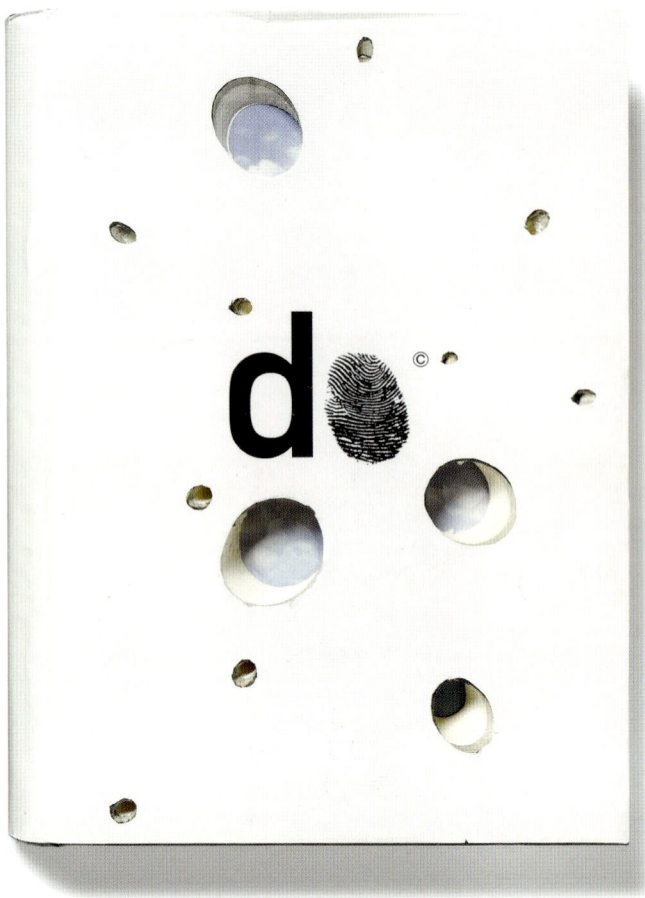

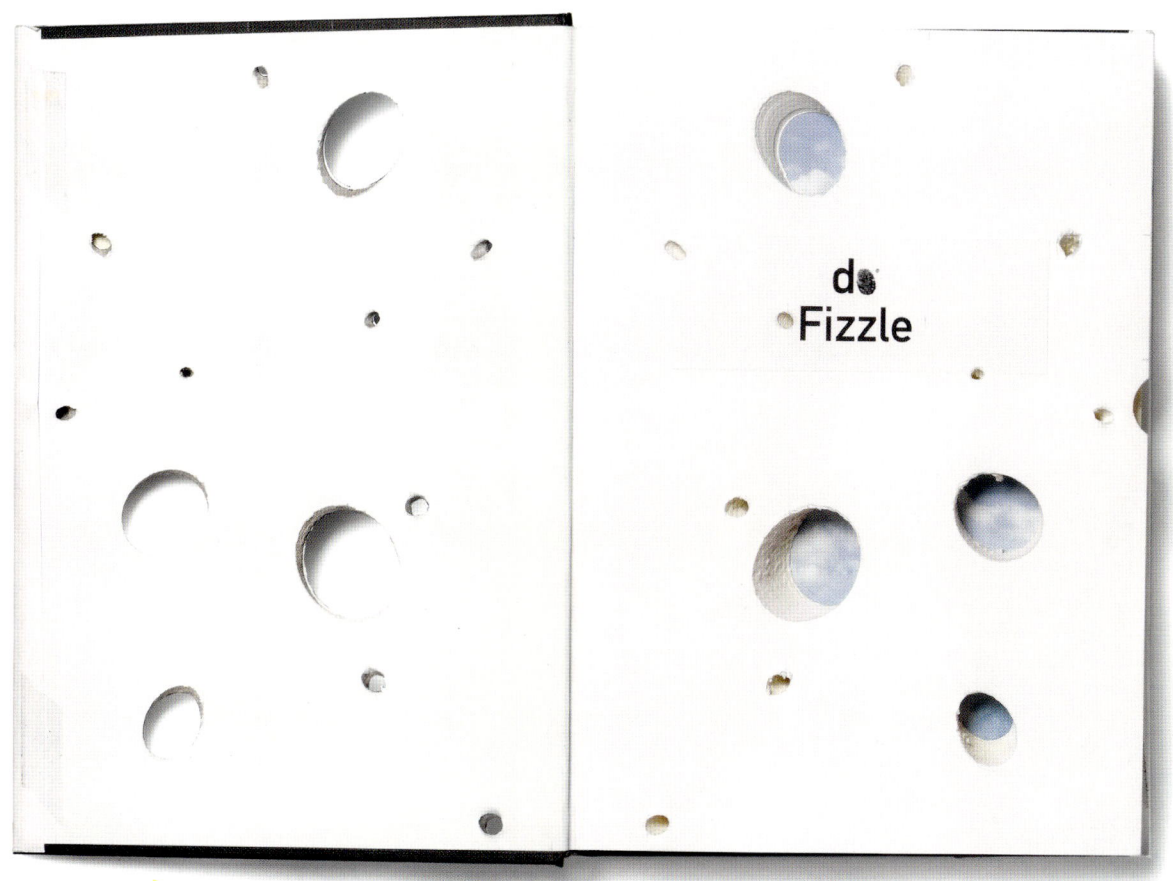

do
Fizzle

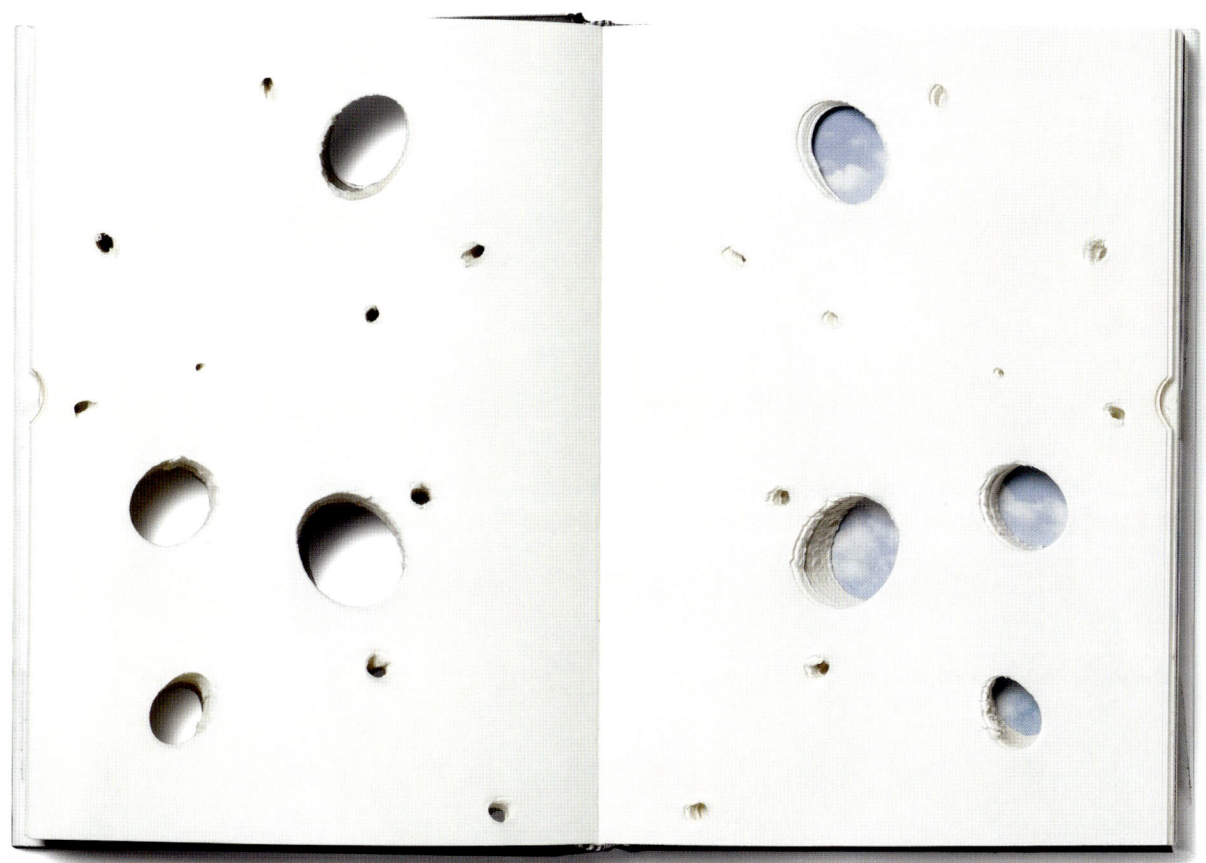

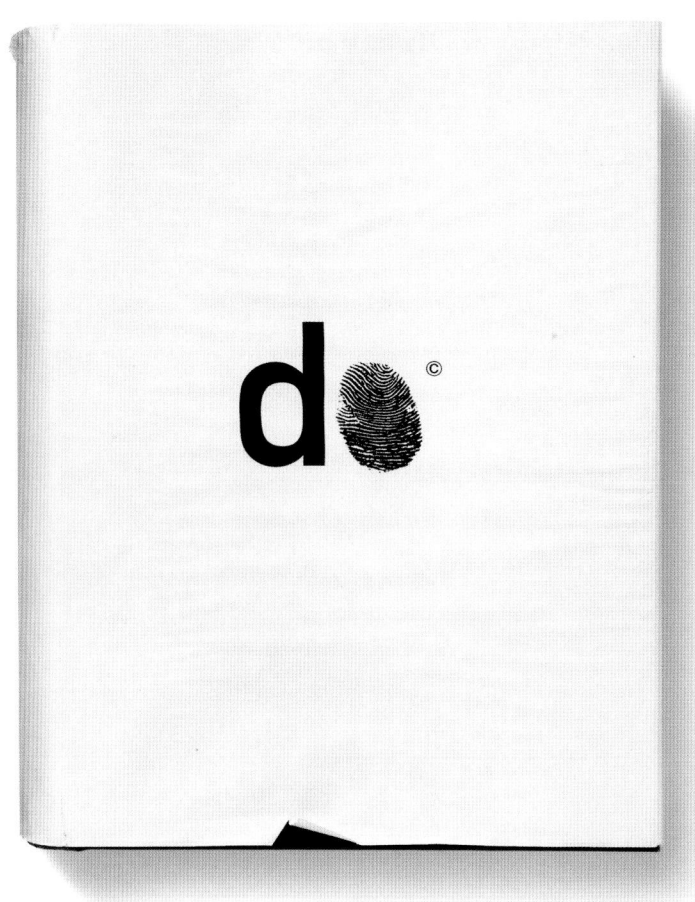

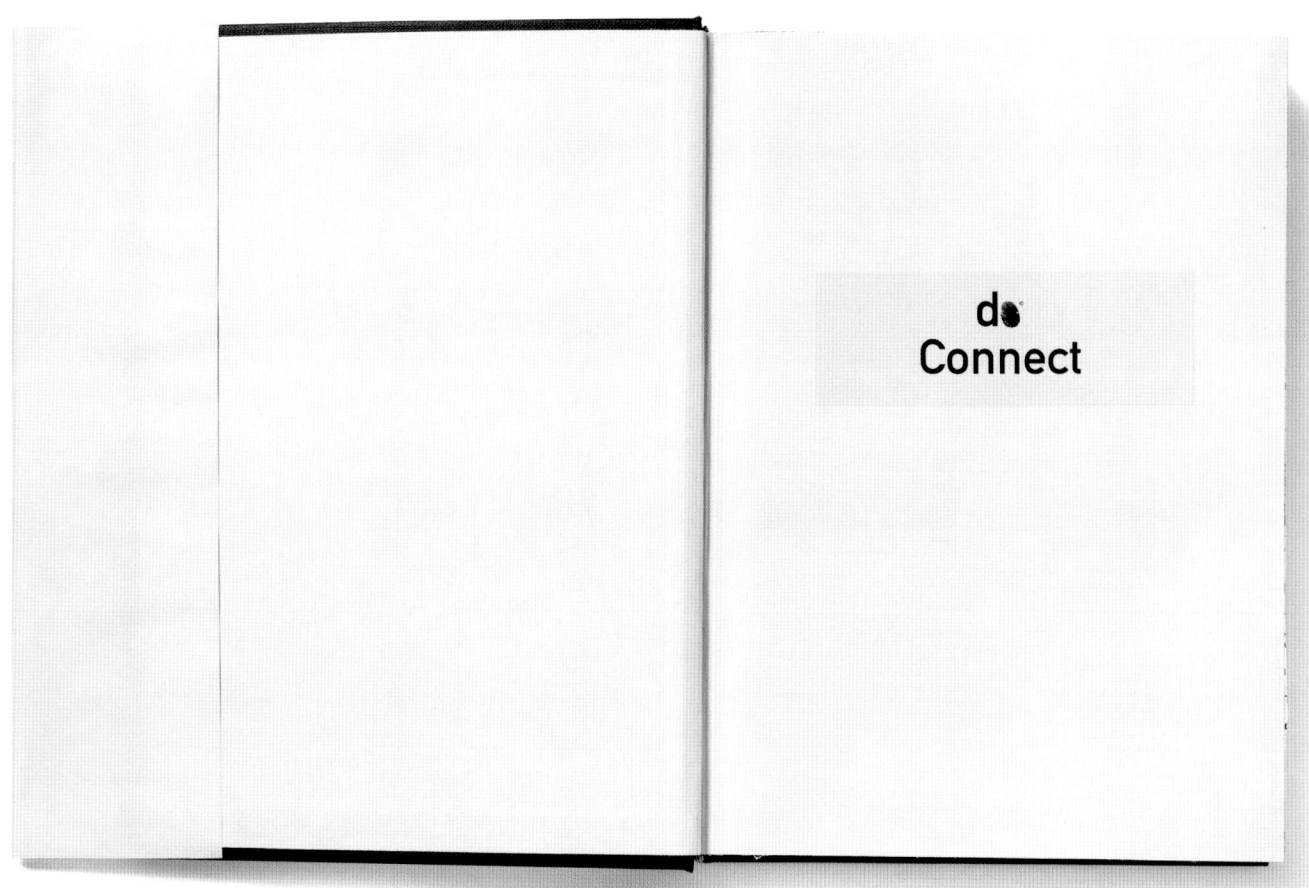

do
Connect

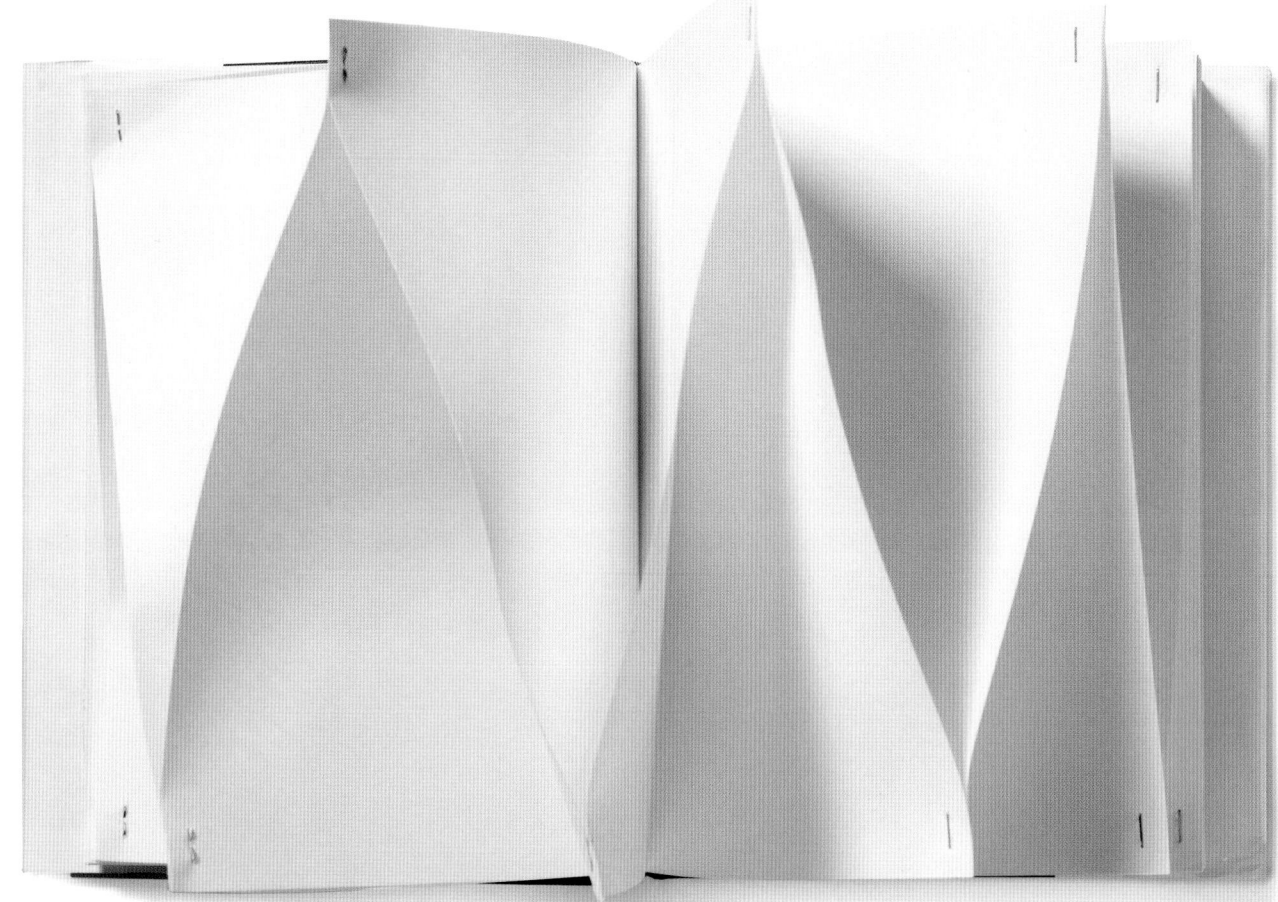

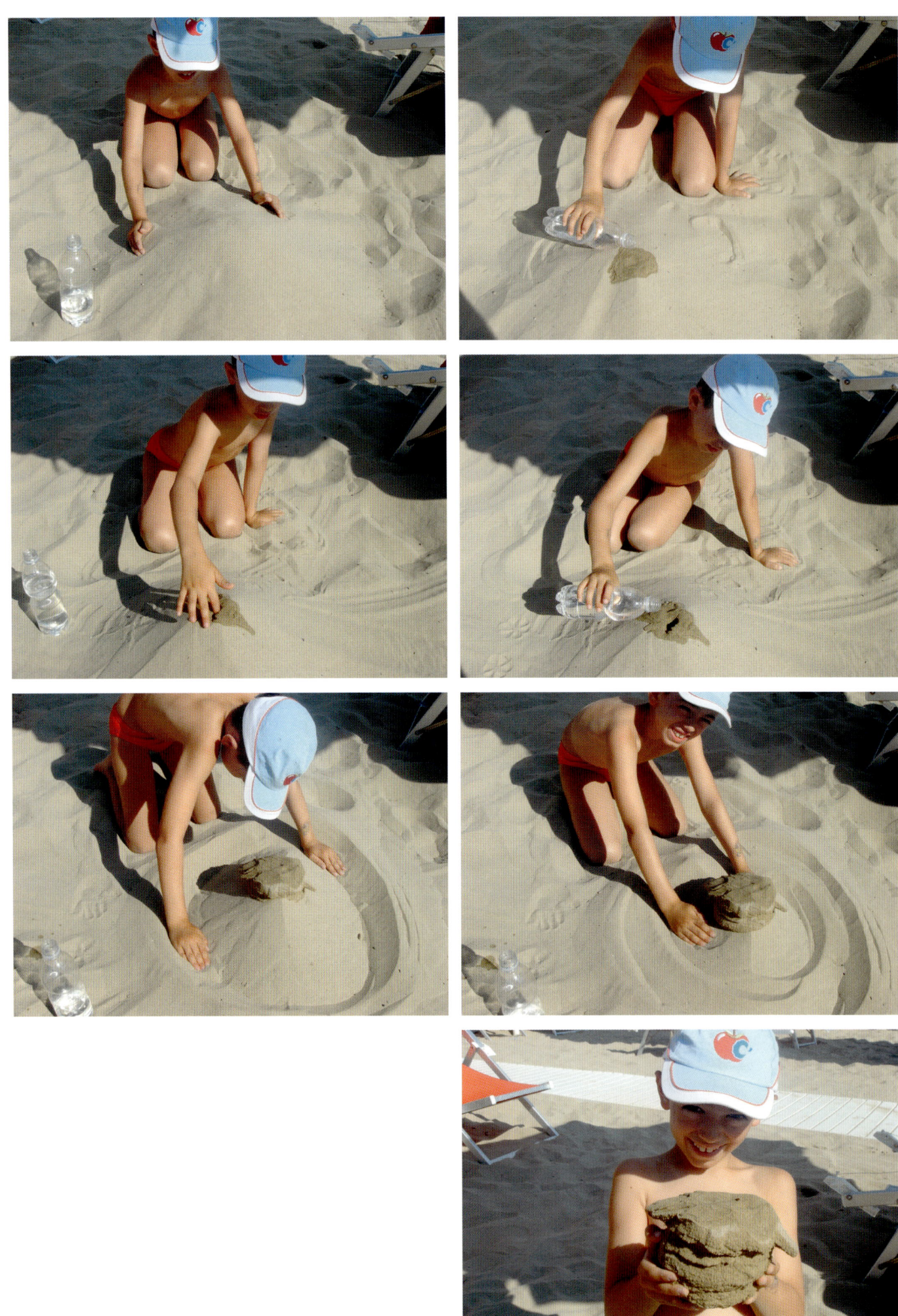

The future is not what it was

(anon)

This is the introduction page to do future, the page where we ~~explain~~ the ~~whole~~ book in one McNugget-sized chunk. ~~It's called~~ ~~and it's in~~ ©ook form.

do

~~FROM~~ ~~laser~~ mini discboy thingy? ~~If, th~~ ~~t dead, it's just been busy~~ ~~back~~ every letter in the ~~to~~ Z, ~~together to talk about~~ ~~Youth~~

Tough subject.

First cynical reaction would be, there's no such thing; it's just a media soundbite. This is, after all, a time when grey-faced politicians turn up at music awards for the votes, and grandmothers gulp ecstasy to cure their migraines.

Whoever coined the term youth culture (probably the same person who invented "downsizing") is missing the point, anyway. There is no such thing. Stick it in the plural and we're closer to the truth. There are, after all, 3,456,234 (approx.) youth cultures clumsily making it in the world today.

So we try our best to avoid any kind of bombastic explanation of youth culture as it stands. Besides, doing so would make it out of

FUT URE

~~d~~ ~~fo~~ ~~k hit th~~ ~~nting pre~~ ~~In~~ ~~creati~~ ~~mments~~ ~~onal s~~ ~~jo~~ ~~ys, journalism, idea~~ ~~ights, fac~~ ~~ures, and in a kind~~ ~~o~~ ~~celebration of the~~ ~~at adult~~ ~~acy (in the U~~ ~~at~~ ~~2~~ ~~d the number of h~~ ~~hool dro~~ ~~29%, you'll~~ ~~p~~ ~~d the odd~~ ~~ing msta~~ ~~Y~~ ~~d the la~~ ~~book - do~~ ~~which had th~~ ~~d~~ ~~effect of mixin', r~~ ~~h' and me~~ ~~sin' as many~~ ~~p~~ ~~as possible. You'll~~ ~~e a goo~~ ~~er have join~~ ~~w~~ ~~healthily illustrates~~ ~~nt w~~ ~~king with do~~ ~~fo~~ ~~ryone - hence over t~~ ~~s or so, you'll~~ ~~contributions from photographe~~ ~~signers, kids, dads, te~~ ~~rs,~~ students, art directors, marketers, writers, internet designers, ~~chemists and 1 Prime Minister. A big thank-you to all who put~~ ~~th~~ ~~ains on p~~

~~A~~ ~~h anything~~ ~~outh c~~ ~~e (~~ ~~term ag~~ ~~so~~ ~~p~~ ~~will hit th~~ ~~rk wit~~ ~~ry precis~~ ~~thers w~~ ~~iss~~ ~~co~~ ~~tely. Th~~ ~~f the~~ ~~you disa~~ ~~with n~~ ~~ng, then~~ ~~w~~ ~~not done~~ ~~b.~~

~~C~~ ~~st piece o~~ ~~)infor~~ ~~on~~ ~~you on you~~ ~~t~~ ~~n~~ ~~ge, and t~~ ~~l start~~ ~~e b~~ ~~ostradamus~~ ~~hesied~~ ~~5~~ ~~rs ago t~~ ~~orld W~~ ~~will~~ ~~on July 4th~~ ~~9, it~~

1998

do explain

Certain specifics of do.

In the beginning:

Brands have traditionally been developed out of one product. From that one product, the brand then develops similar products. The original product and products then work to create a brand mentality through the way the products are made, marketed and communicated. This then creates the brand image and personality. See: Nike, Apple...

do seeks to change this convention by not creating the product first. Basically, do wants to create the image and personality of a brand before there are any products or services.

With the brand personality and all its traits in place, do then creates products and services. do, as a brand, behaves like a person, and therefore allows lots of room for further exploration in communication, products and services by a great many people.

This is the vitality of do.

Why the name, do?

do defines that which survives, or lives. Therefore, do is about living and of course, doing. do is an inclusive brand, open to the many. do is a contrast to other brands. Other brands are produced by a select few.

do is open for contribution. do is open for working with other companies who seek to do something different or new. As do defines its personality, participants can see do's potential and their own ideas voiced and produced in a do way.

do has a personality that is non-conformist, socially critical, intelligent, self-analytical, and aware. do is empowering. do is forming. do has opinions. do has emotions. We are all getting to know do by doing.

25
~~twenty~~
~~eighteen~~

KesselsKramer:

KesselsKramer is a group of ~~fourteen~~ brains activated in the creation of ideas and solutions for brands and communication. Located in a church called The Divine Providence in the centre of

21 33
2132
~~2131~~

Amsterdam, KesselsKramer is a creative factory that waters brand plants all around the big, blue marble. KesselsKramer works free from the bureaucratic stasis of large advertising structures. A new schema. A dynamic collective able to adapt and think along a plethora of disciplines, KesselsKramer houses filmmakers, writers, strategists, art directors, gnome stimulators, virus marketers and brand scientists from The Netherlands, USA, Turkey, UK, Germany, and Japan. KesselsKramer continues to search and experiment with new ways of working and making communication. One of these experiments is do.

do was born at KesselsKramer. KesselsKramer seeks to wetnurse, feed and help formulate the first steps of do. This means that KesselsKramer wishes to create communication around do and then initiate the first products around do with partners. KesselsKramer has a strong role in the rearing of do, however, it is KesselsKramer's plan to relinquish control of do, and allow for a do foundation to take over. This foundation will oversee the production of products, services and communication. This foundation will be the life-support system for do.

Process:

do is in now in its first orbit: the building of do. The care for a new brand. The development. We are communicating through editorials, actions, and this second do book. We are contacting lots of people, like you, and gathering energy and support.

This orbit will never end.
This is the constant pulse of do.
A continuing circle.

When do's orbit is in a steady rhythm, then products and services will develop.
This is do's next evolution in orbit. do will produce tangible reproductions of the personality do has communicated. Contact.

A next evolution in orbit will include more commercial endeavours. Commercial projects might mean do working with other companies, foundations, brands, art, products, services and...

do will gather participants. At this point, maybe there are several do projects in action.

Time is relative, but if you would like, contact do about a linear time-line.

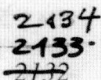

DO R€WARD:
WAIT TILL THIS BOOK IS OUT OF PRINT,
S€LL IT T€N TIM€S ITS PRIC€

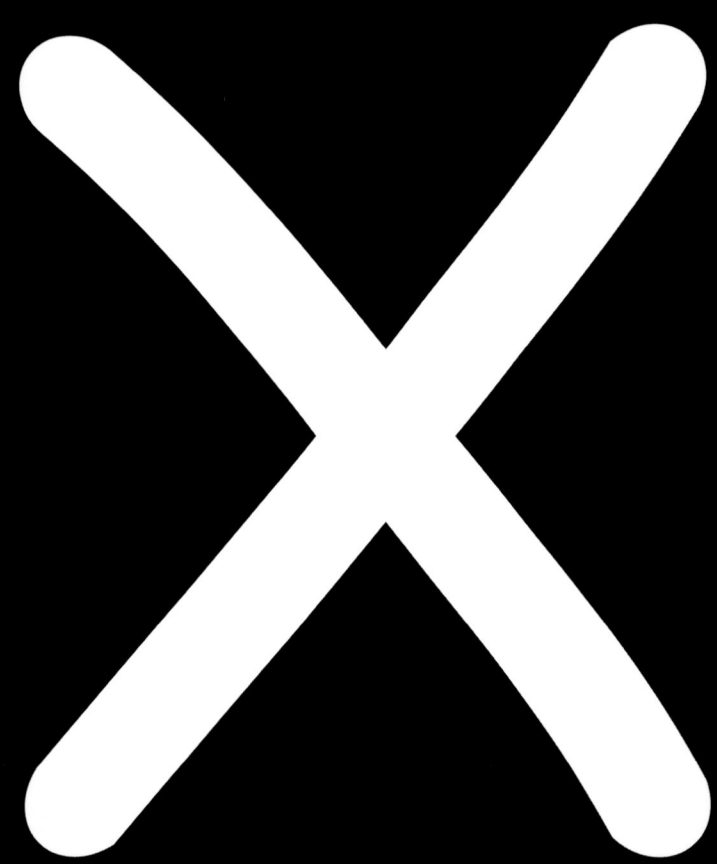

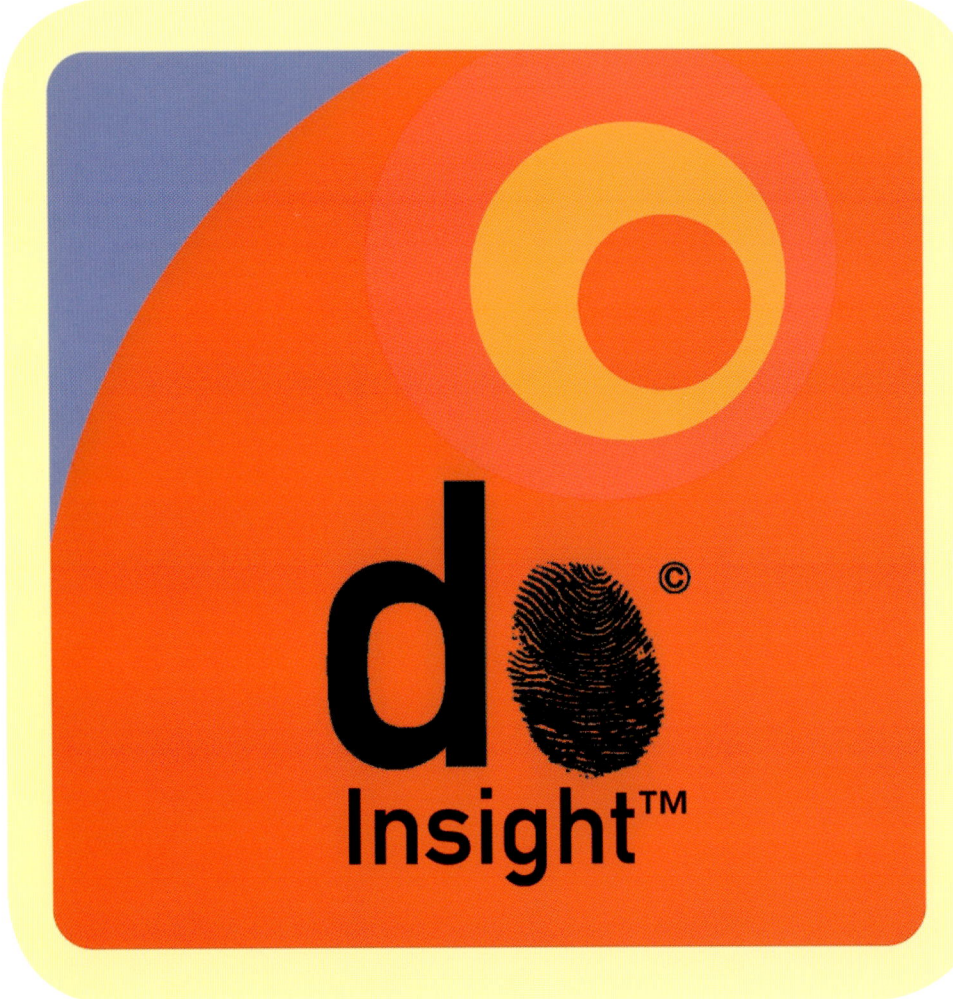

do© Insight™

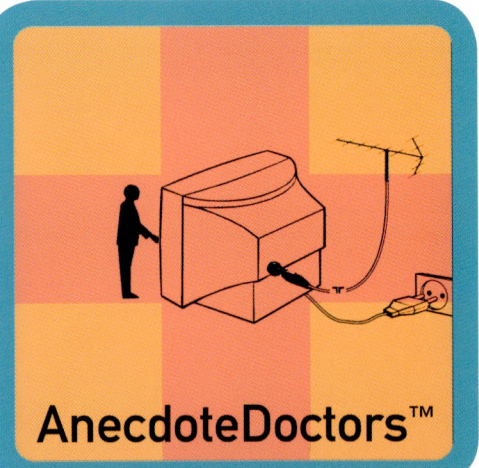

AnecdoteDoctors™

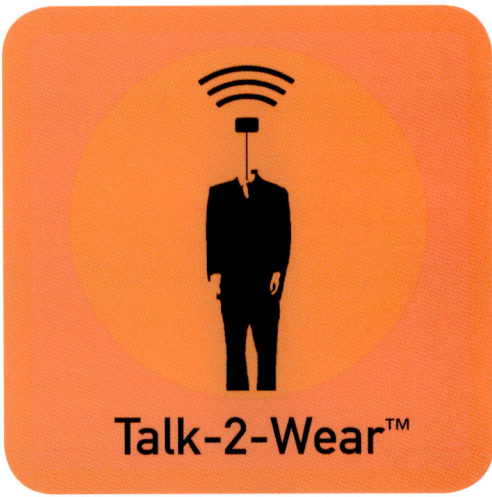

Talk-2-Wear™

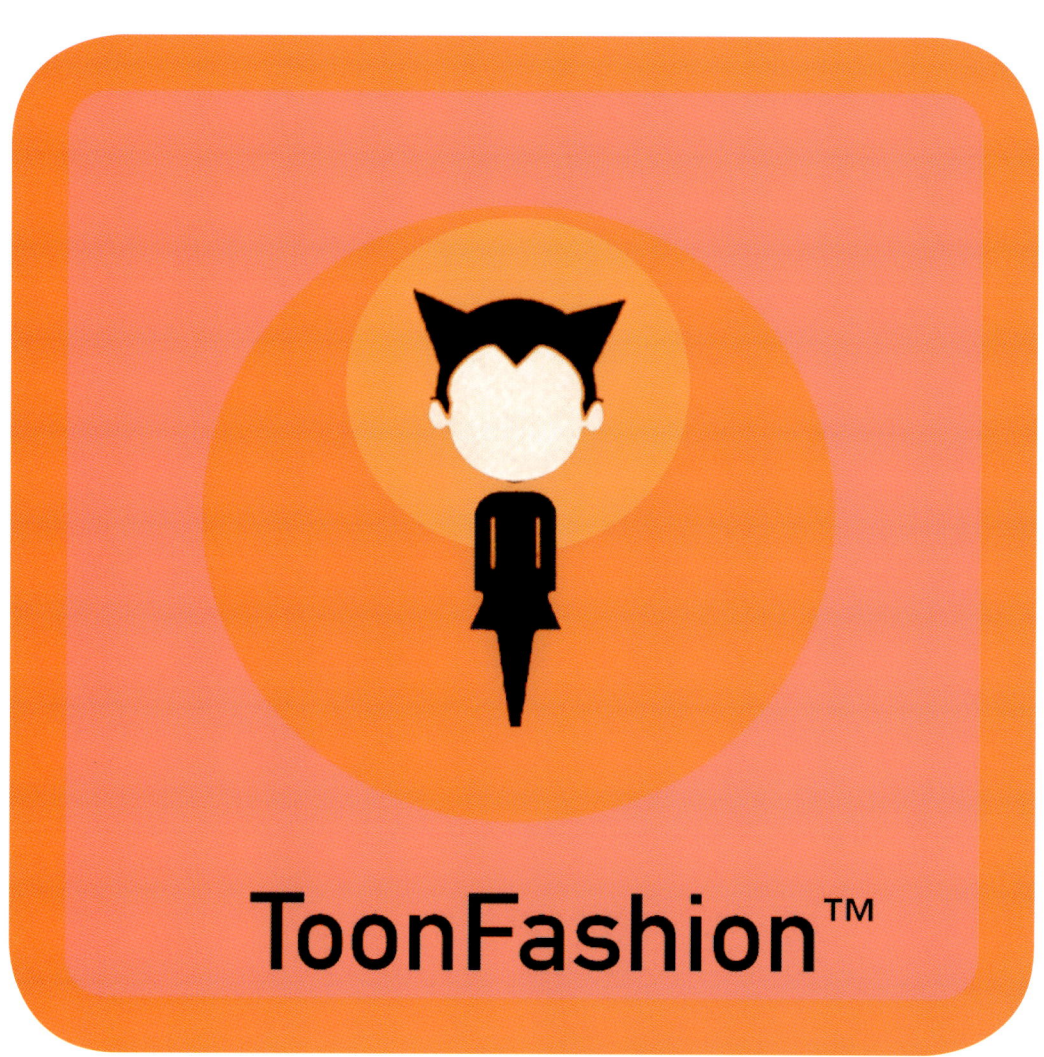

ToonFashion™

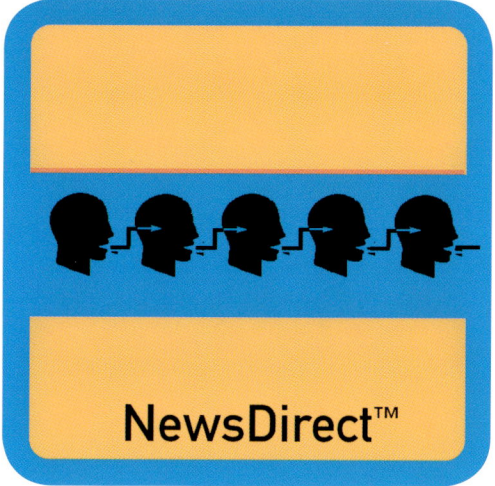

NewsDirect™

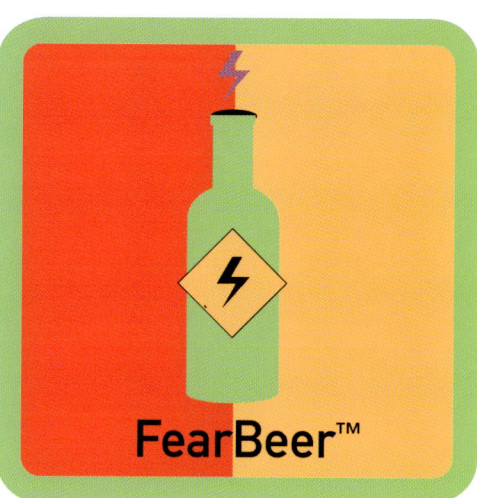

FearBeer™

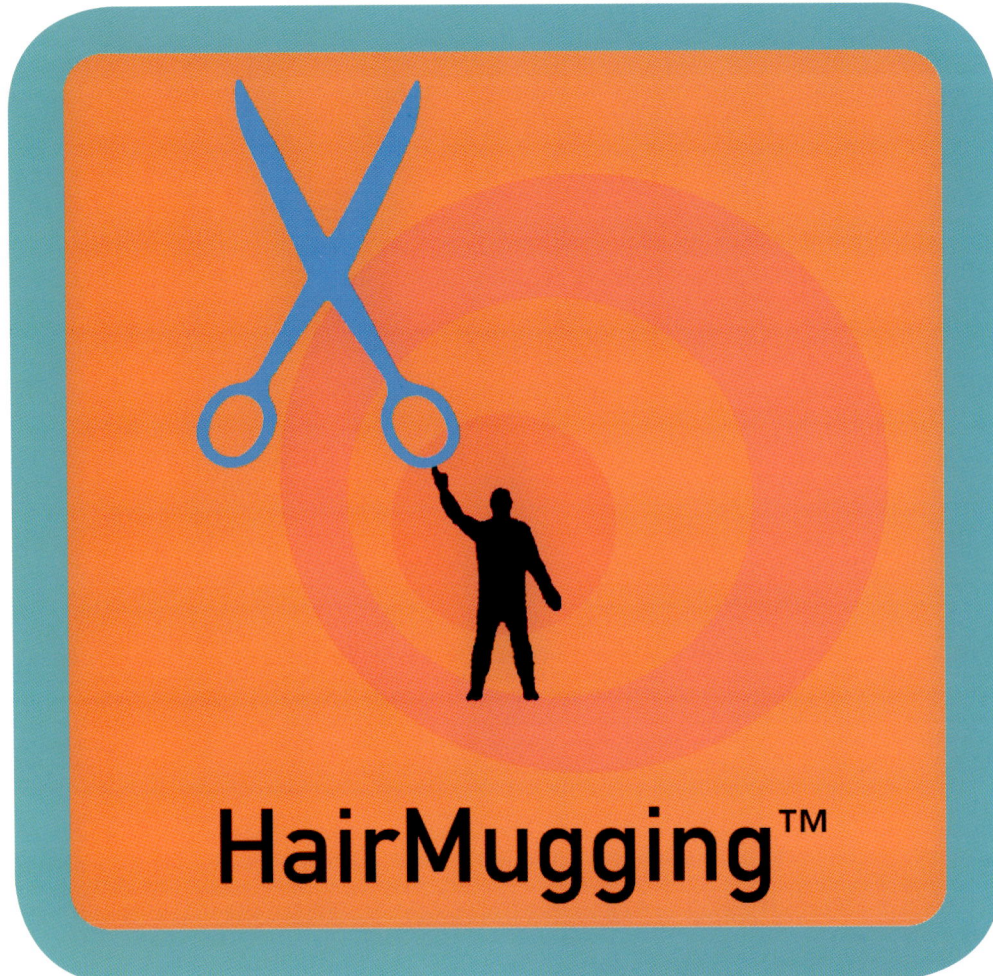

HairMugging™

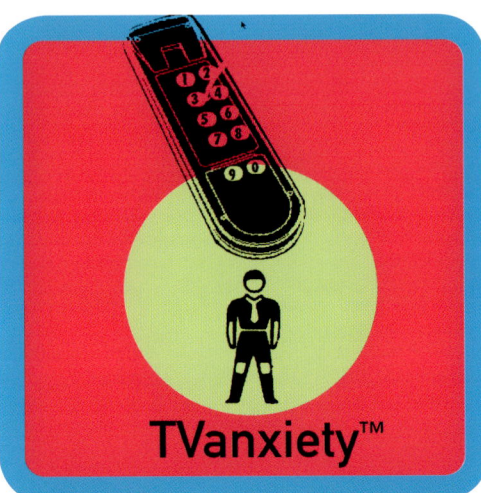

TVanxiety™

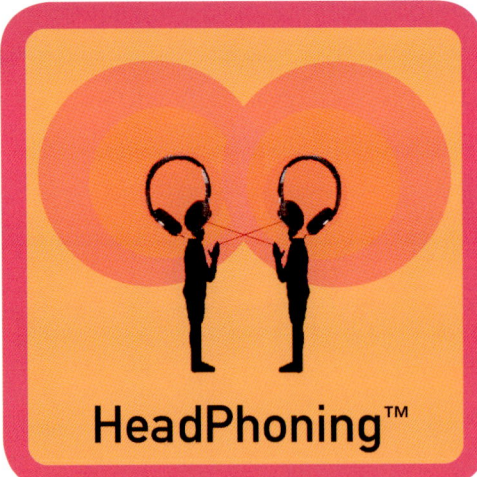

HeadPhoning™

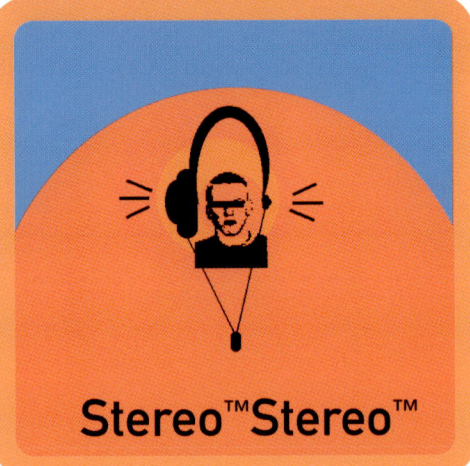

Stereo™Stereo™

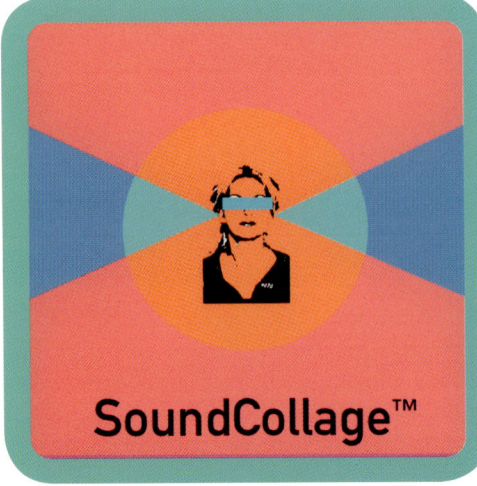

SoundCollage™

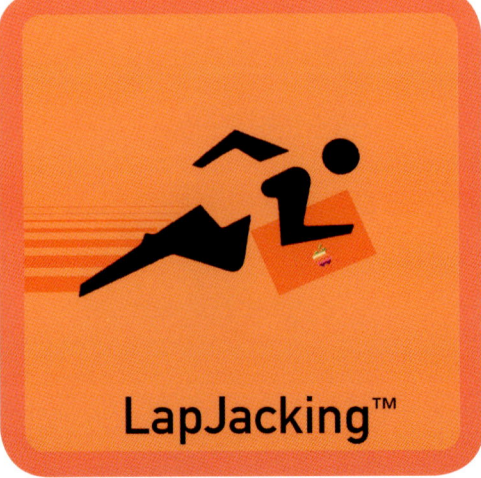

LapJacking™

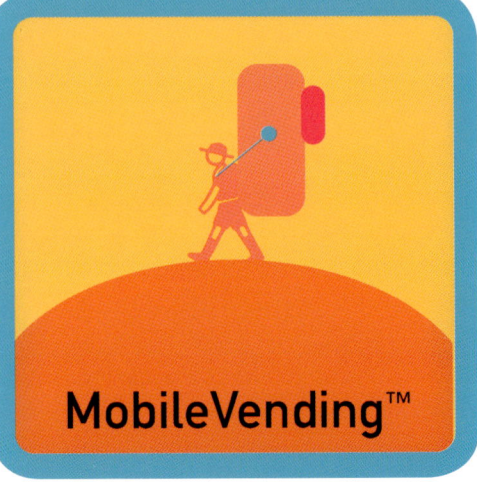

MobileVending™

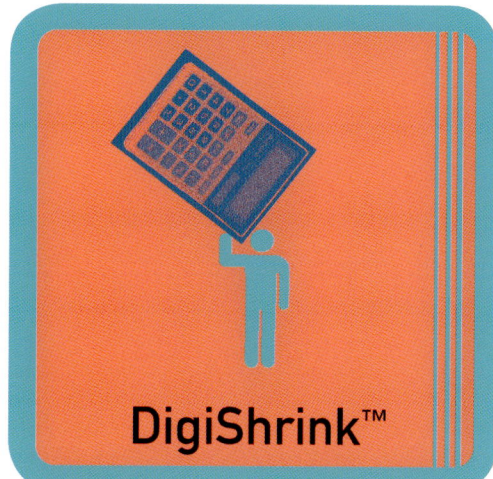

DigiShrink™

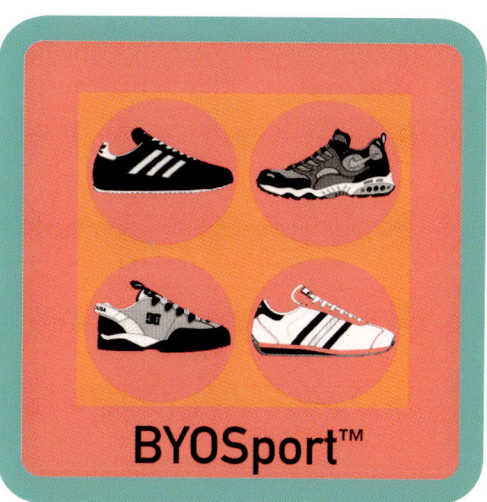

BYOSport™

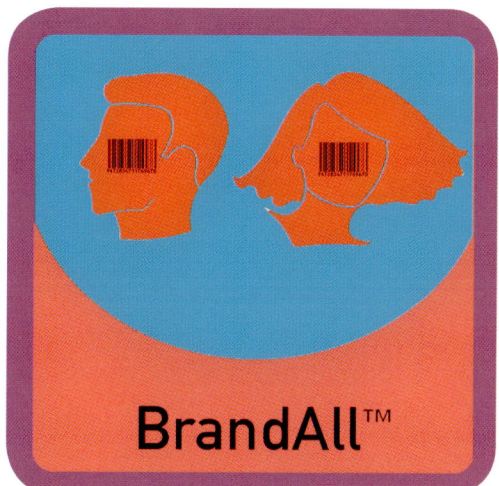

BrandAll™

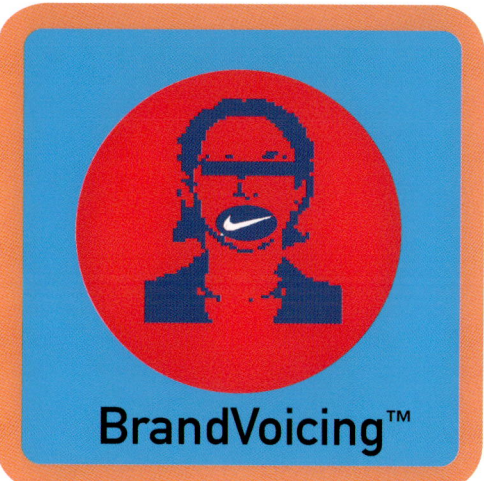

BrandVoicing™

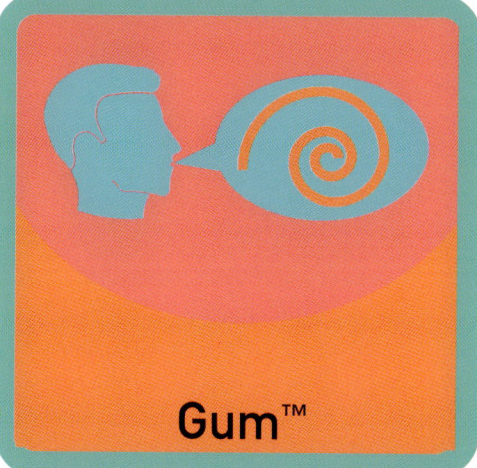

Gum™

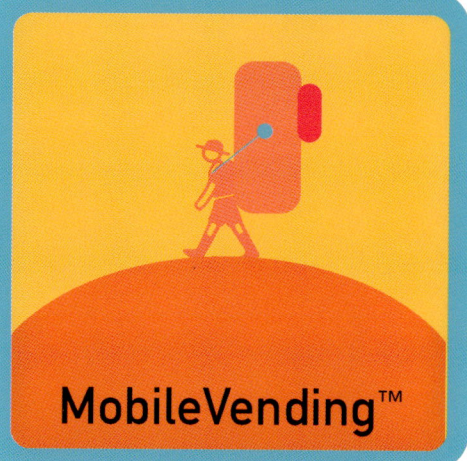

MobileVending™

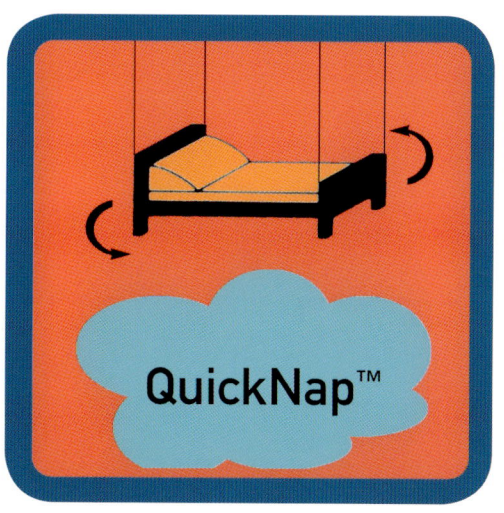

QuickNap™

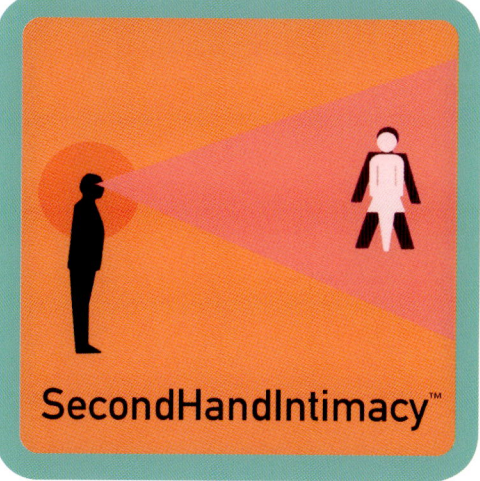

SecondHandIntimacy™

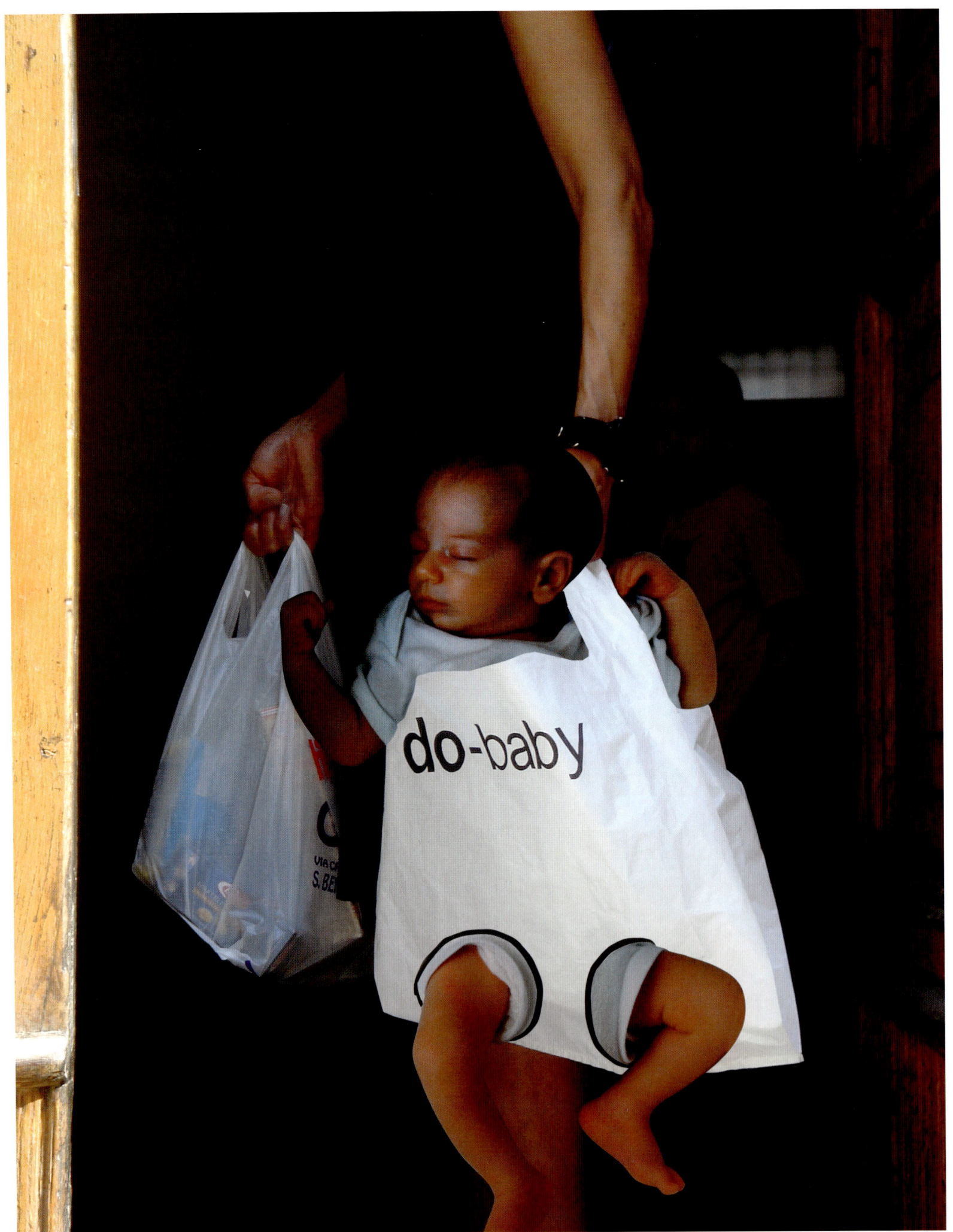

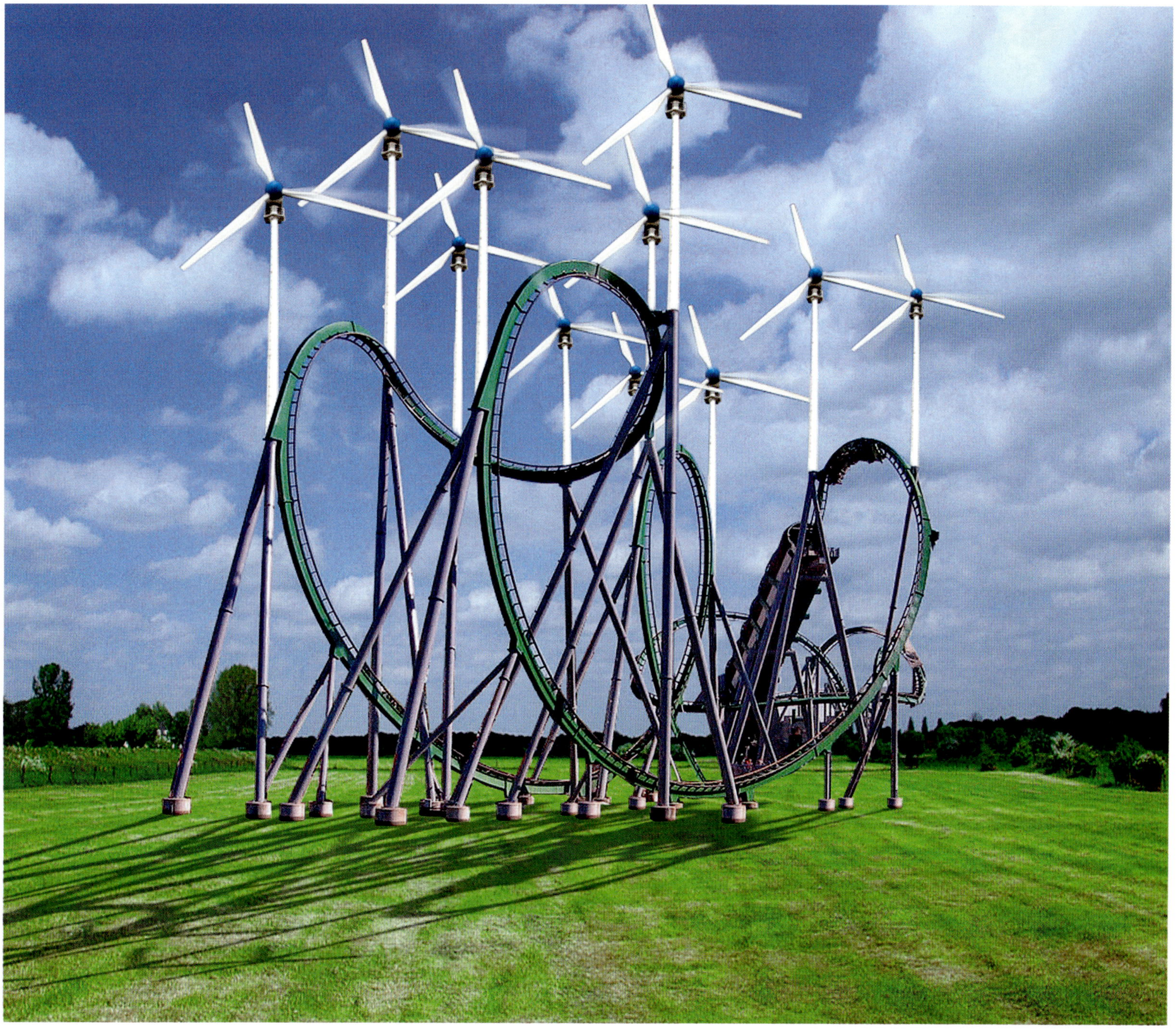

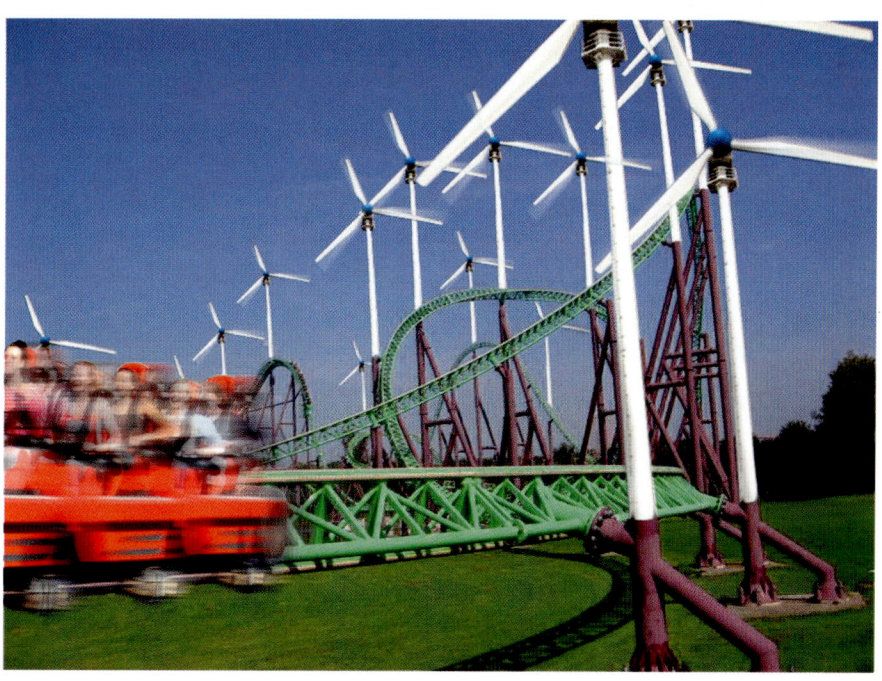

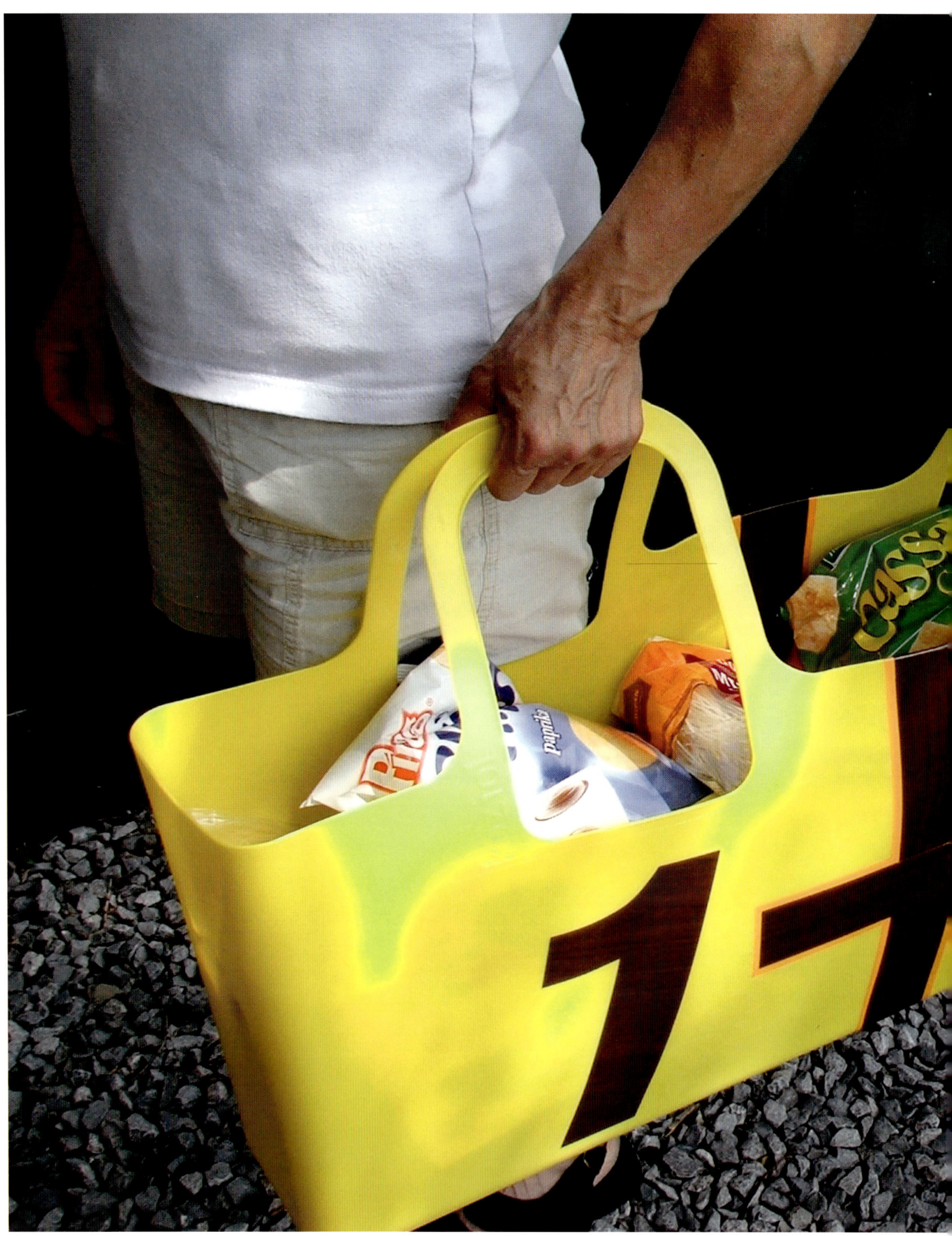

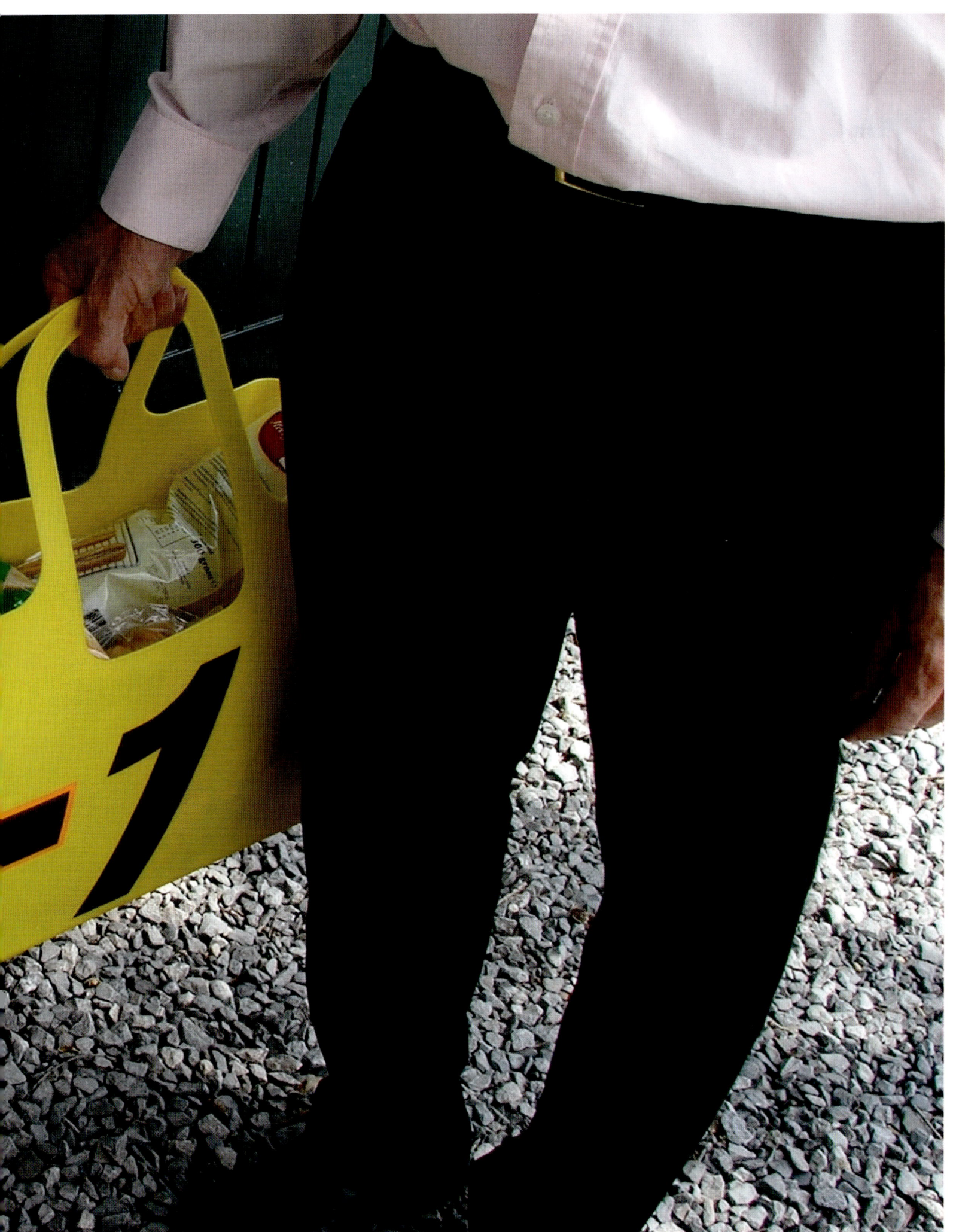

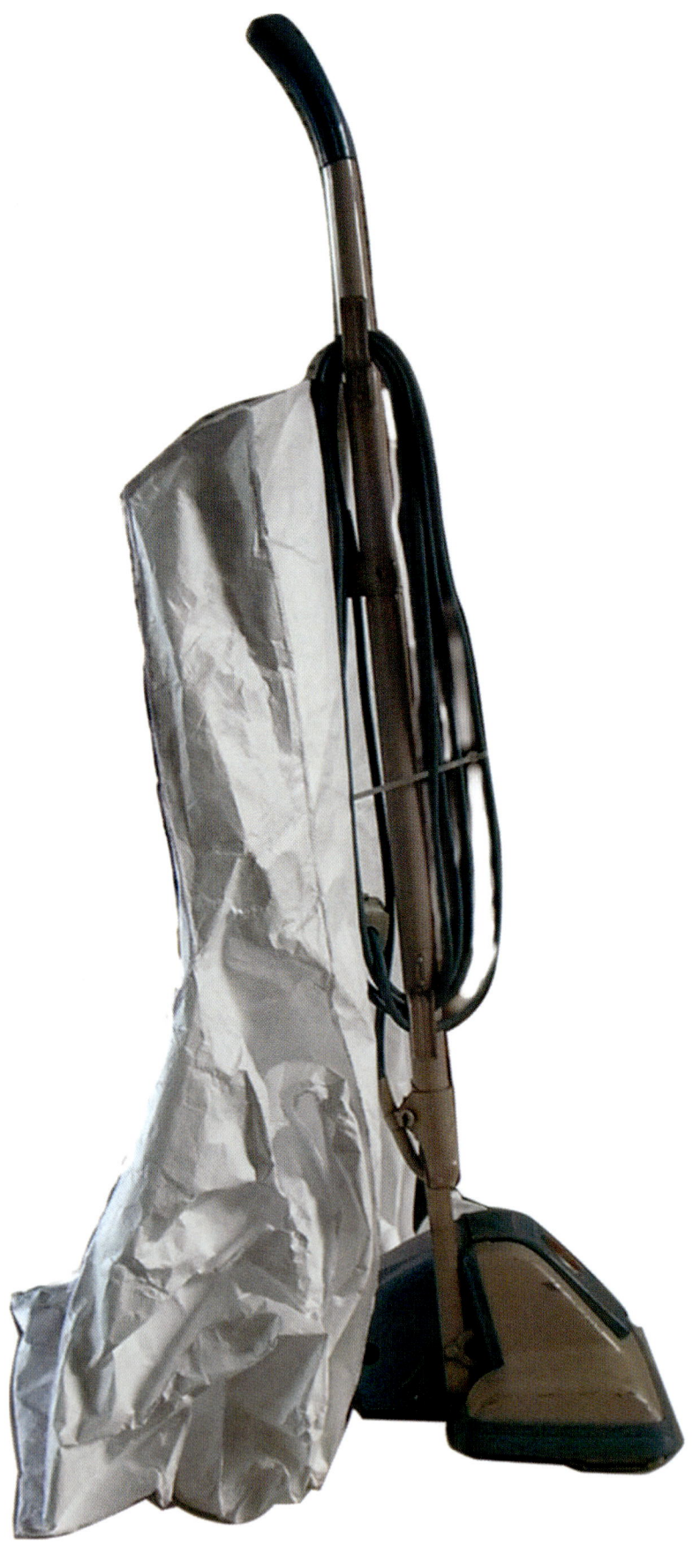

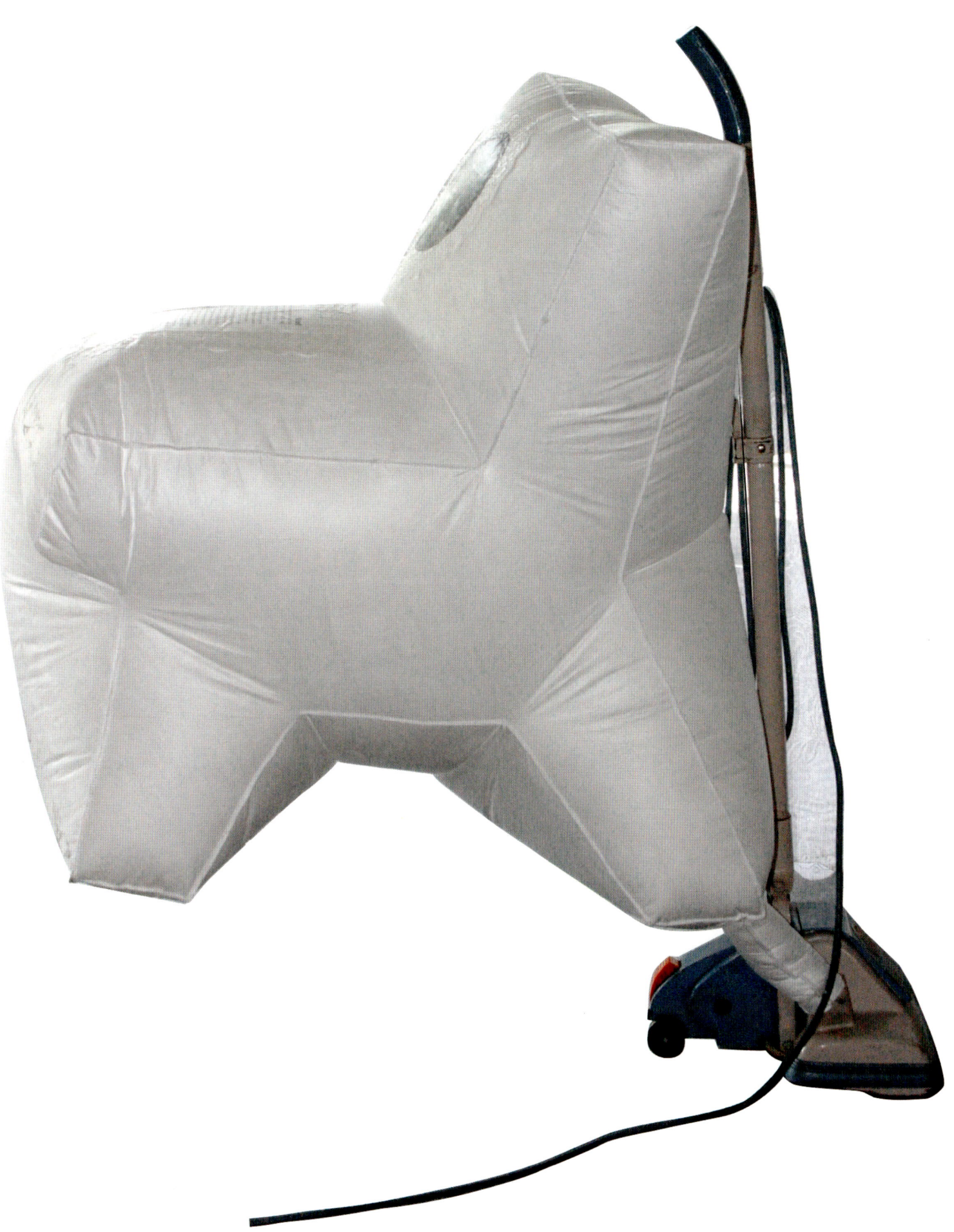

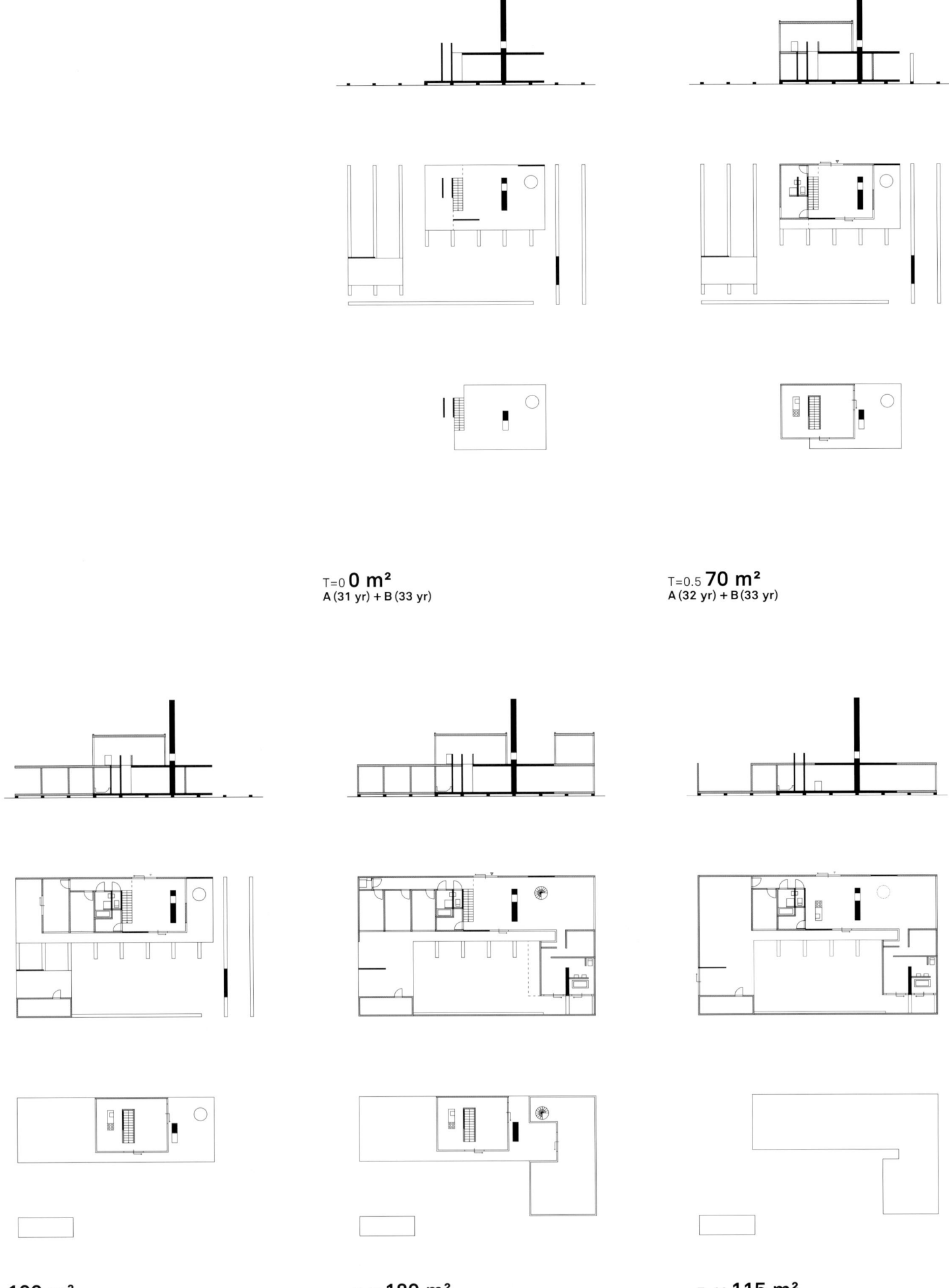

T=0 **0 m²**
A (31 yr) + B (33 yr)

T=0.5 **70 m²**
A (32 yr) + B (33 yr)

T=7 **100 m²**
A (38 yr) + B (40 yr) + C (5 yr)

T=16 **180 m²**
A (47 yr) + B (49 yr) + C (14 yr) + D (8 yr) + E (6 yr)

T=30 **115 m²**
A (61 yr) + B (63 yr)

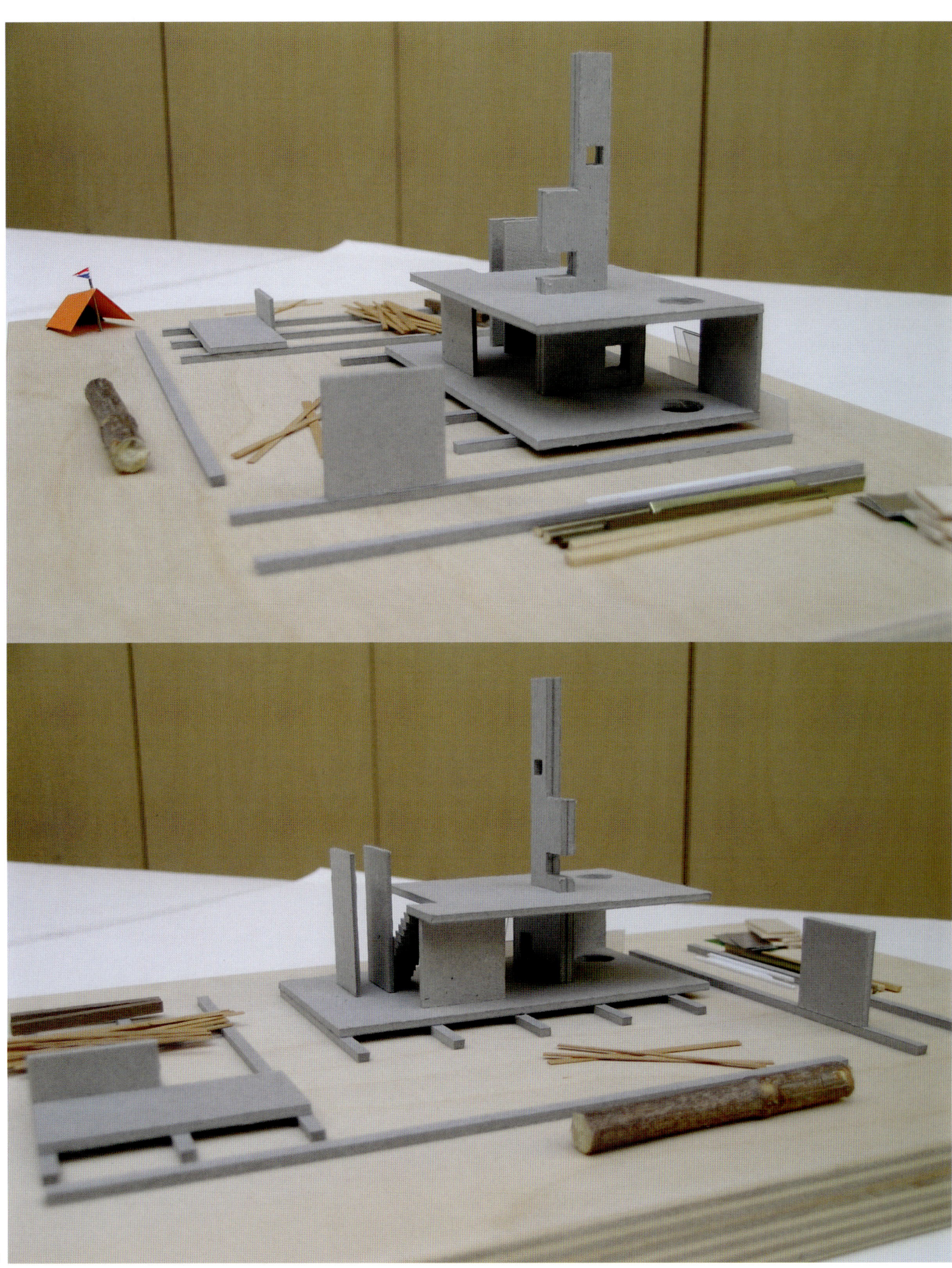

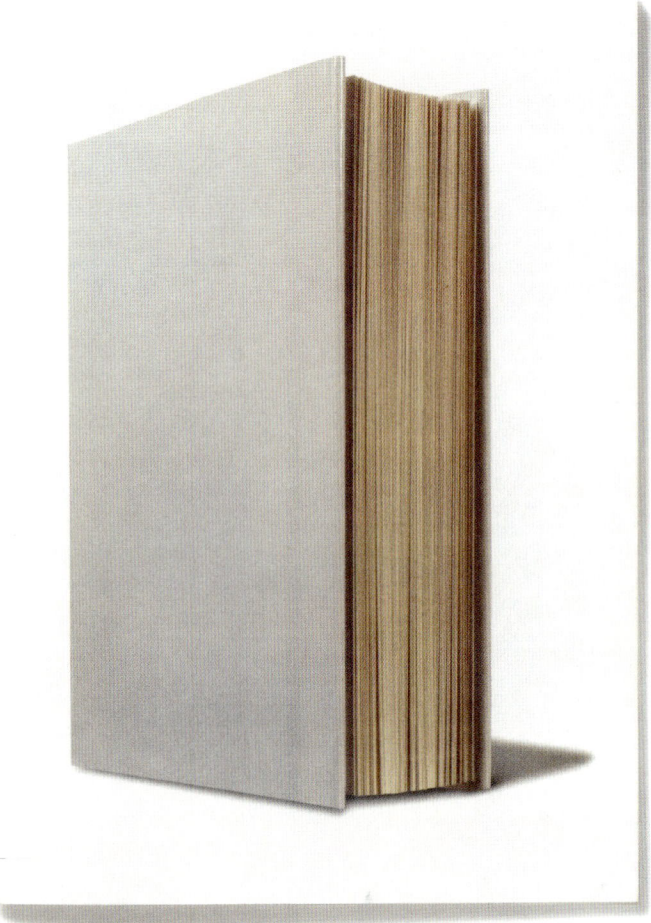

 000.002

do future

A journey into youth trends of today and tomorrow, do future is written by do and 30 other contributors from around the world. The book, jammed full of information, disinformation, stories, trends, brand strategies, questions, essays and ideas, also includes a 600-strong research group experiment which formulates an intriguing platform for trends and brand directions. If you don't know what FearBear™ is, if you want to hear Tony Blair's real vision of the future, if you want to discover the secret of everlasting youth, this book is for you. Life, death, drugs, politics, laundromats, cocker spaniel leashes and much, much more - they all make relevant and often irreverent appearances in do future.

do future 2nd Edition

ISBN 90-803927-3-1

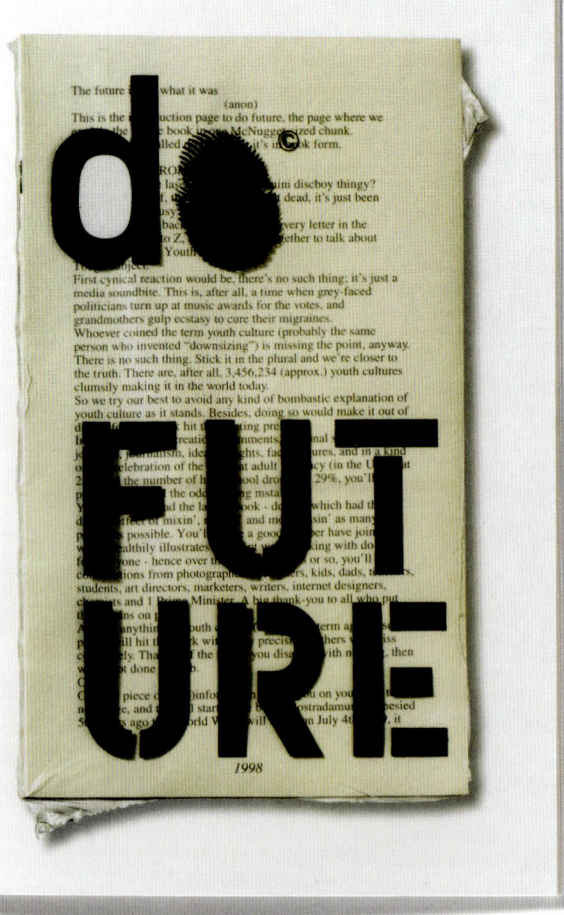

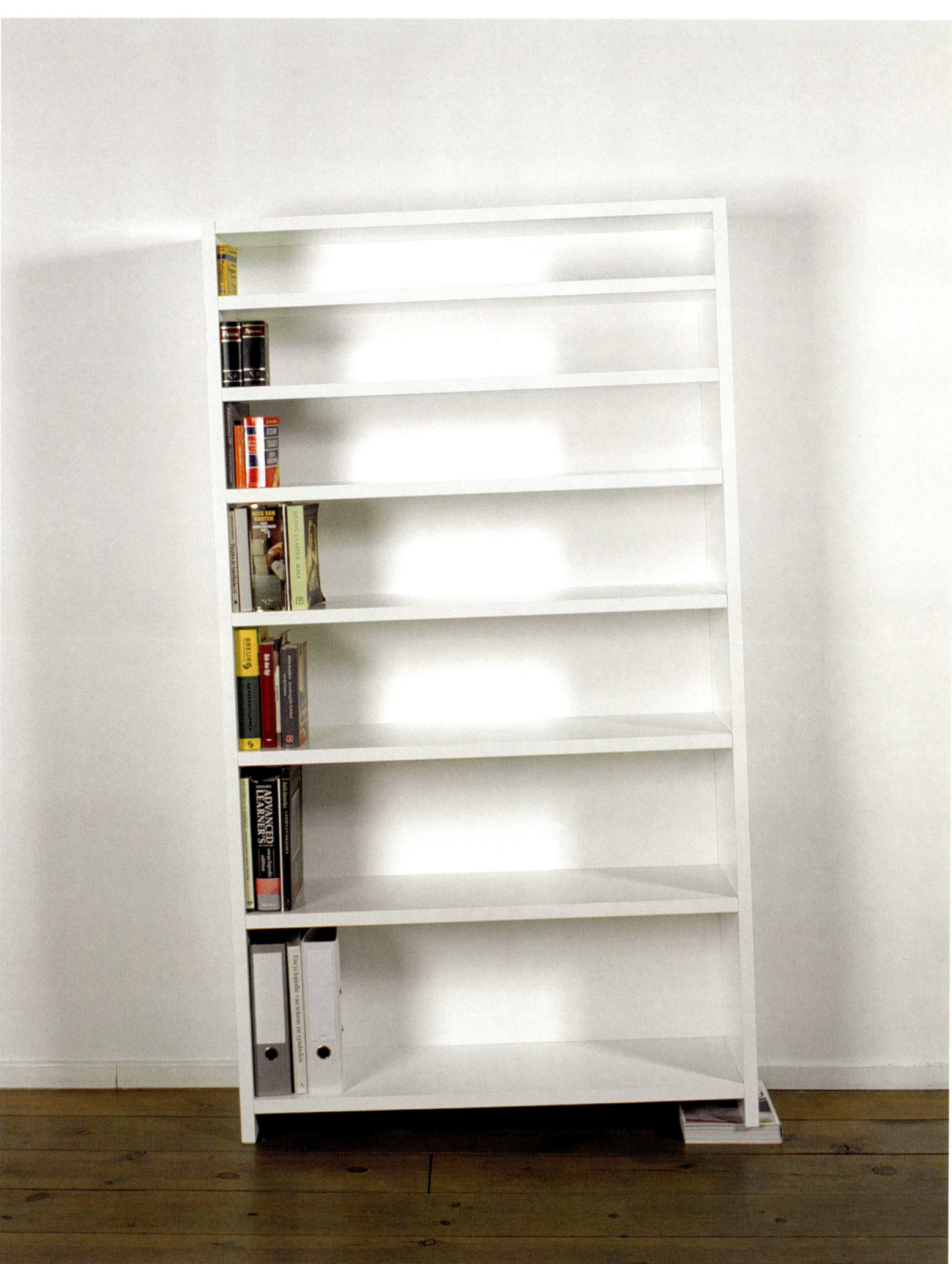

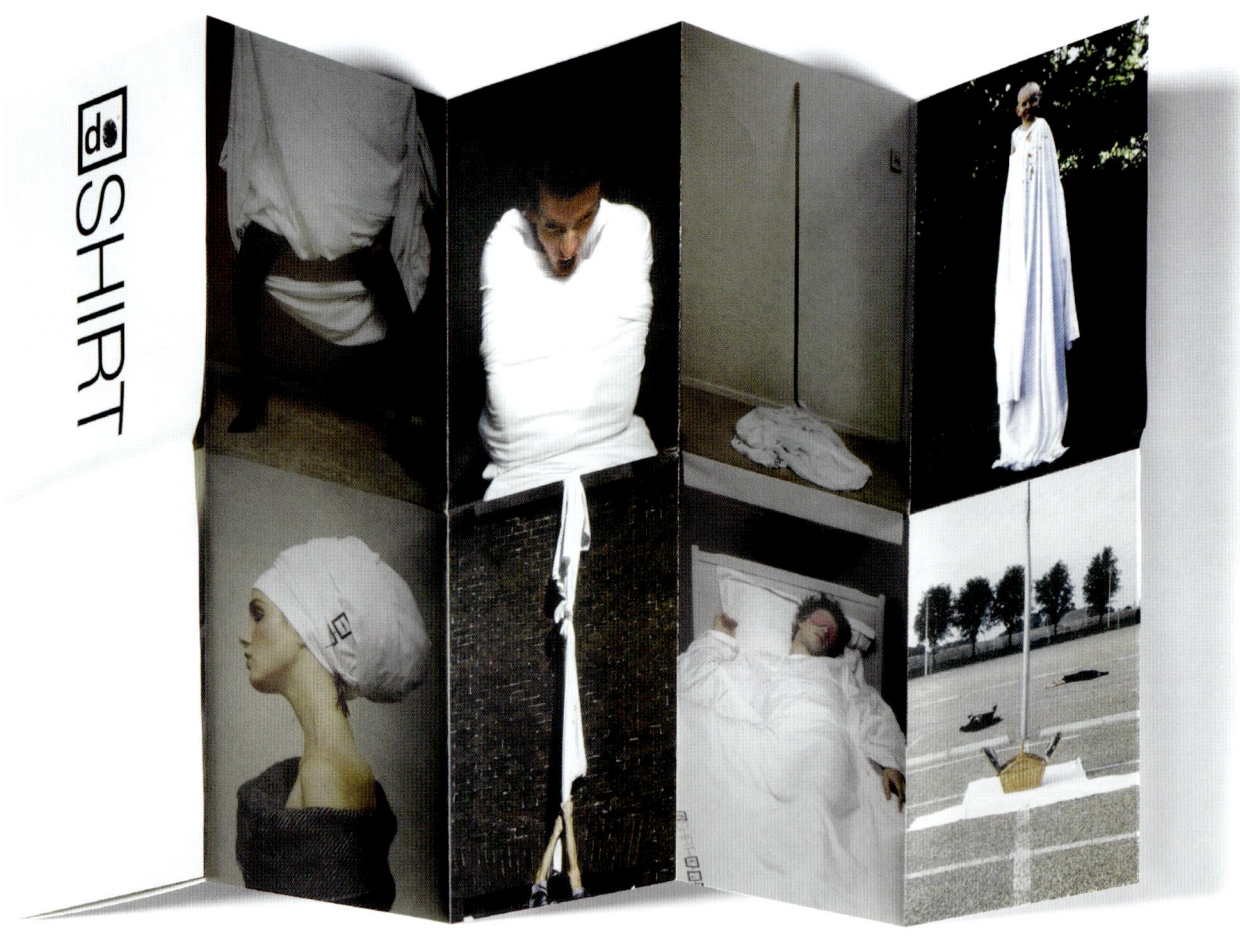

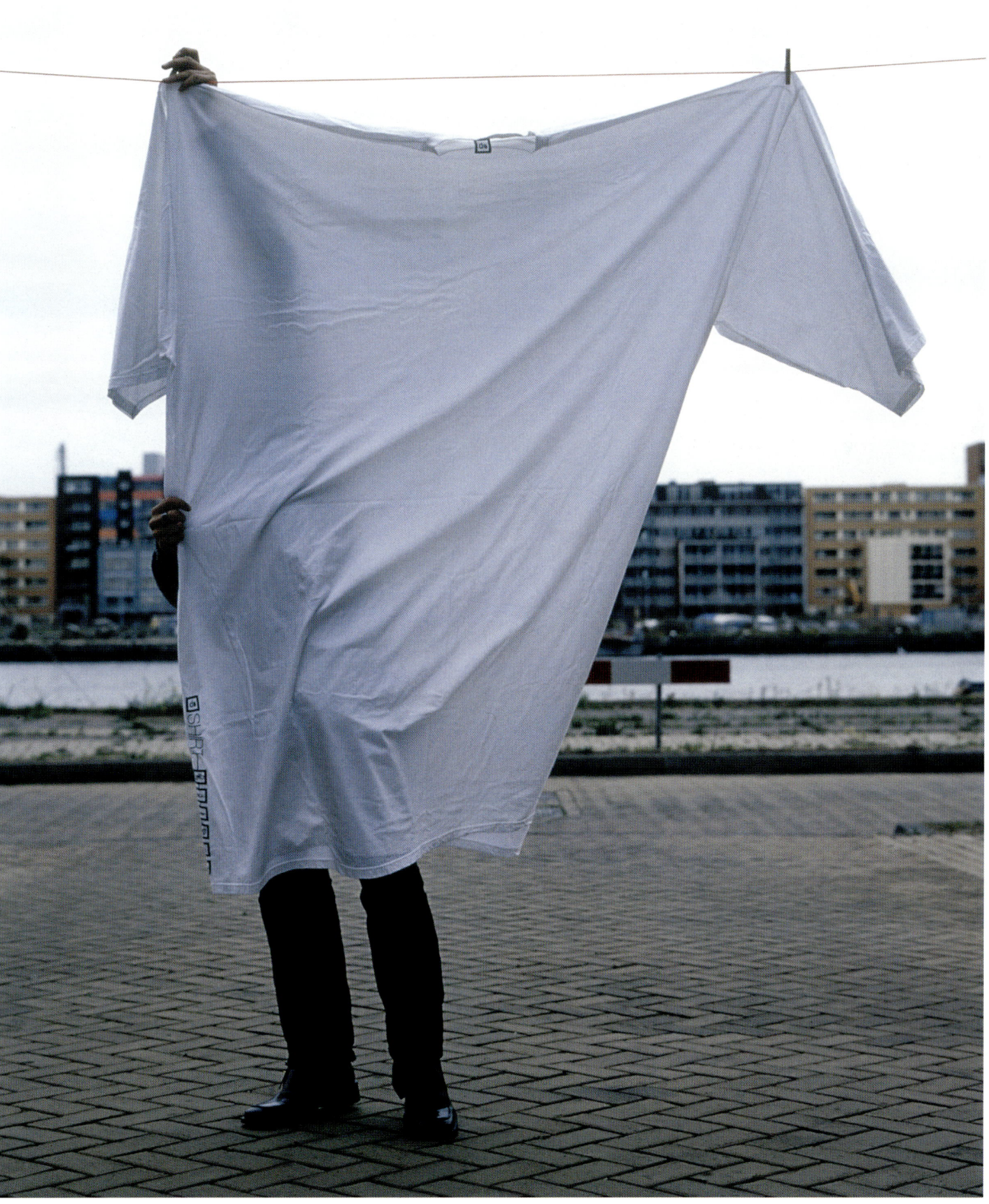

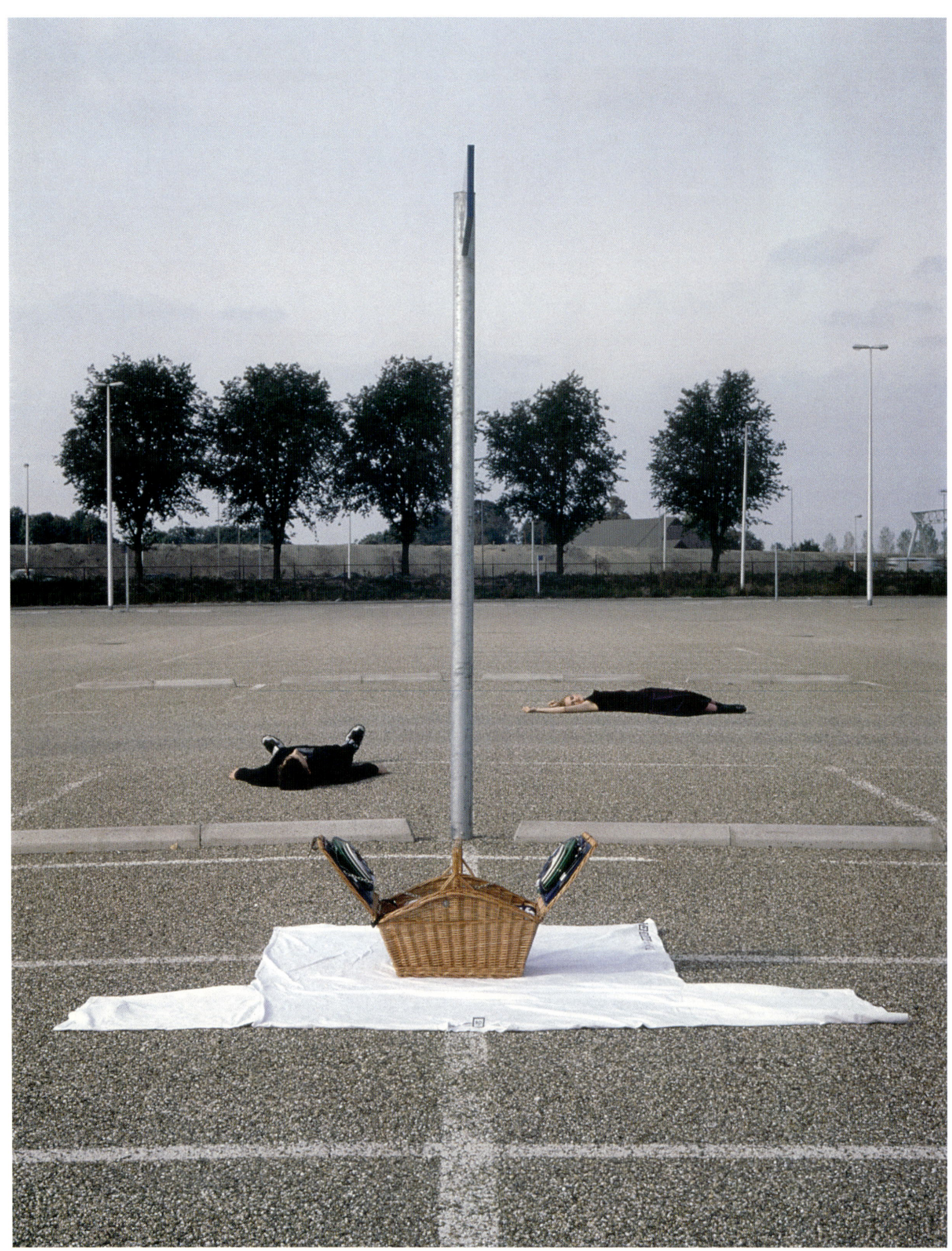

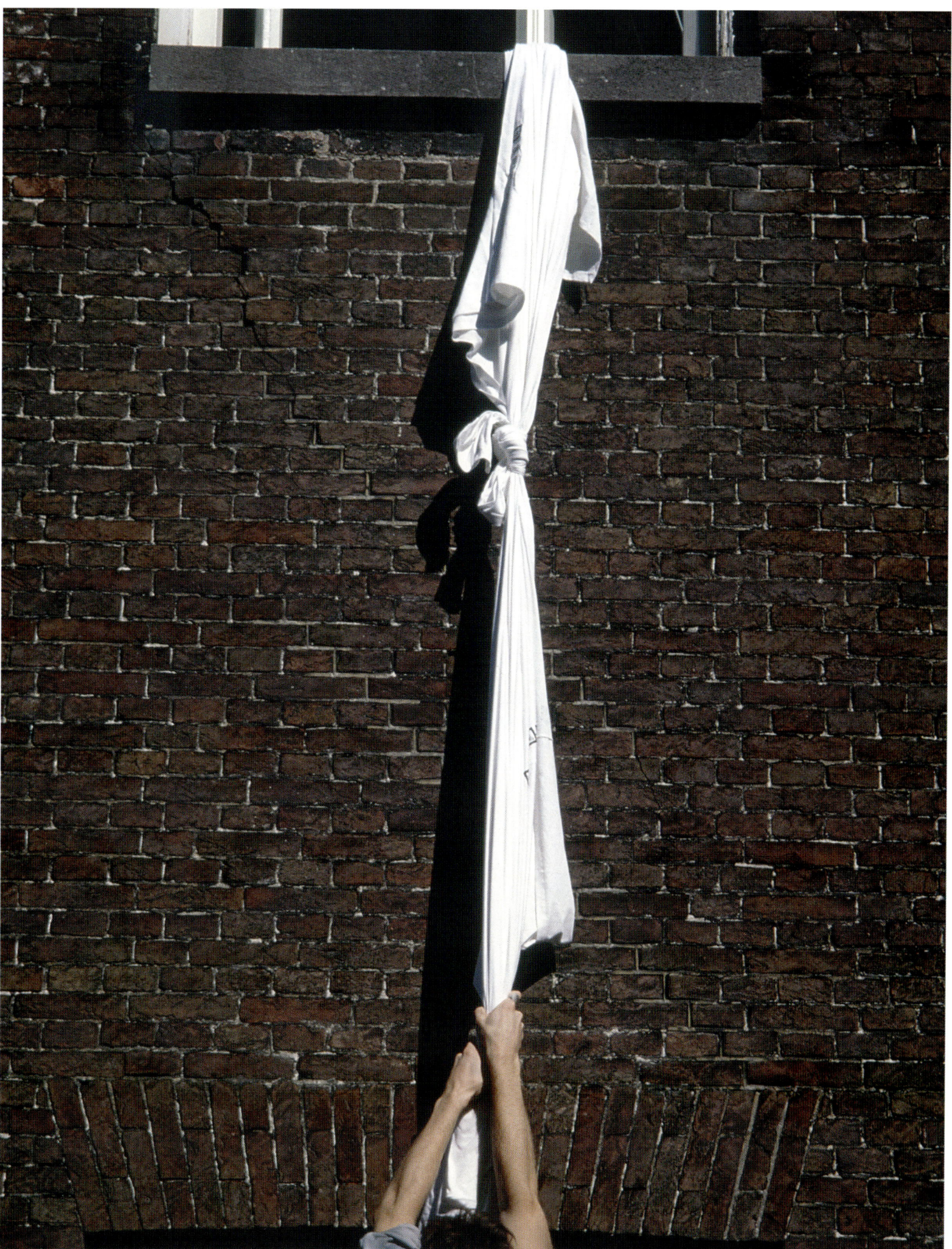

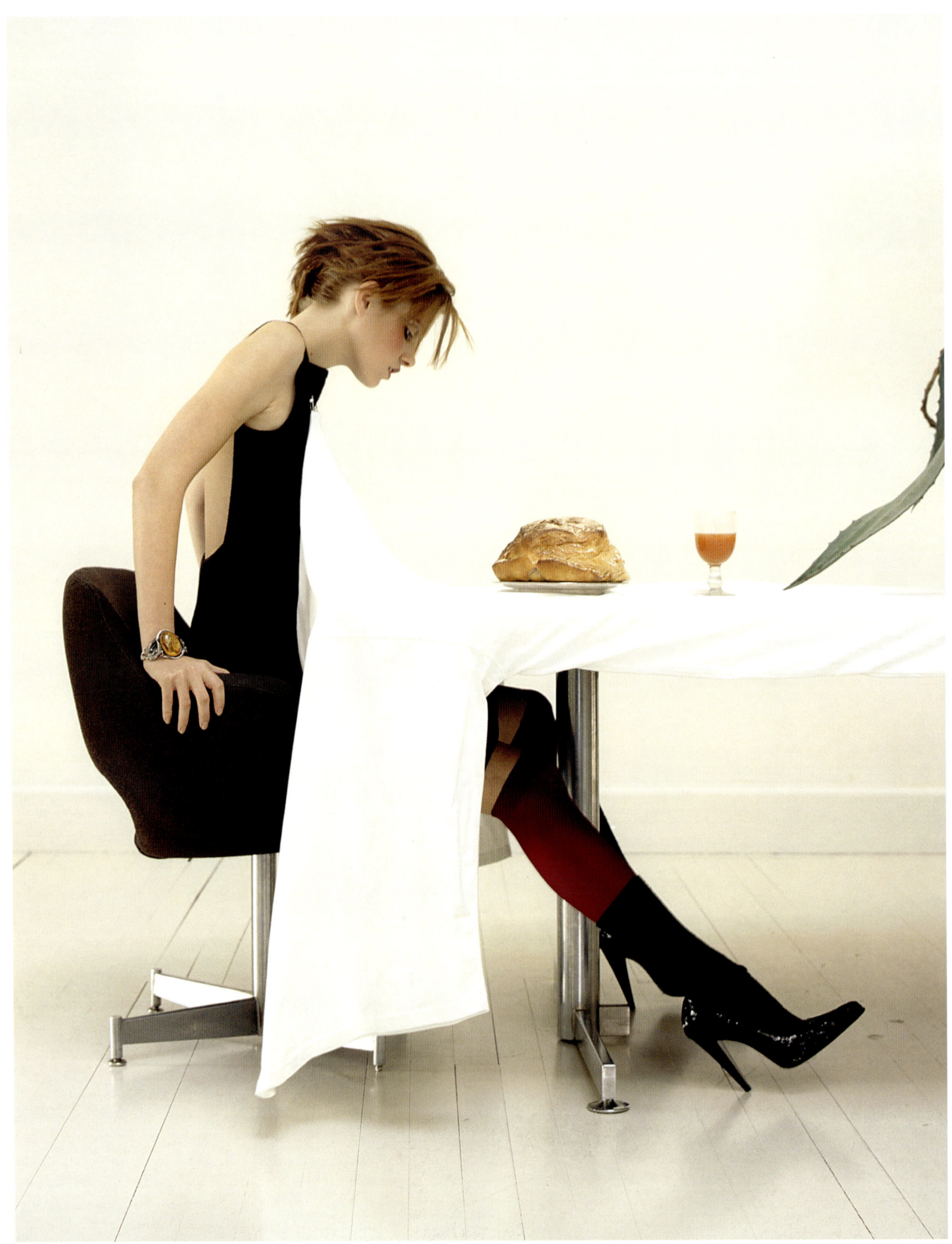

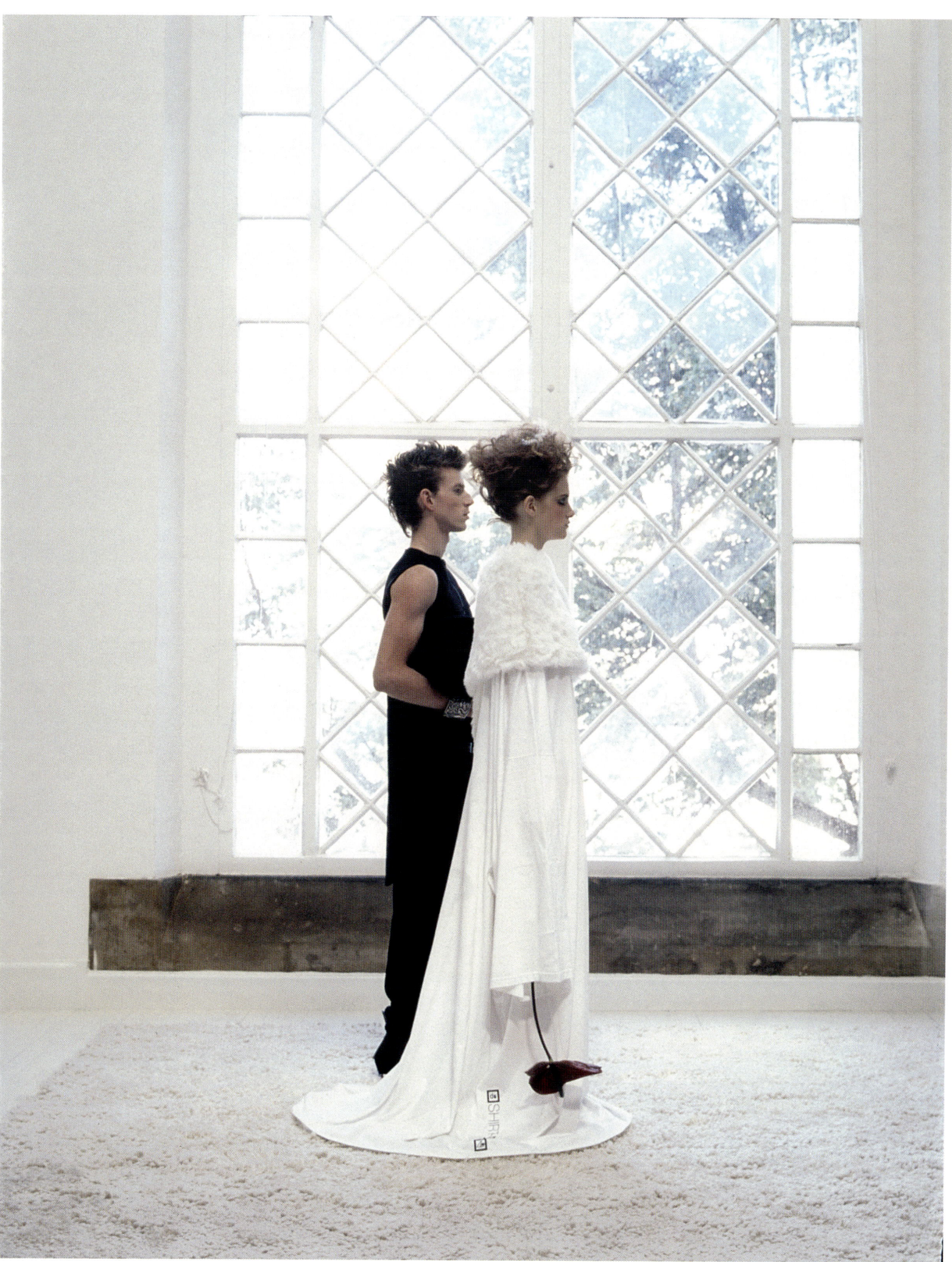

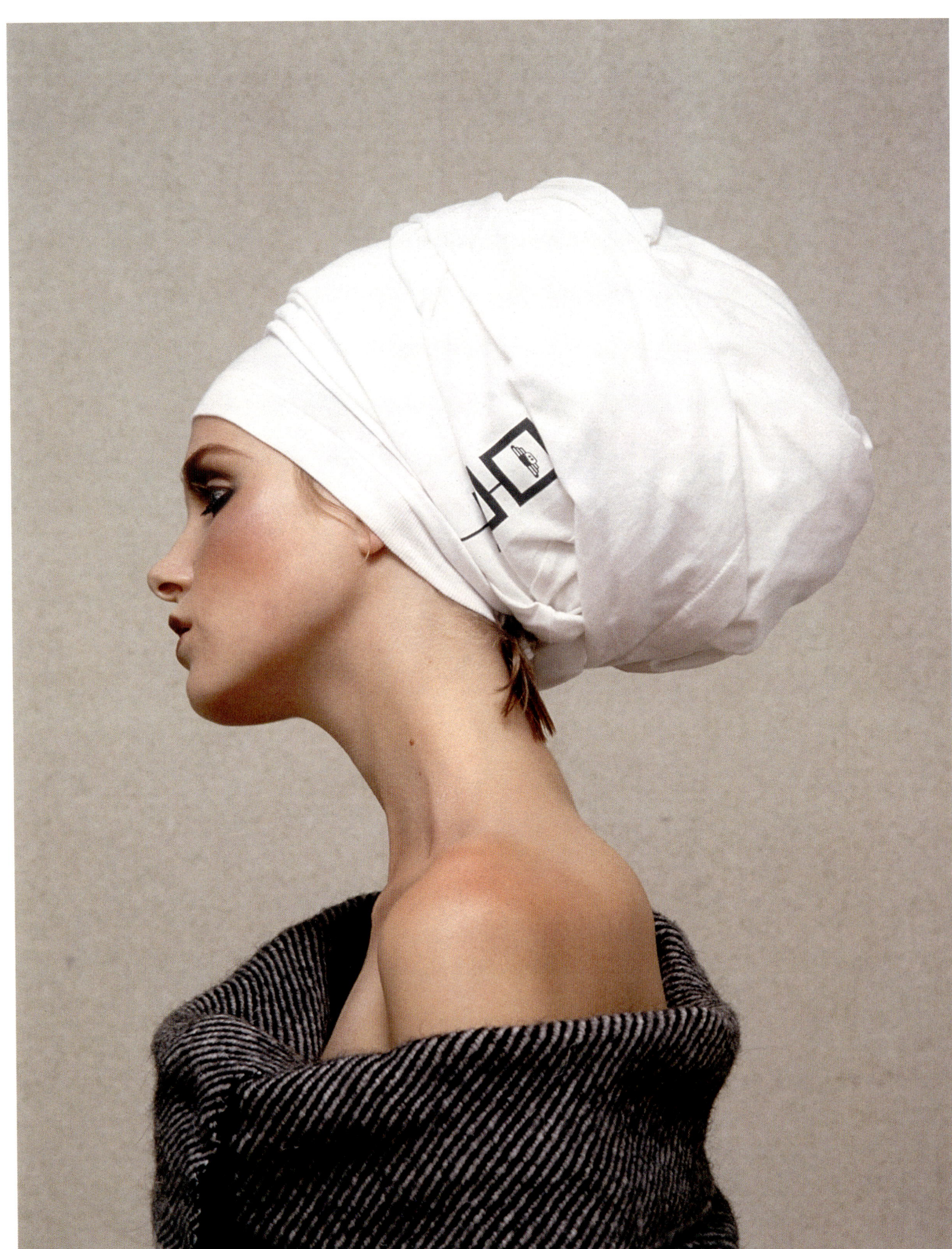

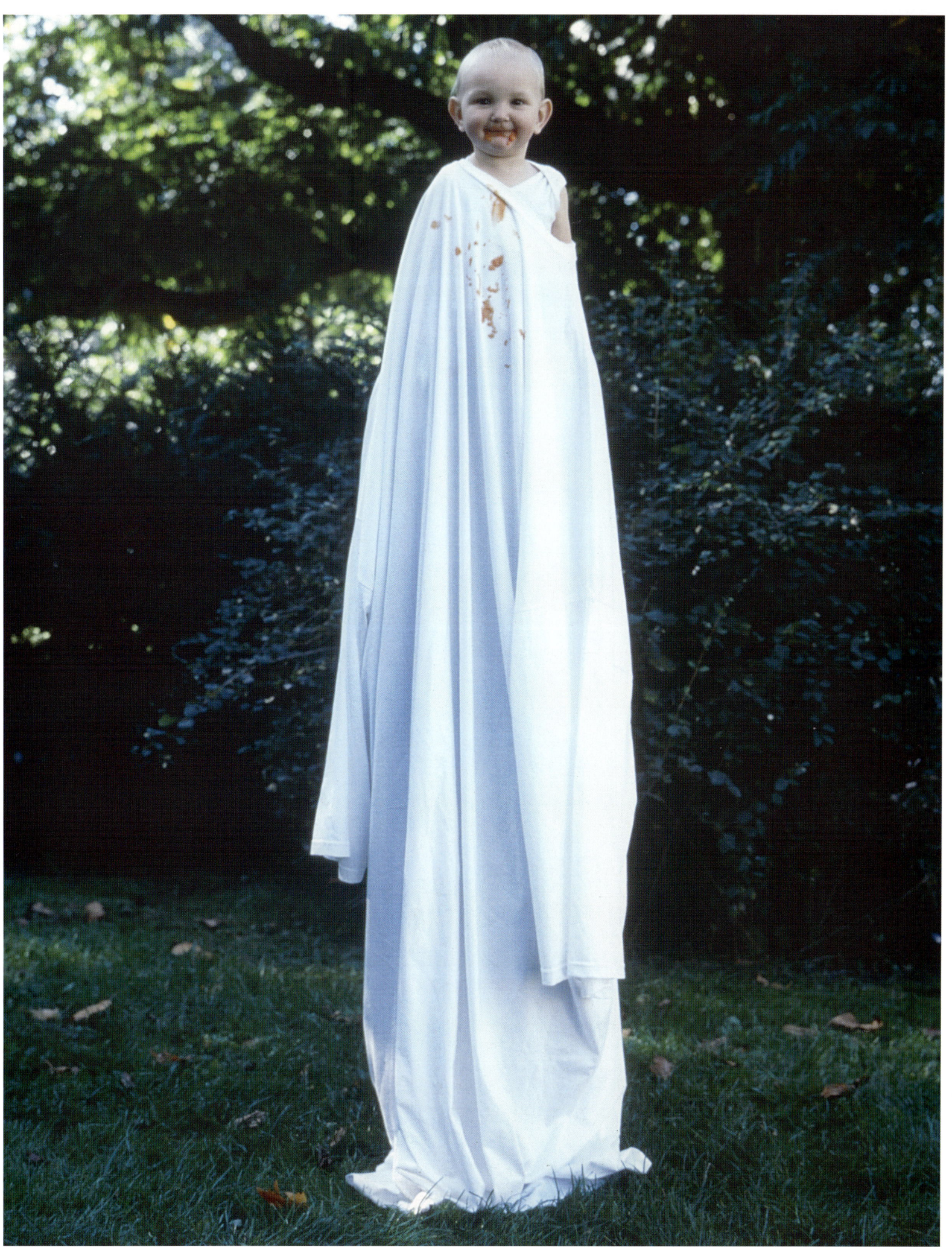

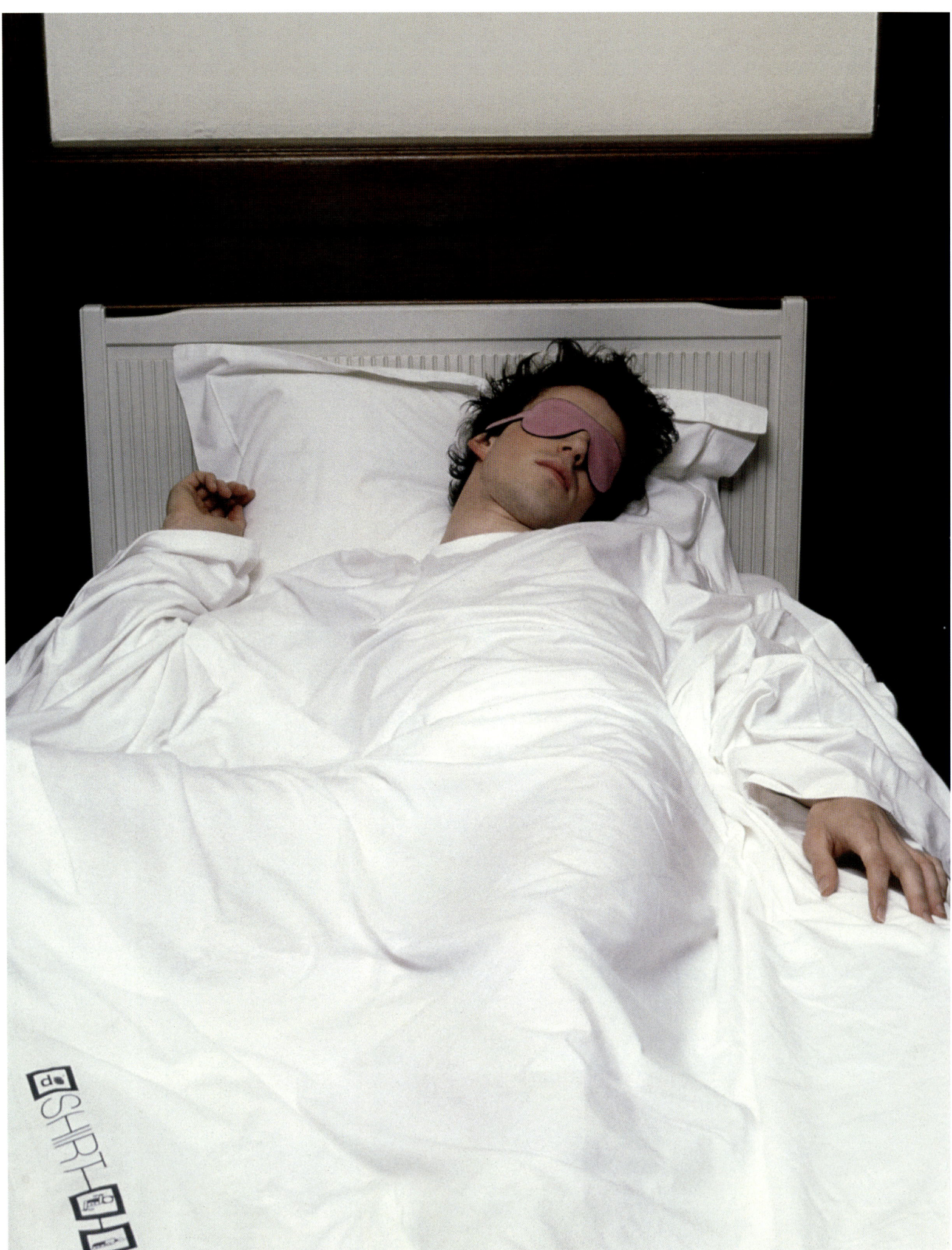

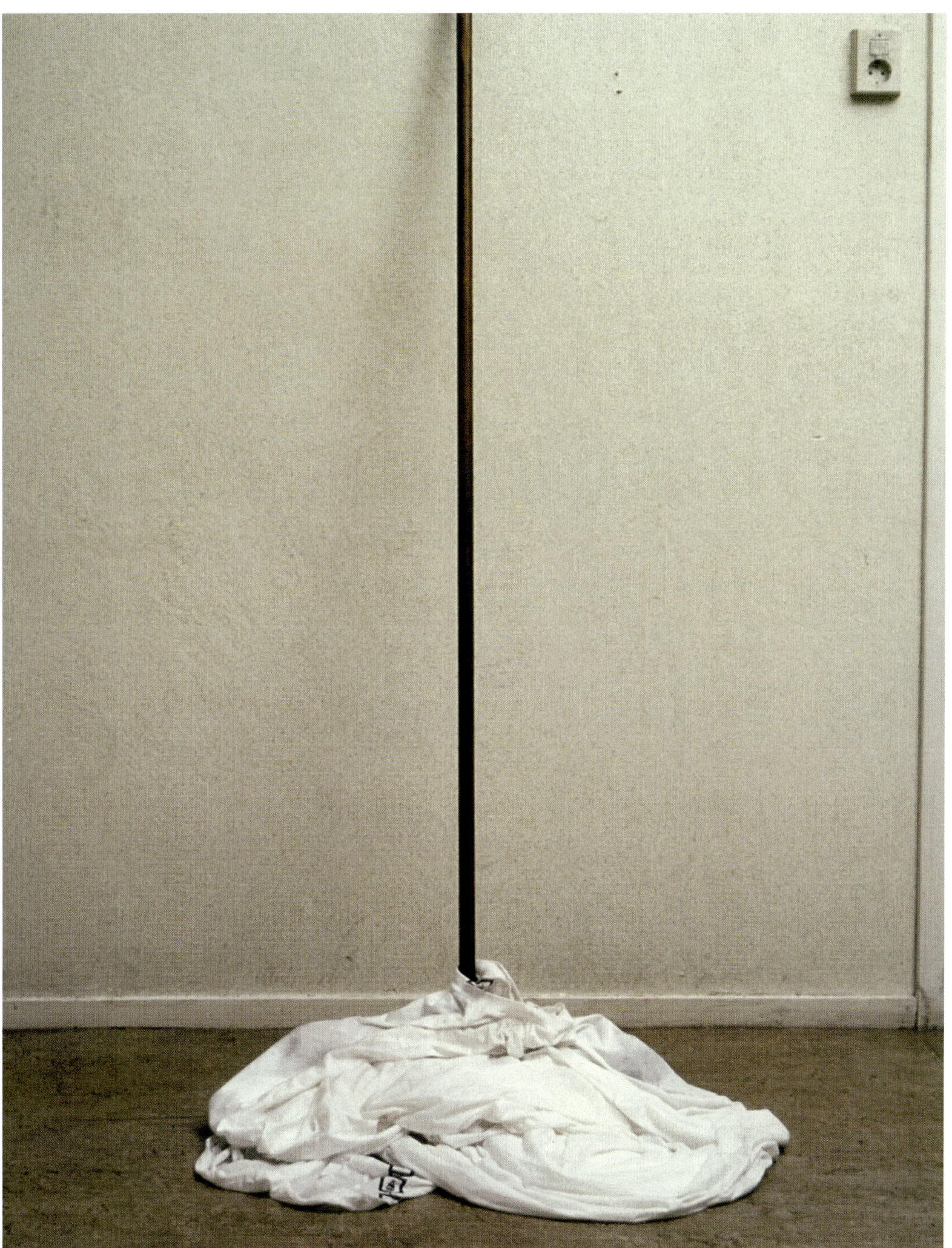

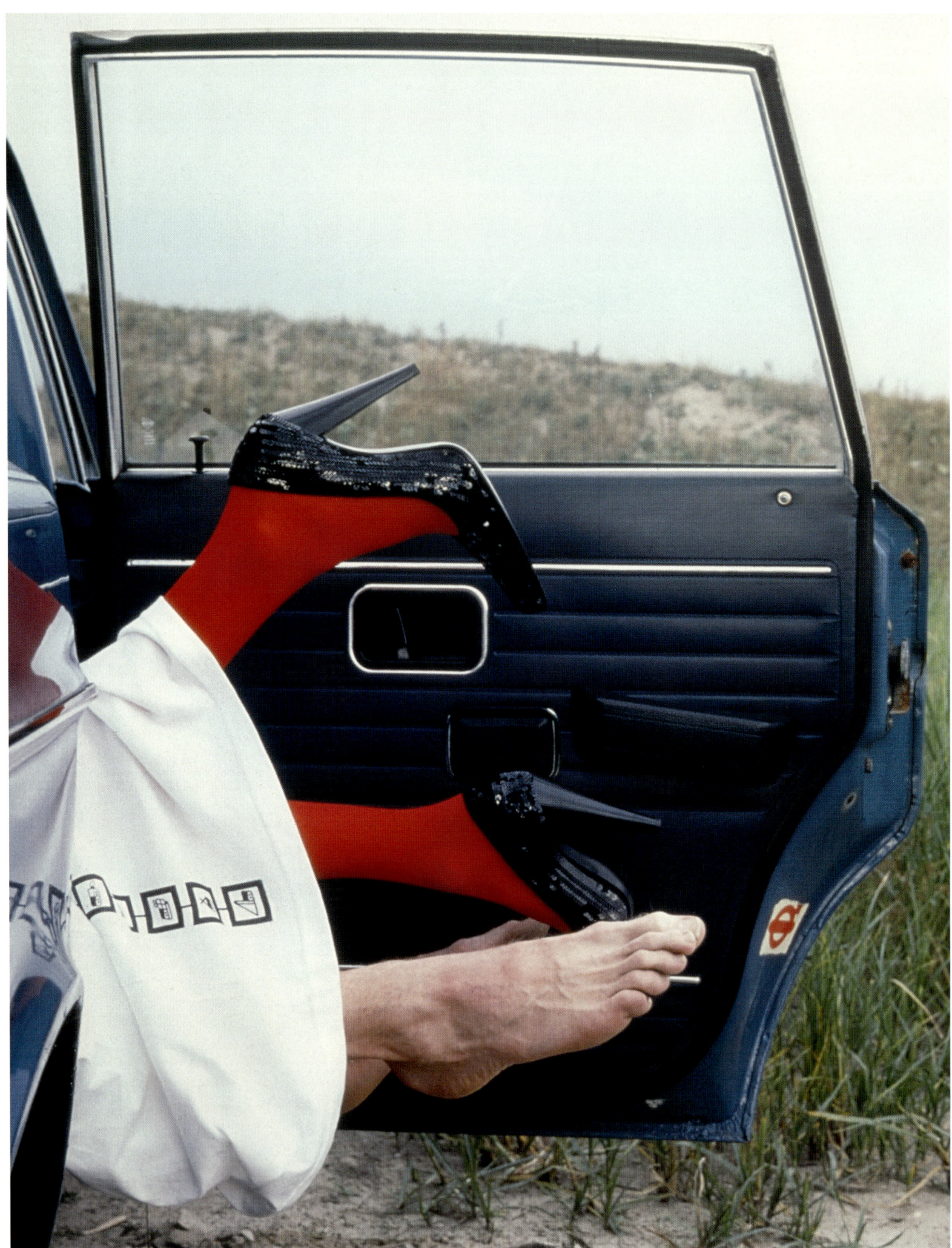

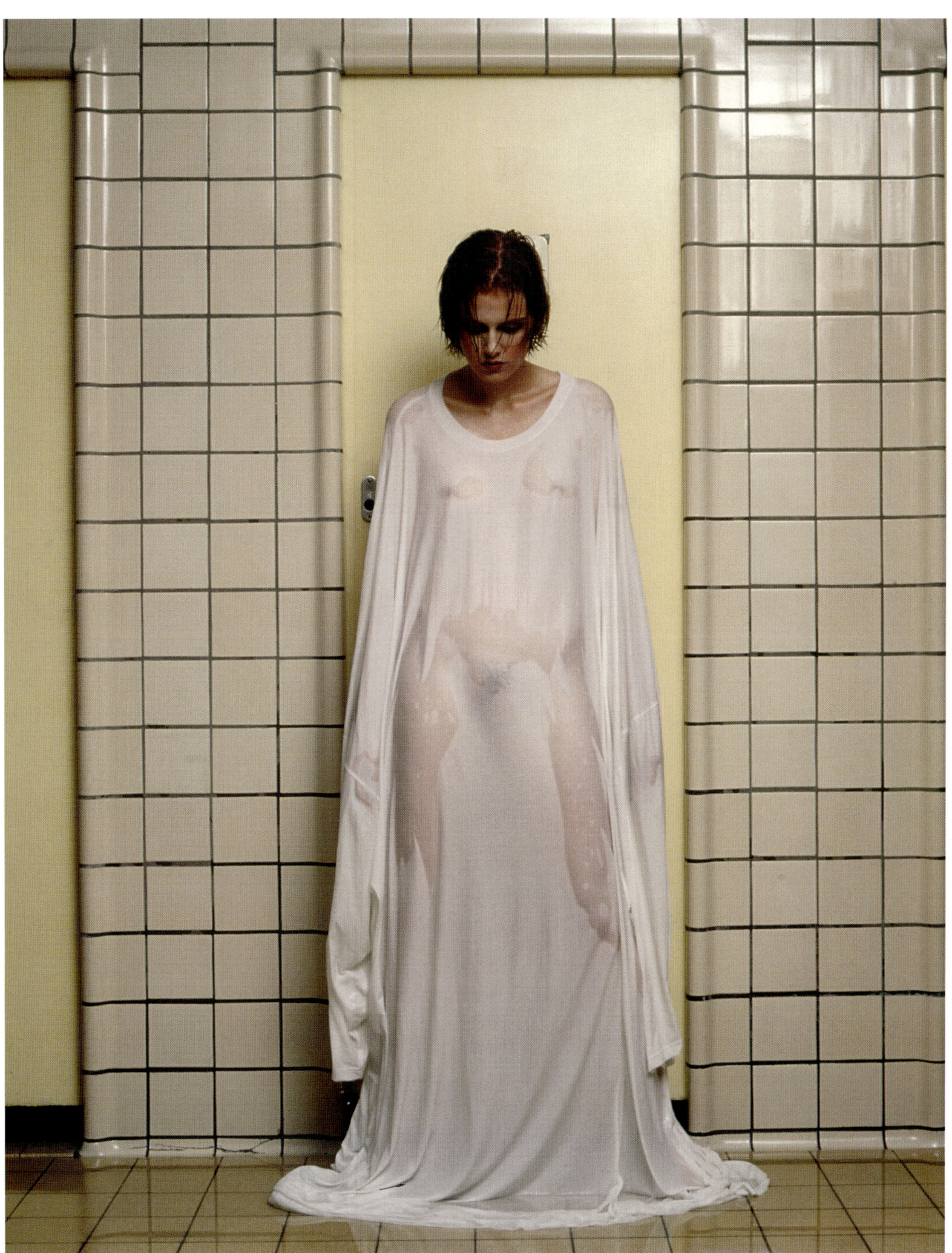

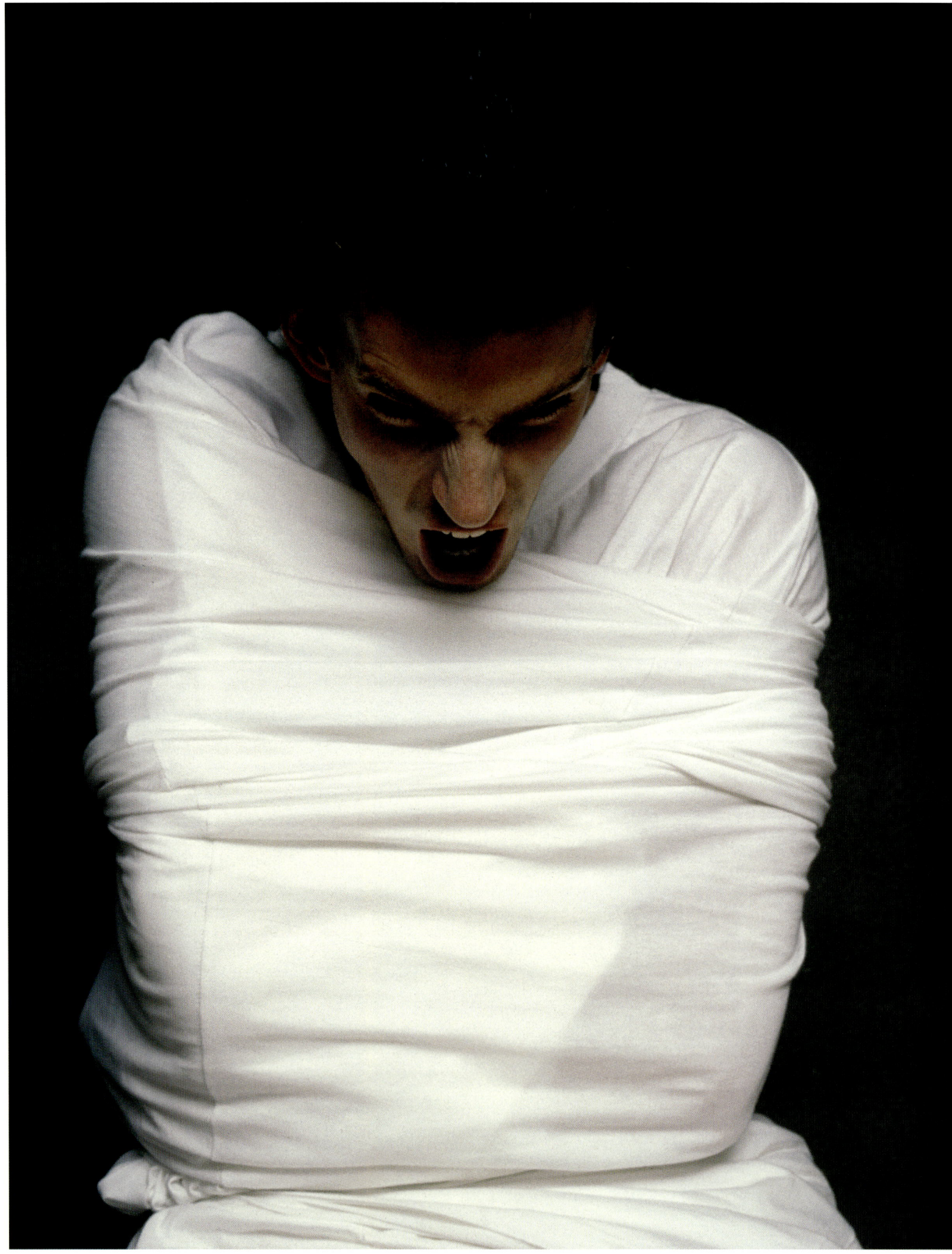

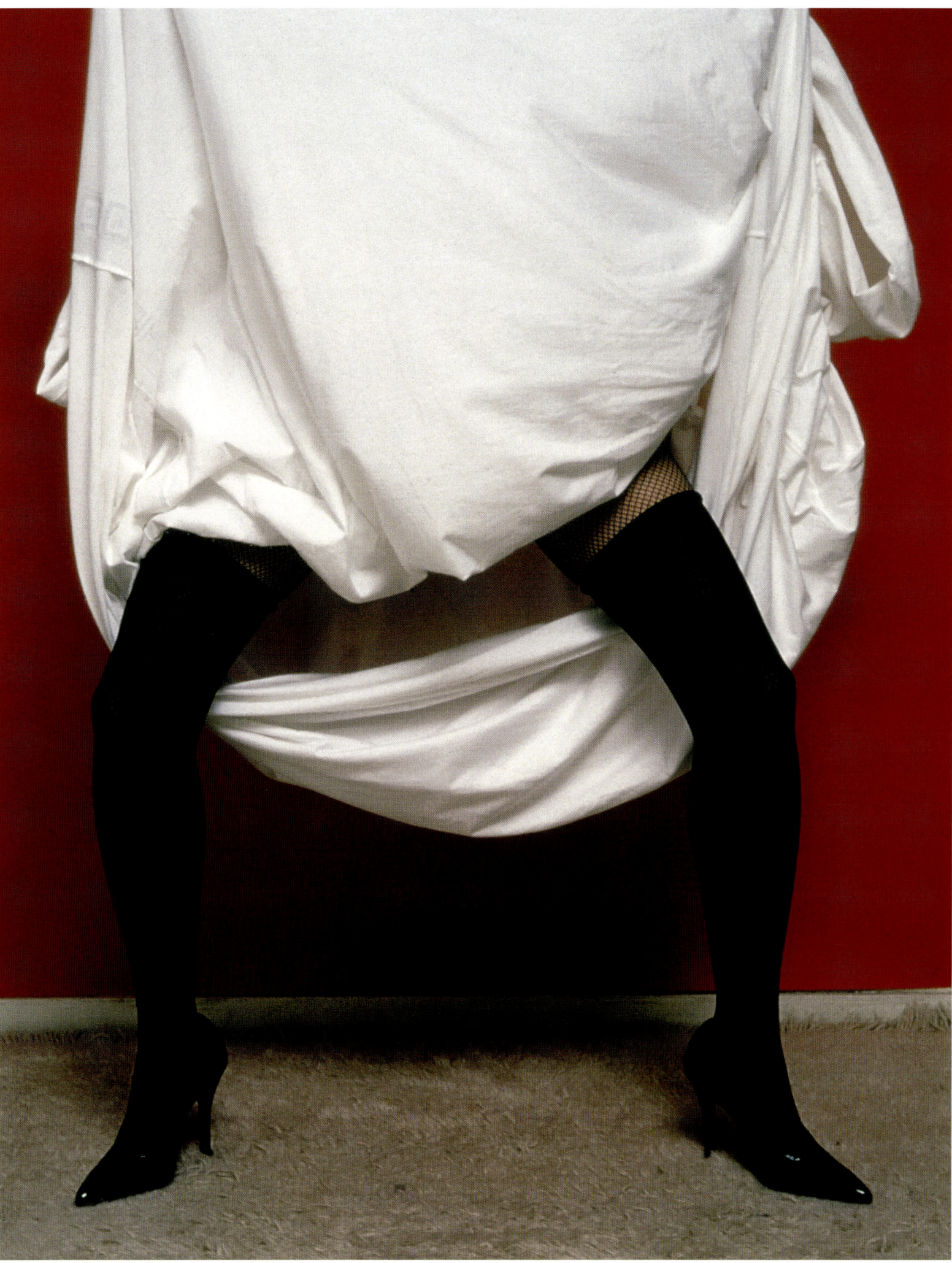

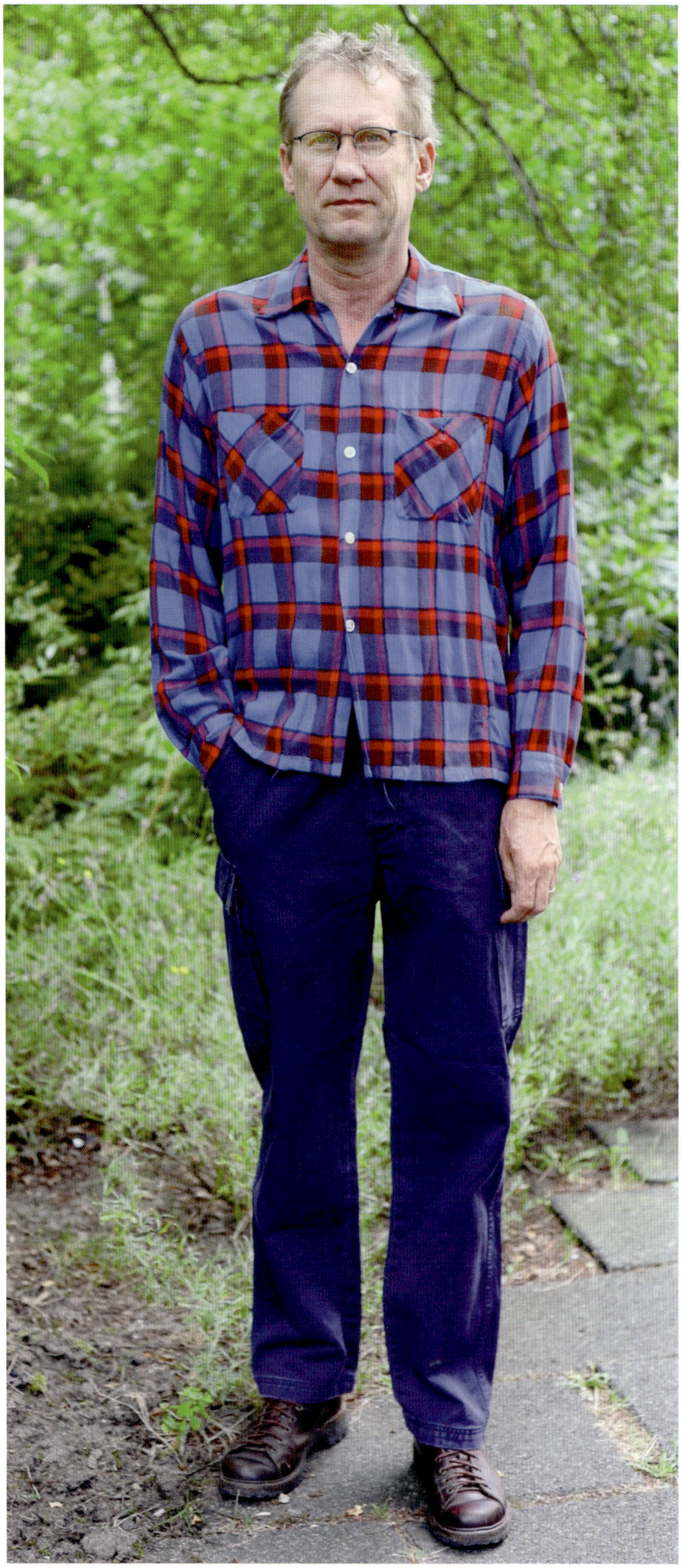

SHIRT 1977
TROUSERS 1986
SHOES 1995

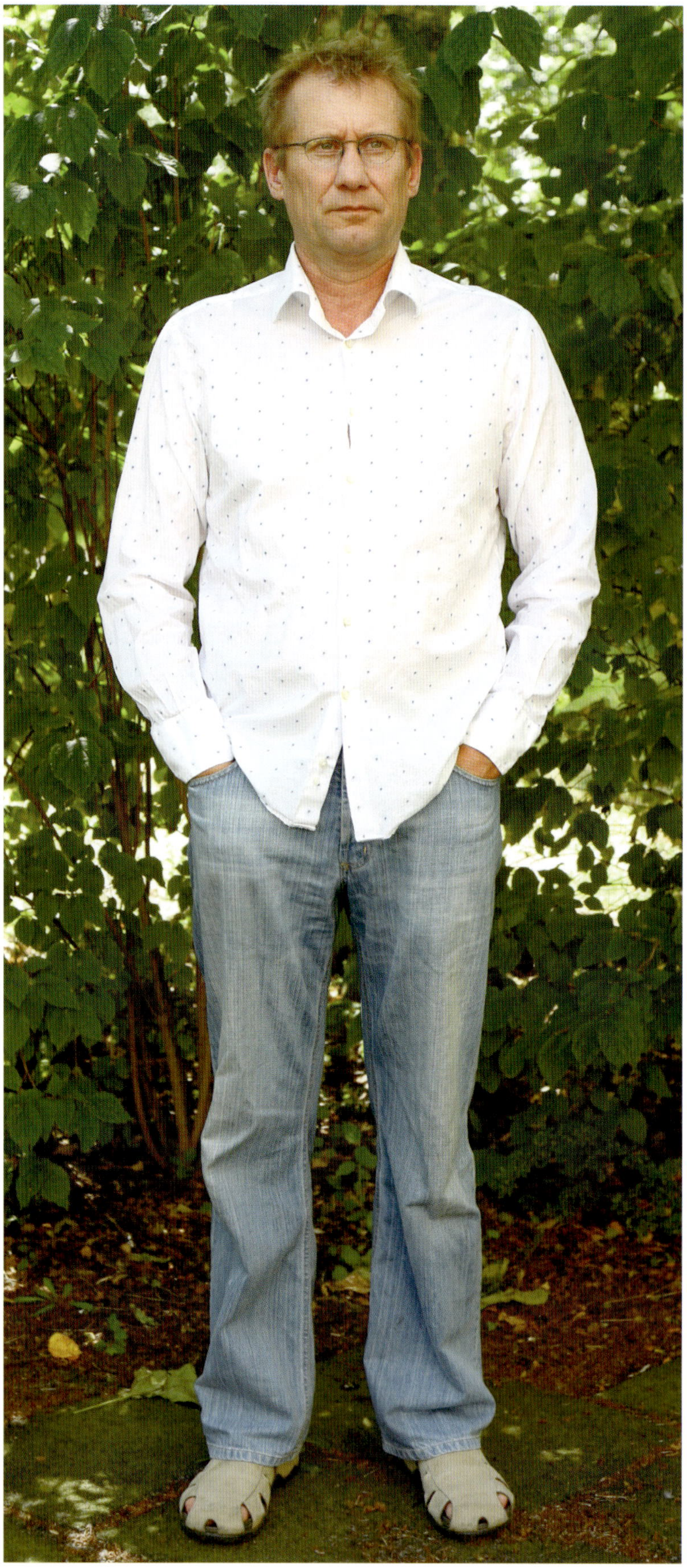

SHIRT 2005
TROUSERS 2005
SHOES 2005

Look in your wardrobe. Find the clothes that you bought the longest time ago and the clothes you bought most recently. Make a picture of yourself in your oldest clothes and one in your newest clothes. Send in your photographs along with the dates that you purchased your clothing items. From the first 24 submissions, I will make a small book which will be sent to you. Hans Eijkelboom, hans.eijkelboom@xs4all.nl, www.photonotebooks.com

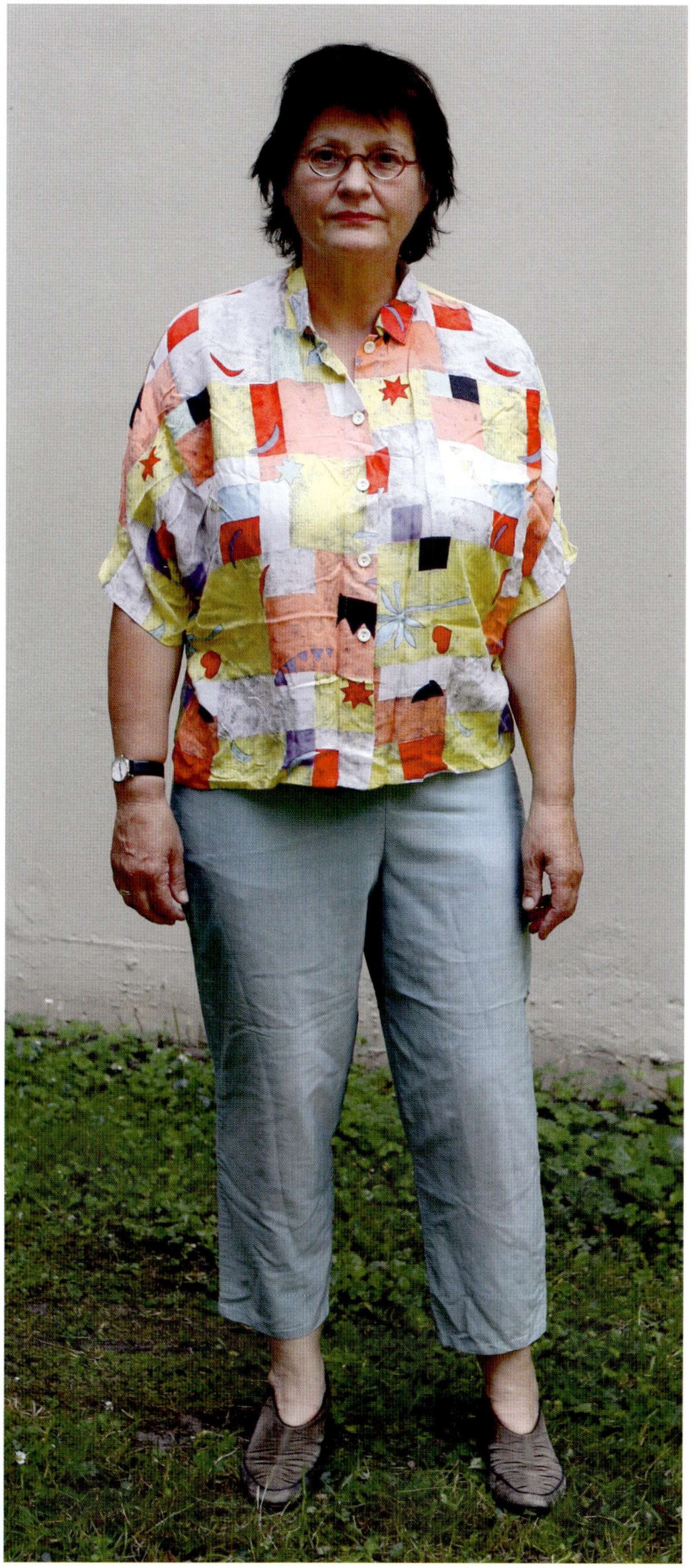

BLOUSE 1980
TROUSERS 1994
SHOES 1990

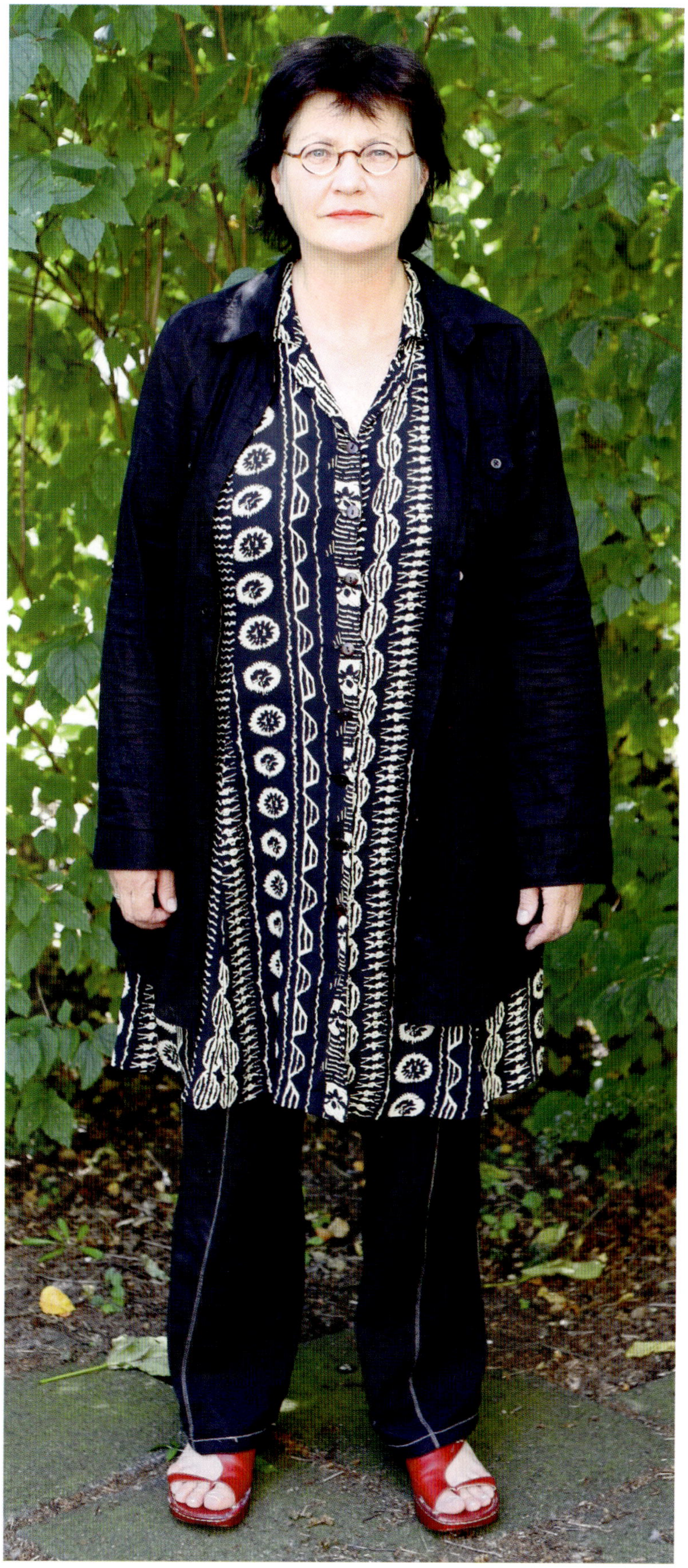

DRESS 2005
TROUSERS 2006
LONG BLOUSE 2006
SHOES 2006

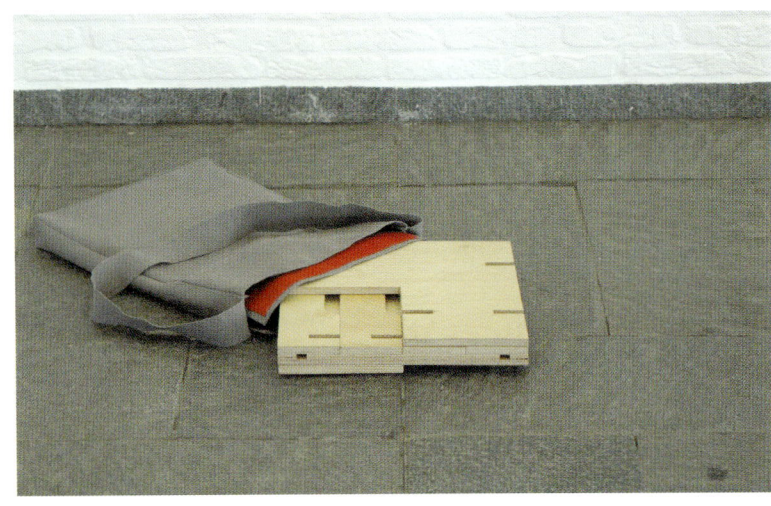
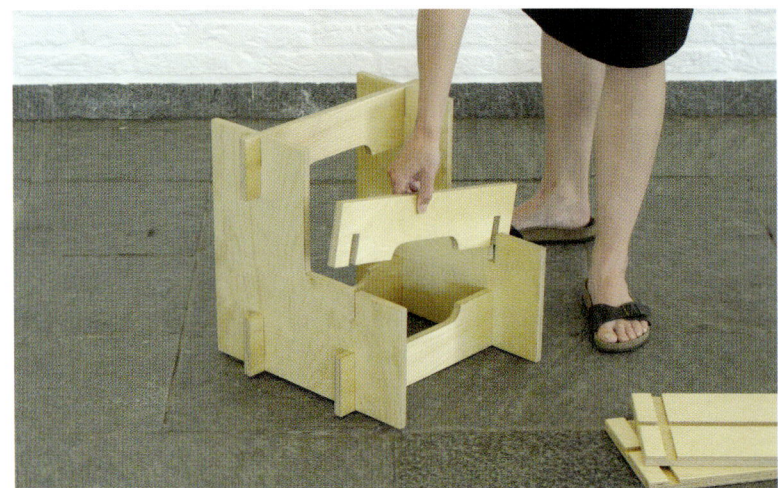
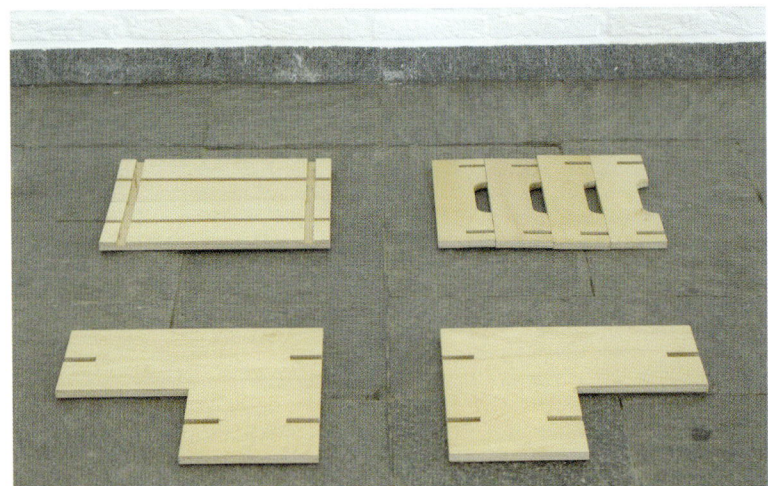
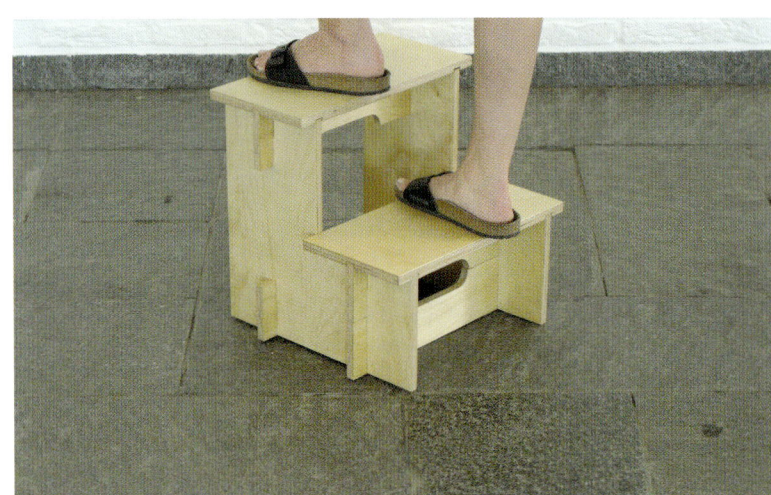
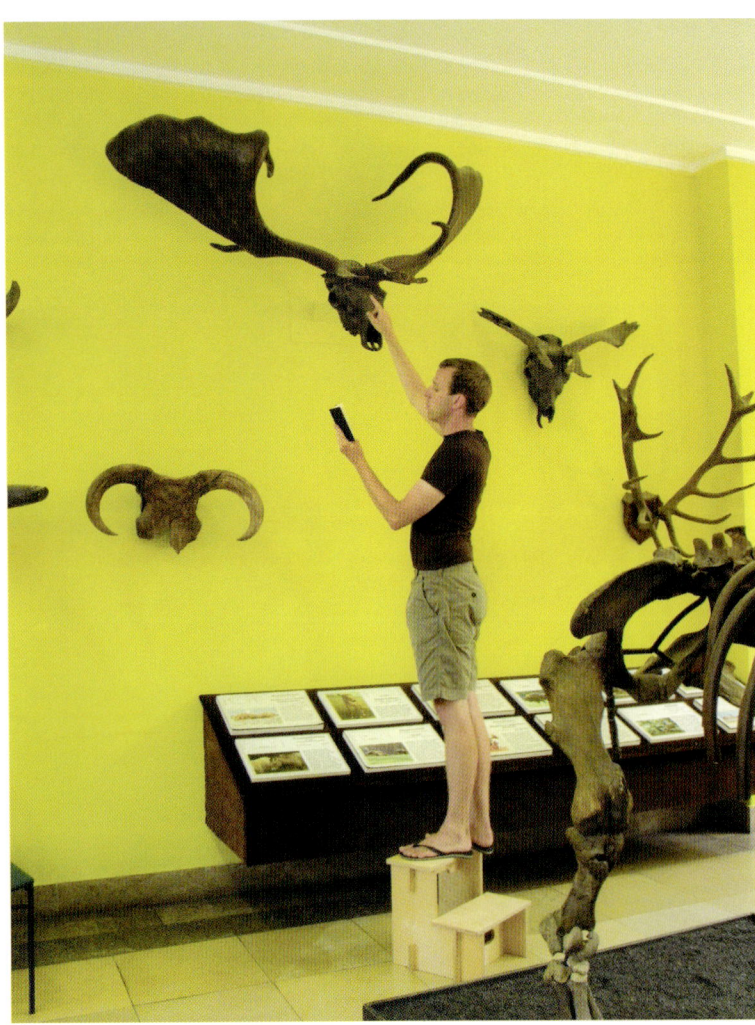
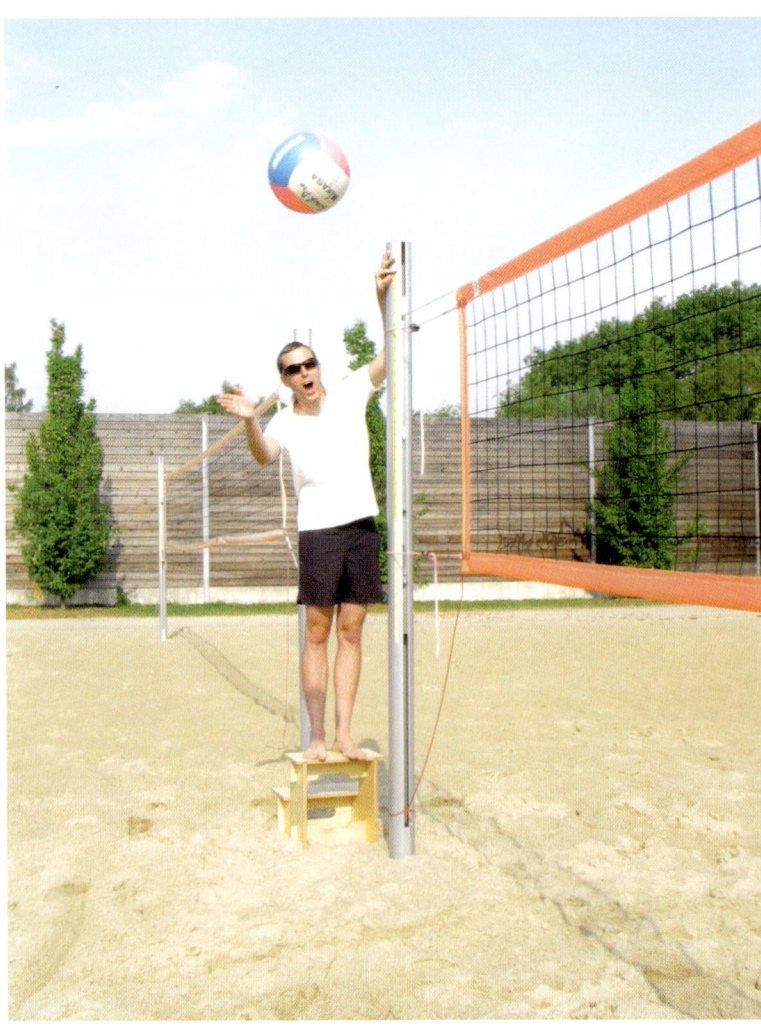

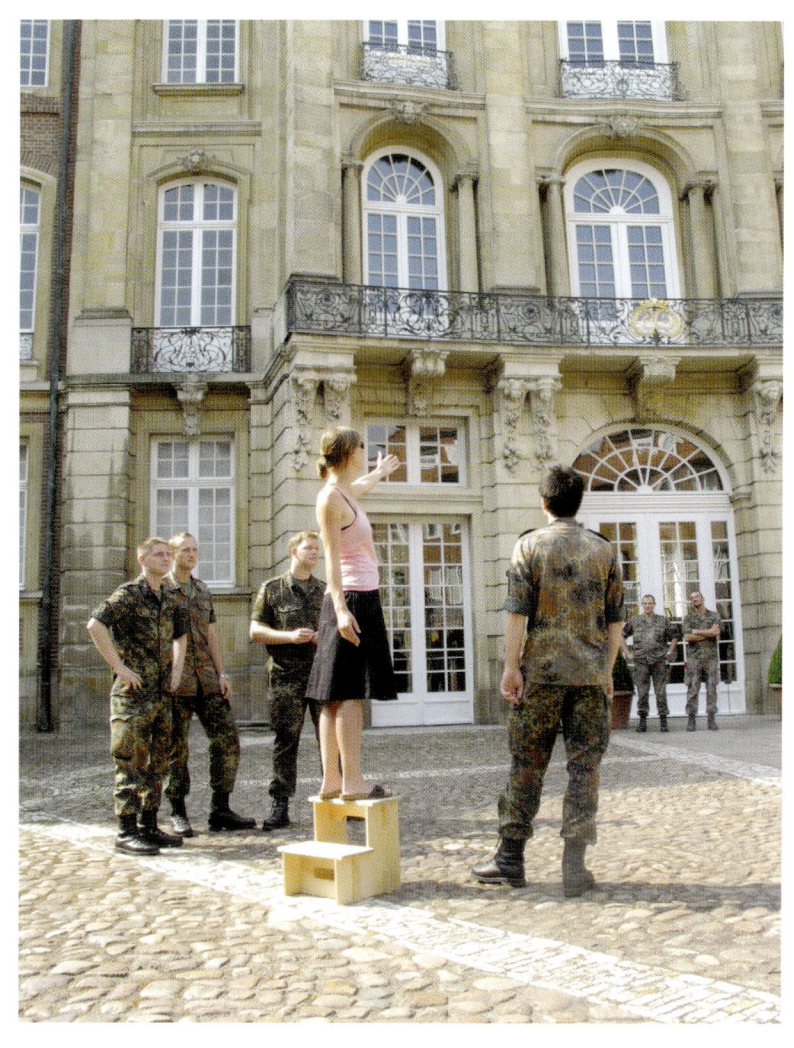
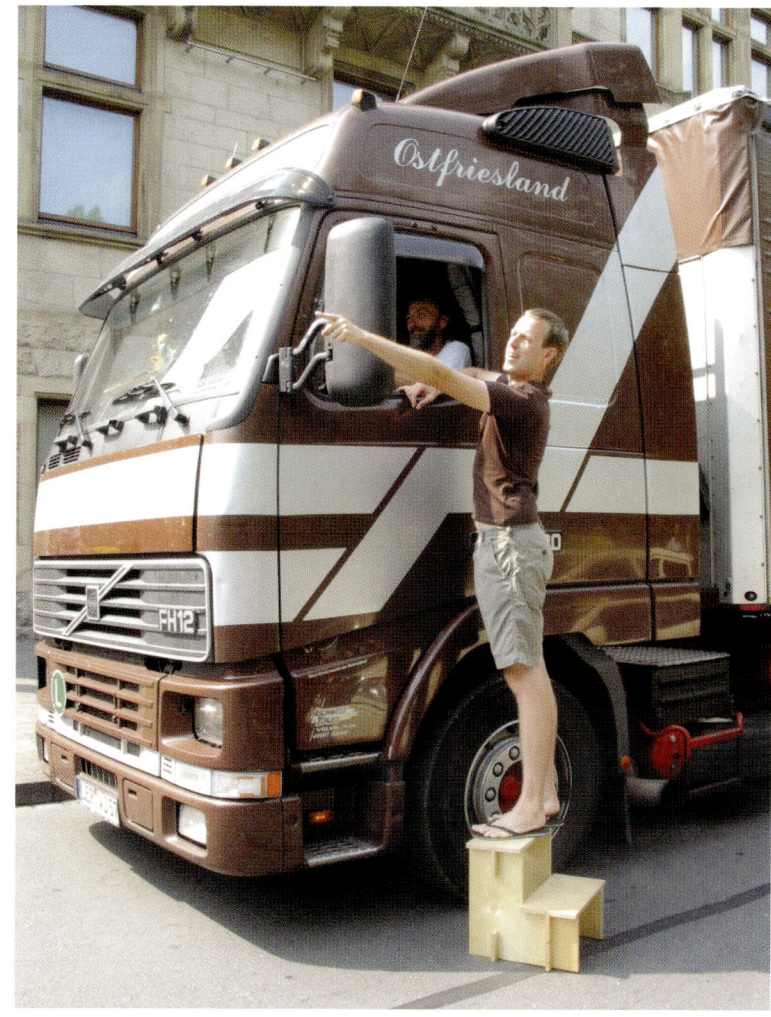
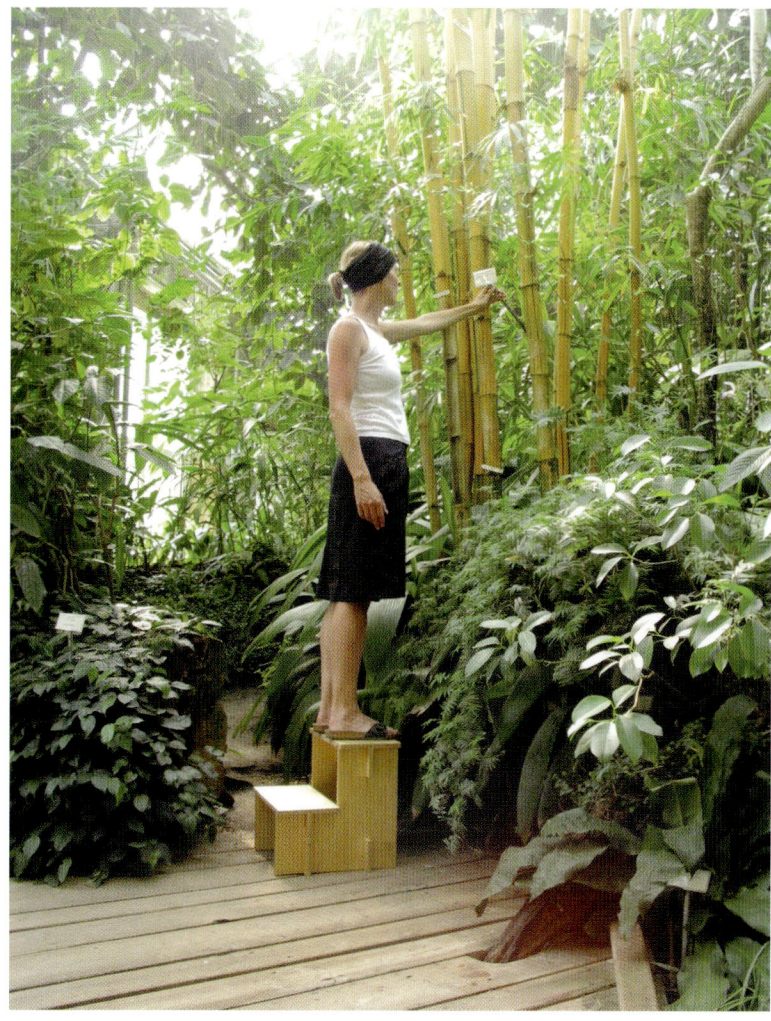
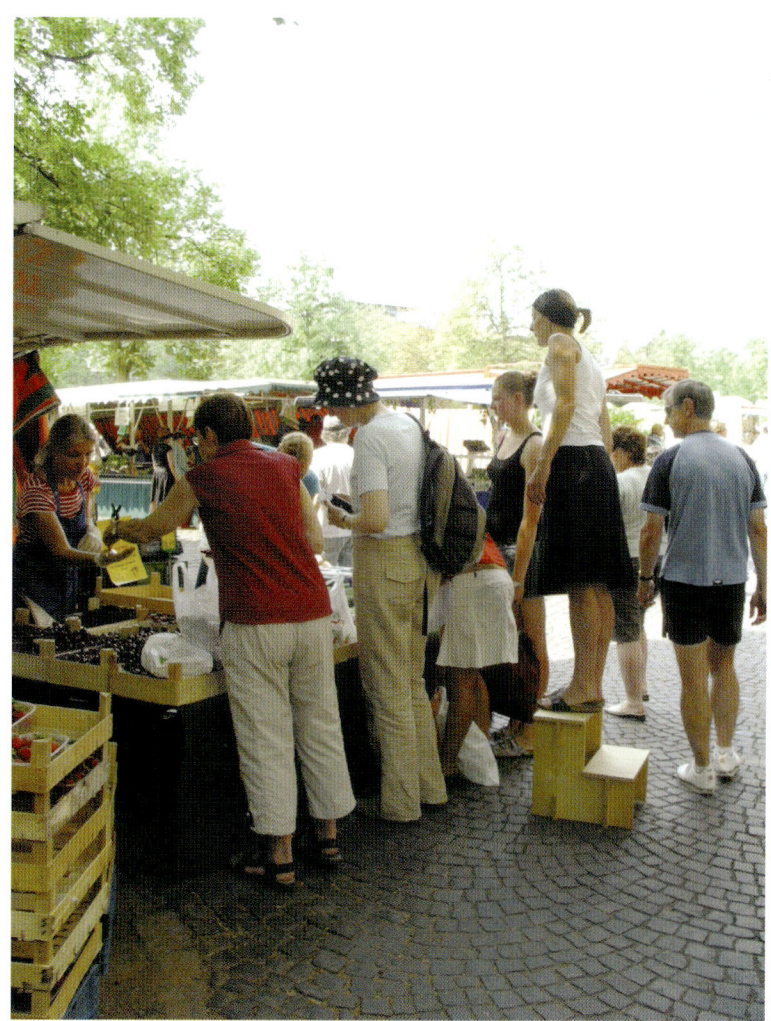

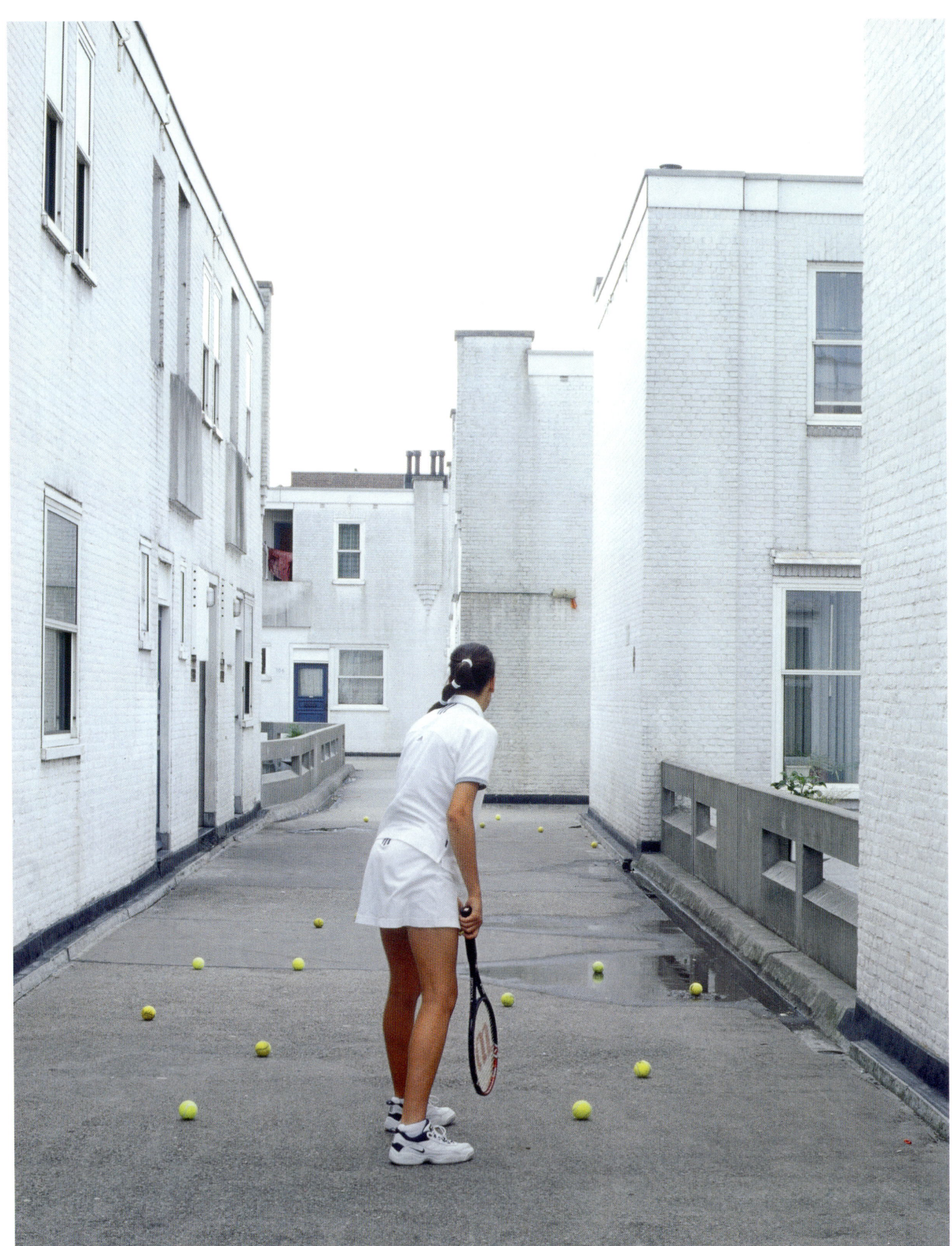

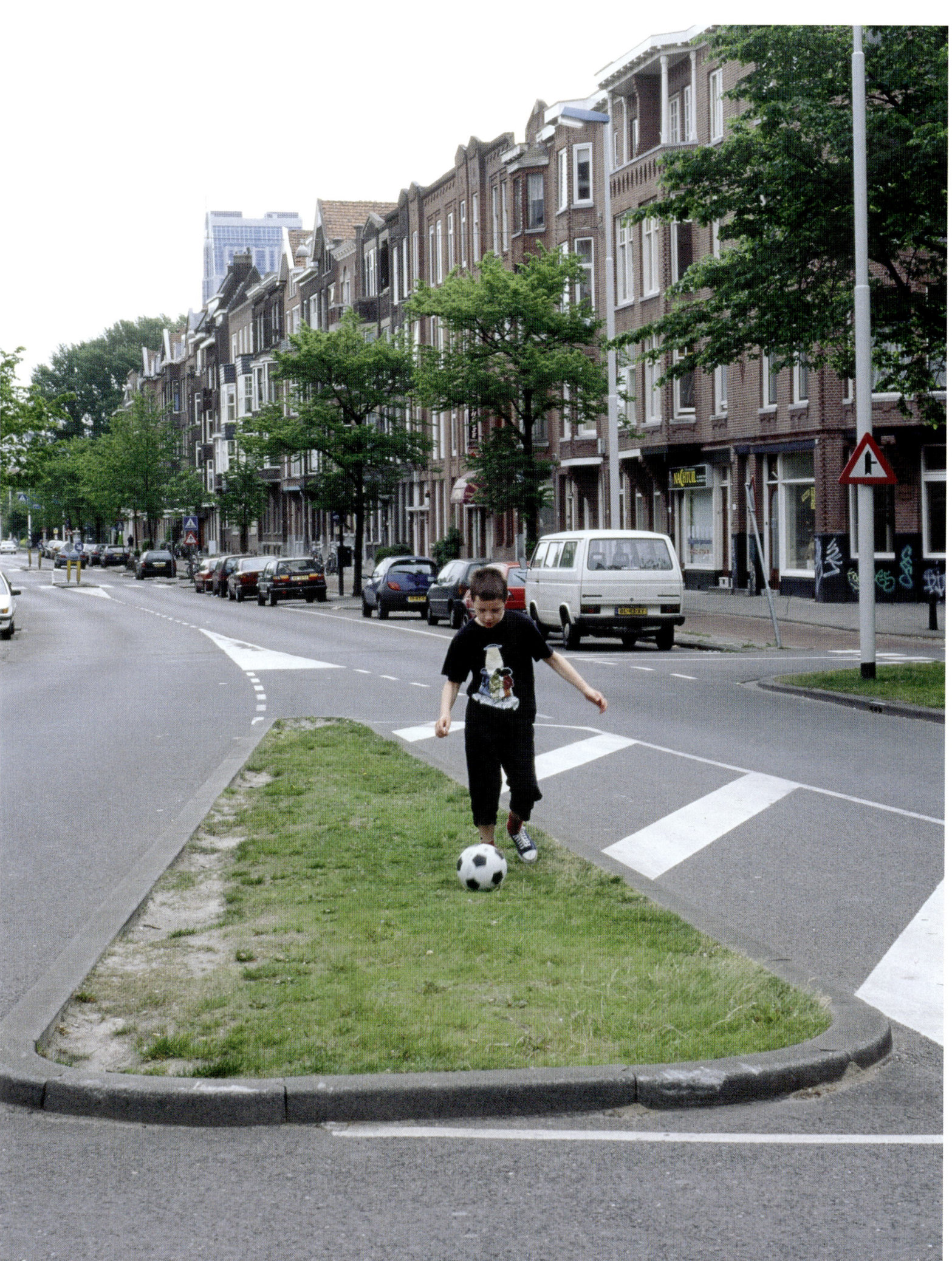

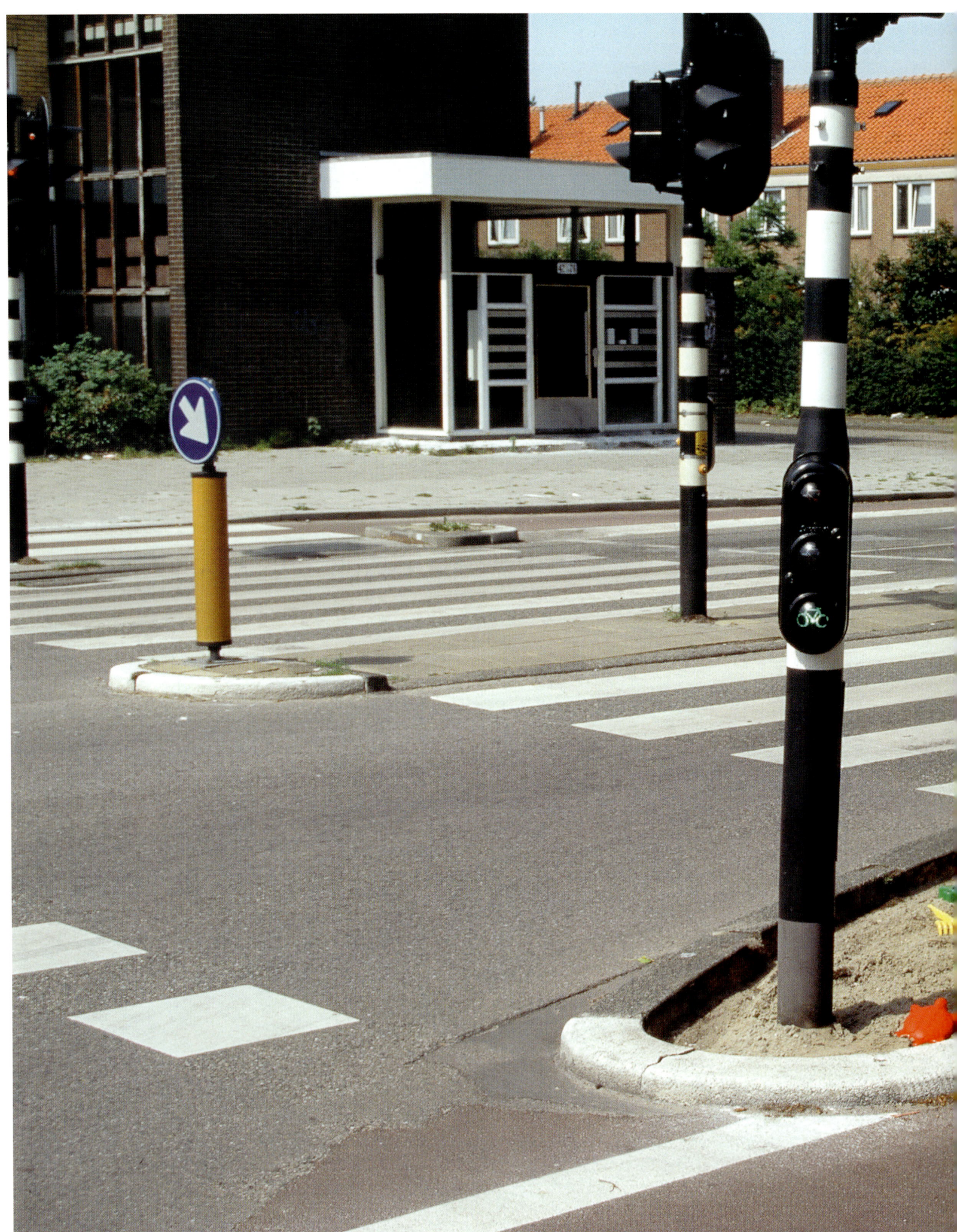

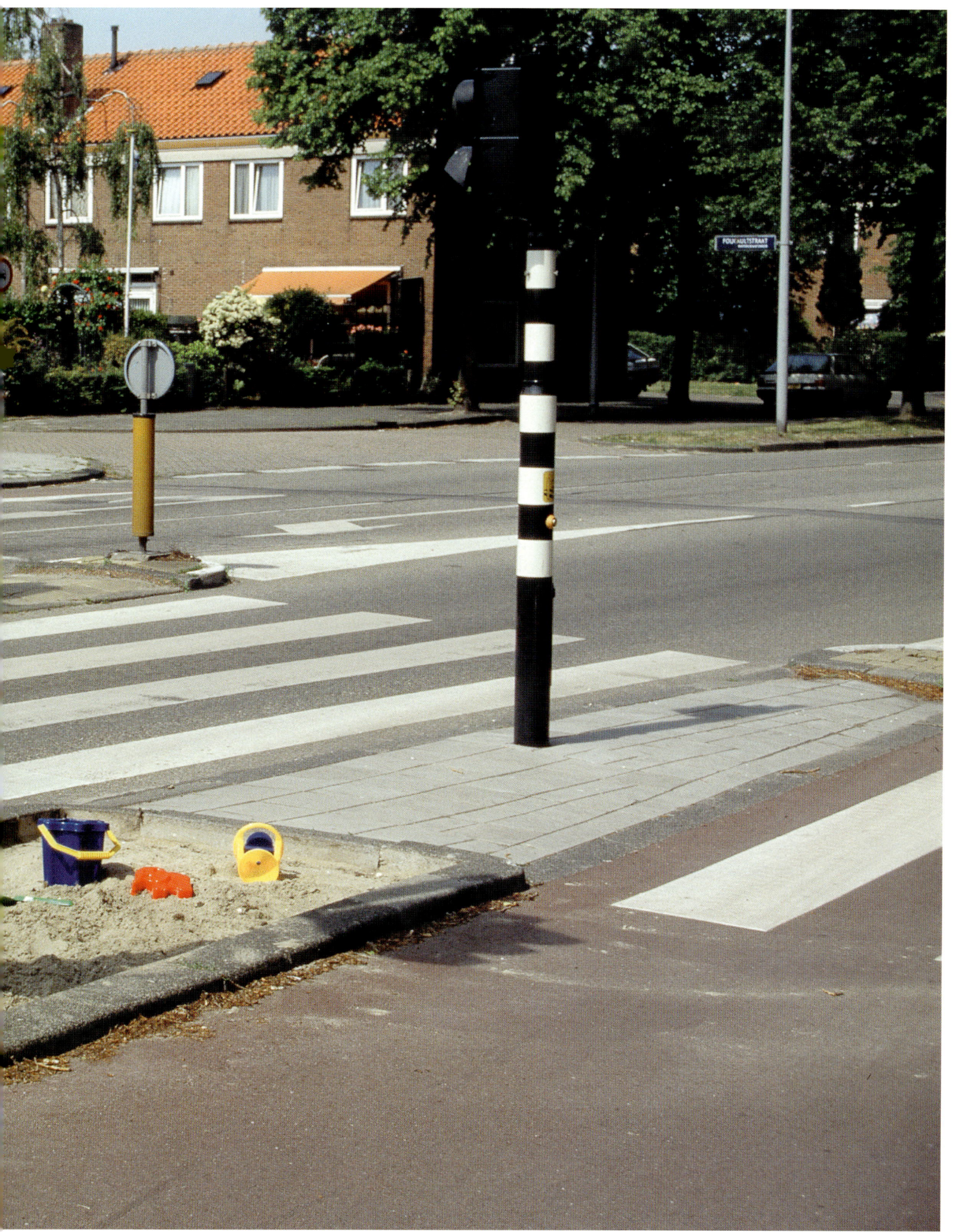

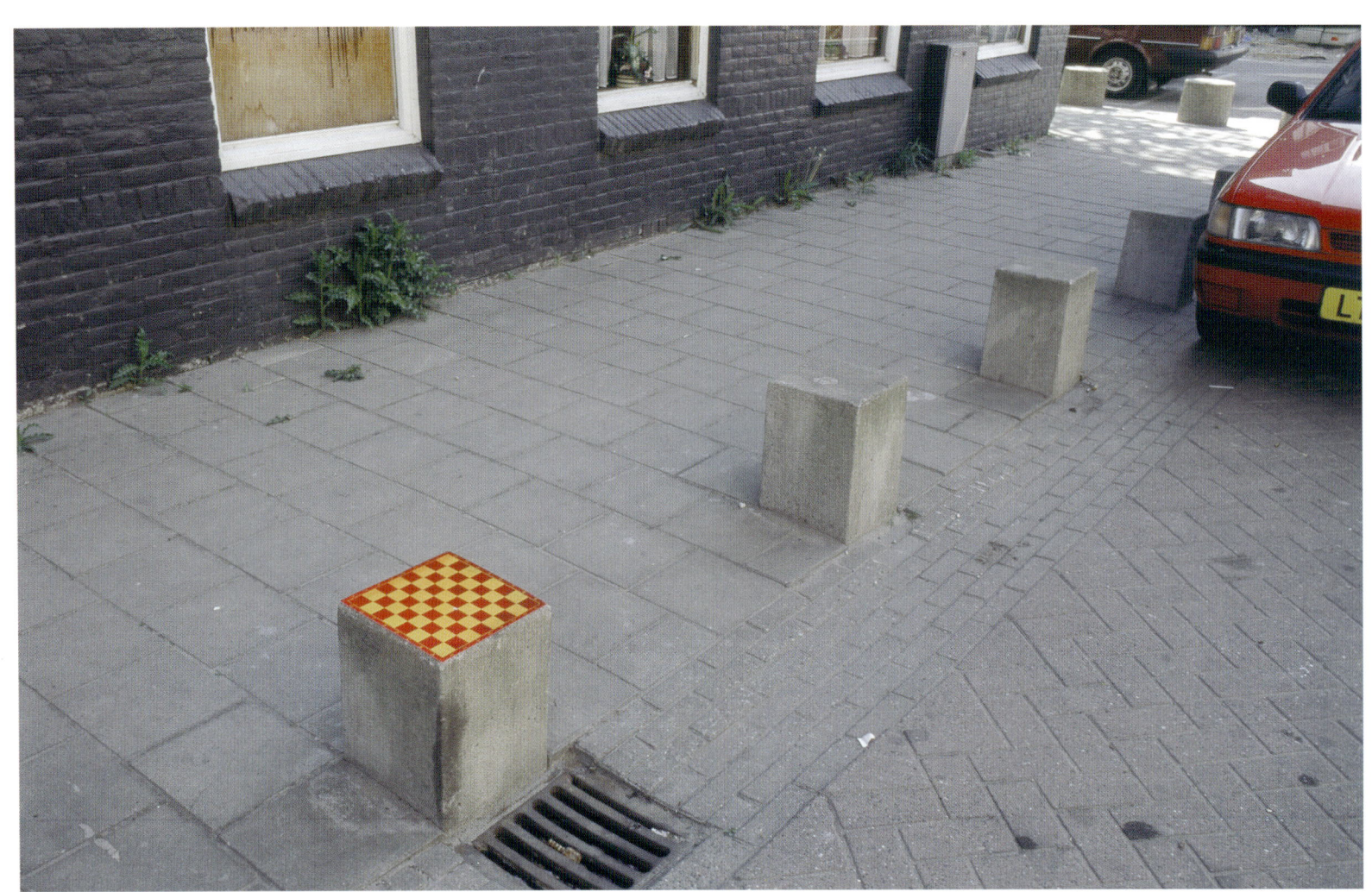

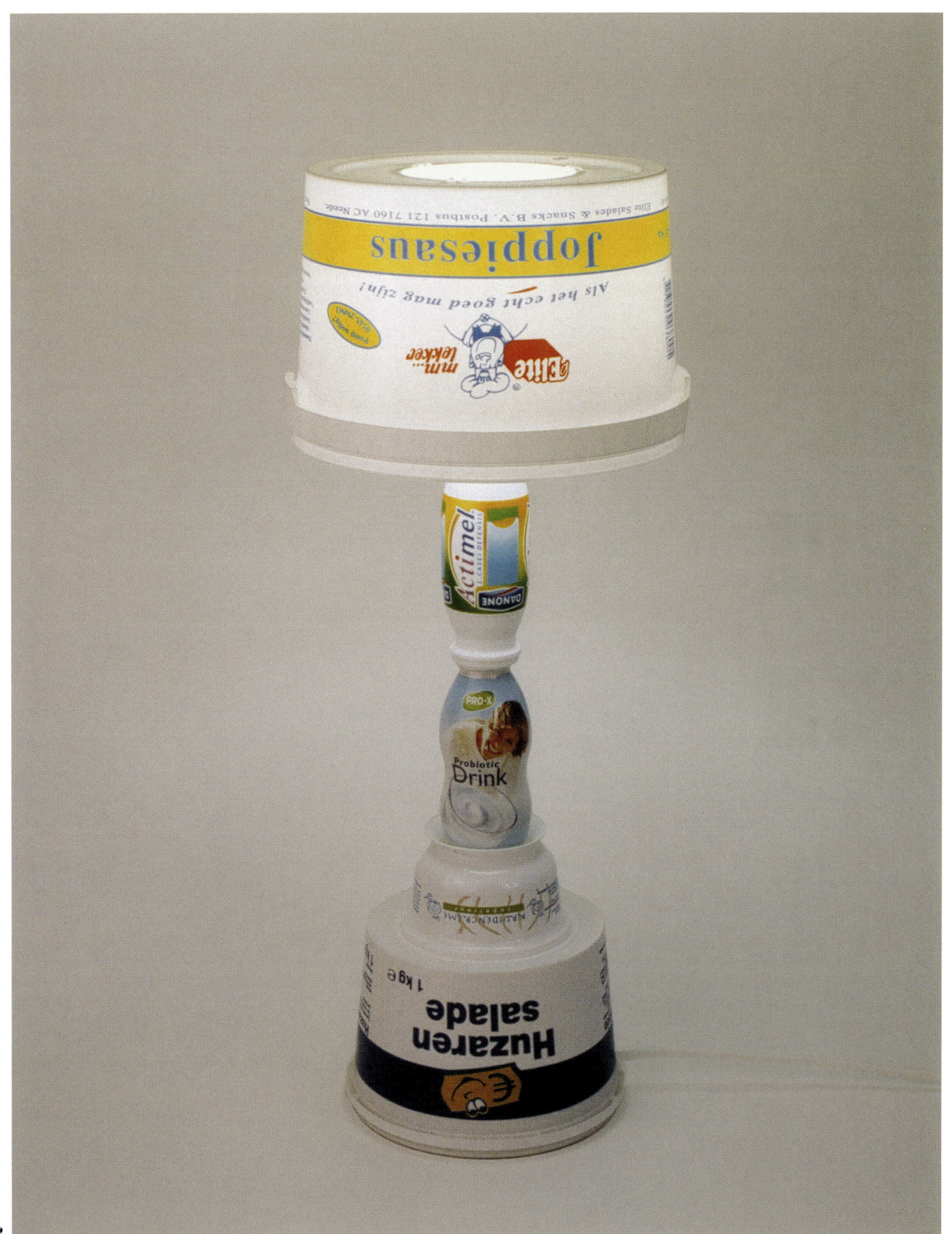

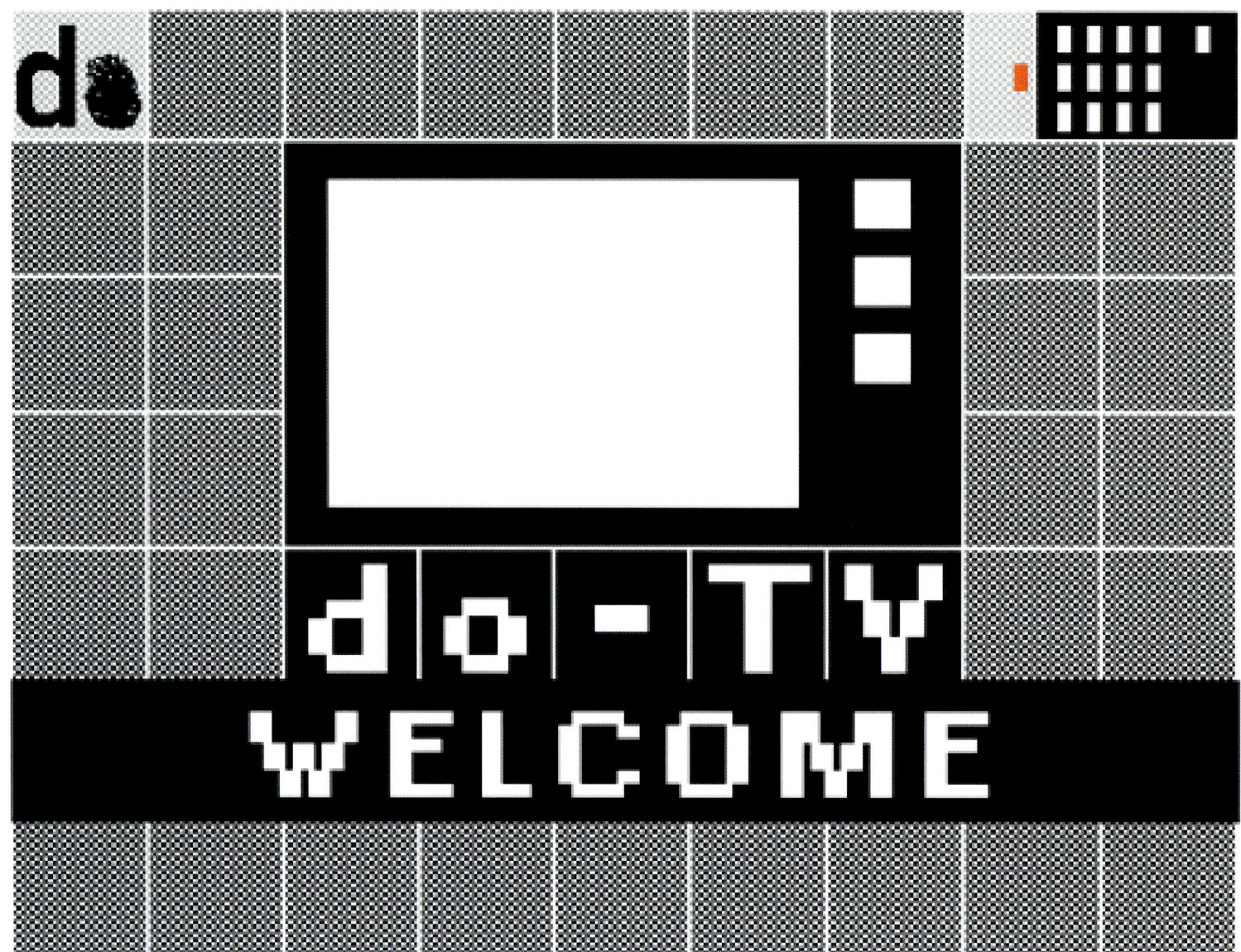

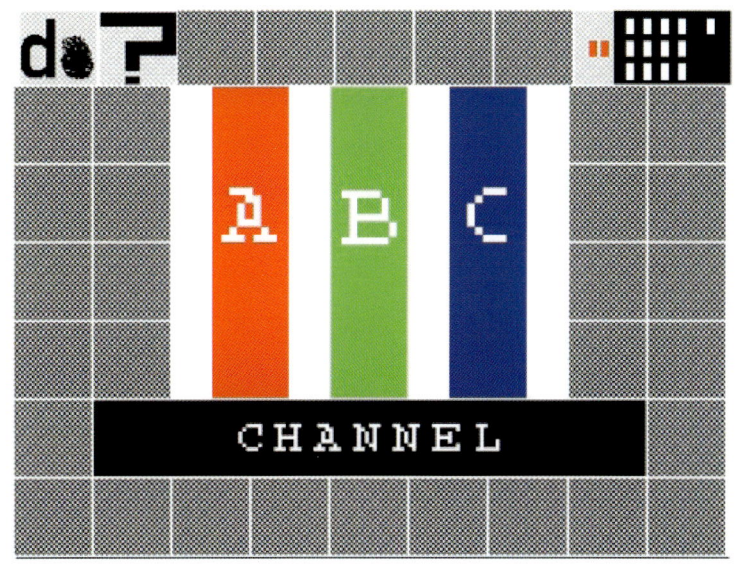

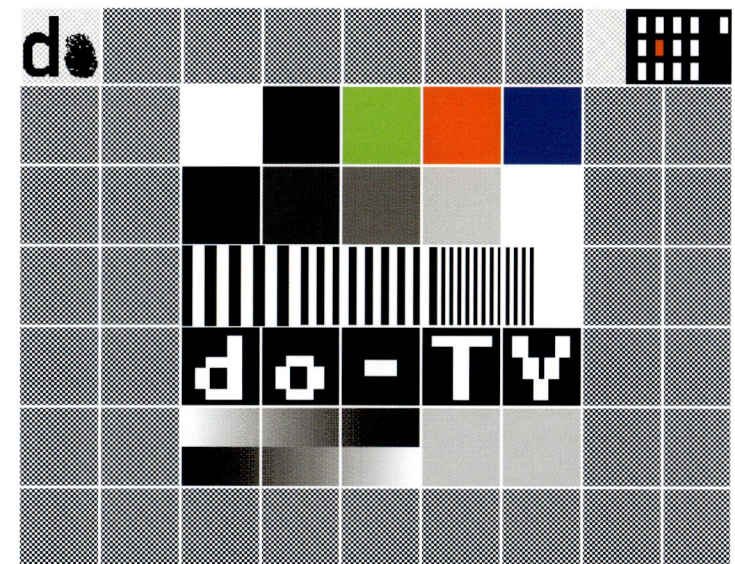

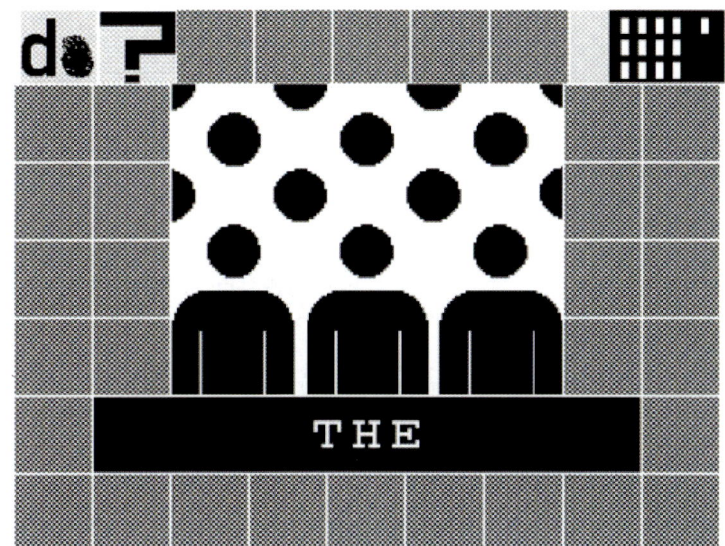

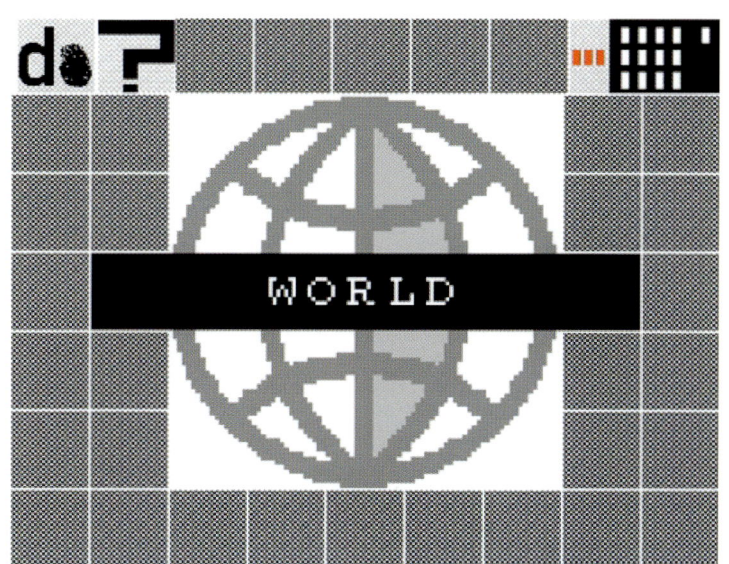

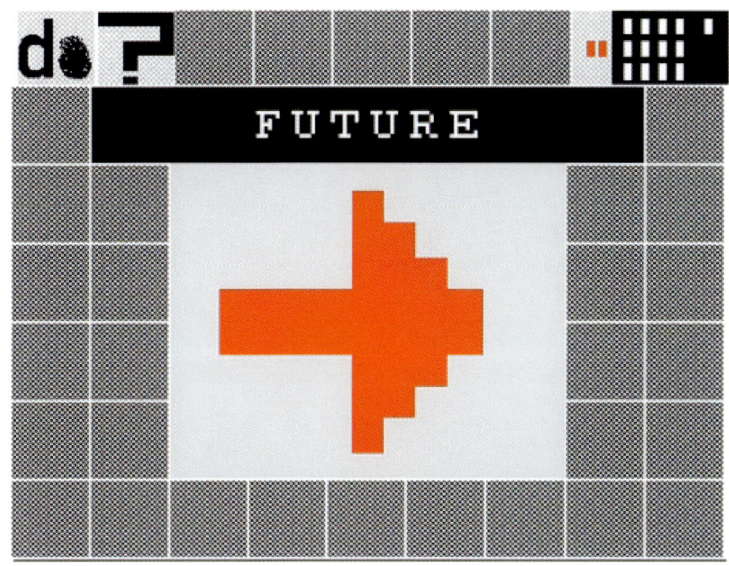

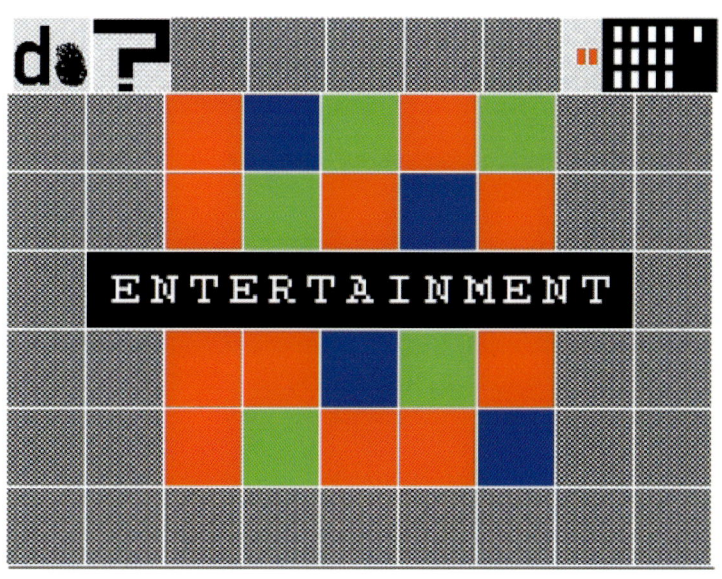

54) do TV

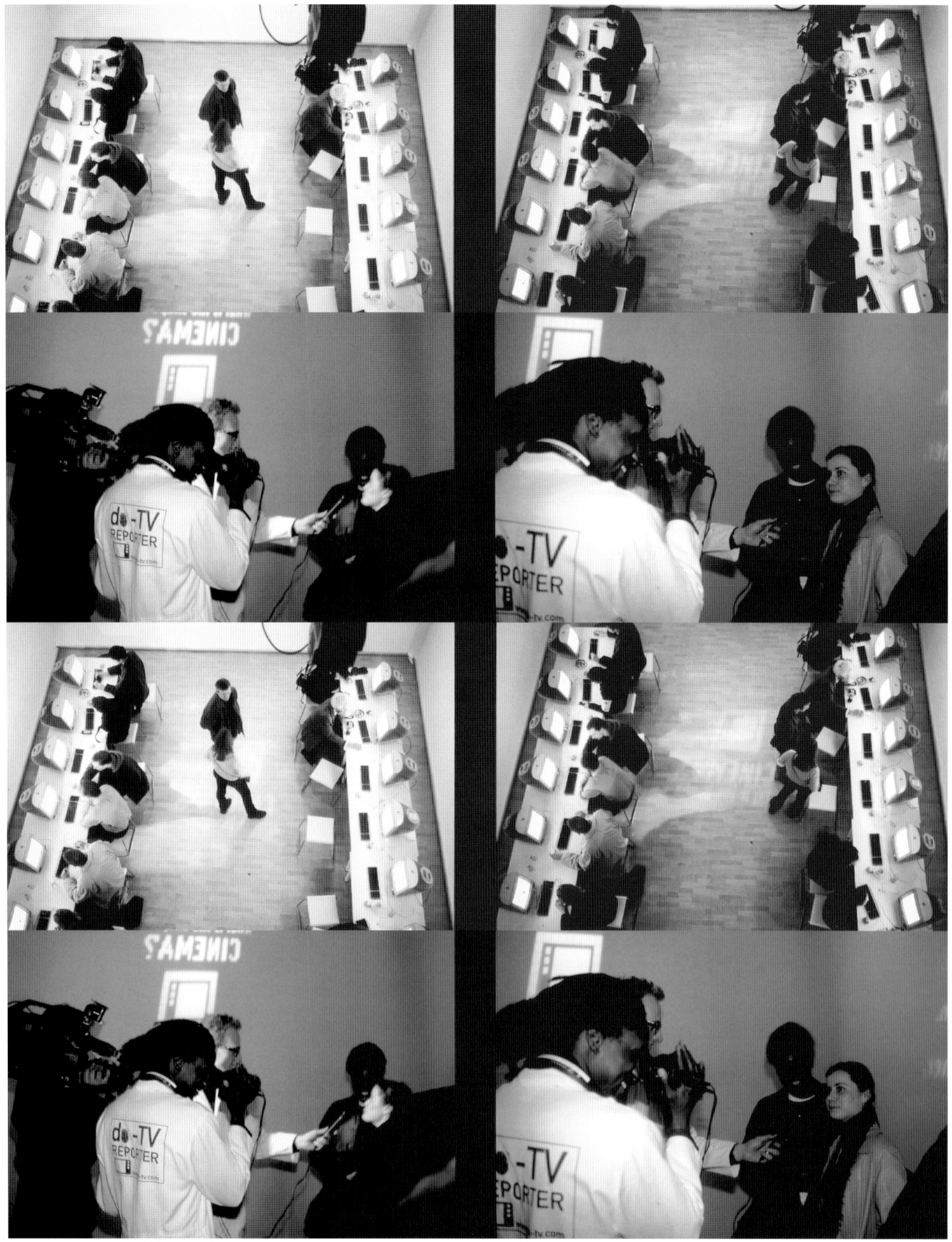

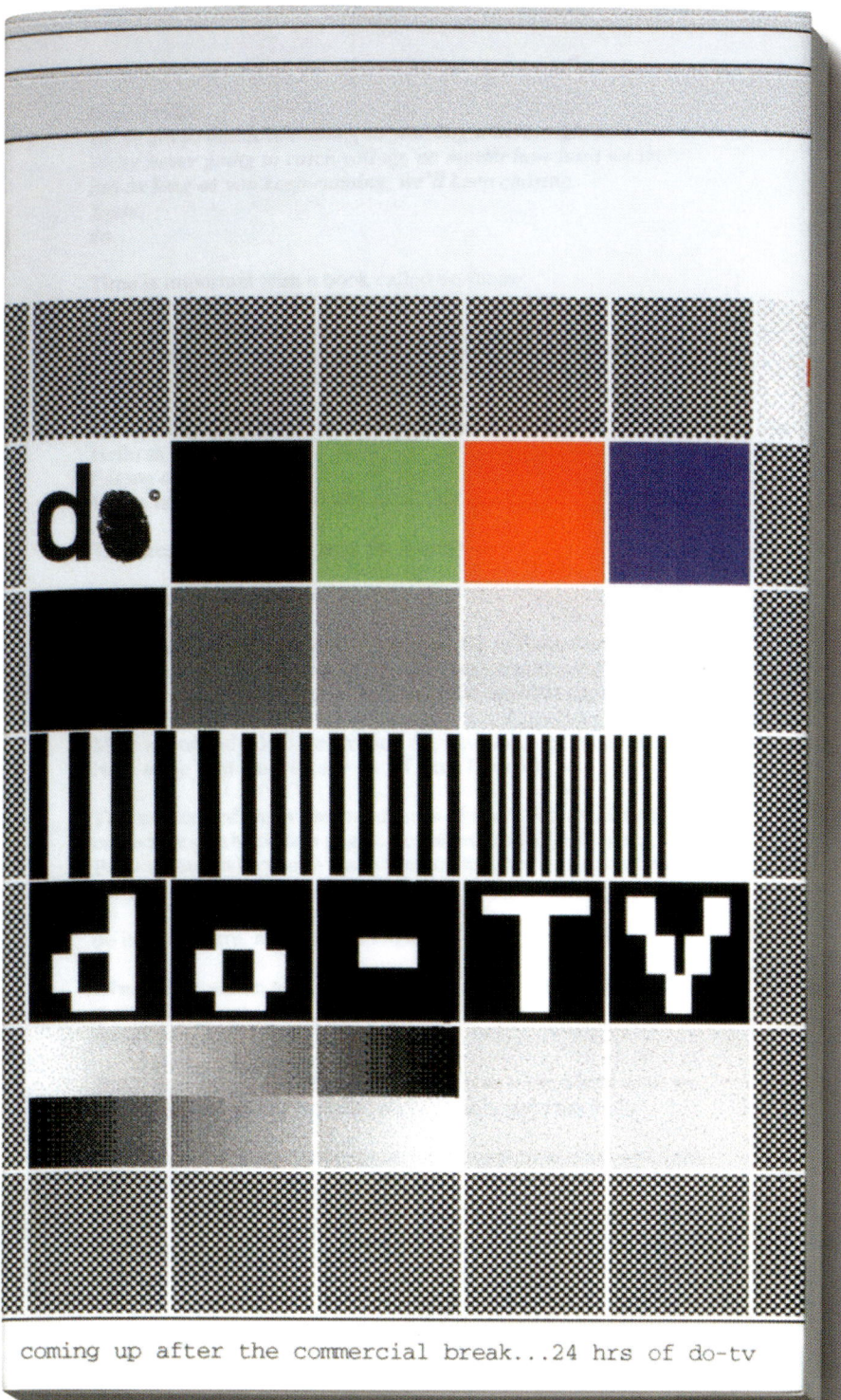

coming up after the commercial break...24 hrs of do-tv

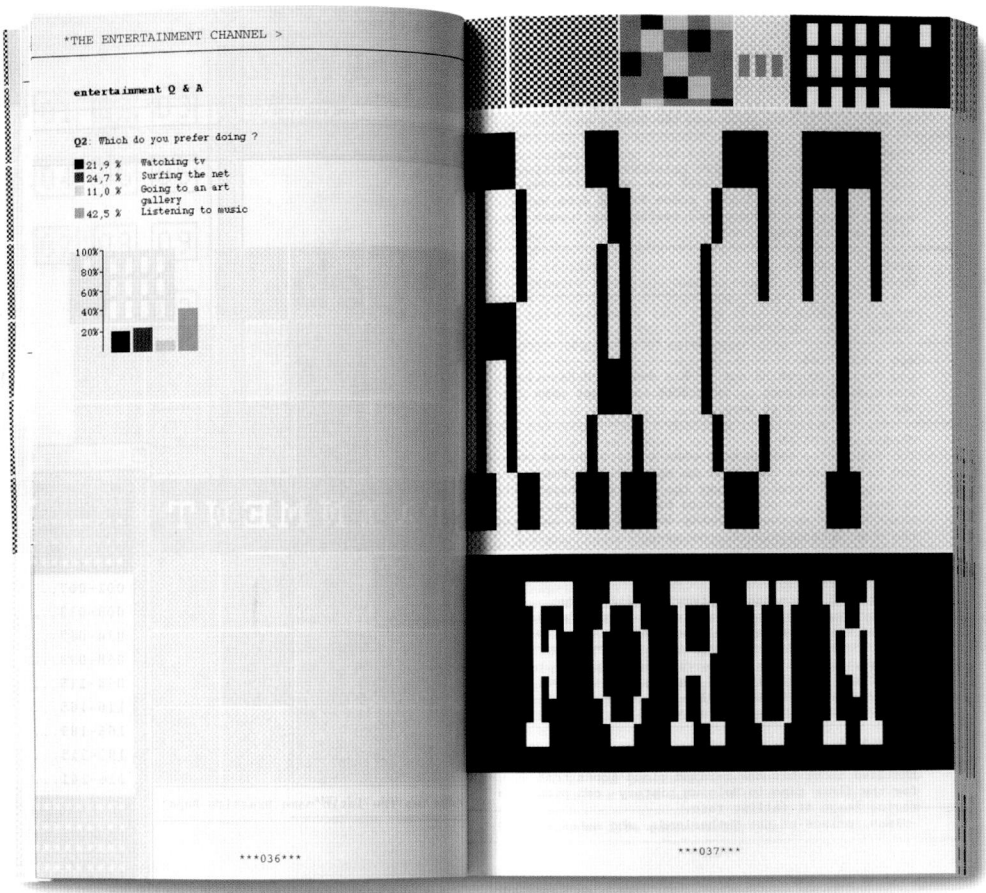

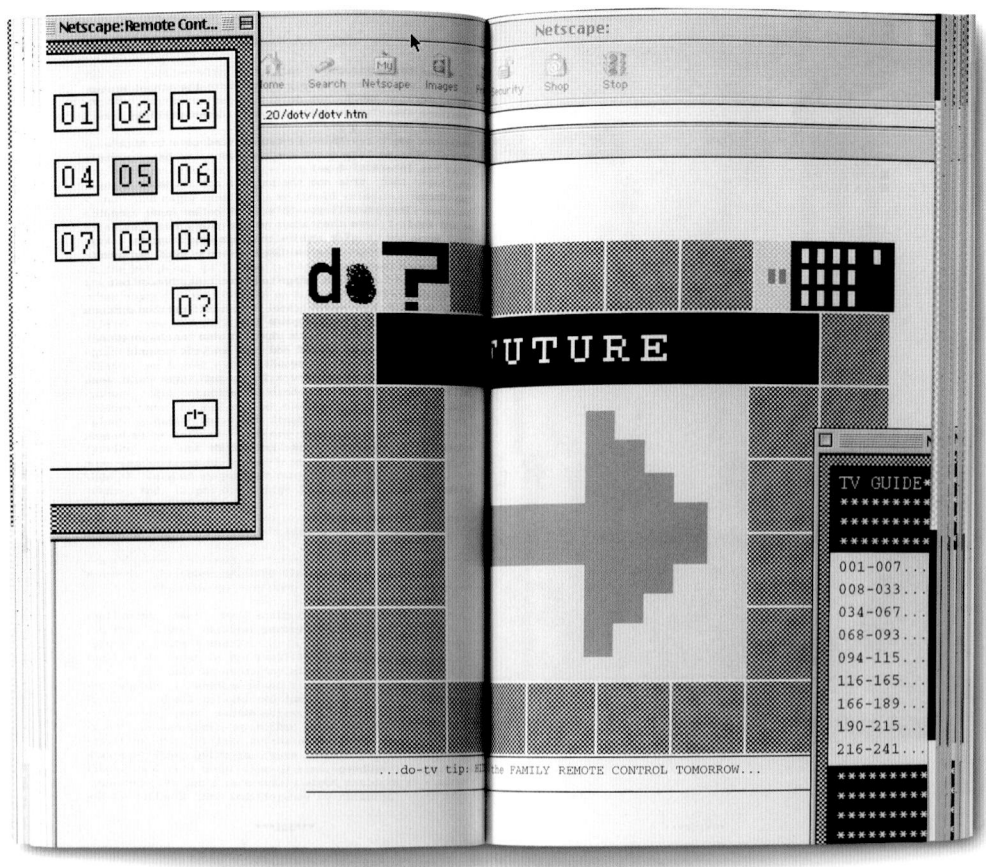

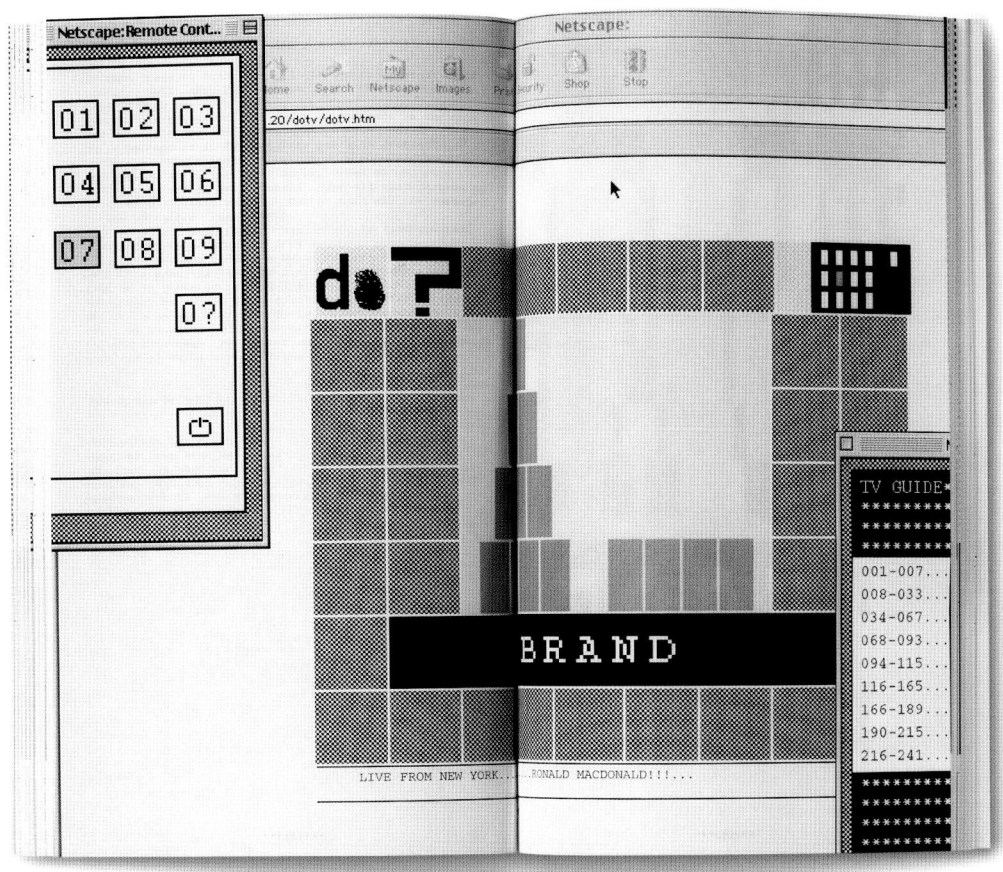

01 02 03
04 05 06
07 08 09
0?

Netscape:

Home Search Netscape Images Pr...curity Shop Stop

.20/dotv/dotv.htm

do ?

BRAND

TV GUIDE*
****
****
****

001-007...
008-033...
034-067...
068-093...
094-115...
116-165...
166-189...
190-215...
216-241...

****
****
****

LIVE FROM NEW YORK... ...RONALD MACDONALD!!!...

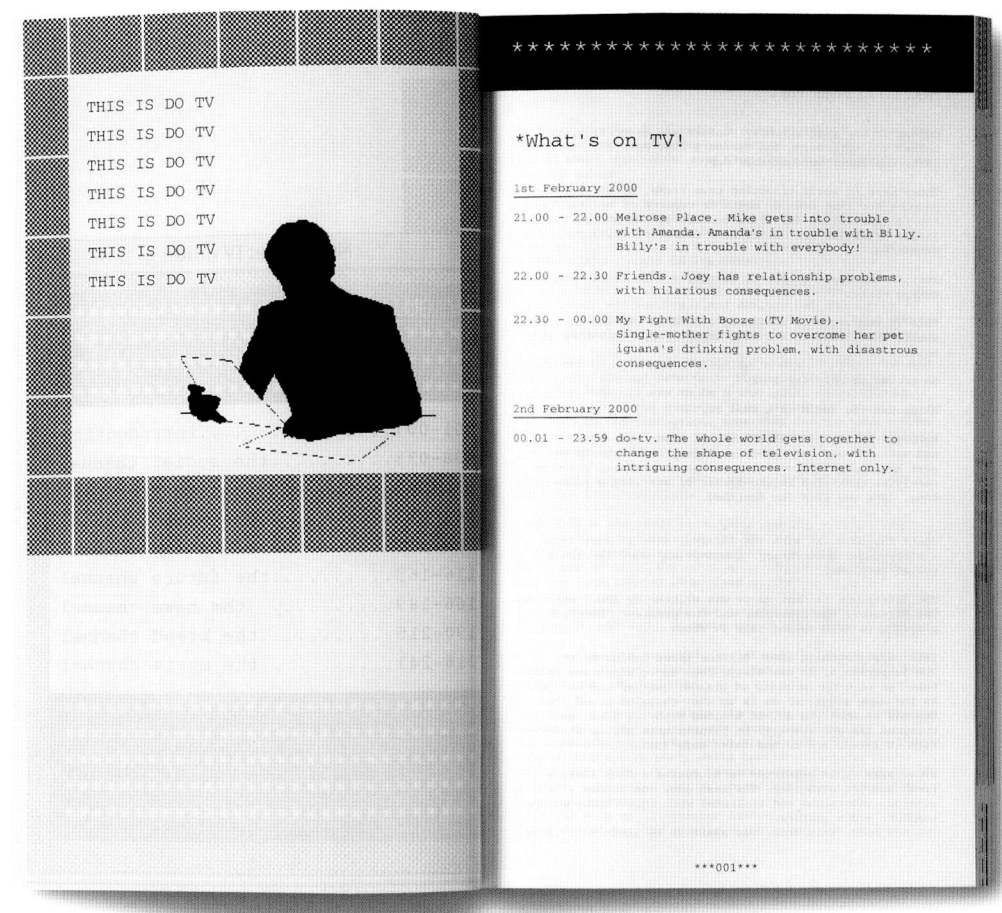

THIS IS DO TV
THIS IS DO TV
THIS IS DO TV
THIS IS DO TV
THIS IS DO TV
THIS IS DO TV
THIS IS DO TV

* *

*What's on TV!

1st February 2000

21.00 - 22.00 Melrose Place. Mike gets into trouble
              with Amanda. Amanda's in trouble with Billy.
              Billy's in trouble with everybody!

22.00 - 22.30 Friends. Joey has relationship problems,
              with hilarious consequences.

22.30 - 00.00 My Fight With Booze (TV Movie).
              Single-mother fights to overcome her pet
              iguana's drinking problem, with disastrous
              consequences.

2nd February 2000

00.01 - 23.59 do-tv. The whole world gets together to
              change the shape of television, with
              intriguing consequences. Internet only.

001

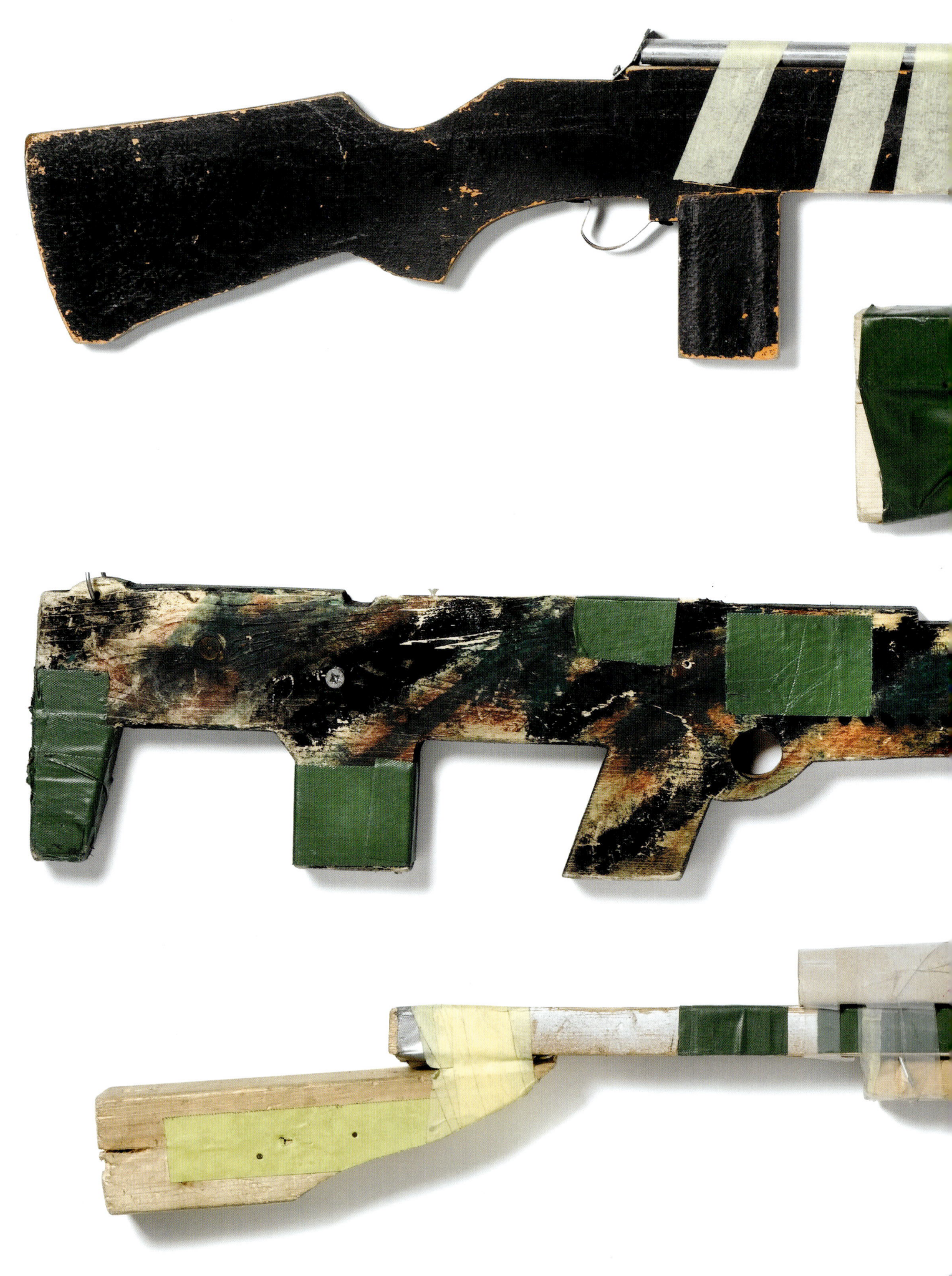

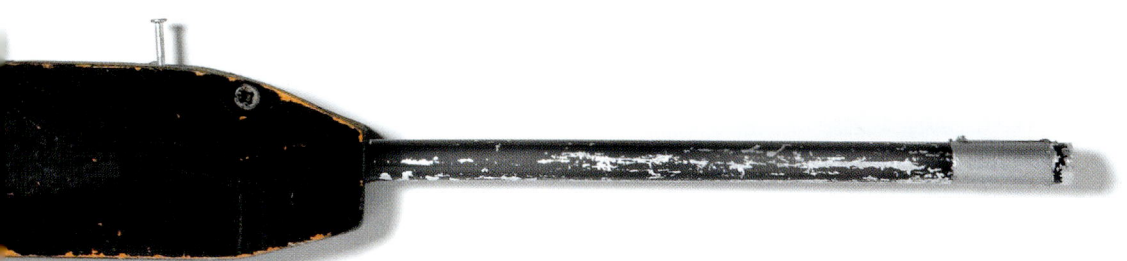

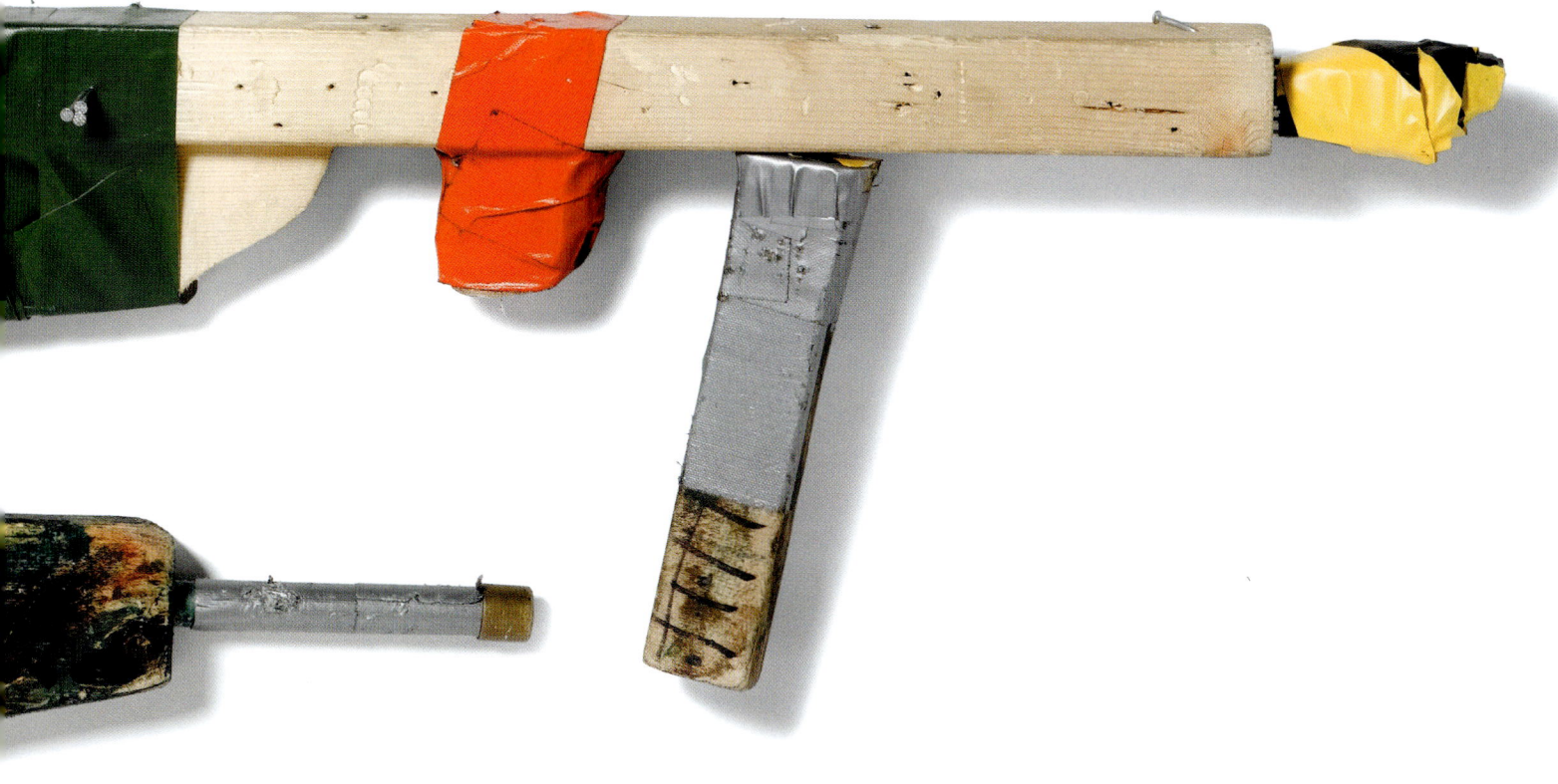

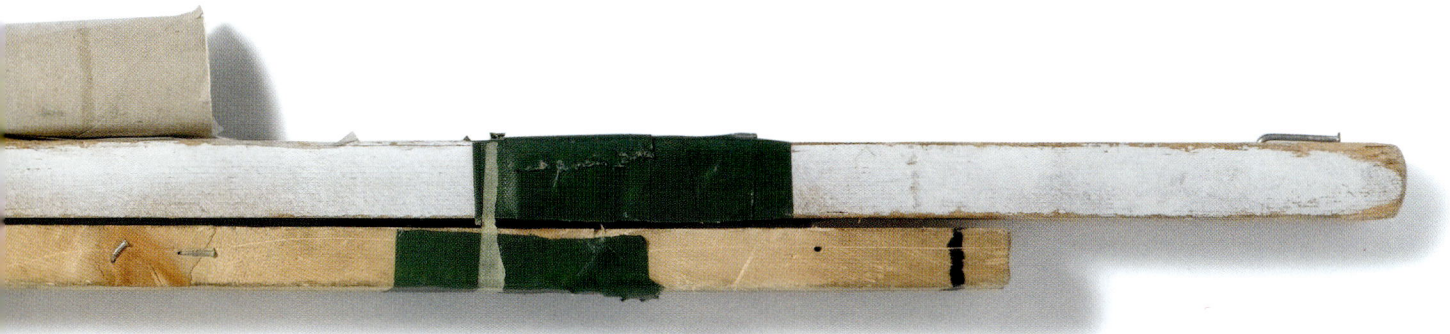

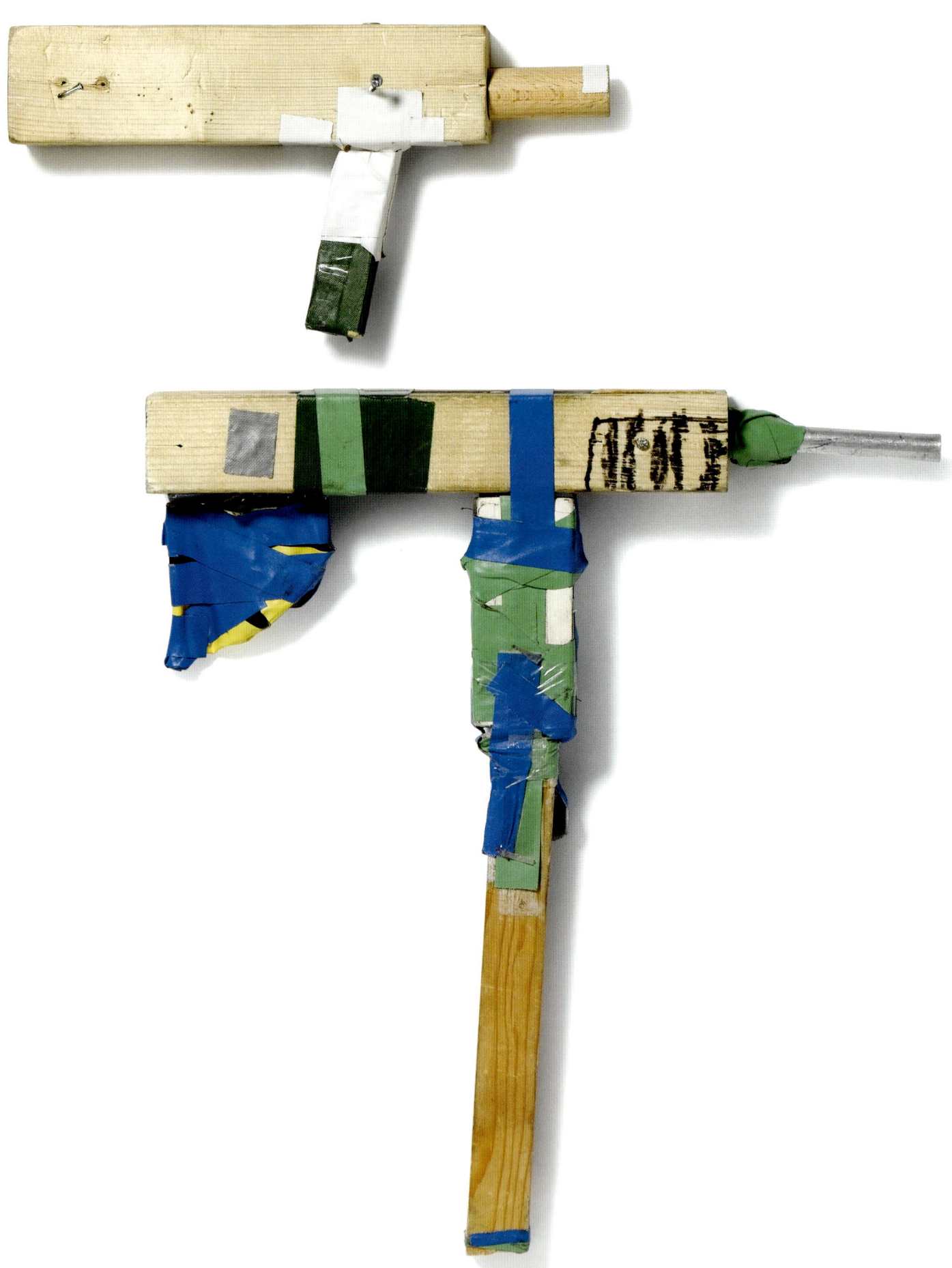

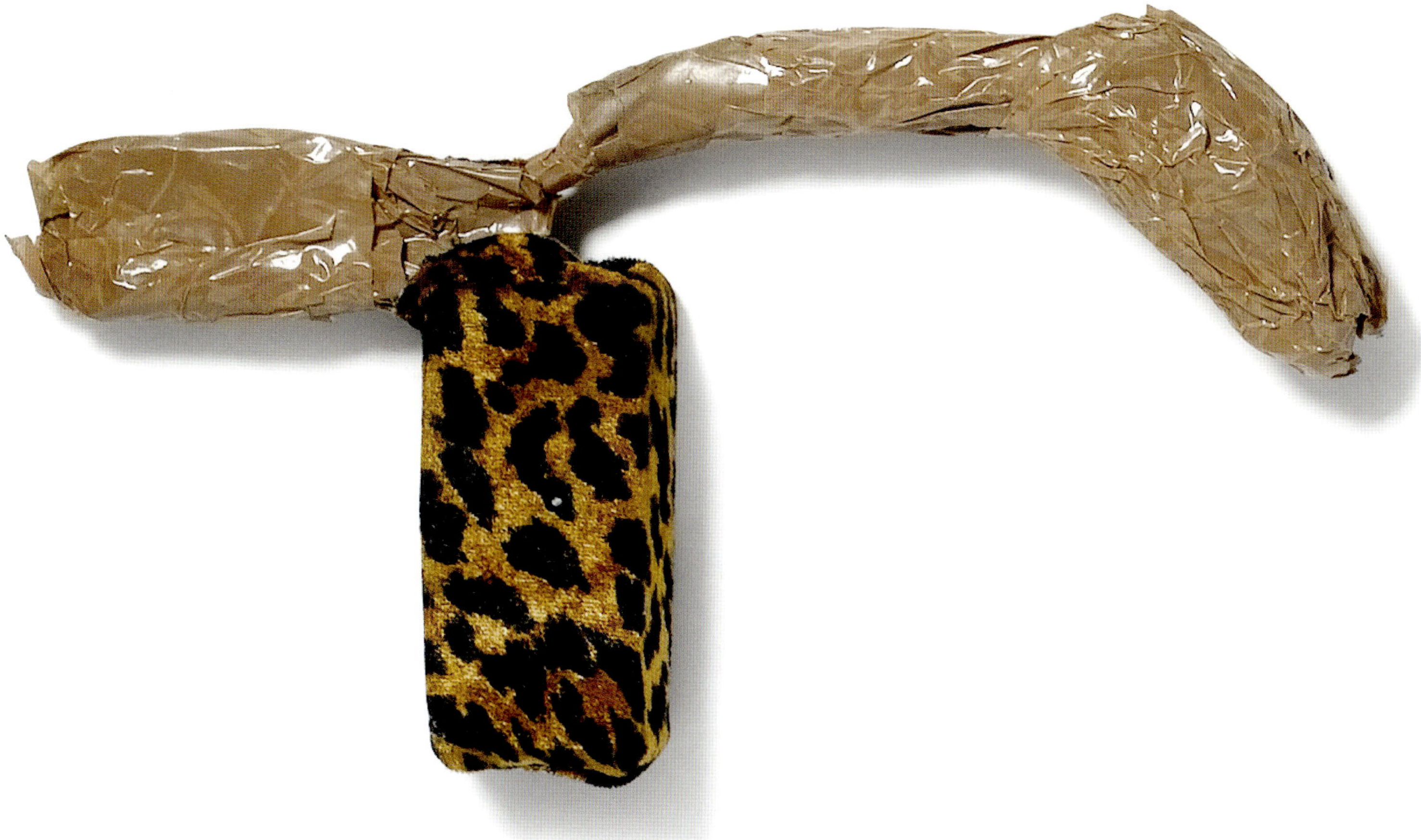

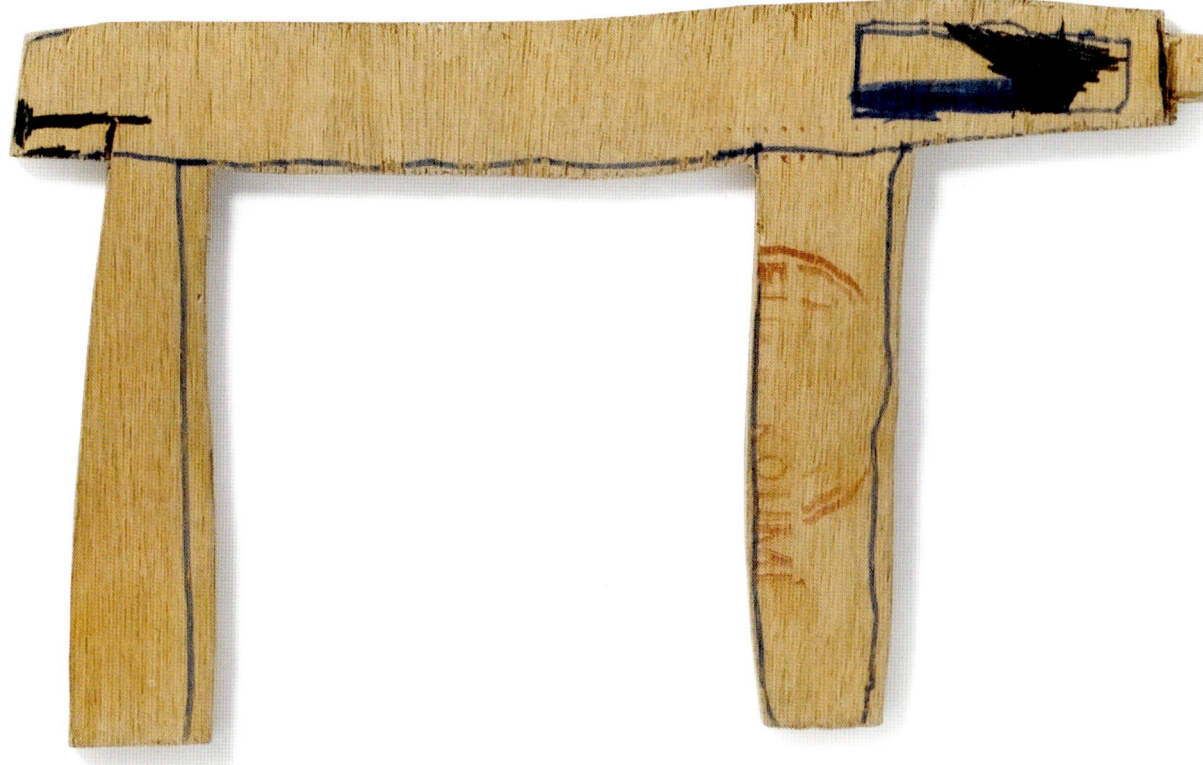

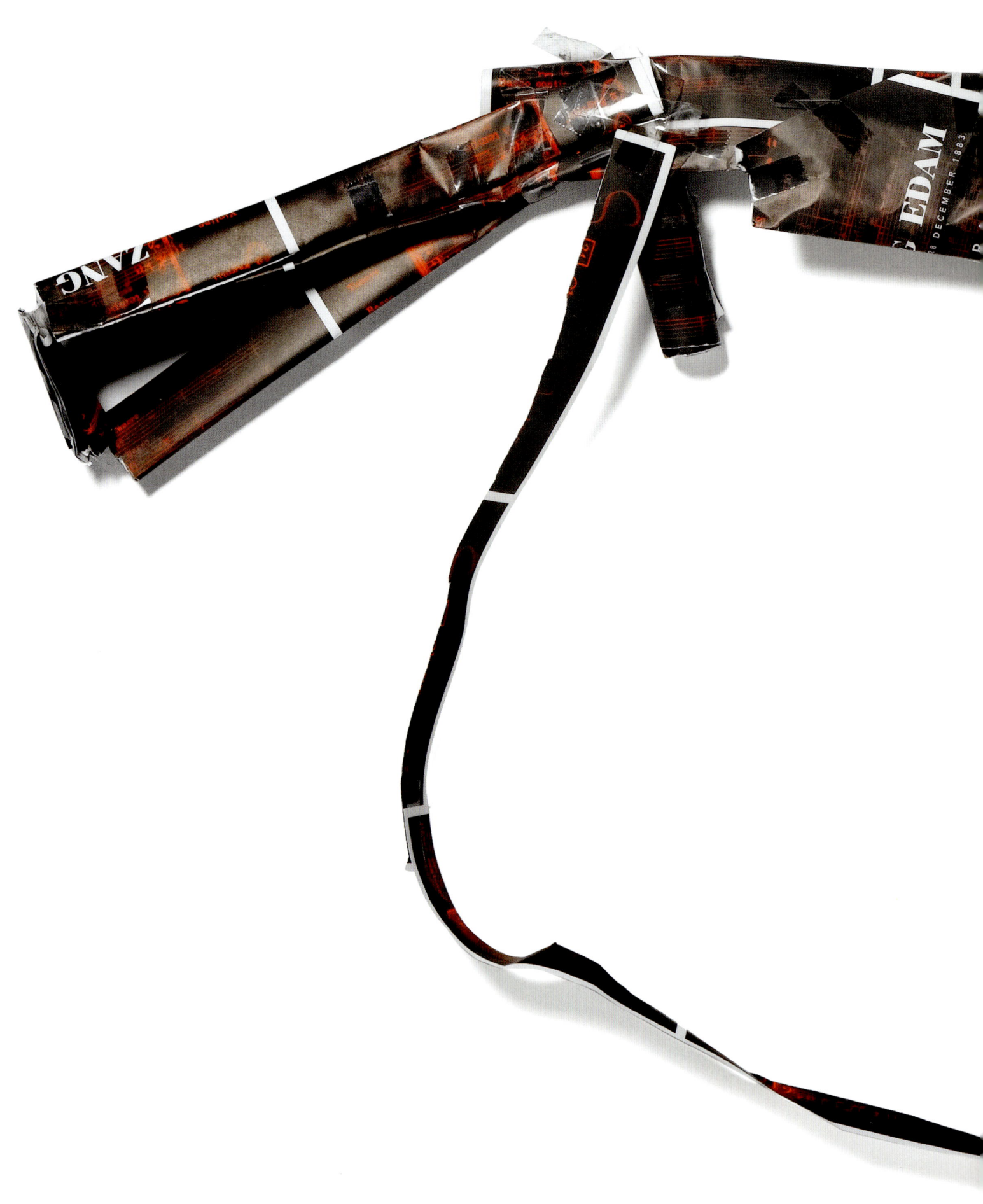

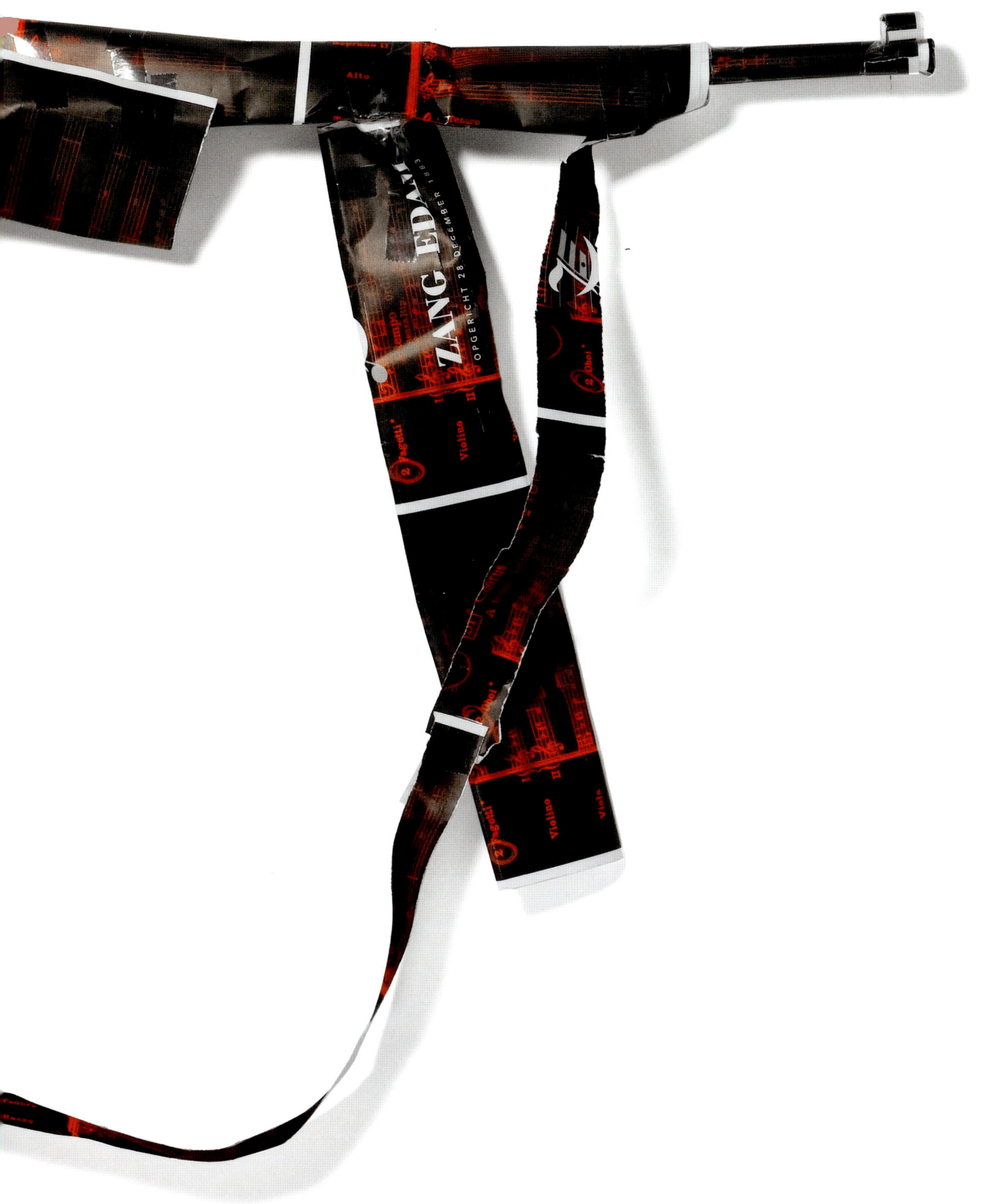

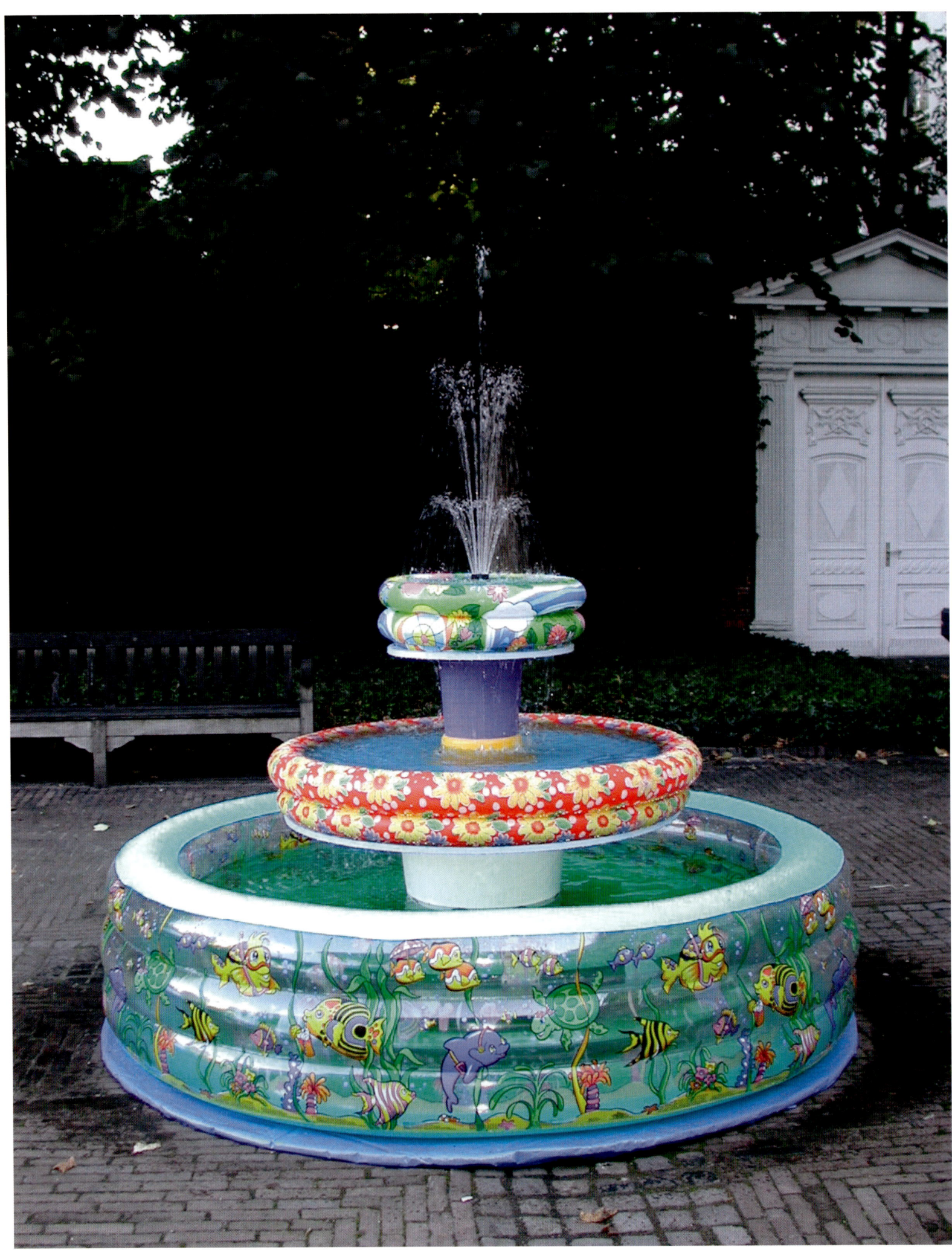

58) do drum

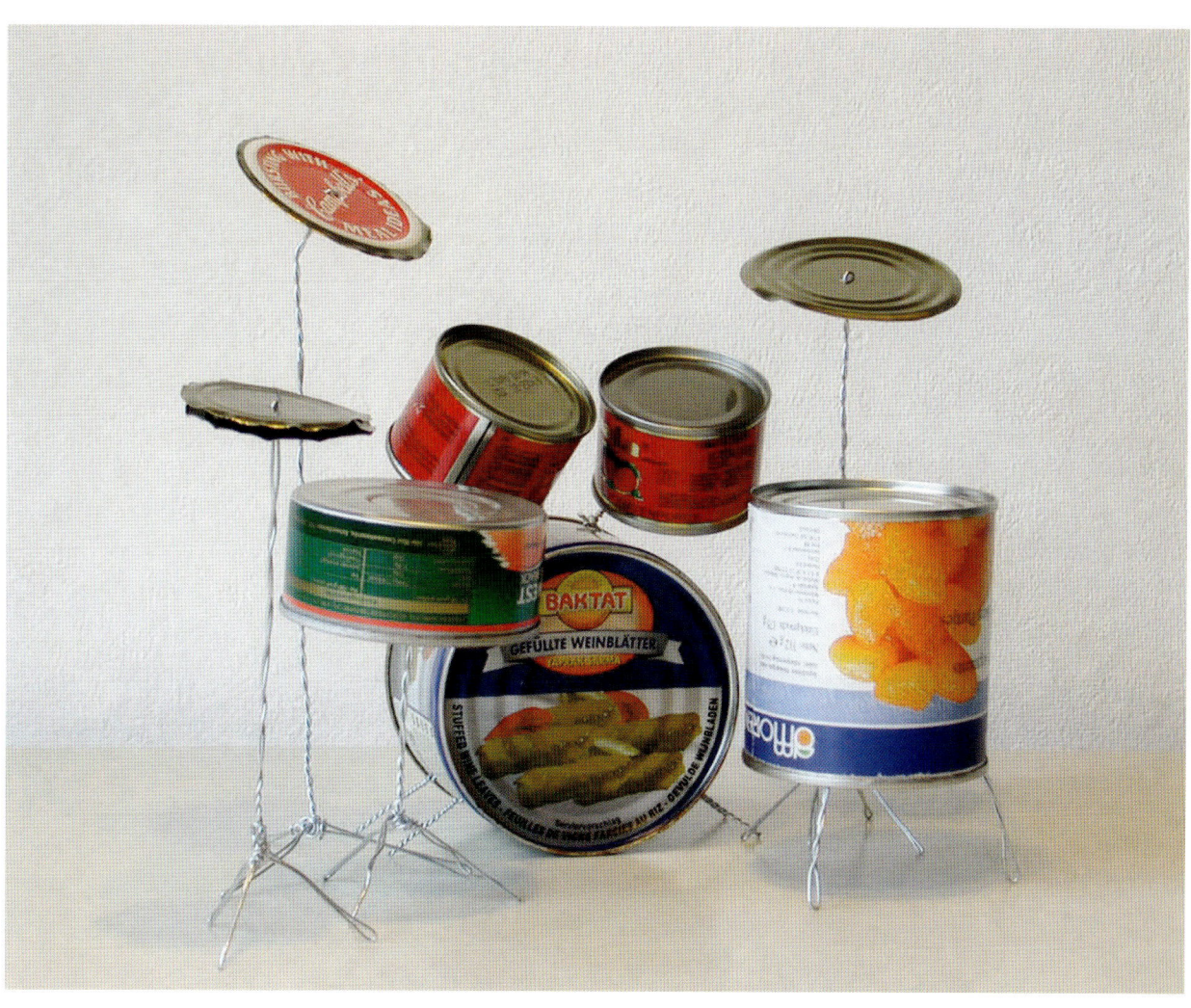

59) do rest

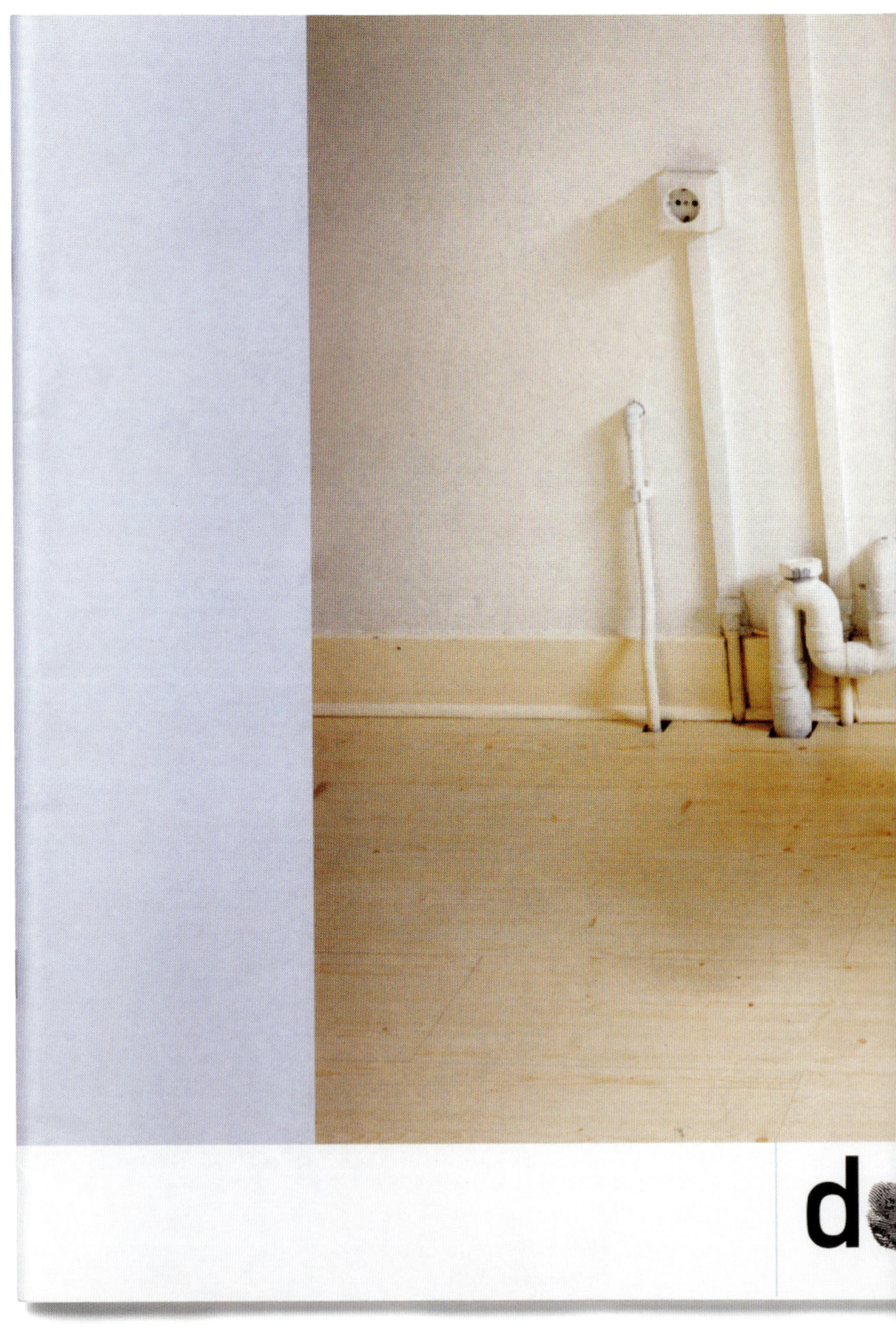

d

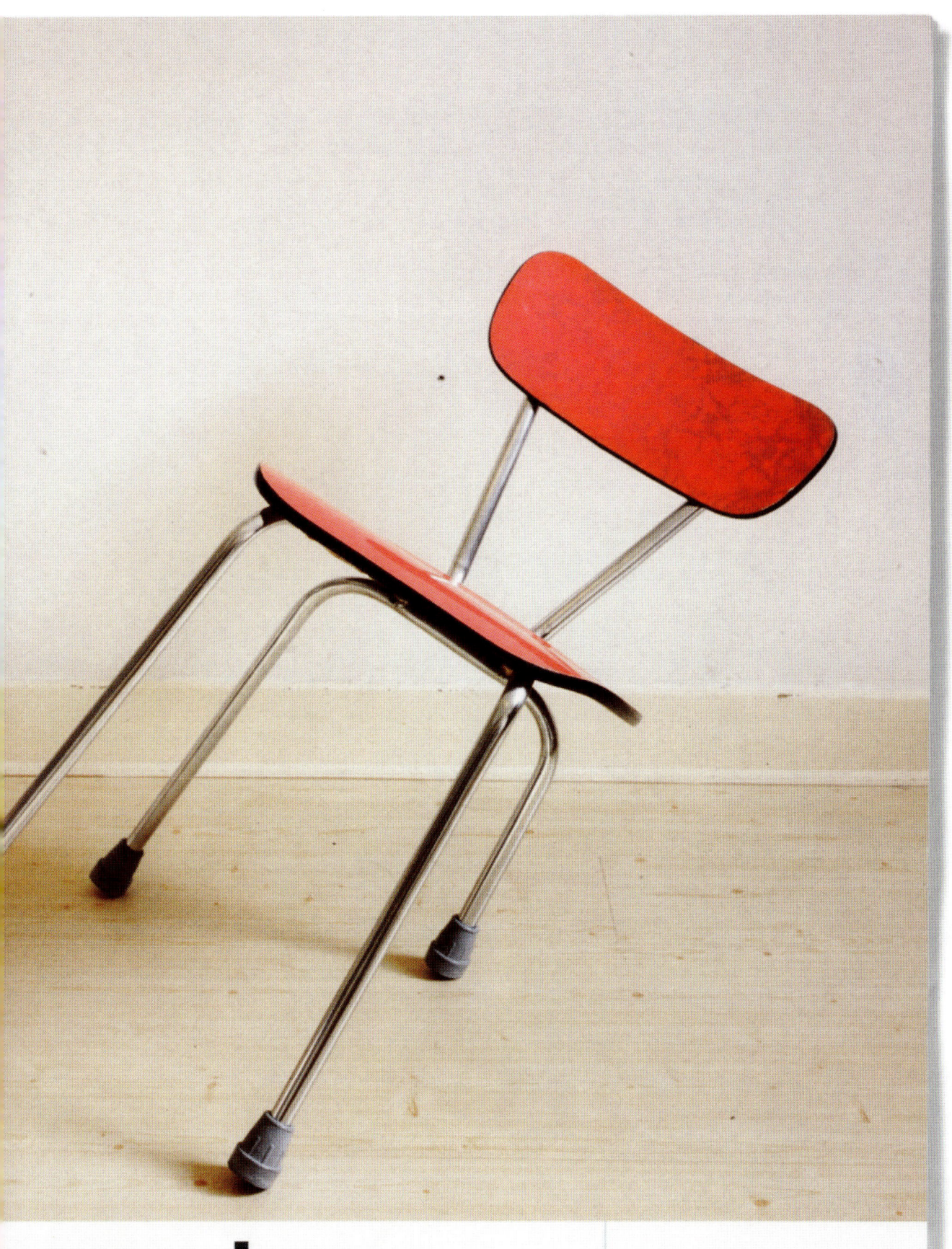

create

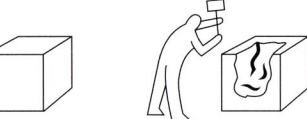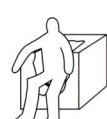

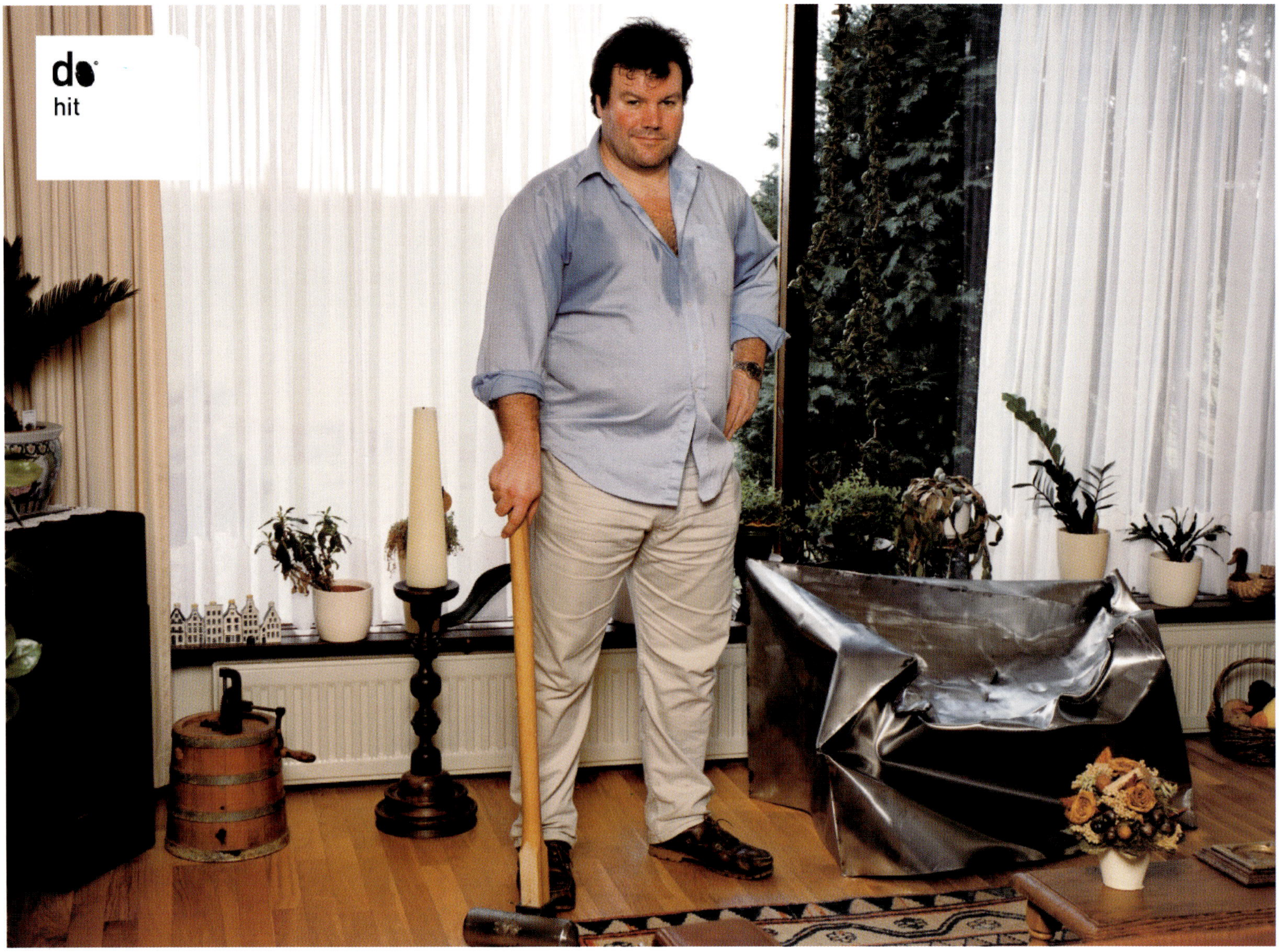

do
hit

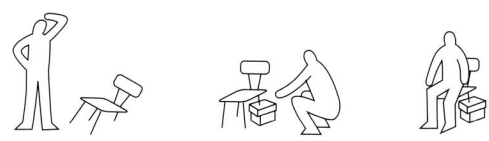

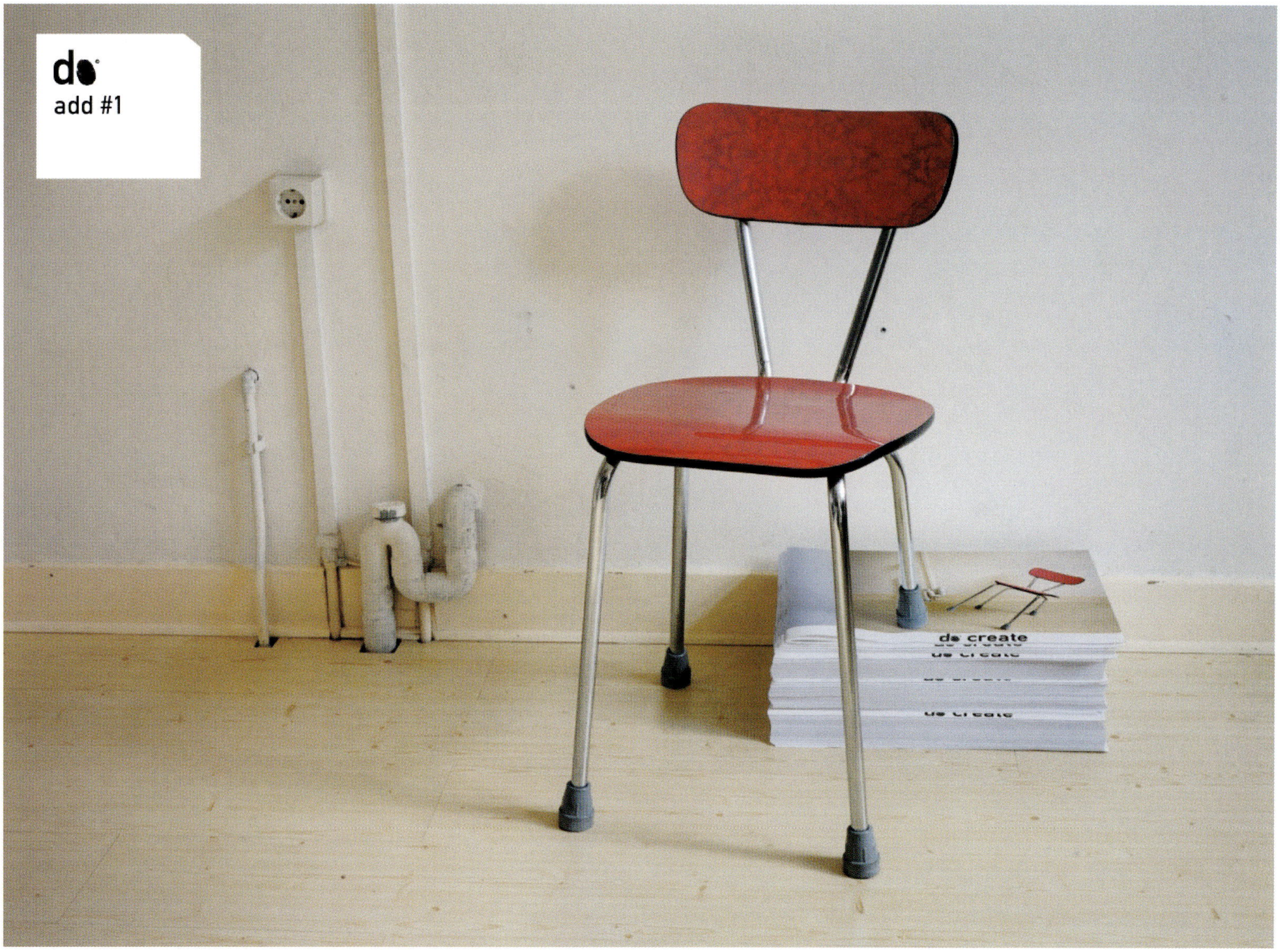

do
add #1

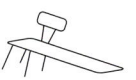 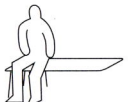 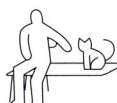

do
add #2

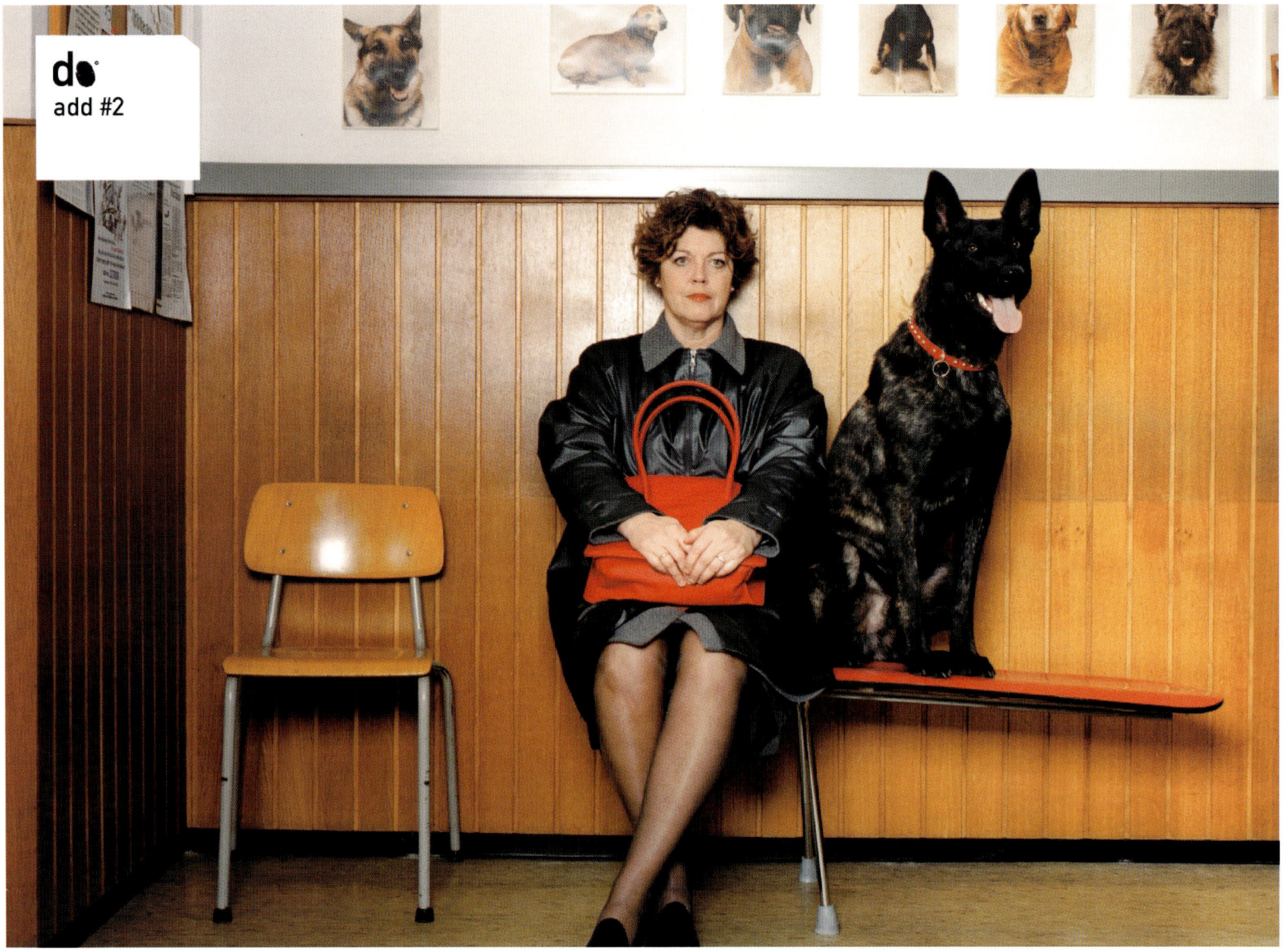

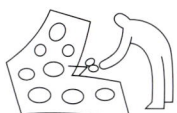 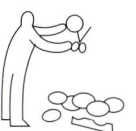 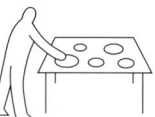

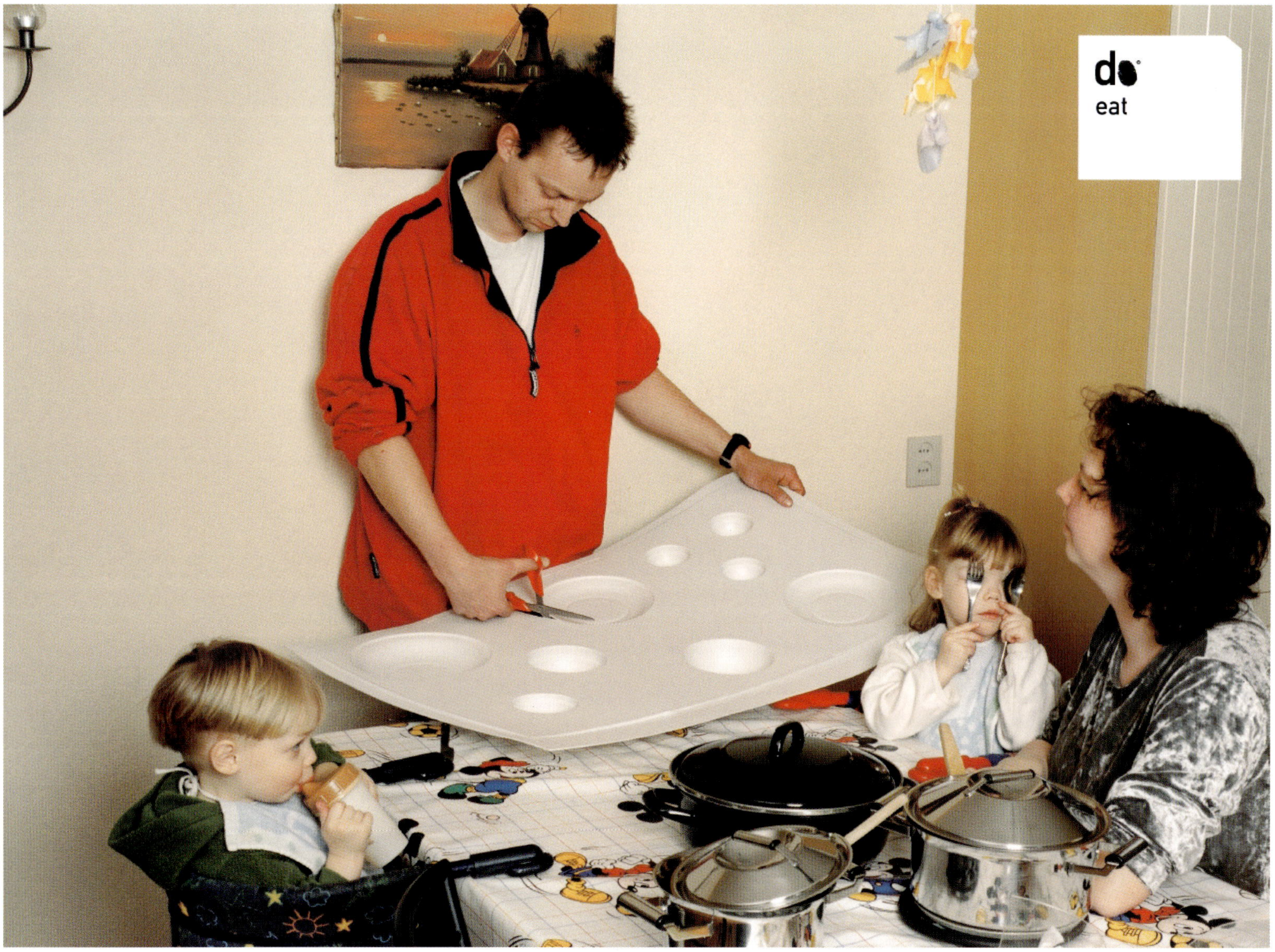

do
eat

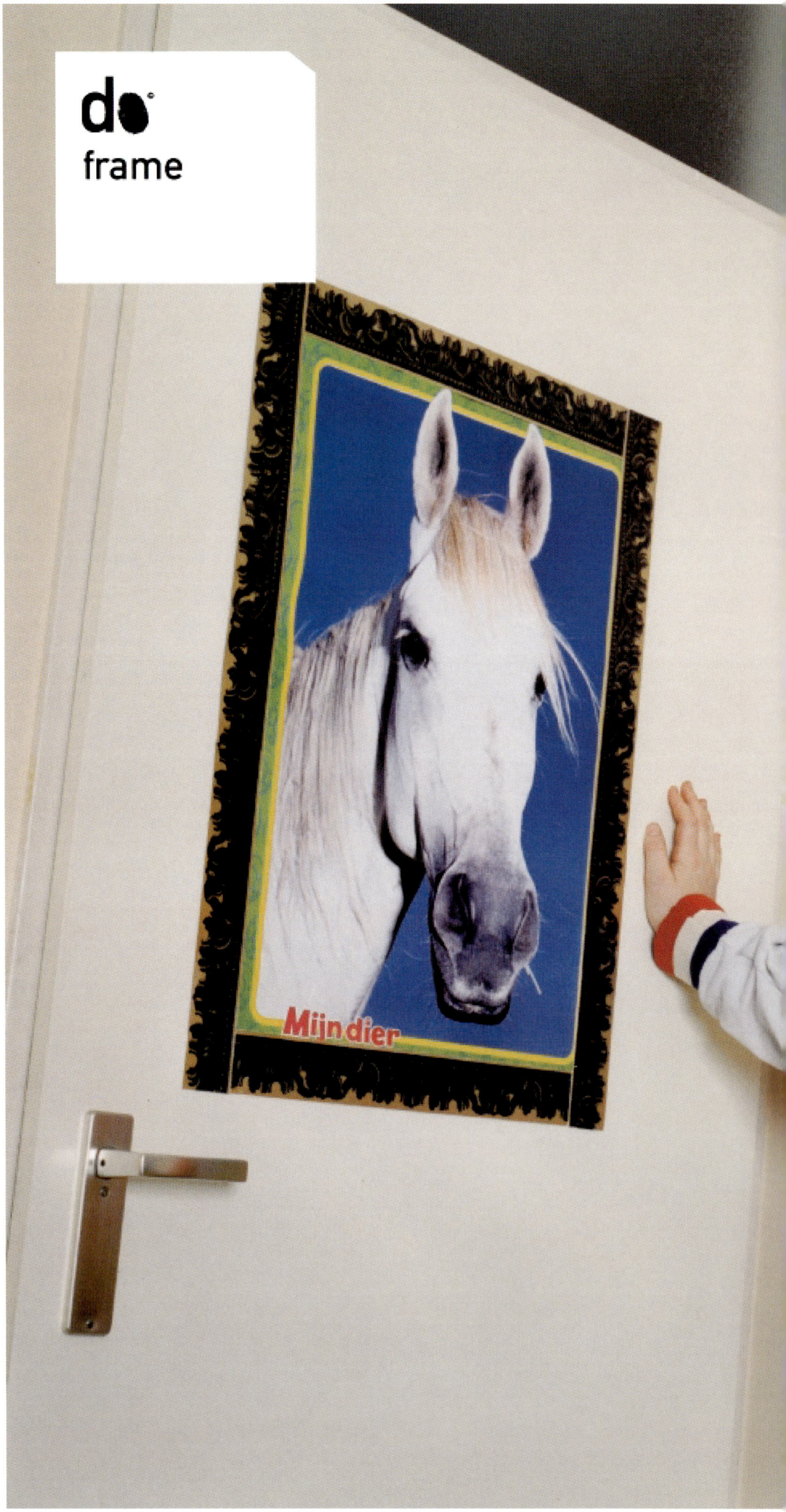

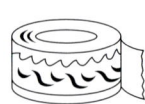

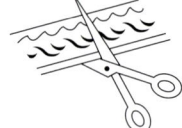

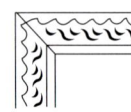

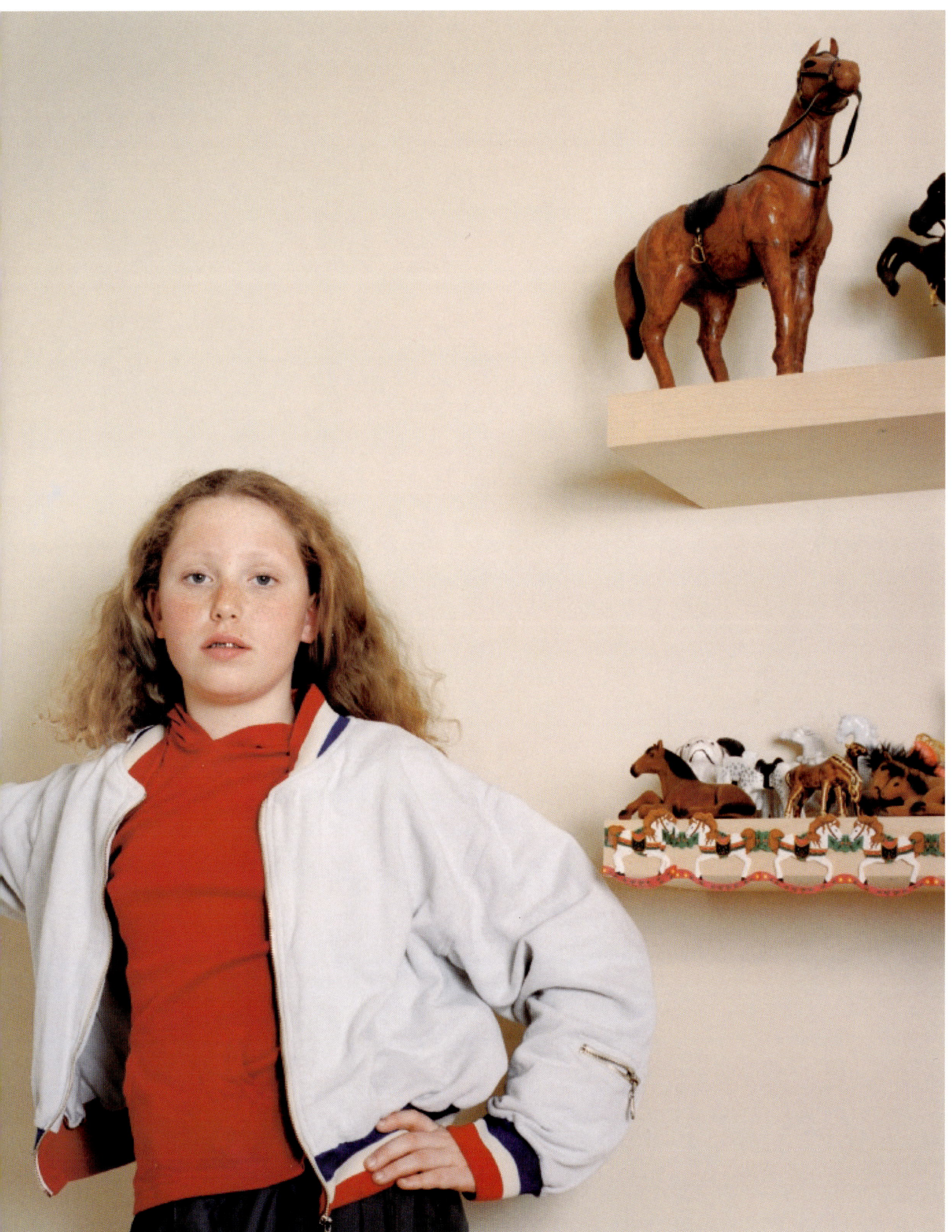

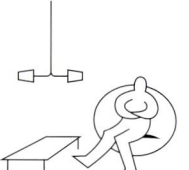 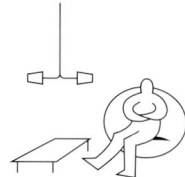 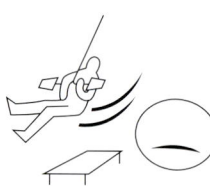

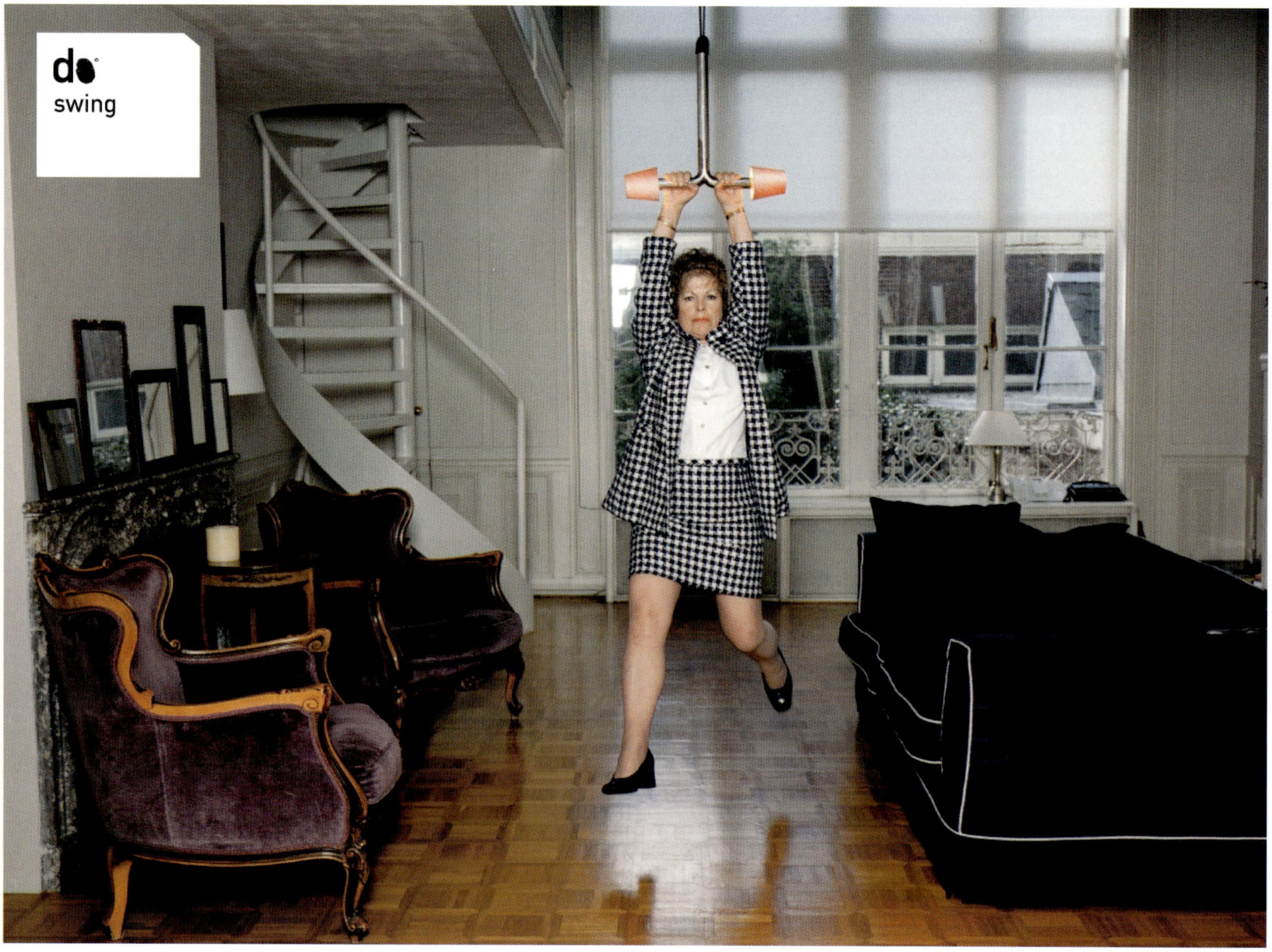

do swing

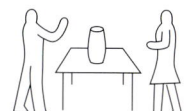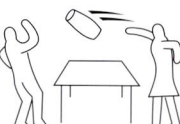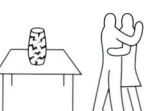

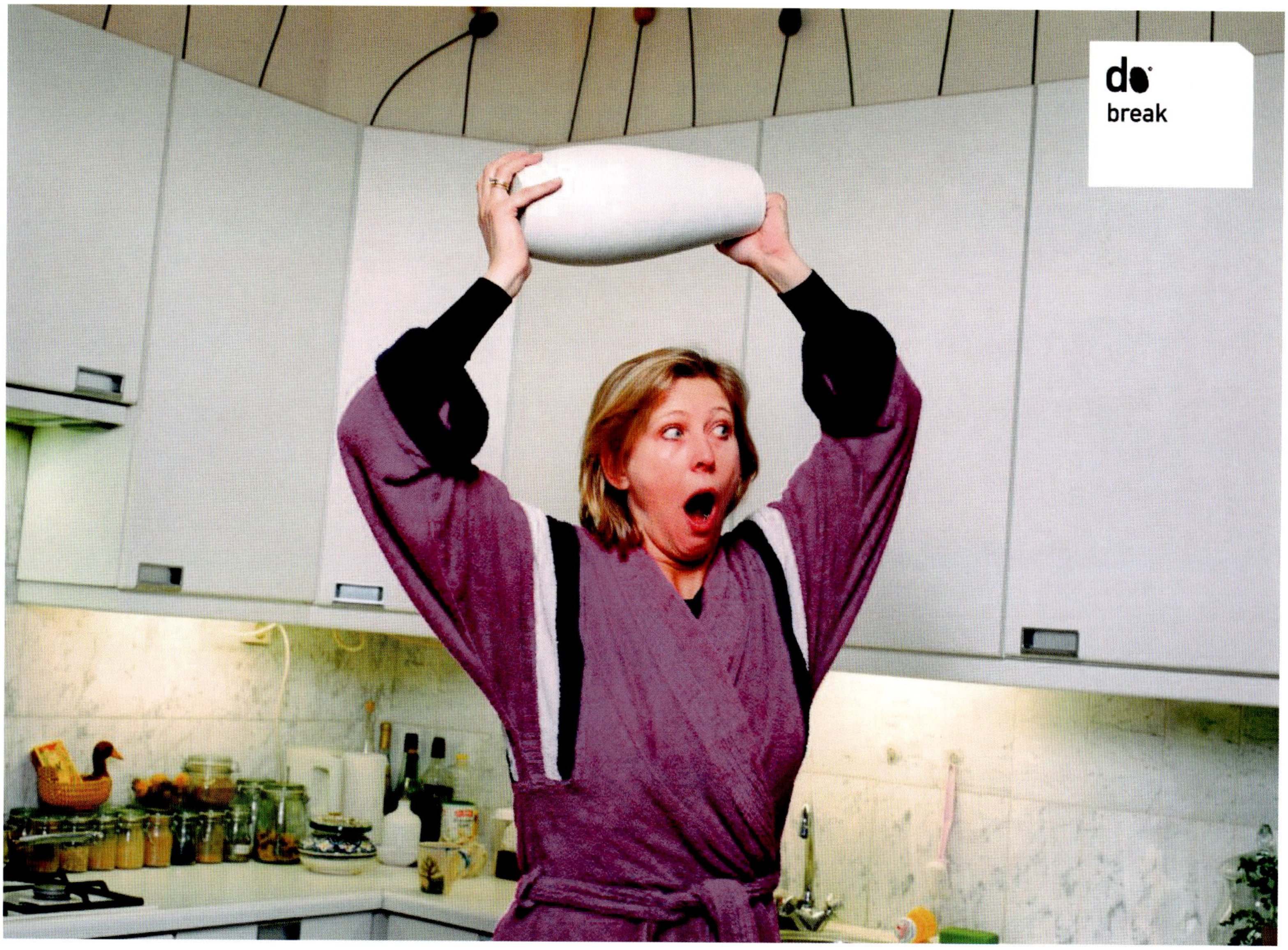

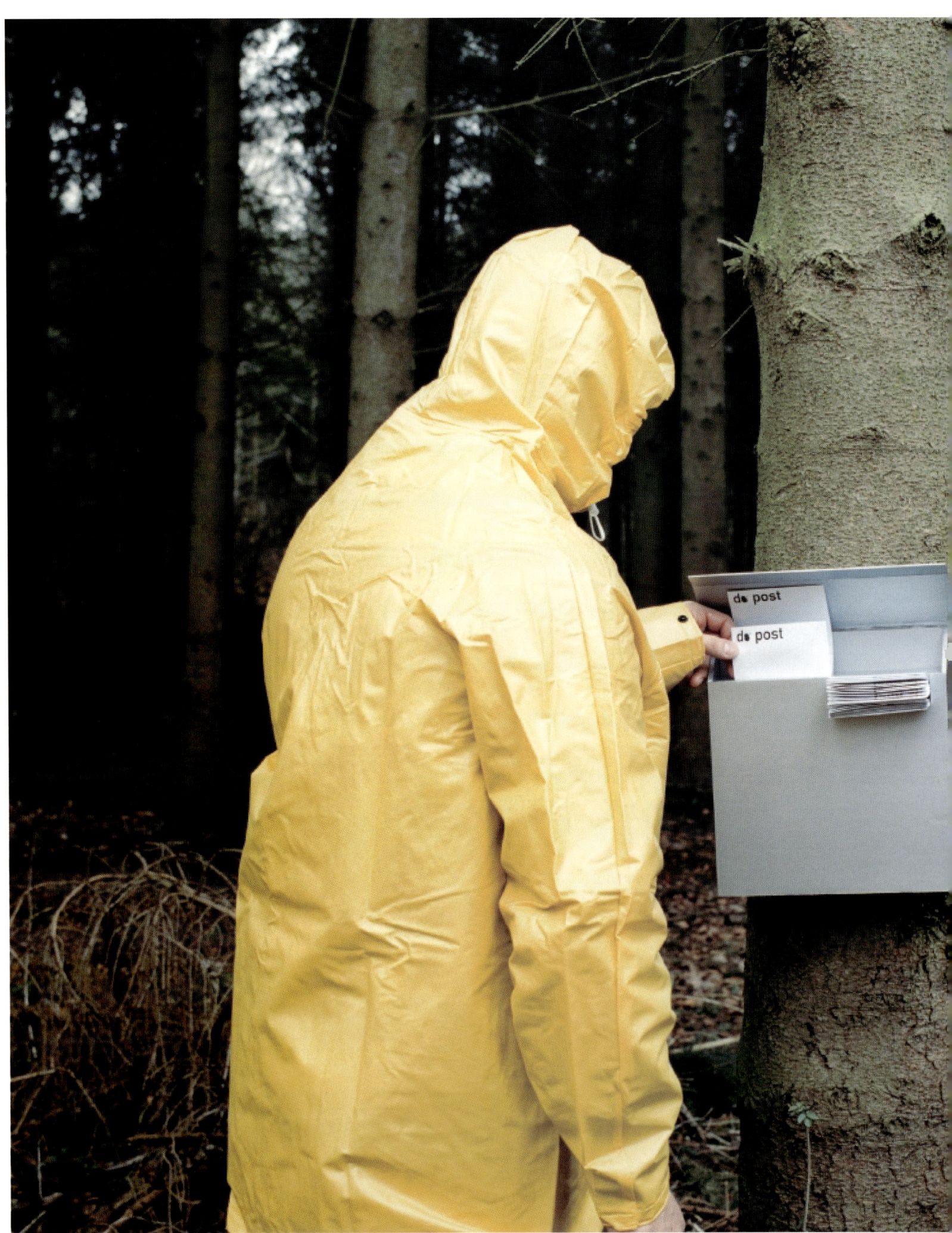

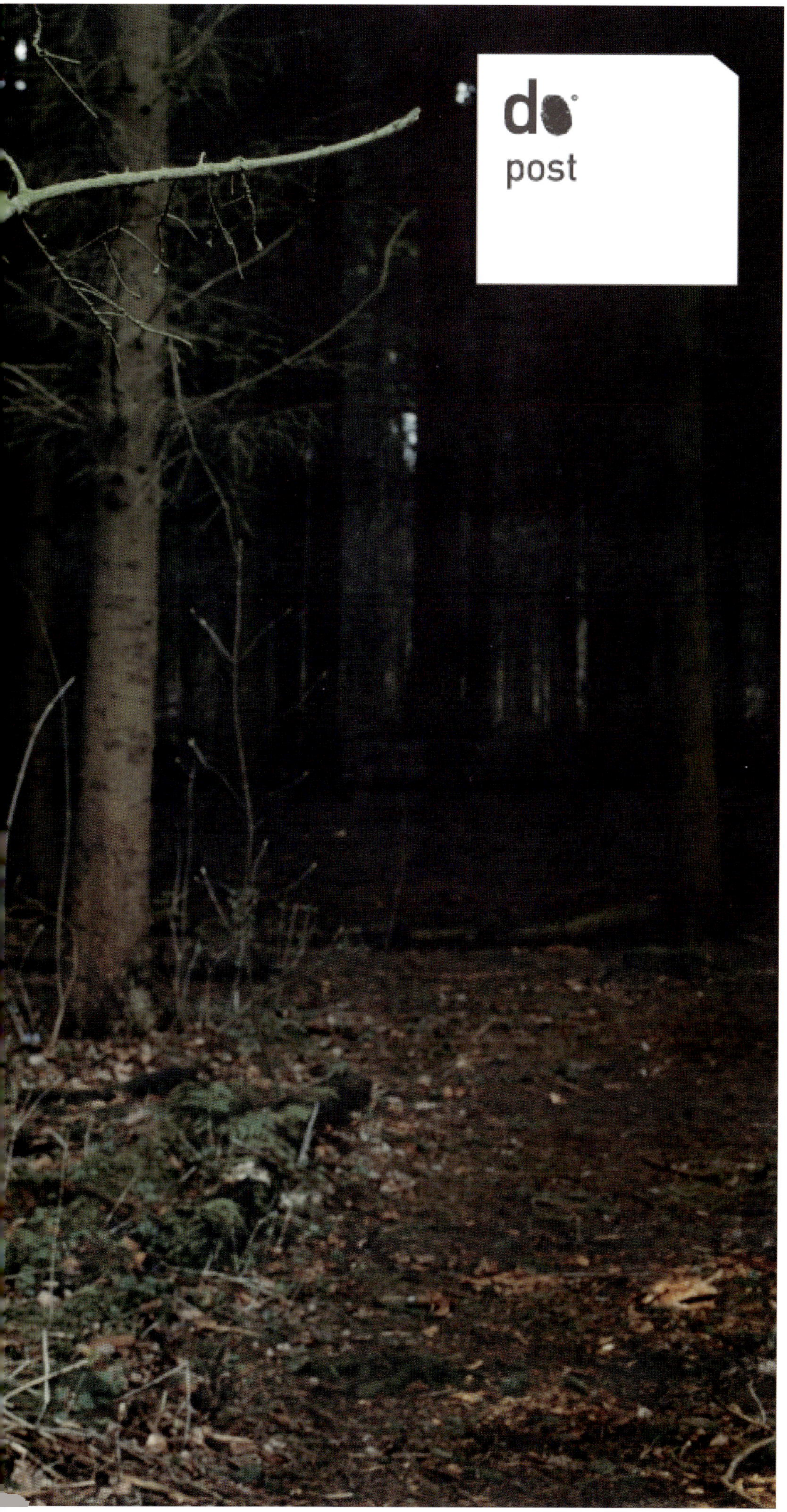

do
post

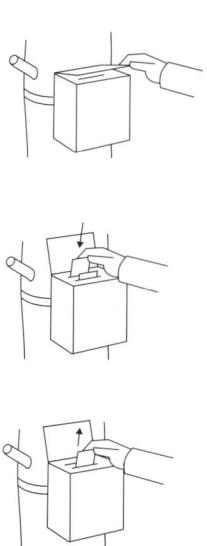

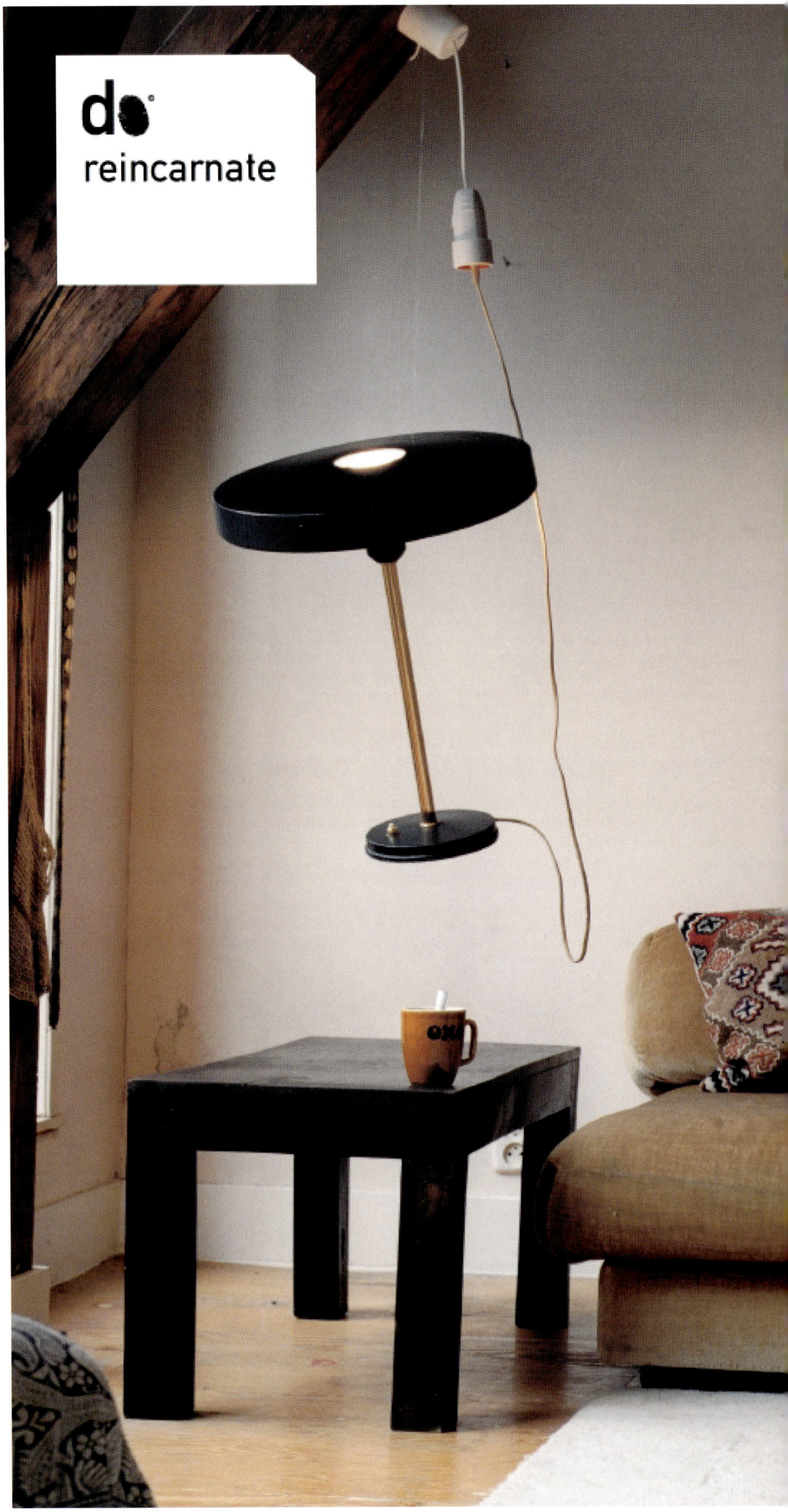

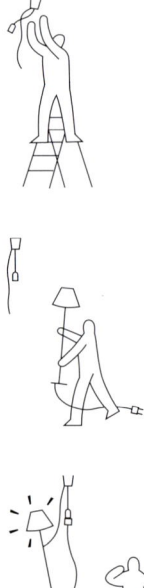

do reincarnate

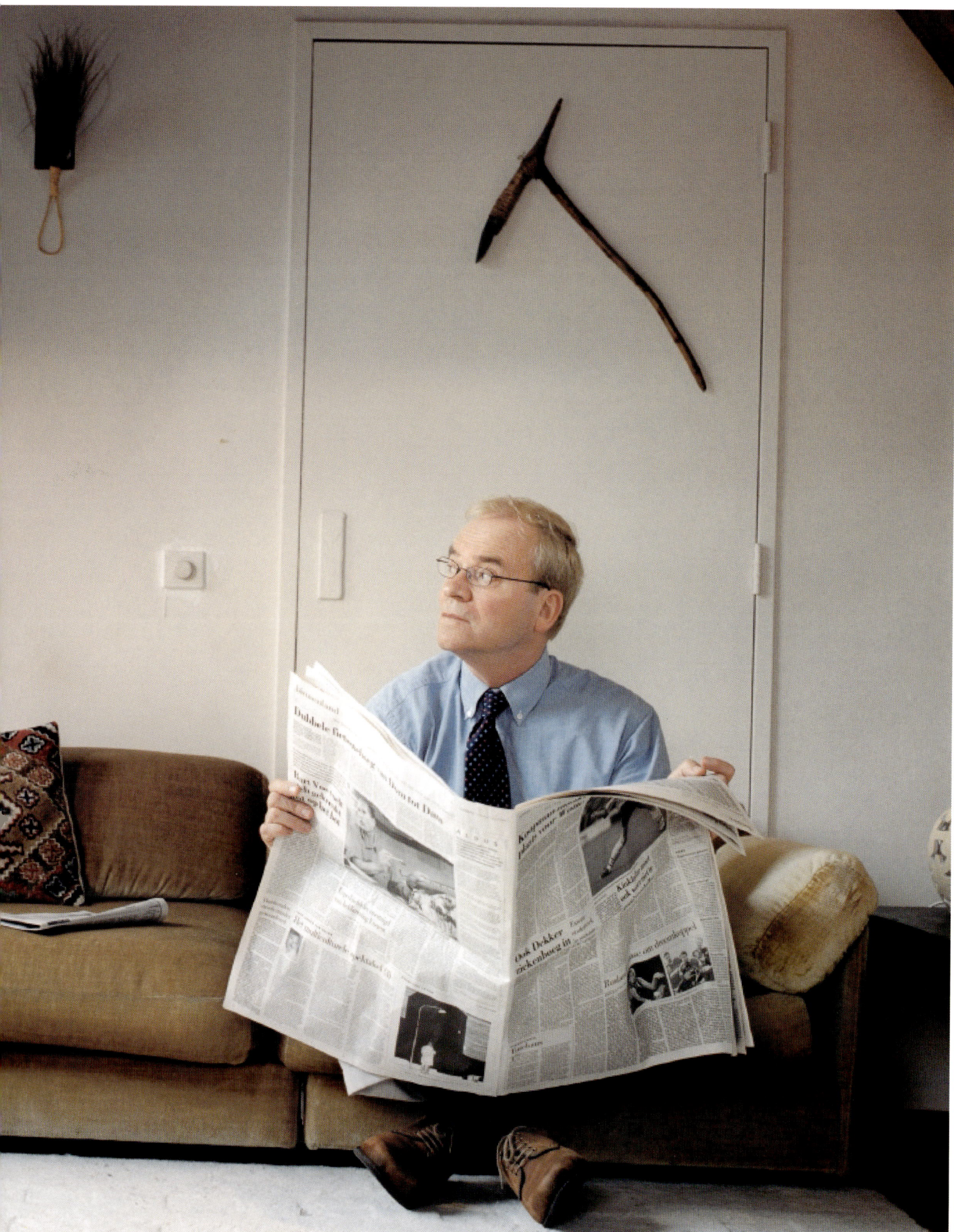

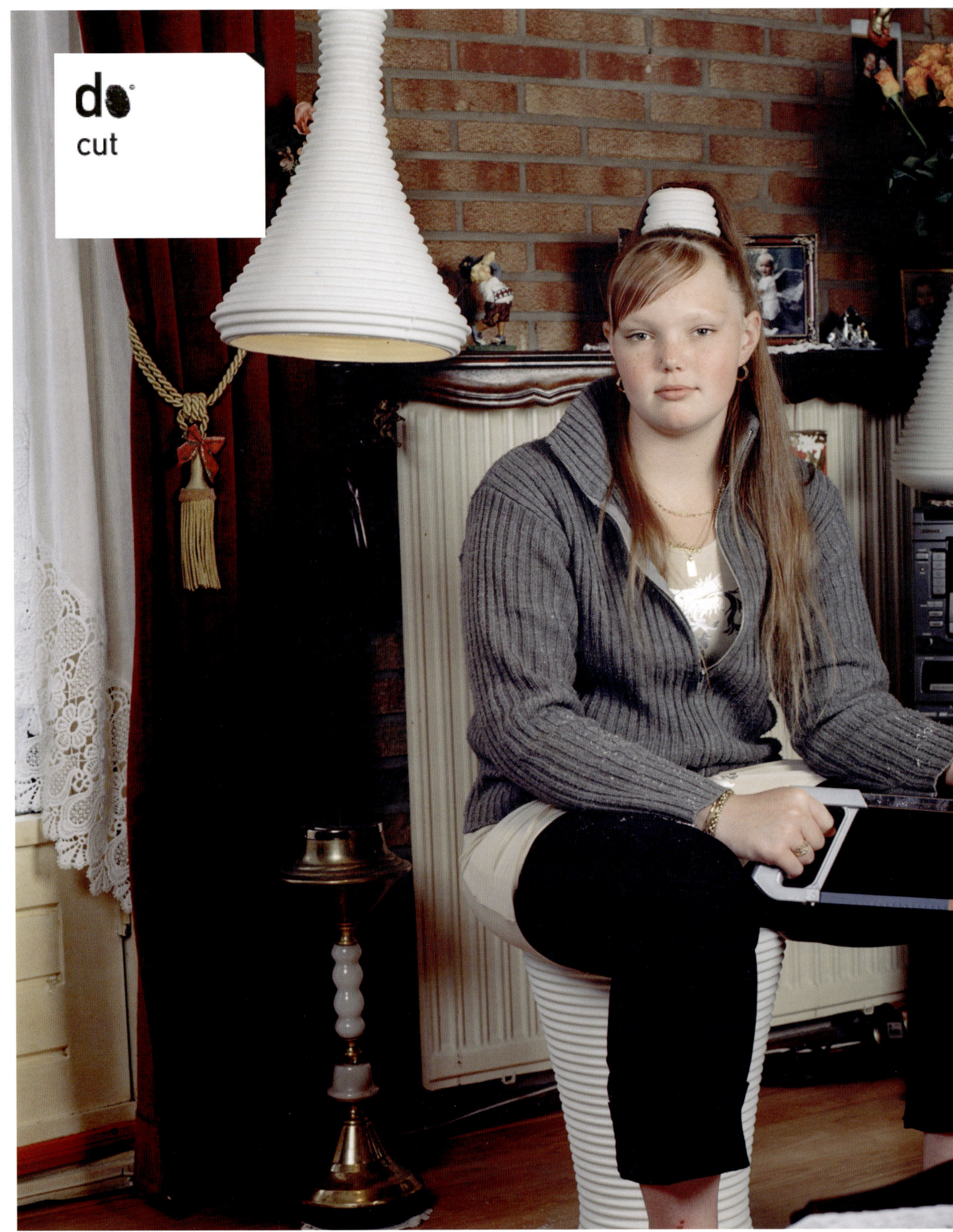

do

cut

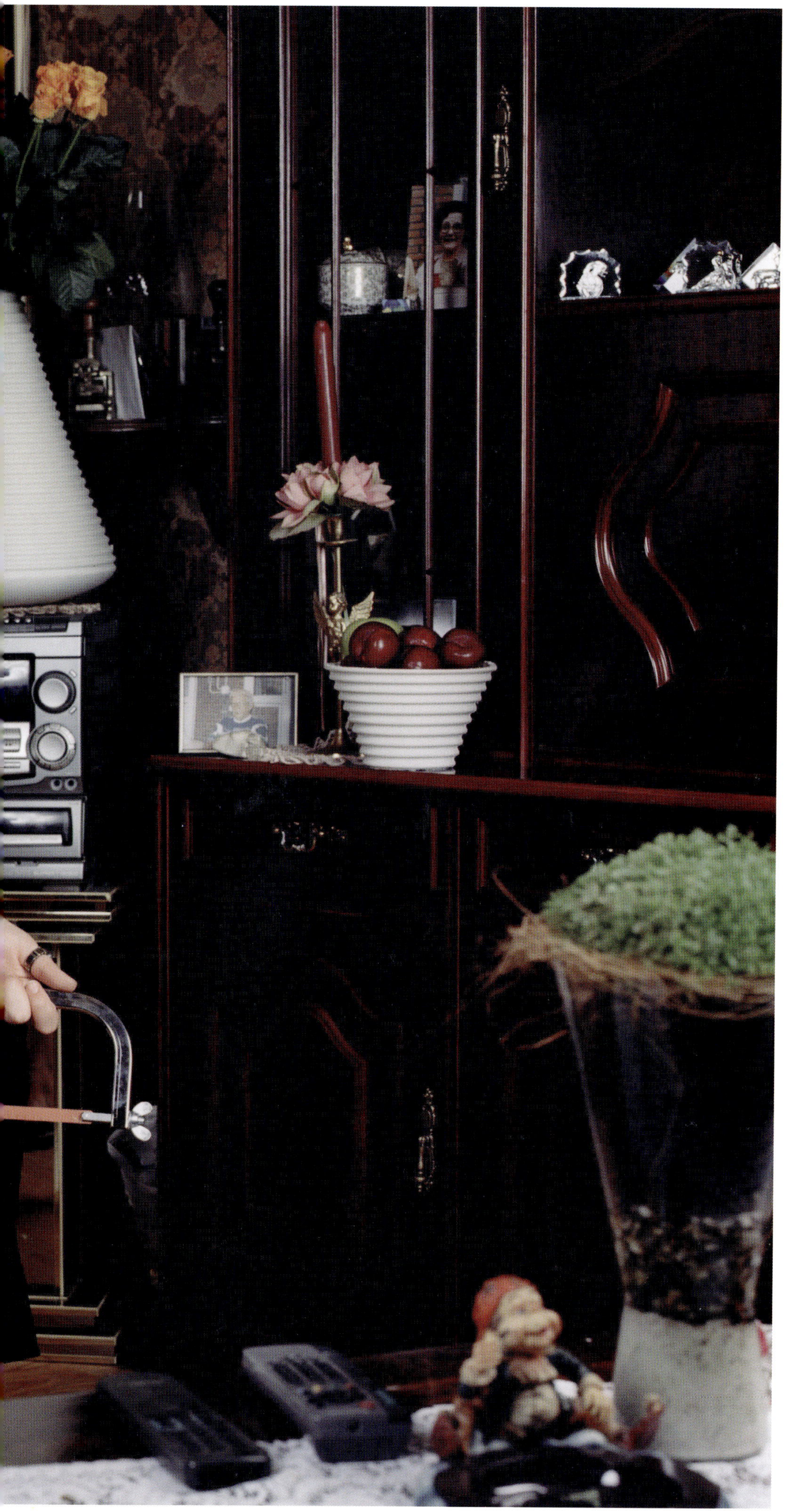

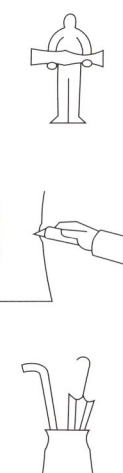

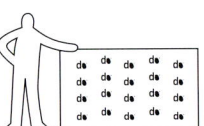 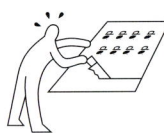 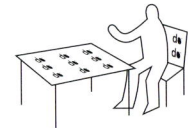

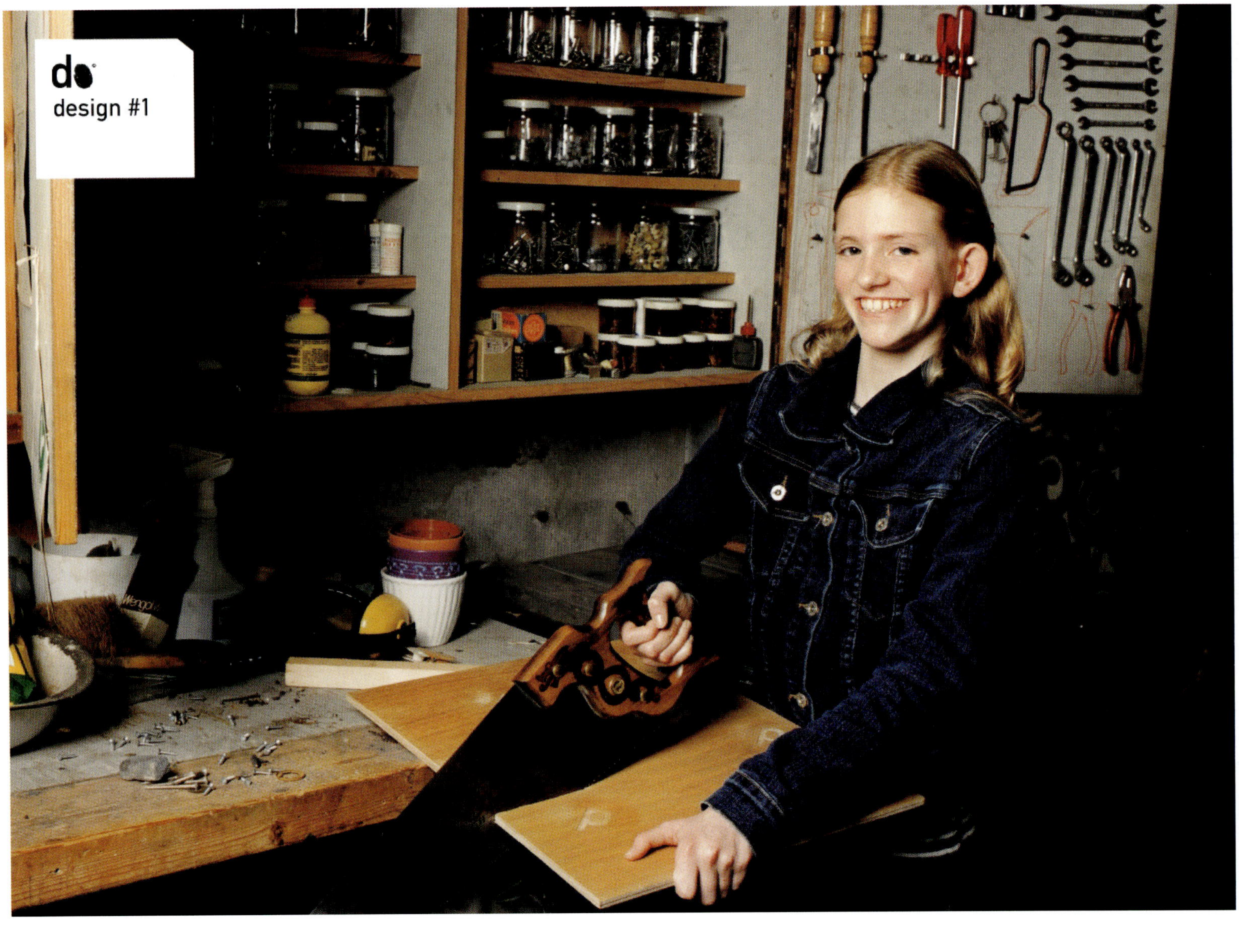

do

design #1

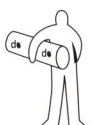 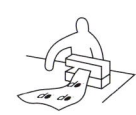 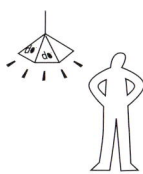

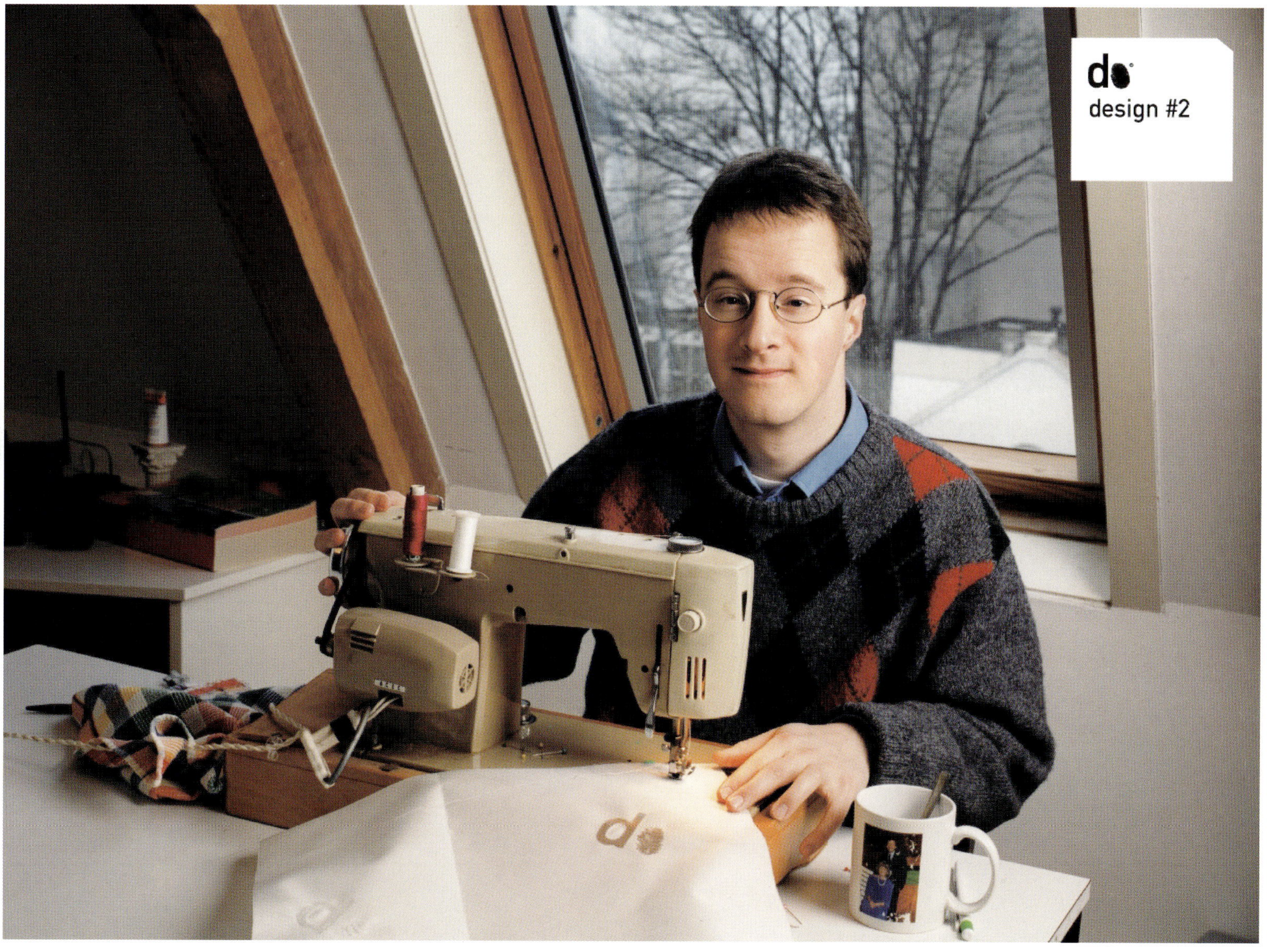

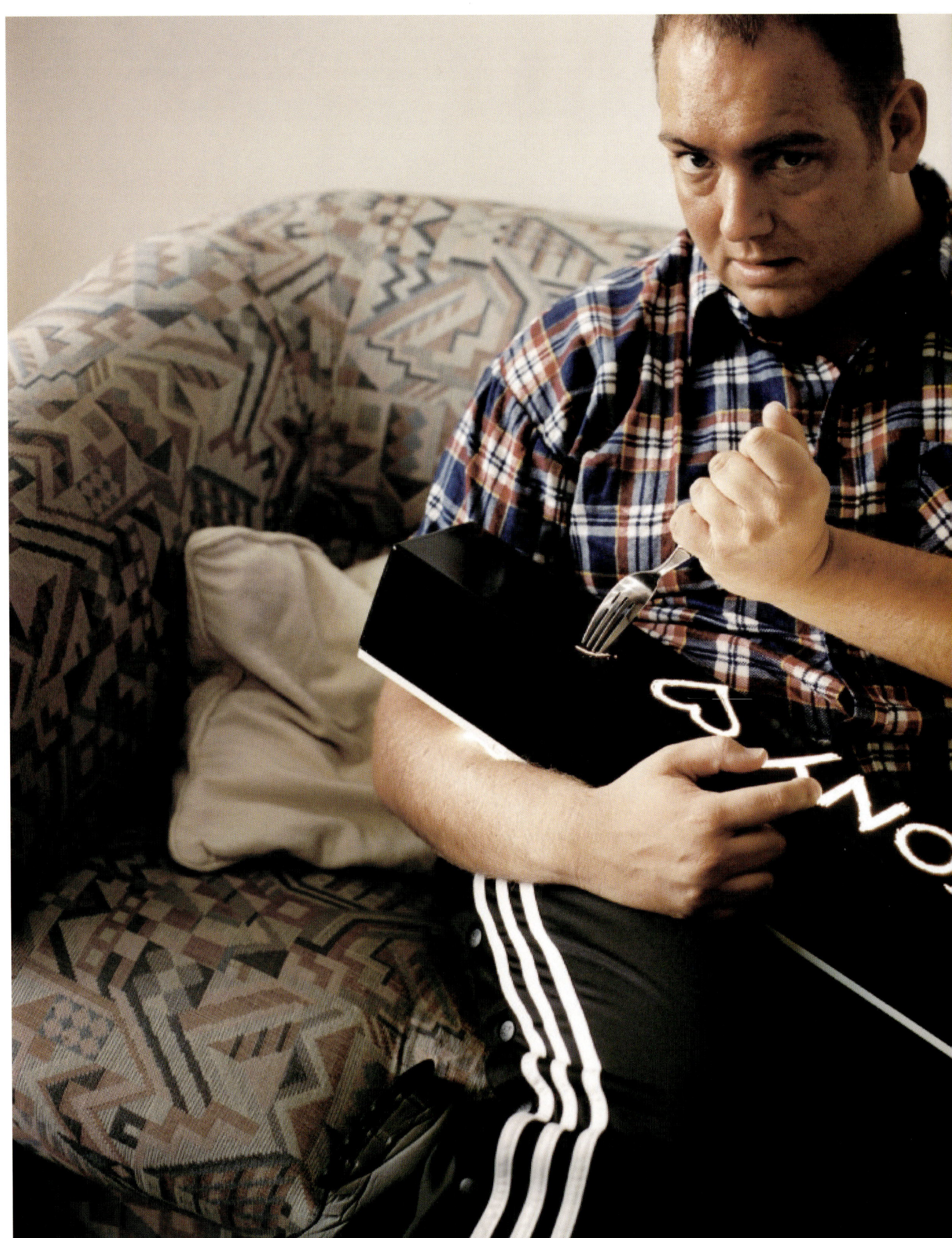

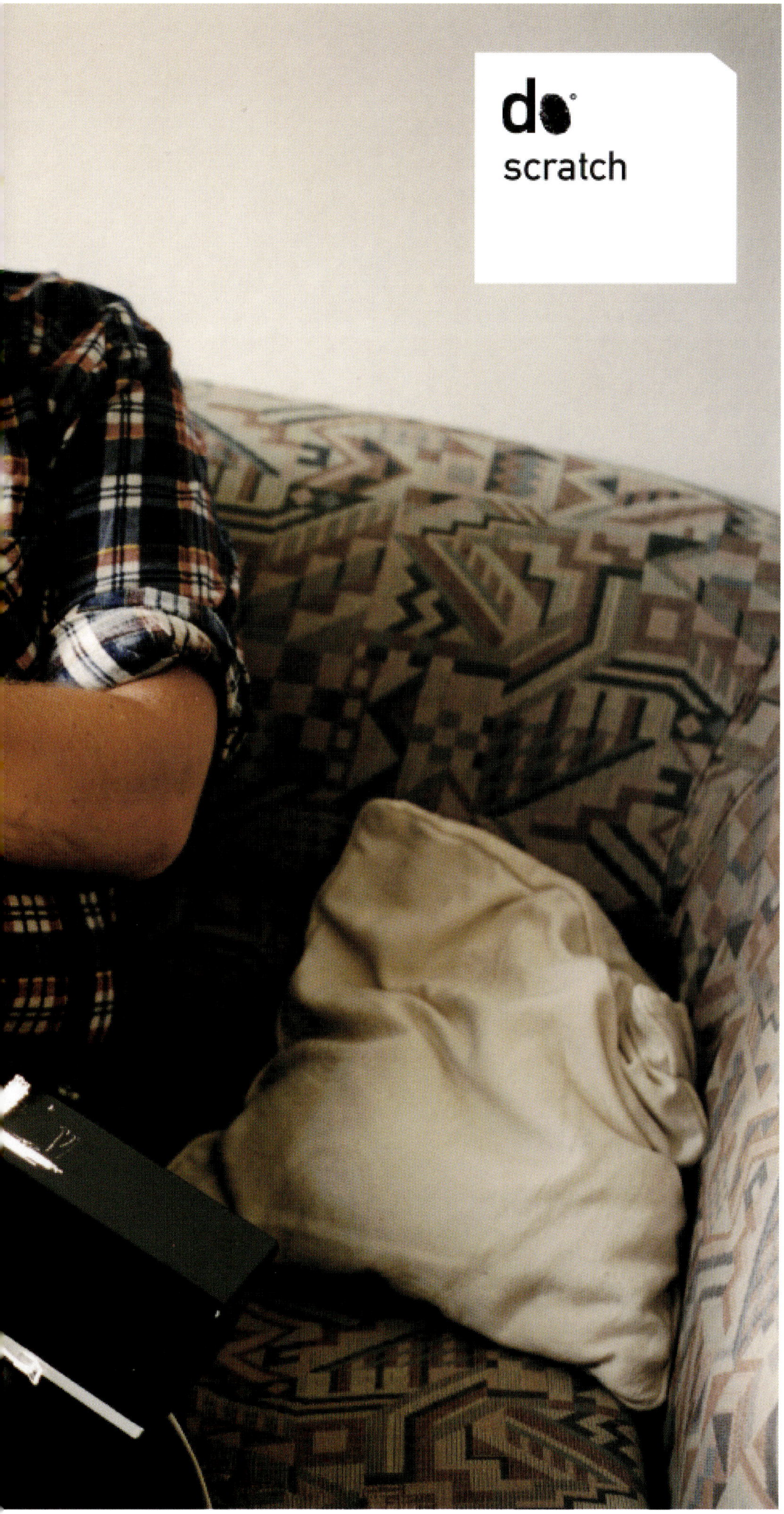

do
scratch

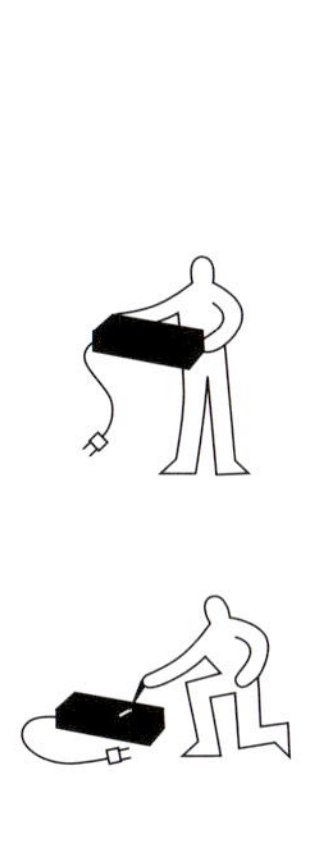

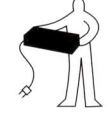

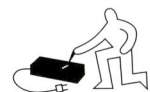

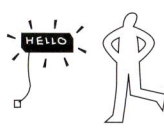

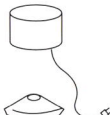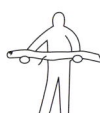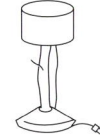

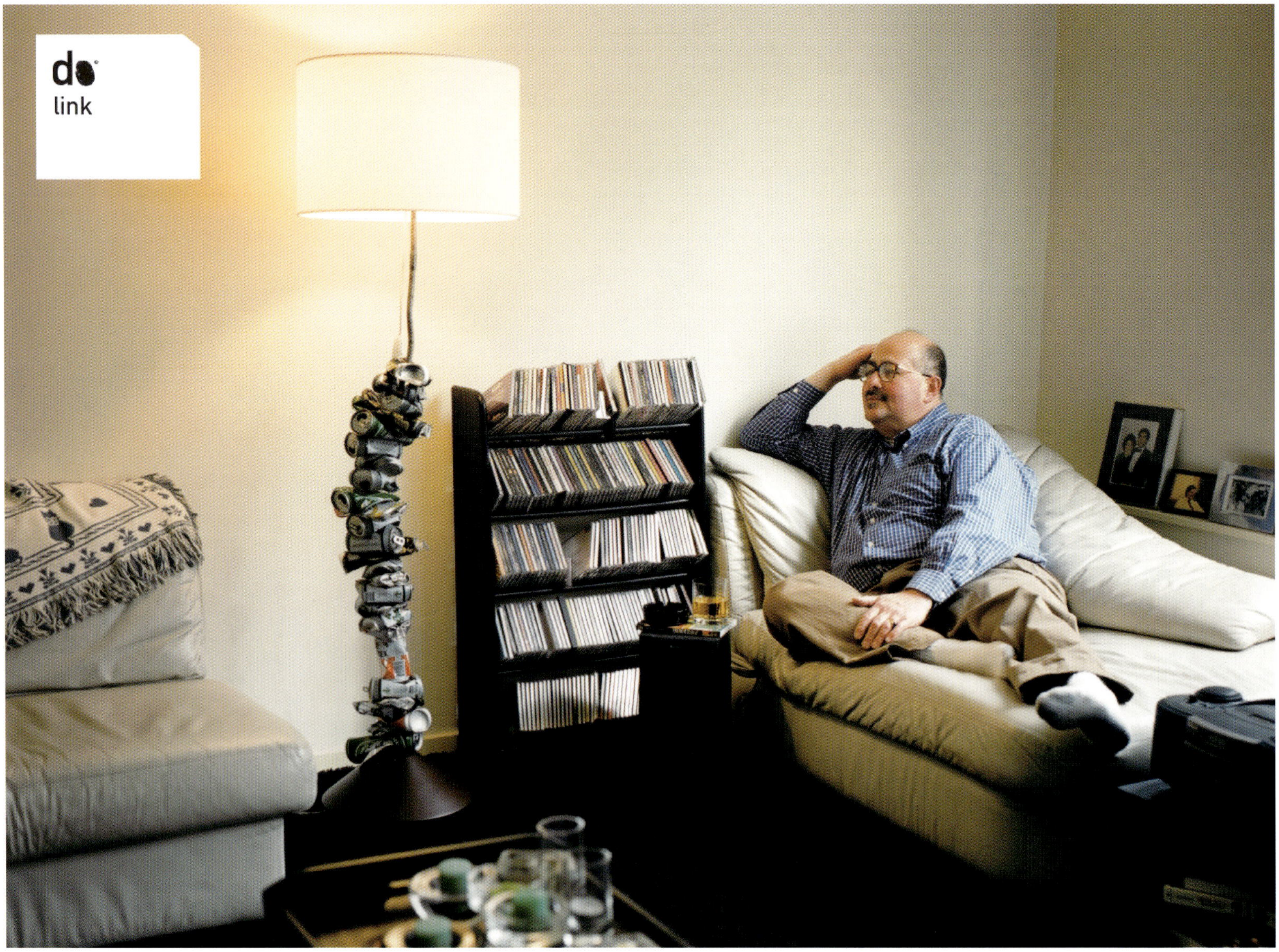

do
link

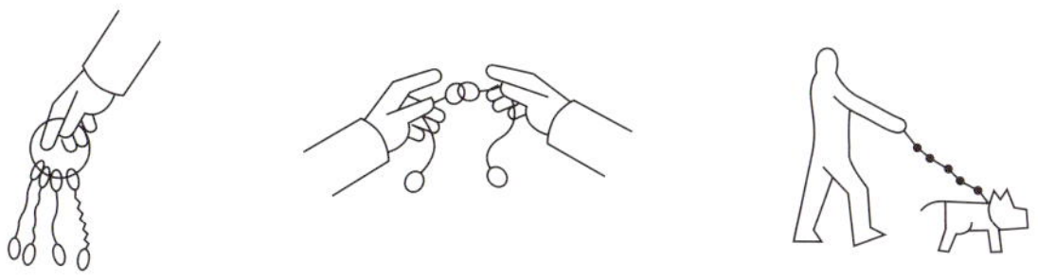

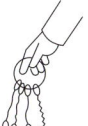 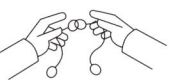 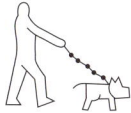

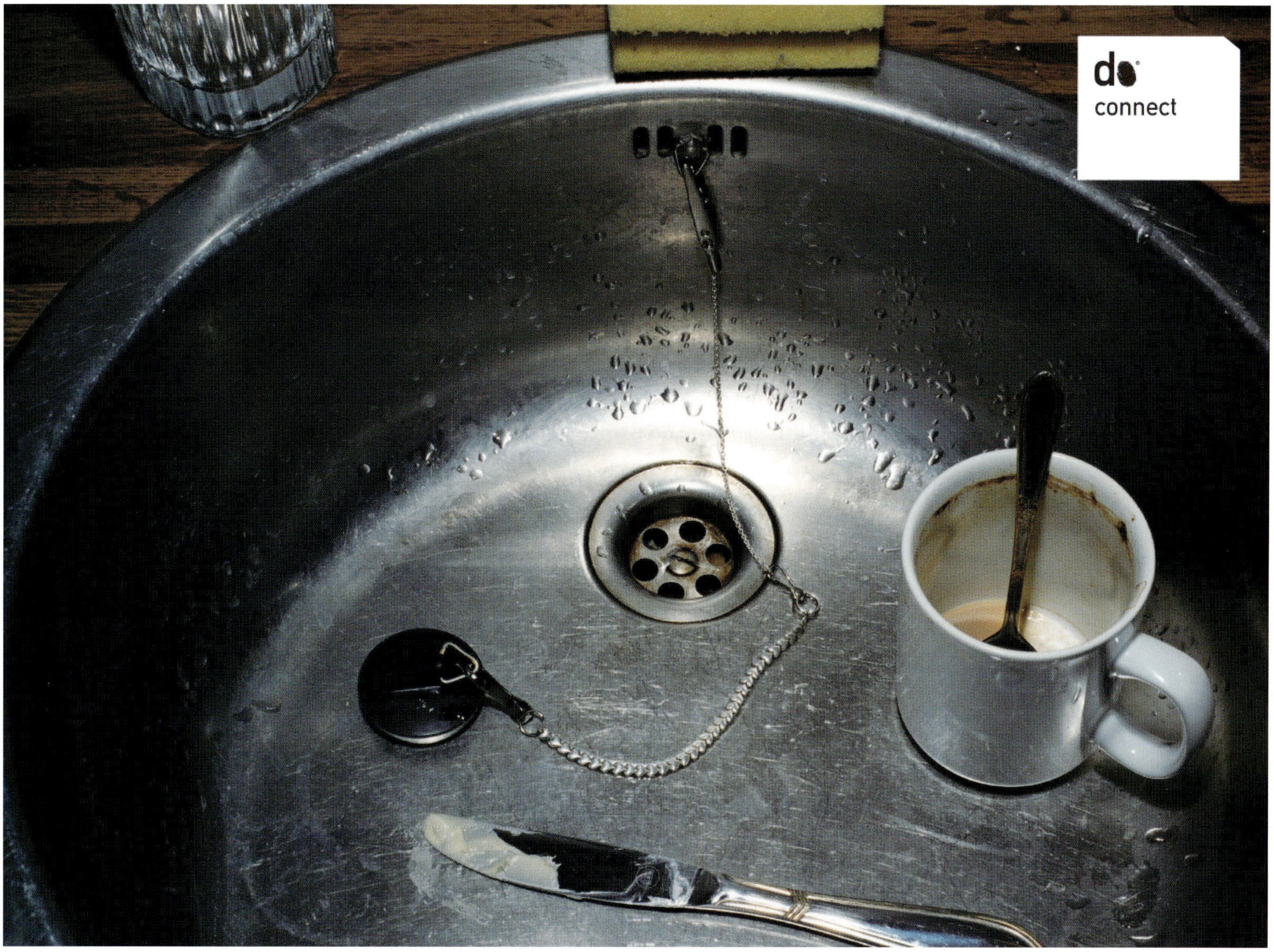

do
connect

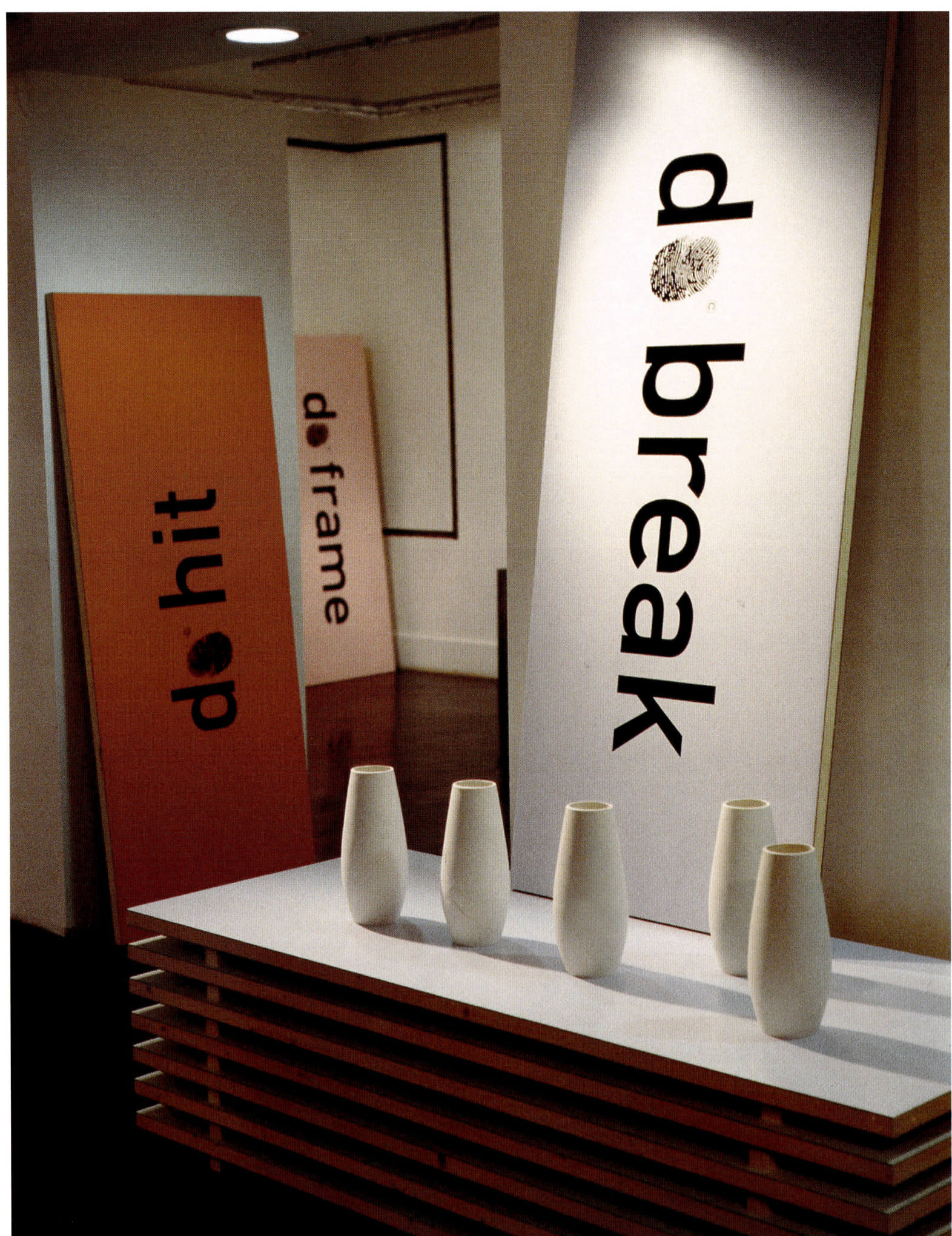

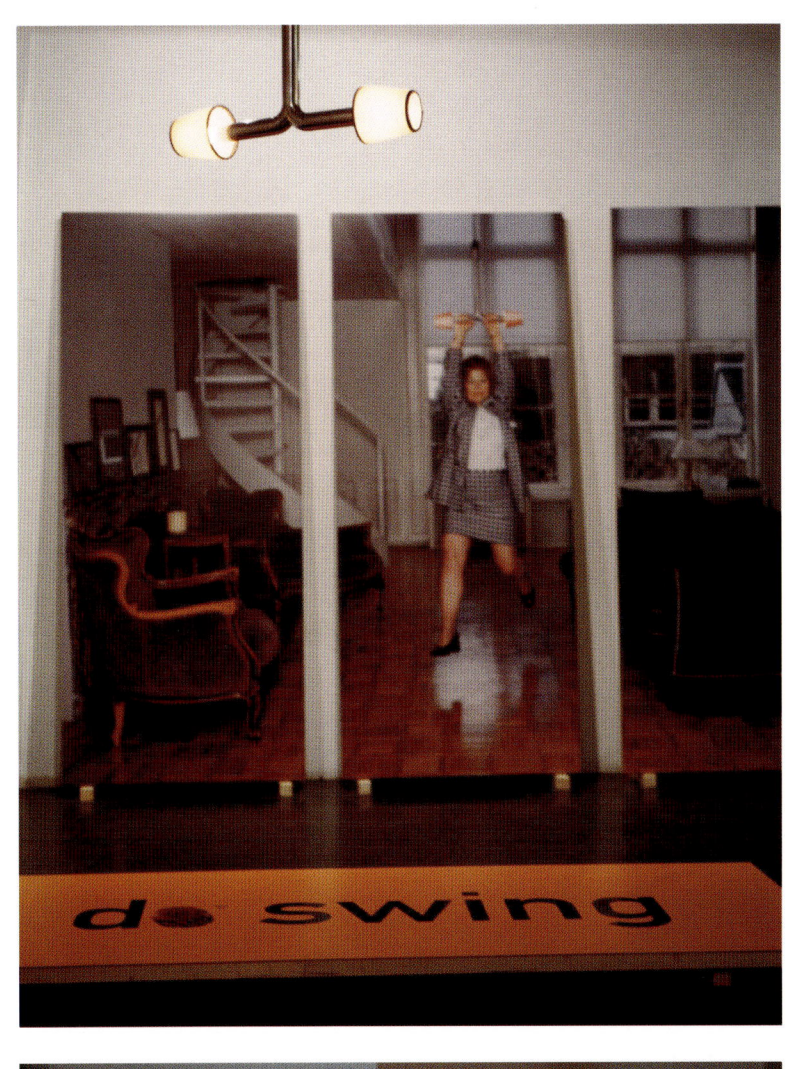

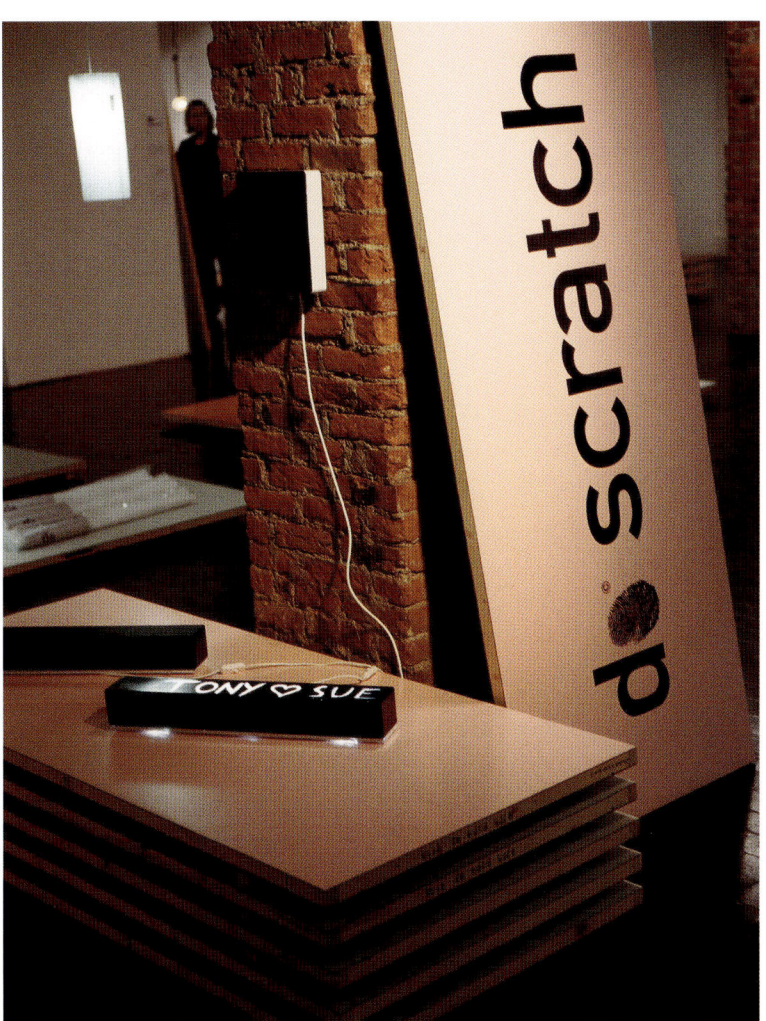

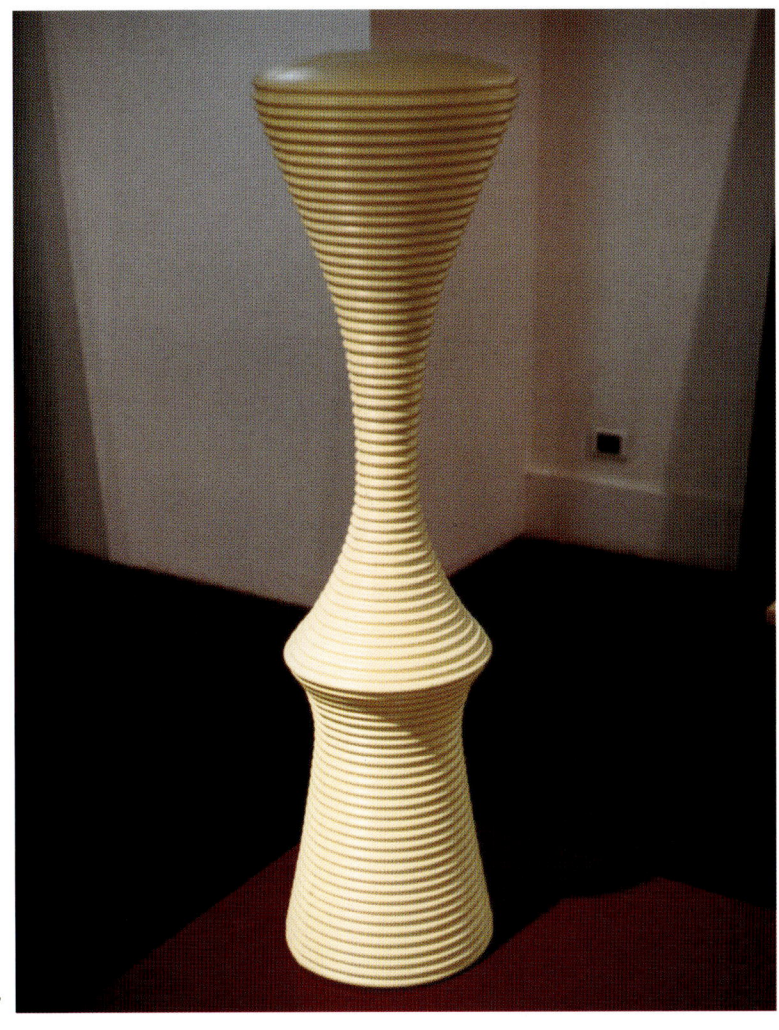

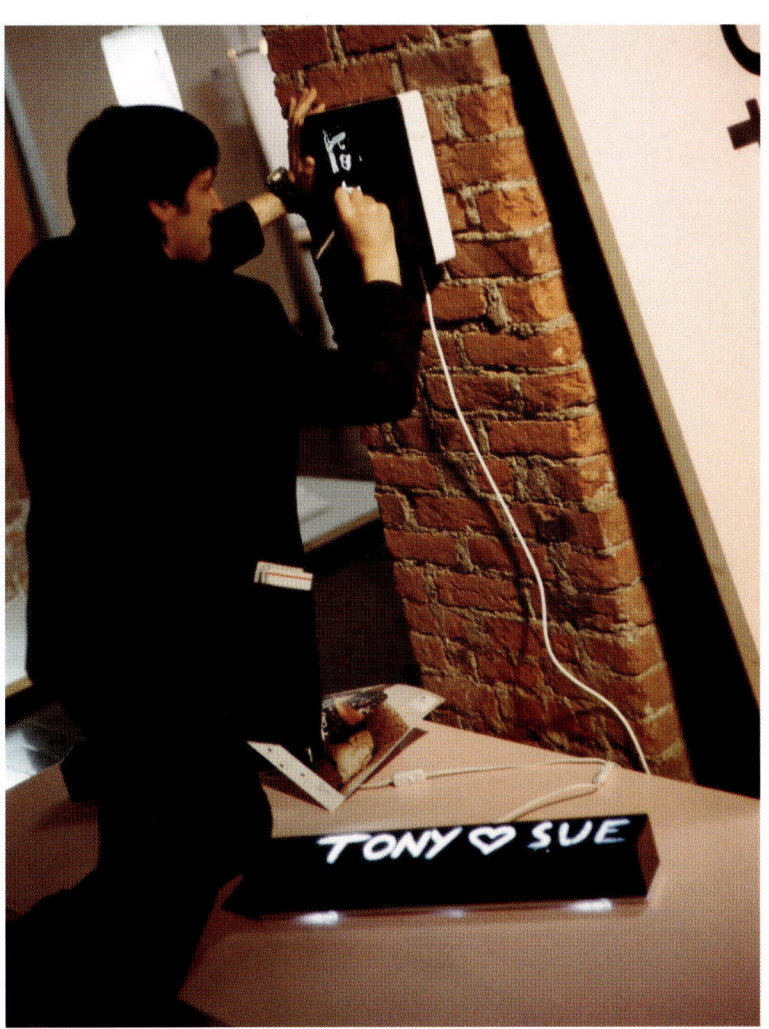

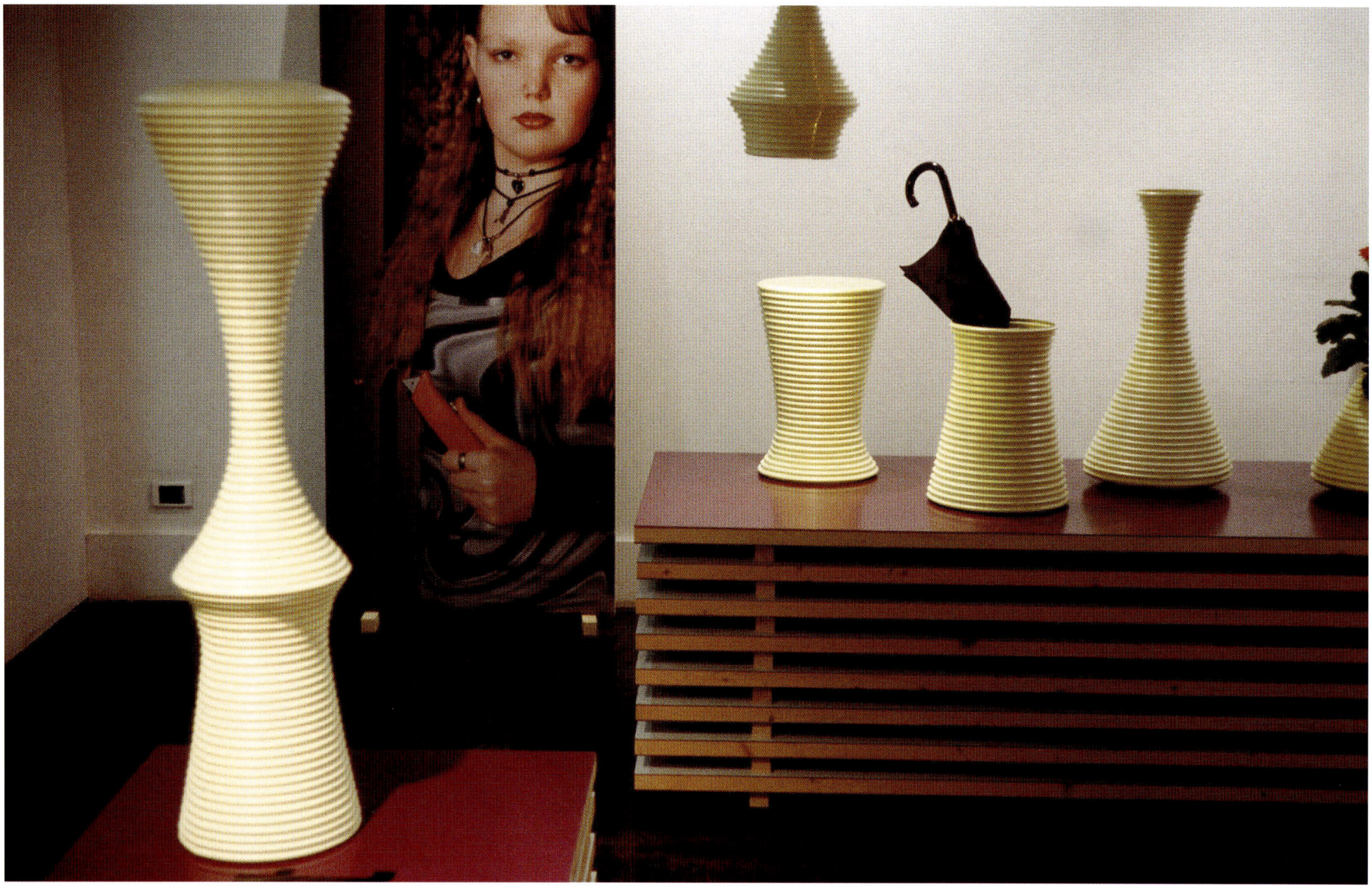

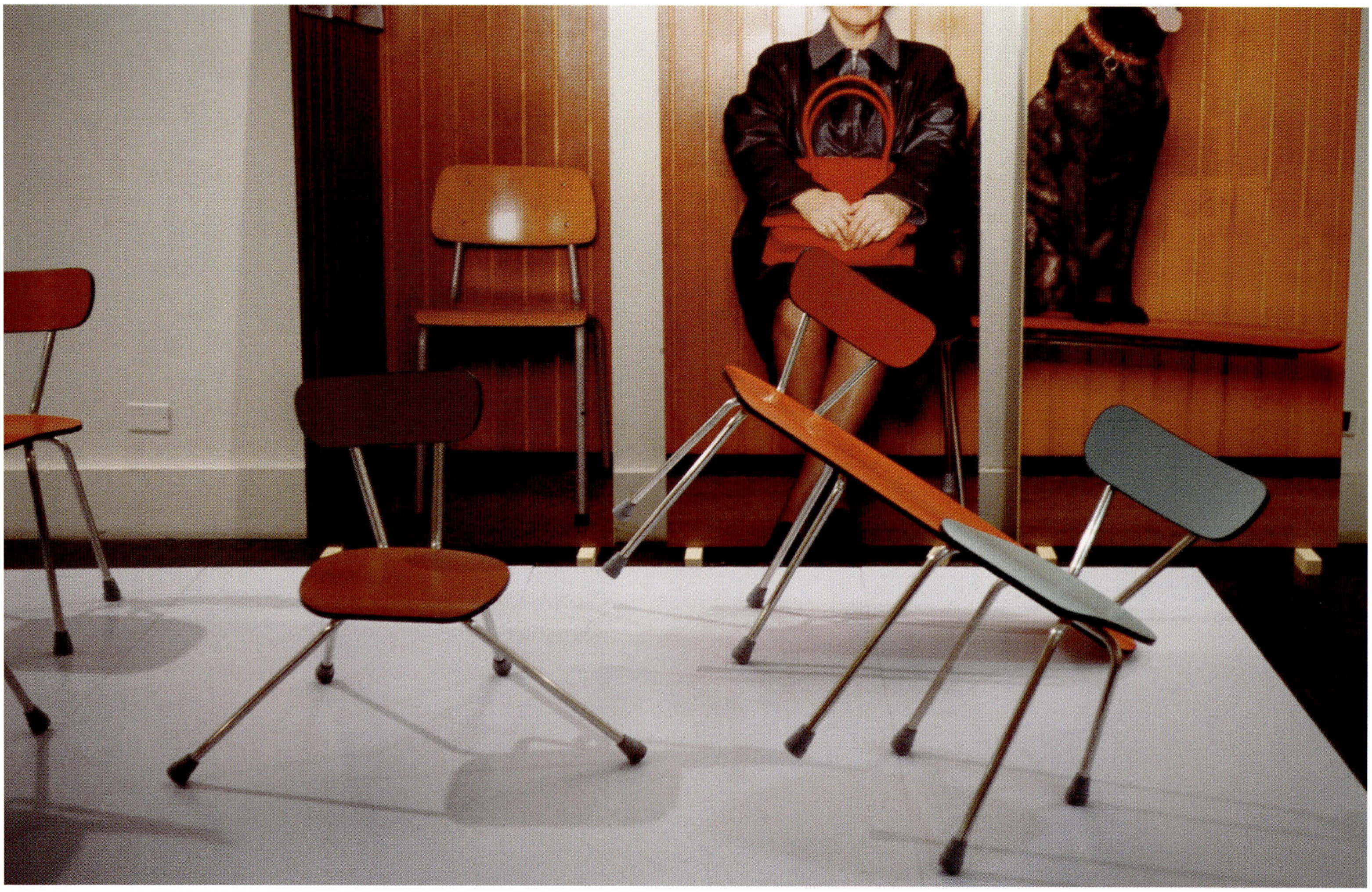

1

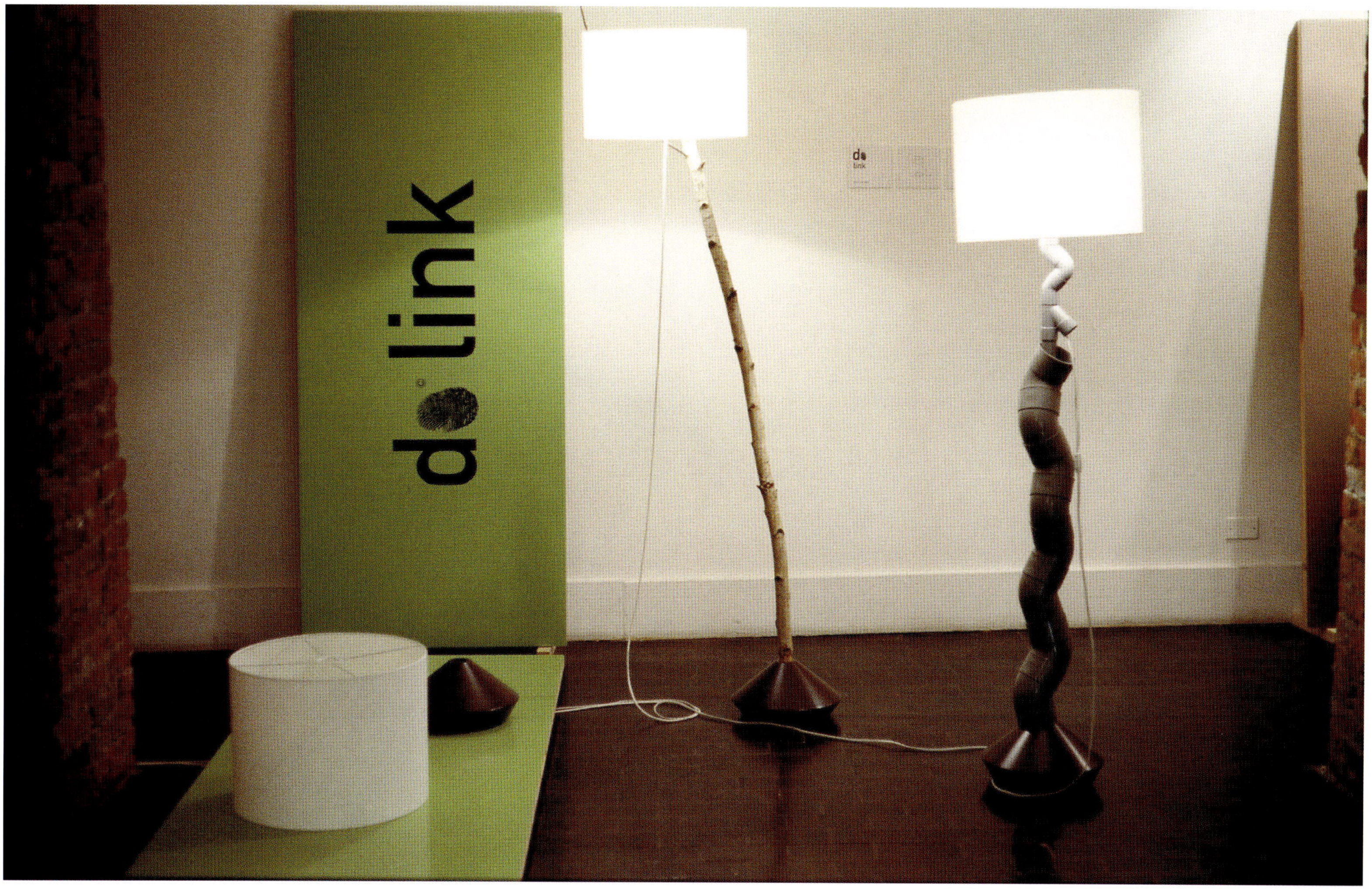
do link

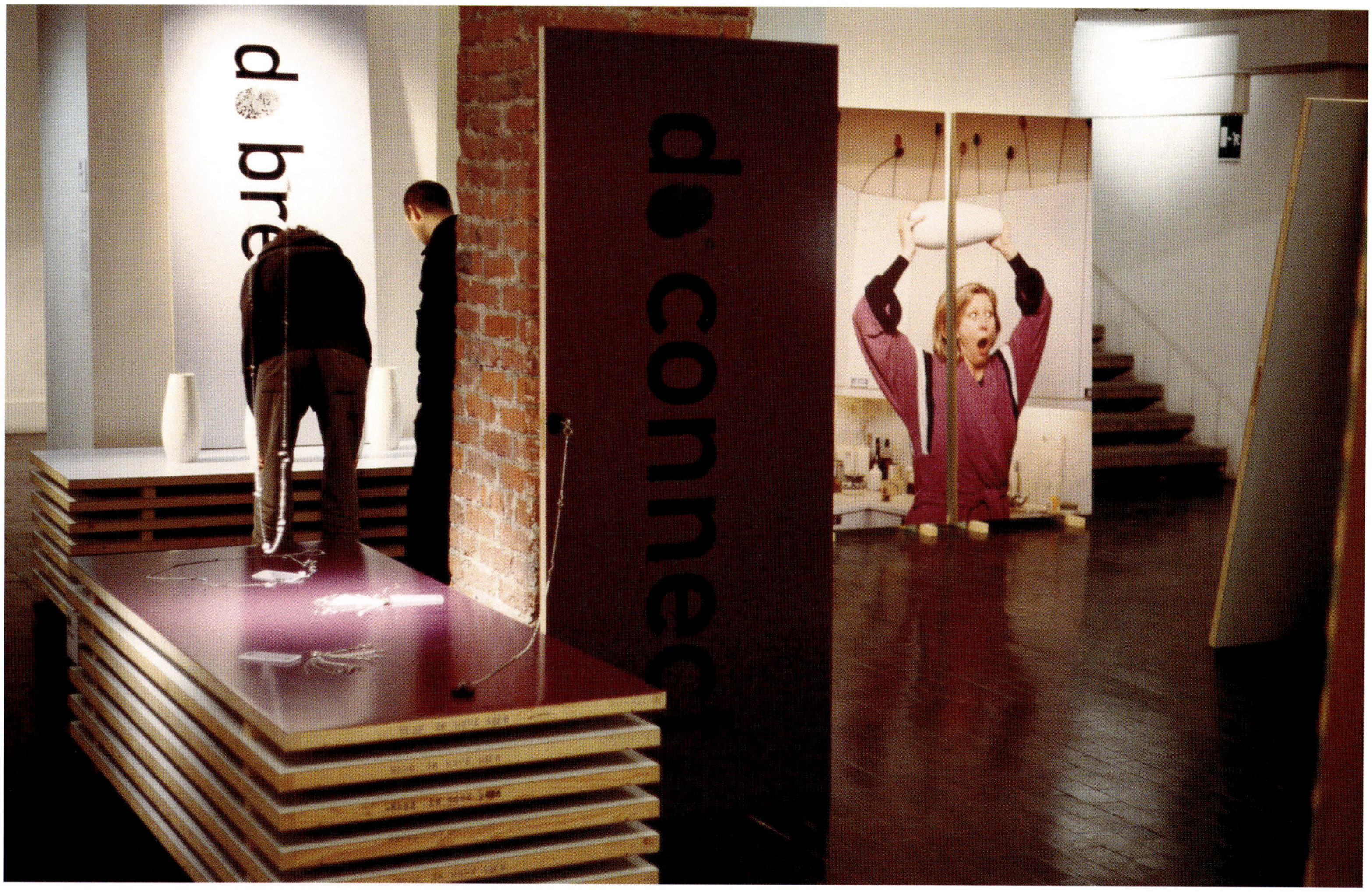
do bre
do connec

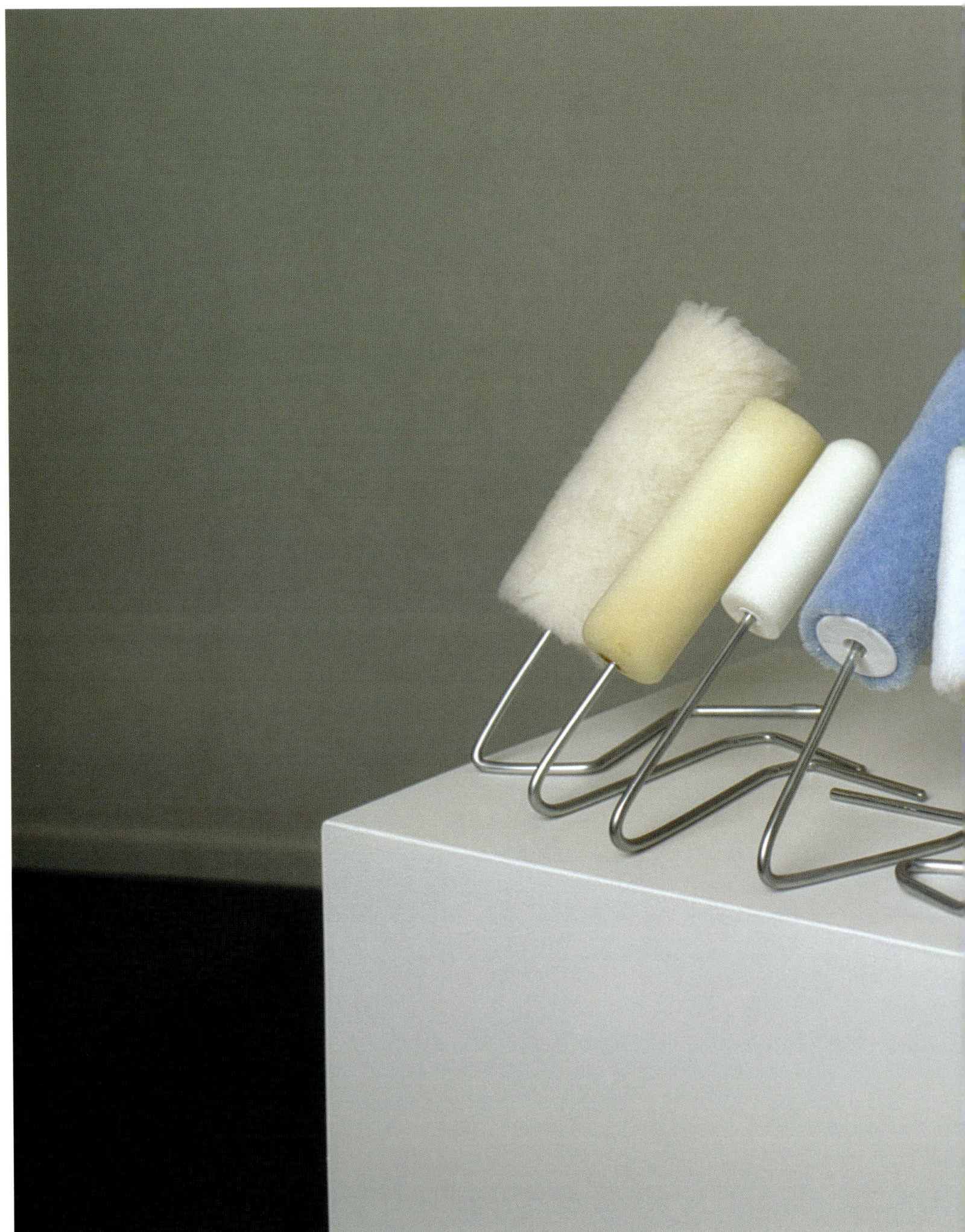

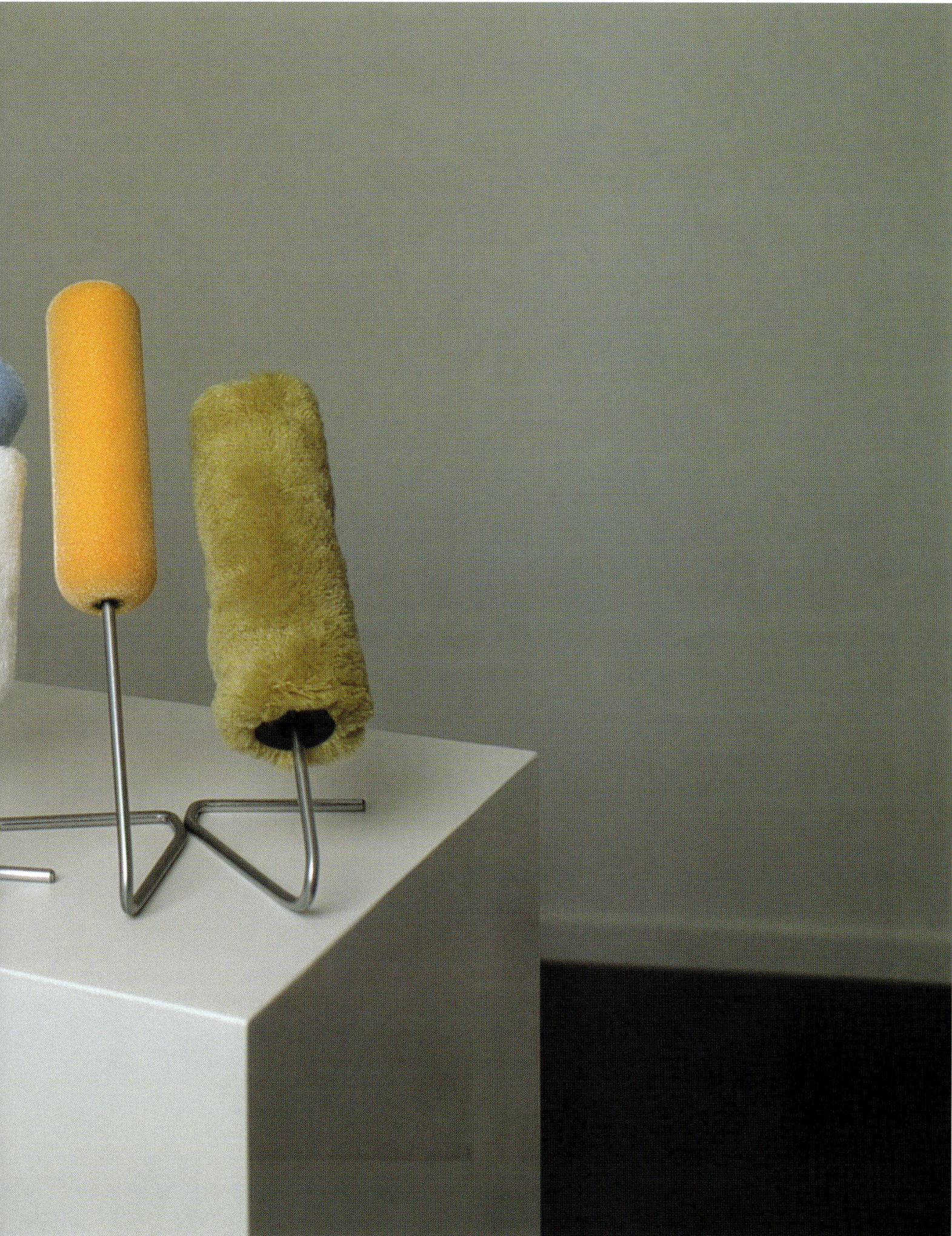

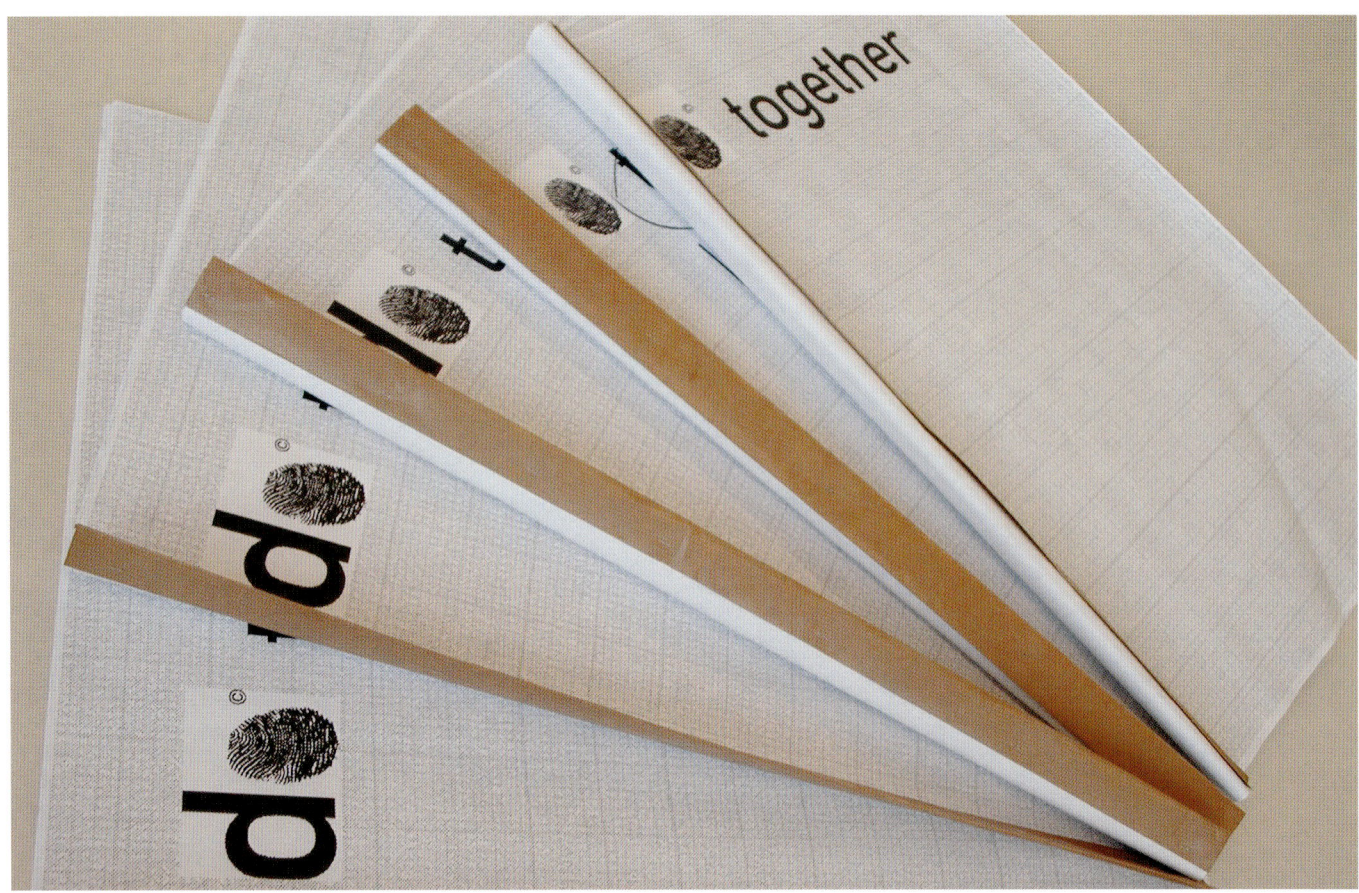

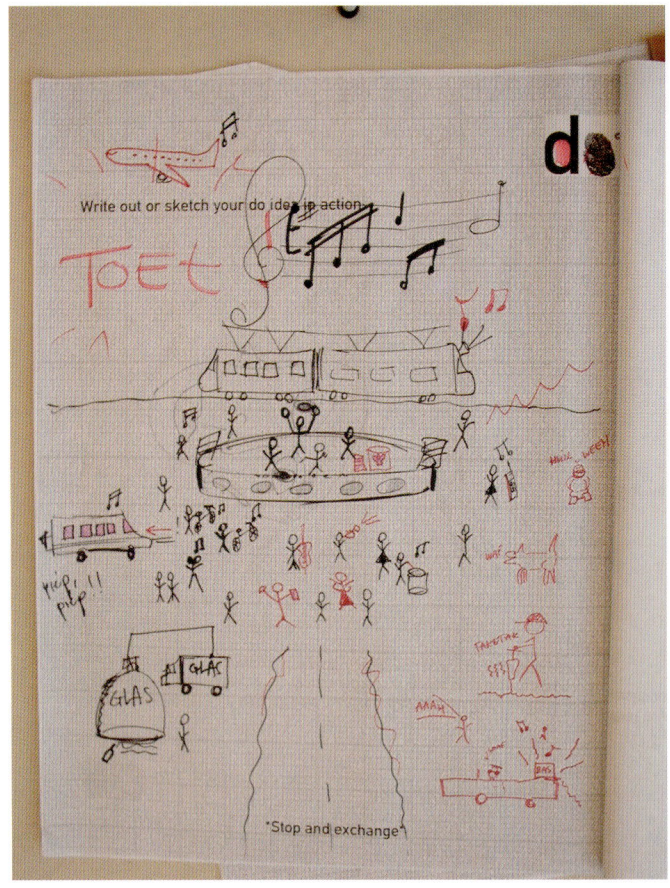

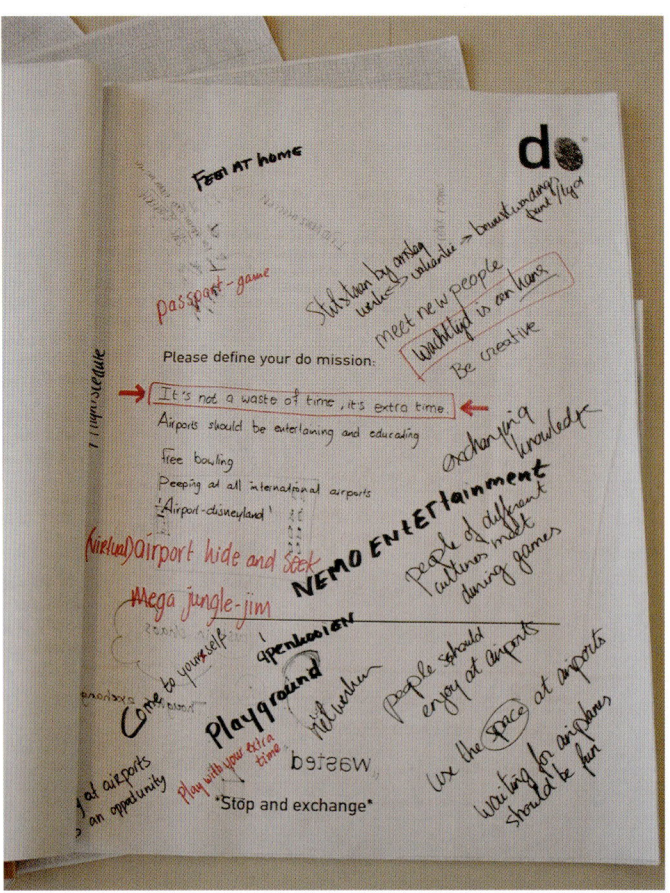

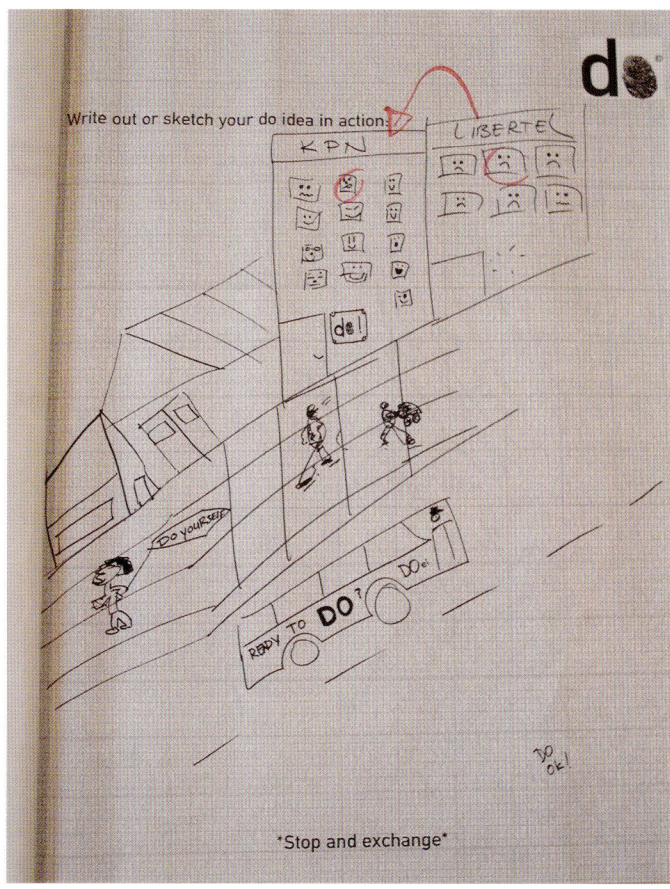

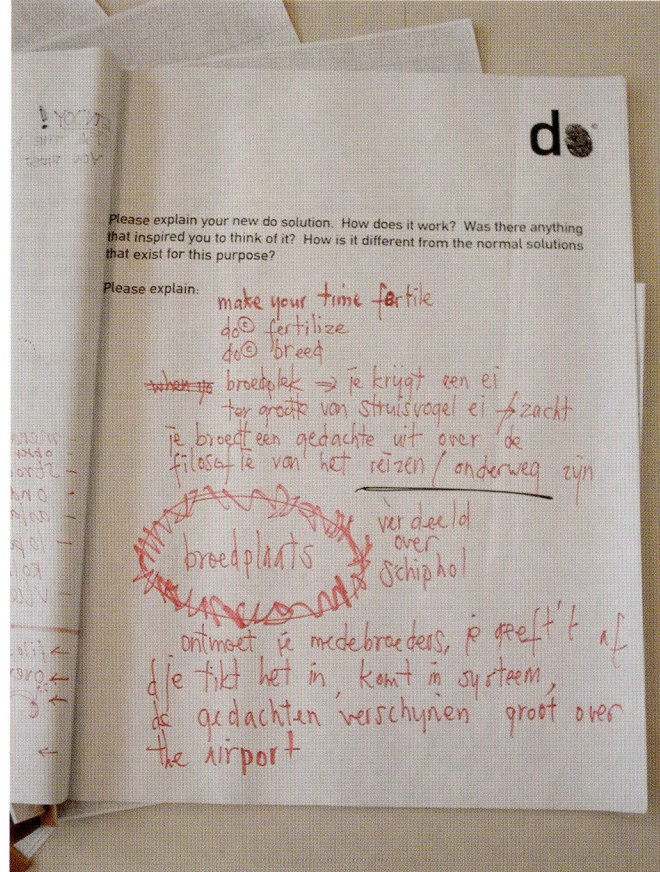

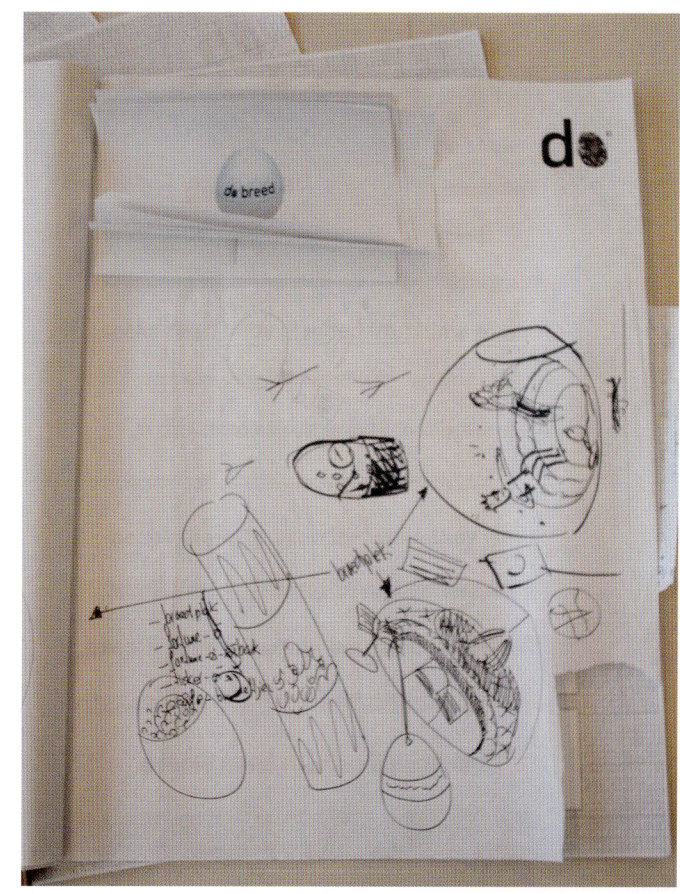

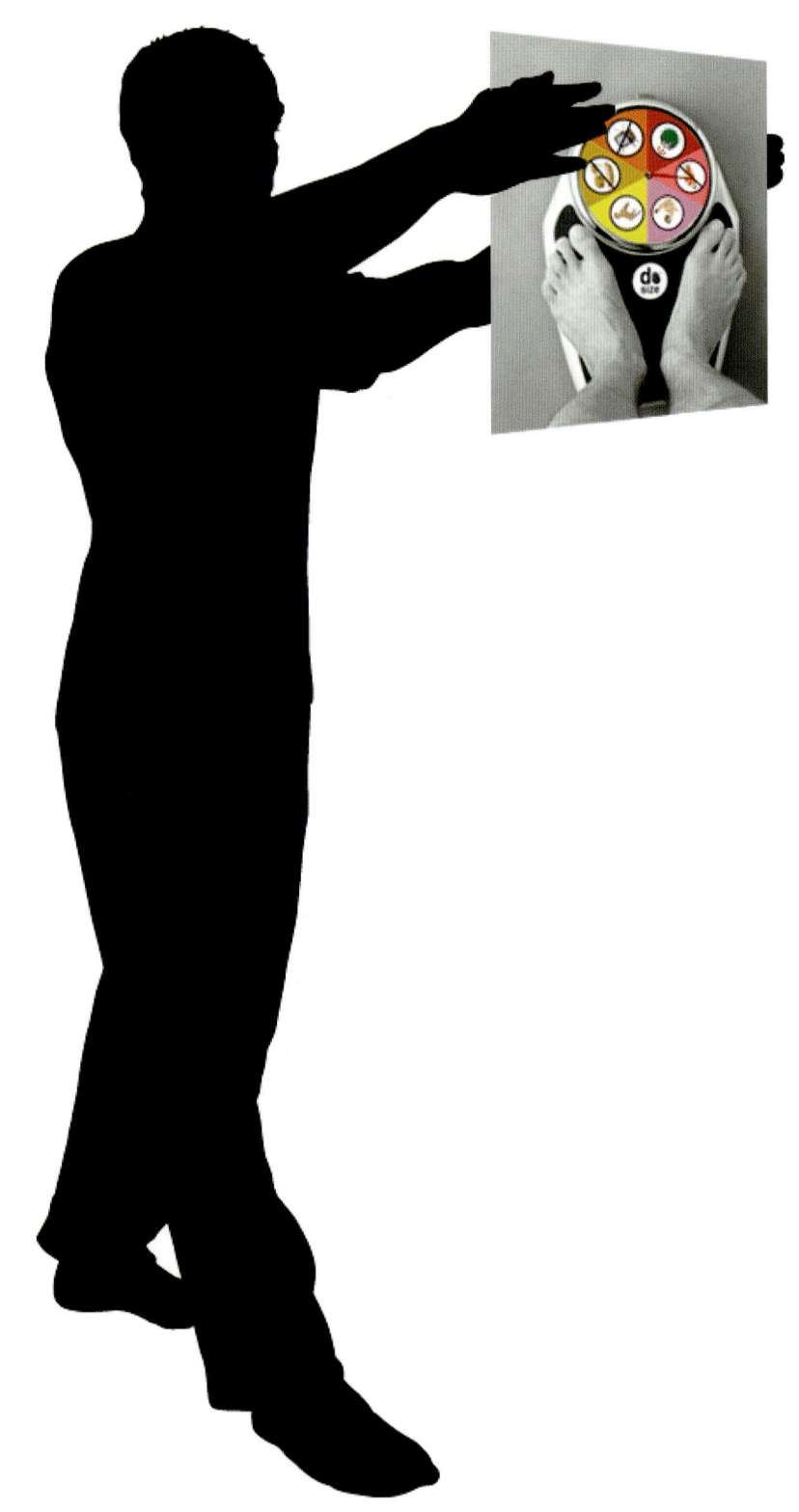

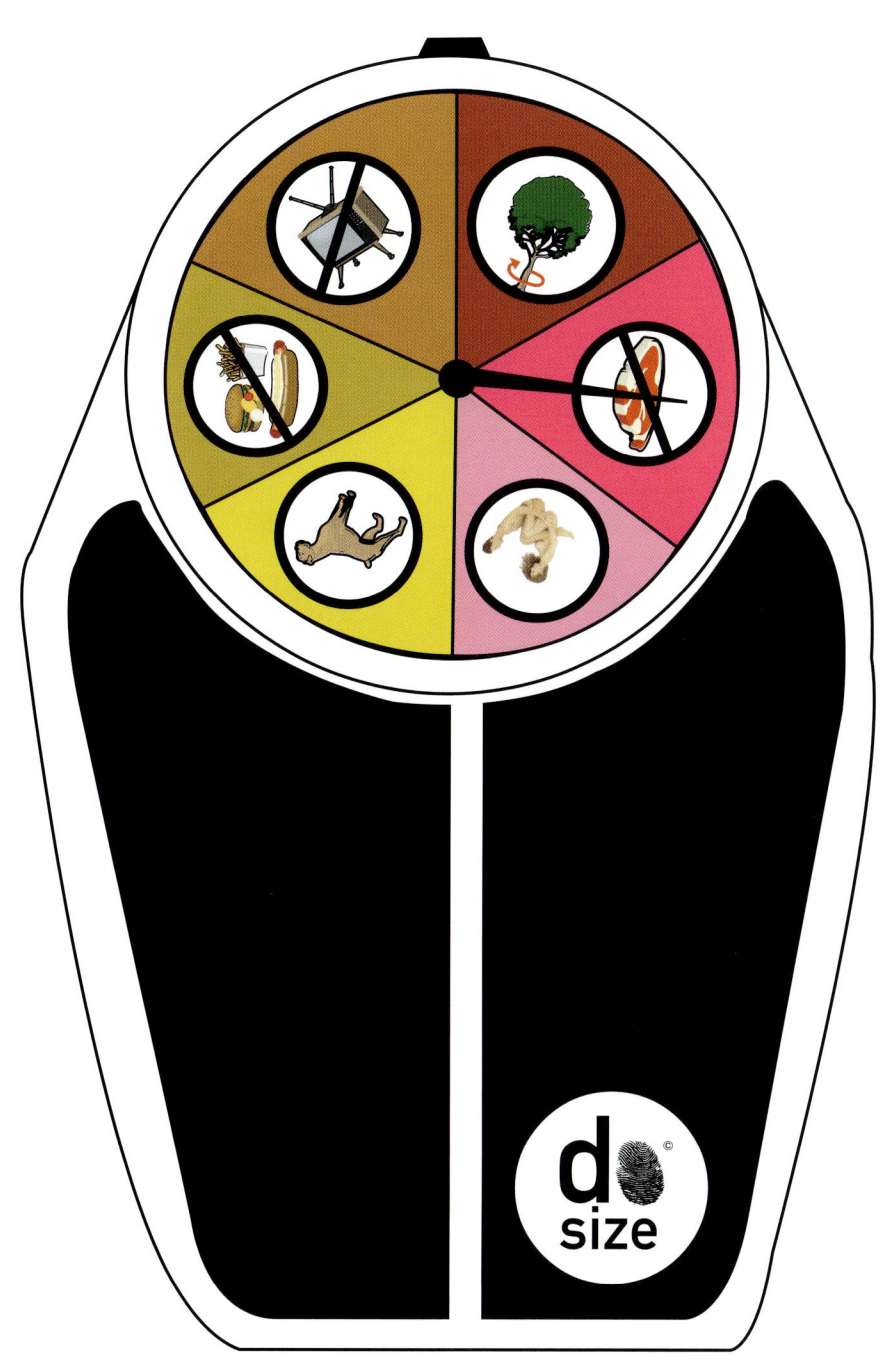

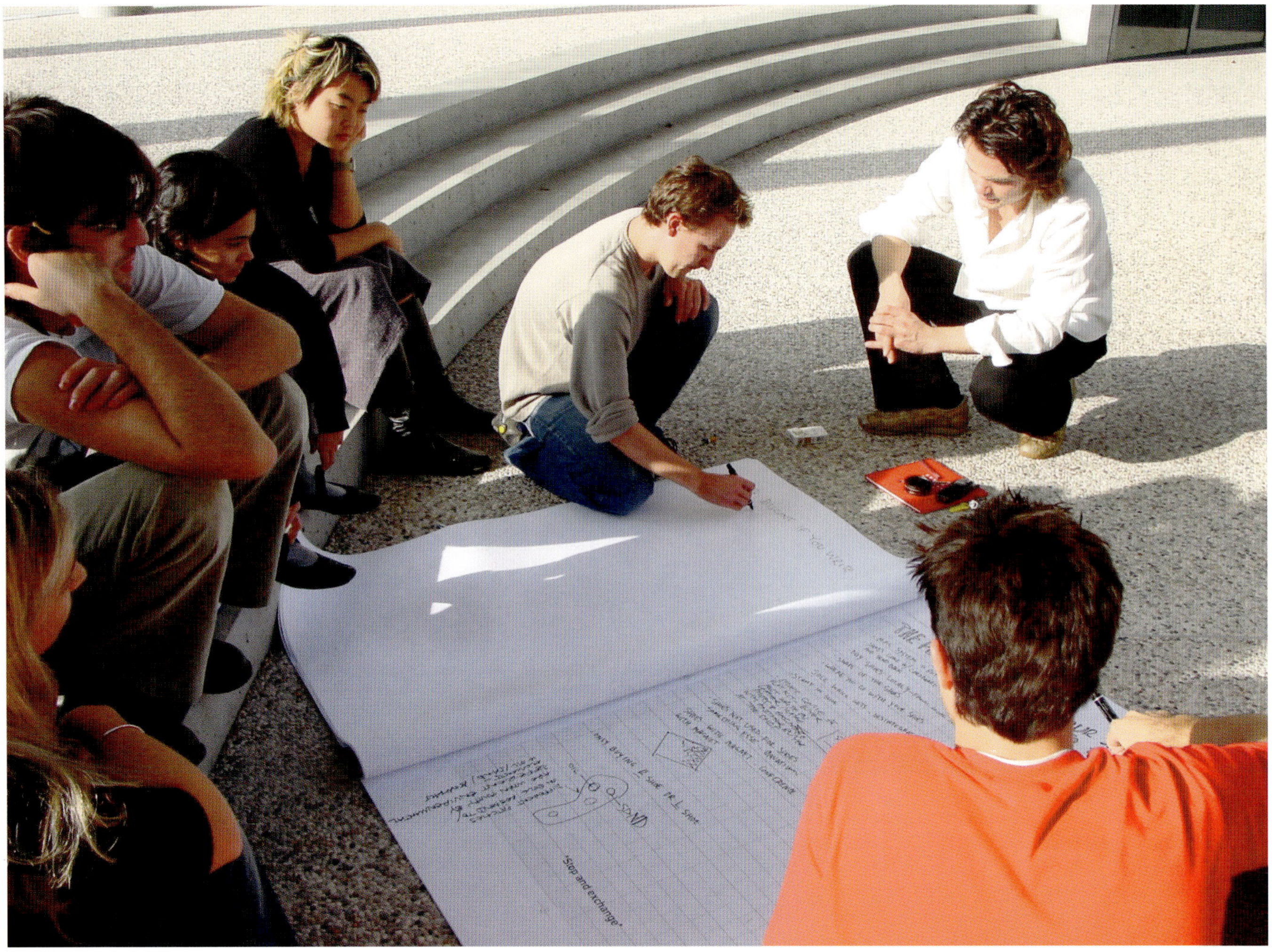
'Stop and exchange'

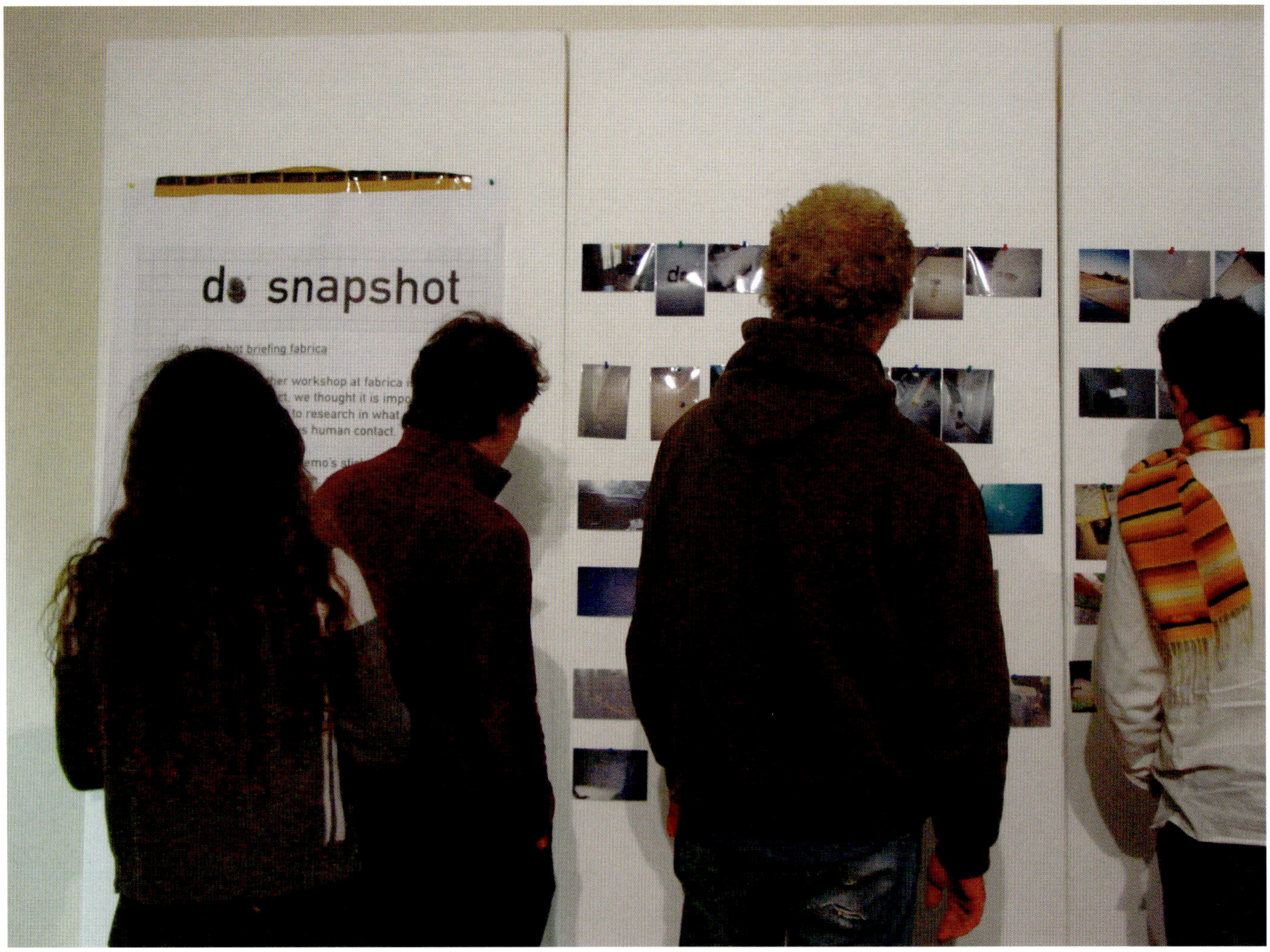
do snapshot

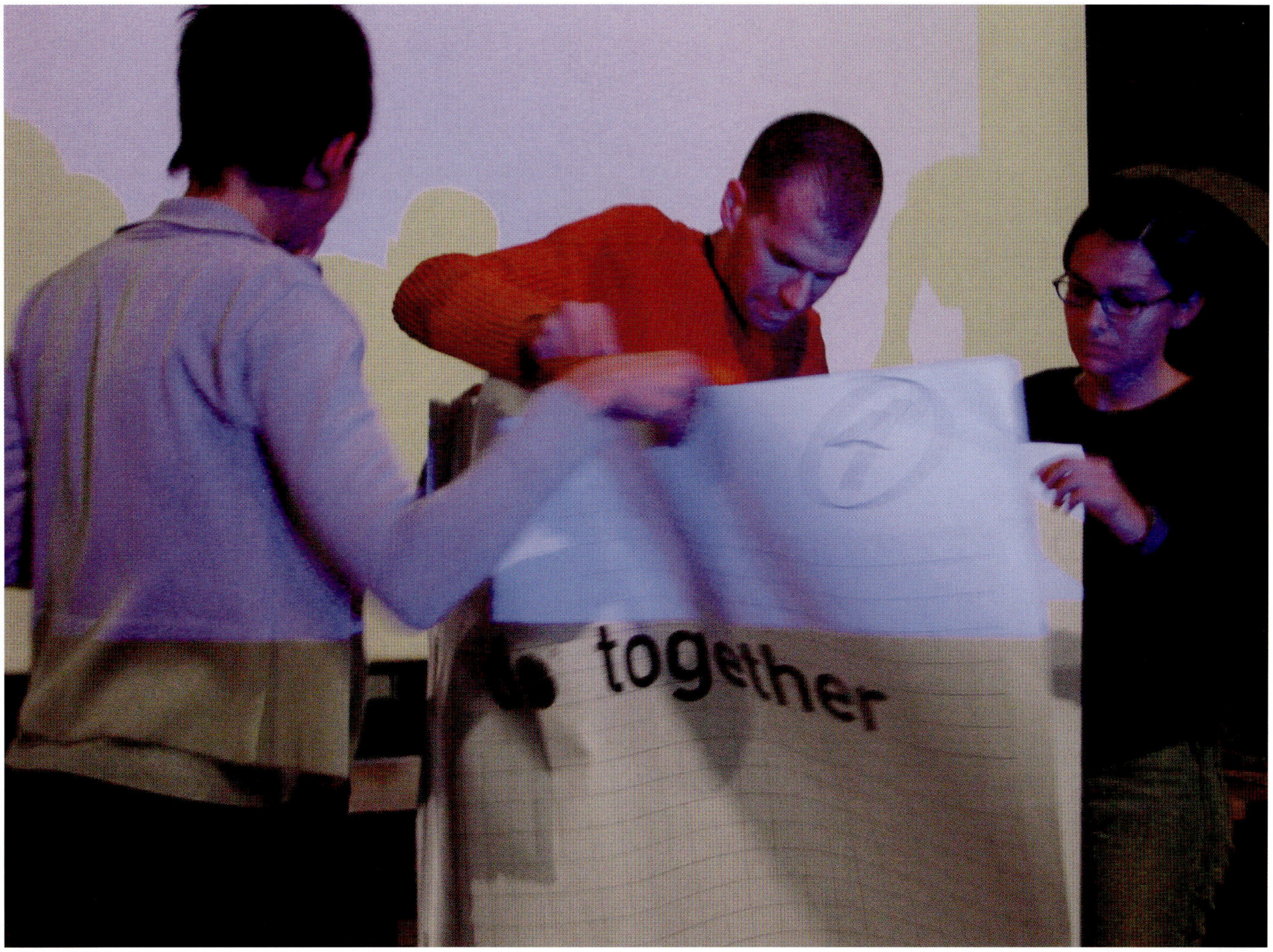
together

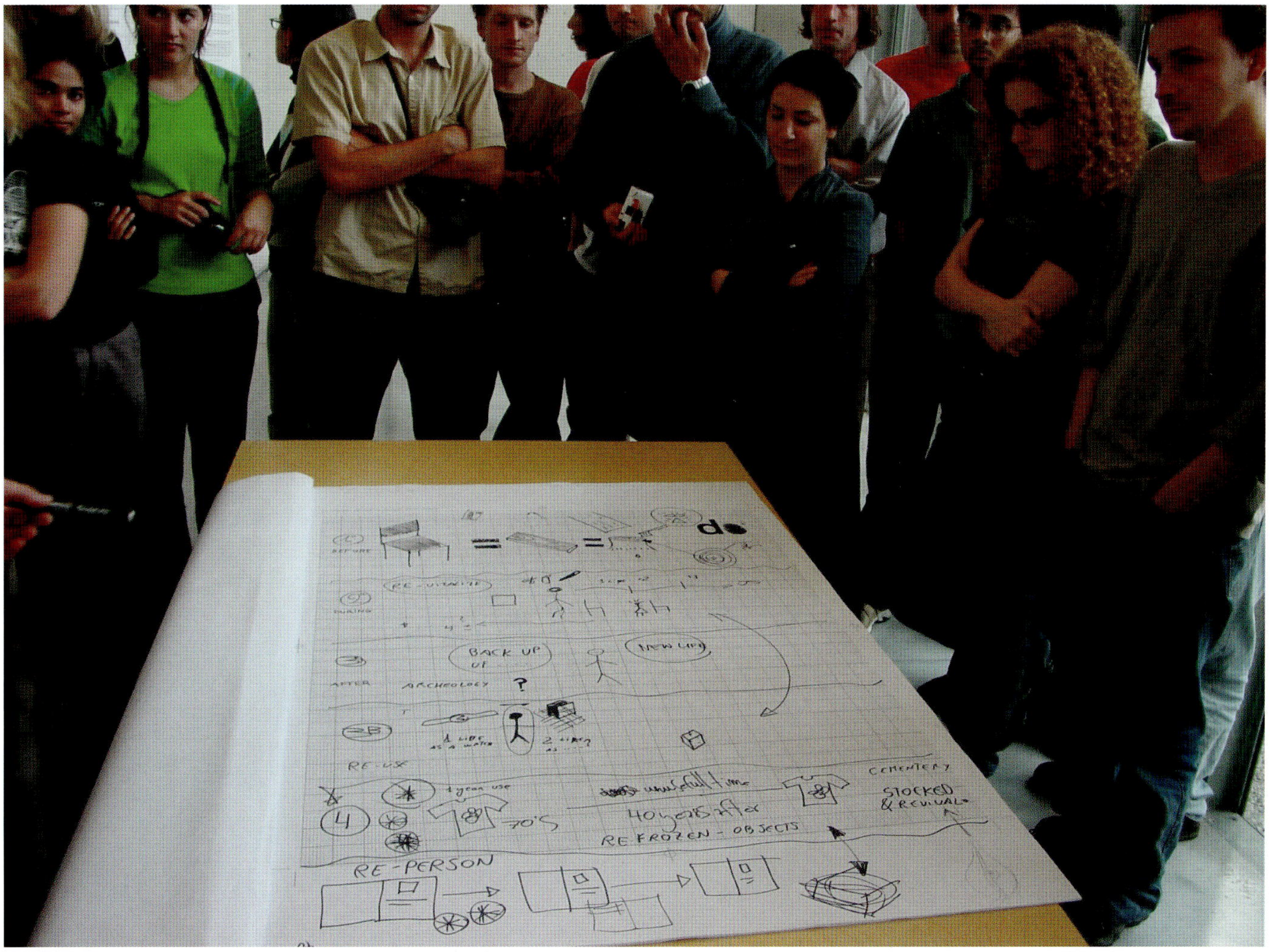
BACK UP
ARCHEOLOGY
RE-USE
CEMENTERY
STOCKED & REVIVALS
70'S
40 years after
RE FROZEN - OBJECTS
RE-PERSON

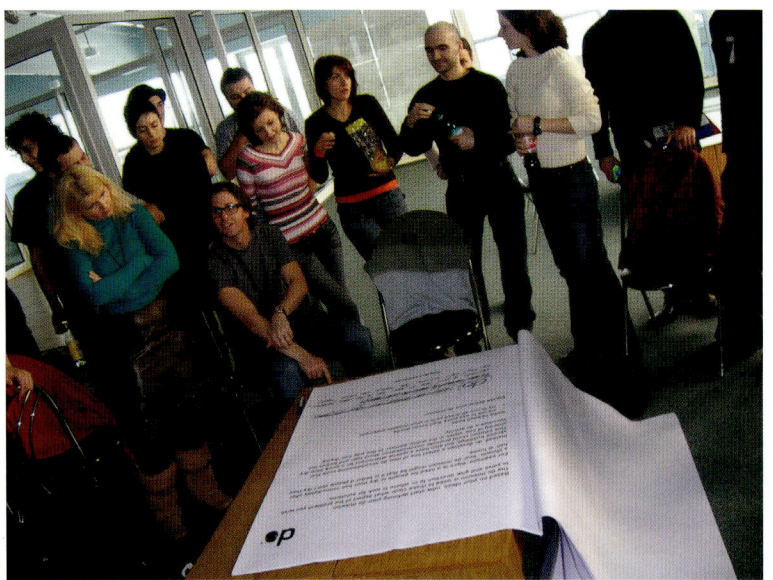

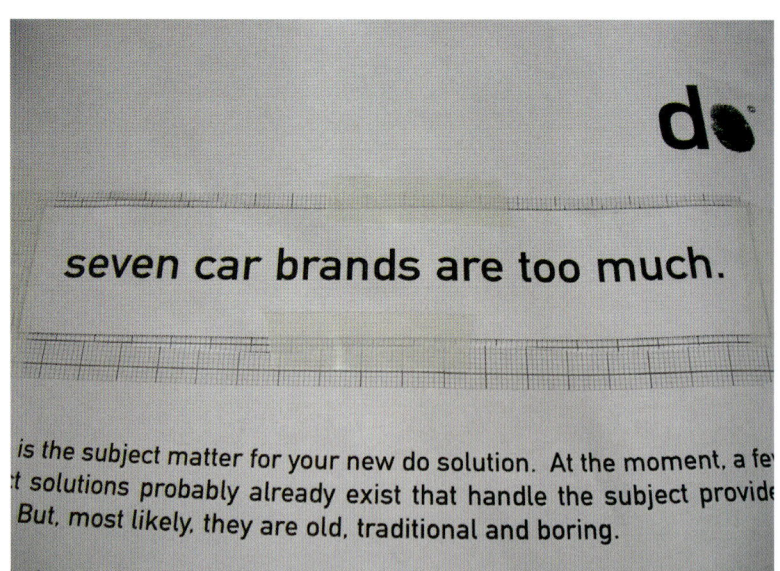

seven car brands are too much.

is the subject matter for your new do solution. At the moment, a fe...
...t solutions probably already exist that handle the subject provide...
...But, most likely, they are old, traditional and boring.

...ution that comes...

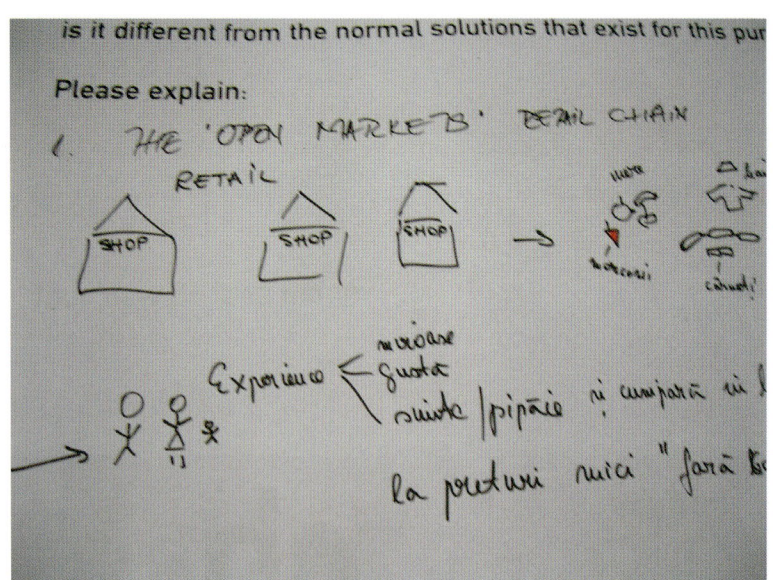

is it different from the normal solutions that exist for this pur...

Please explain:

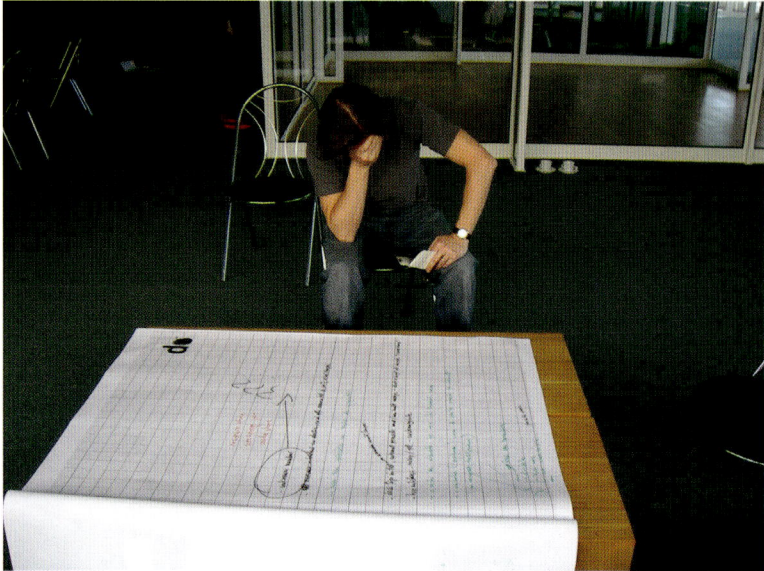

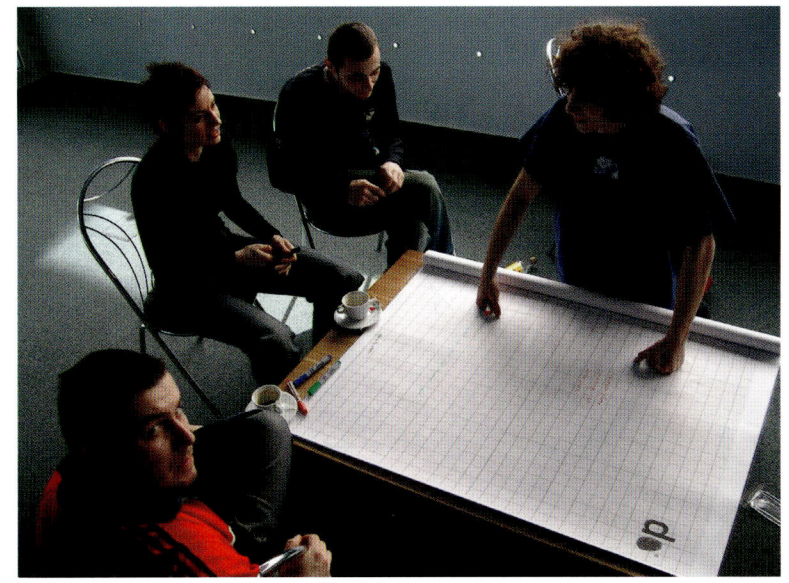

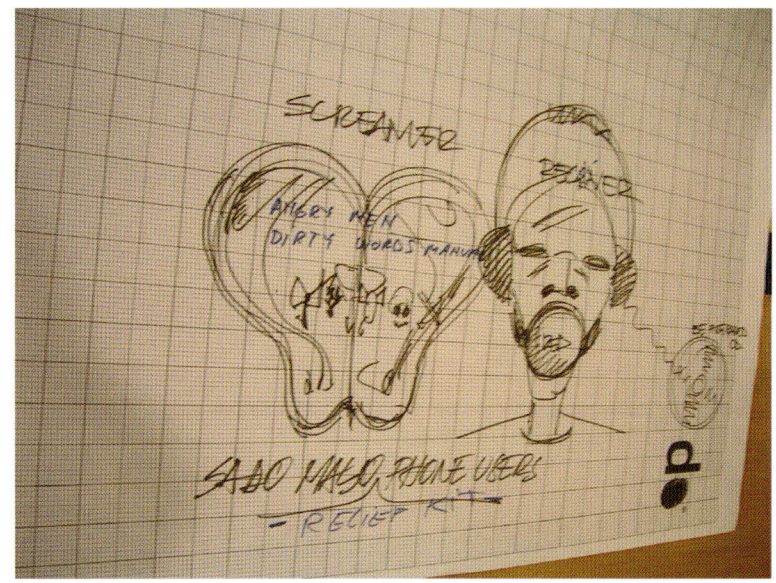

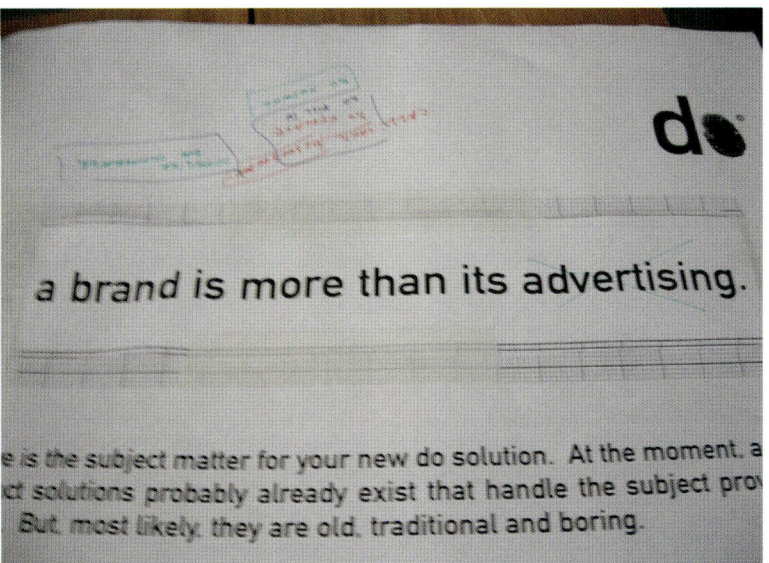

a brand is more than its advertising.

e is the subject matter for your new do solution. At the moment, a
ct solutions probably already exist that handle the subject prov
But, most likely, they are old, traditional and boring.

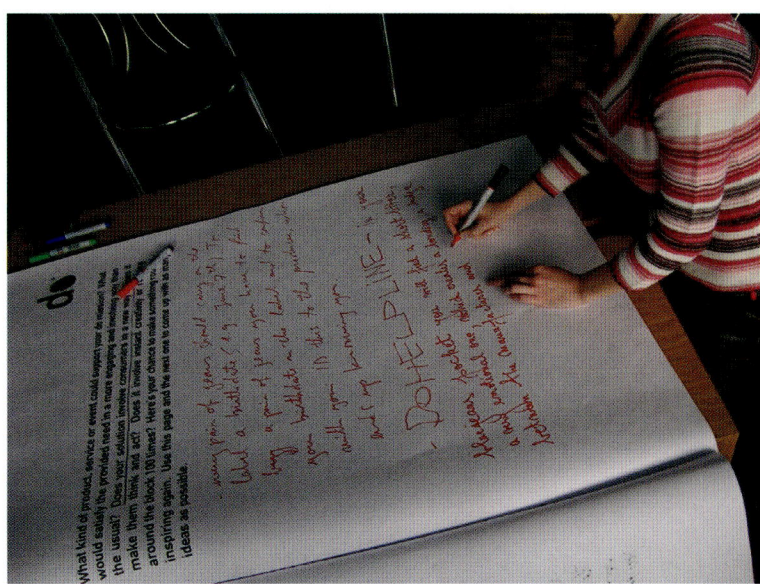

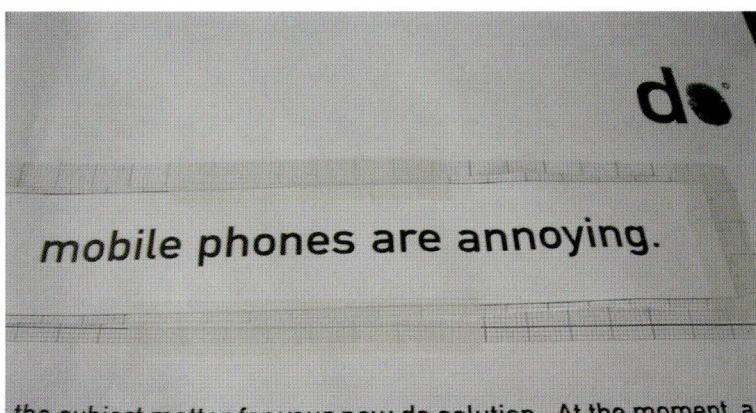

mobile phones are annoying.

the subject matter for your new do solution. At the moment, a
solutions probably already exist that handle the subject prov
ut, most likely, they are old, traditional and boring.

on that comes out of this subject area can be a product, s

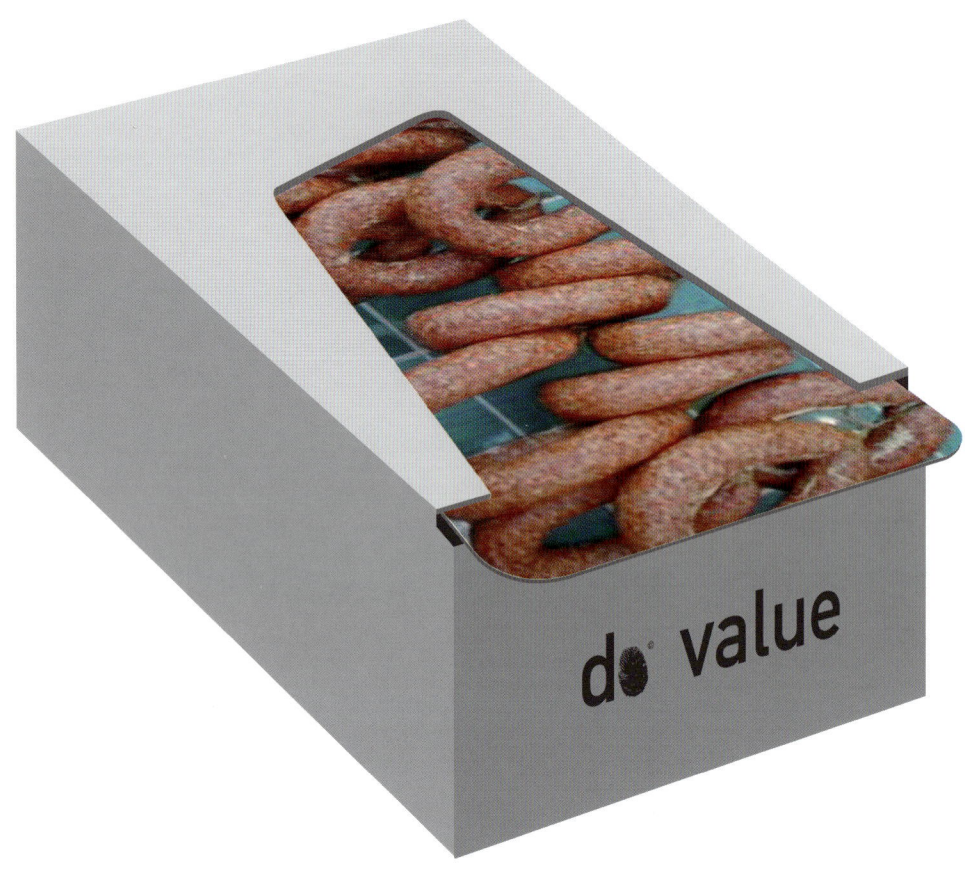

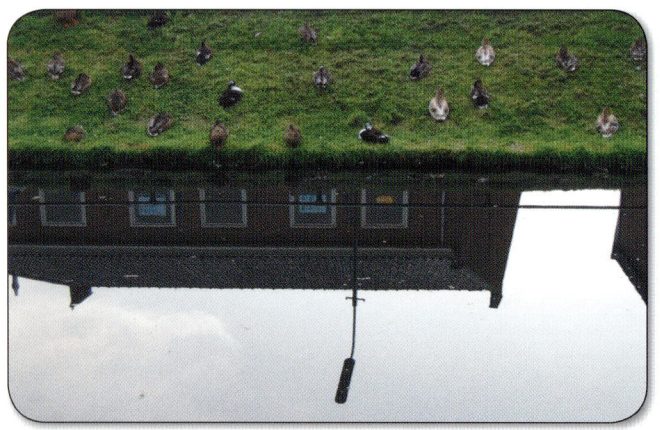

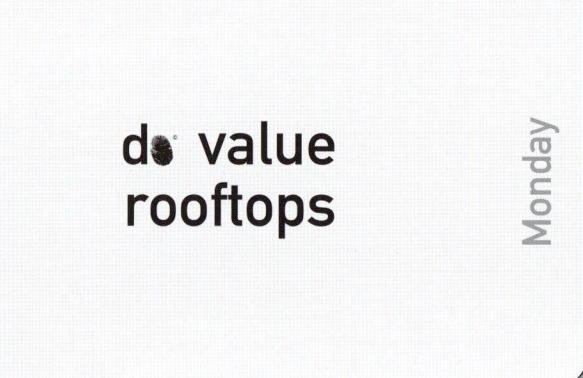

do value
rooftops

Monday

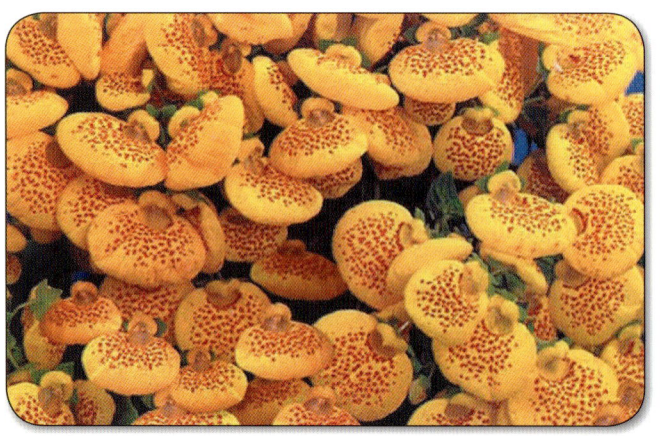

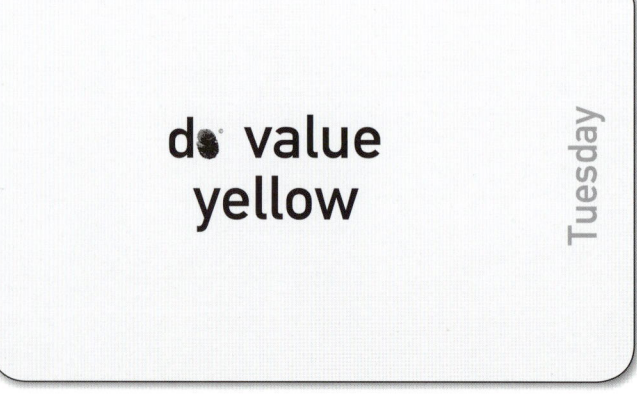

do value
yellow

Tuesday

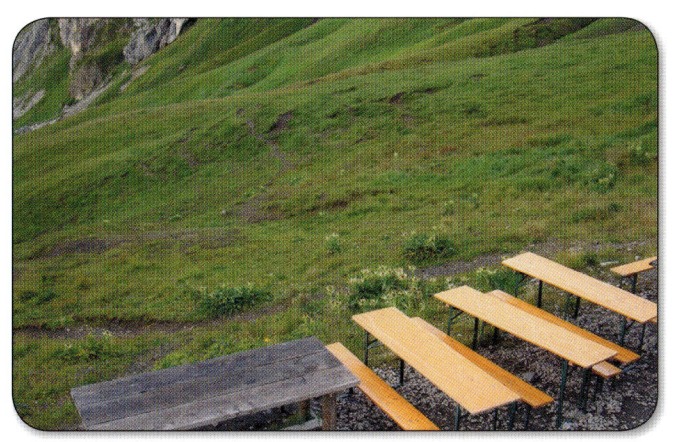

do value
stripes

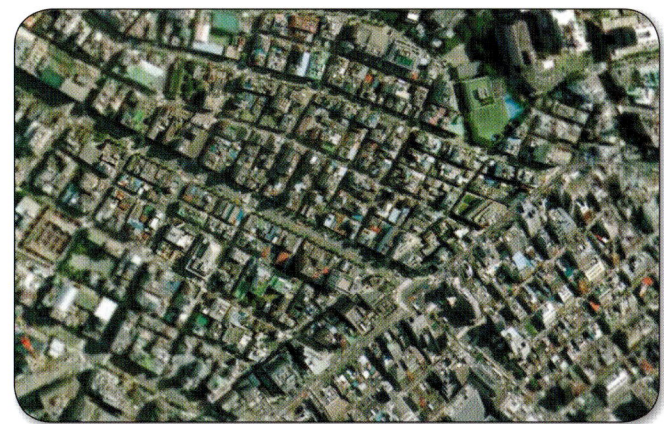

do value
two minutes

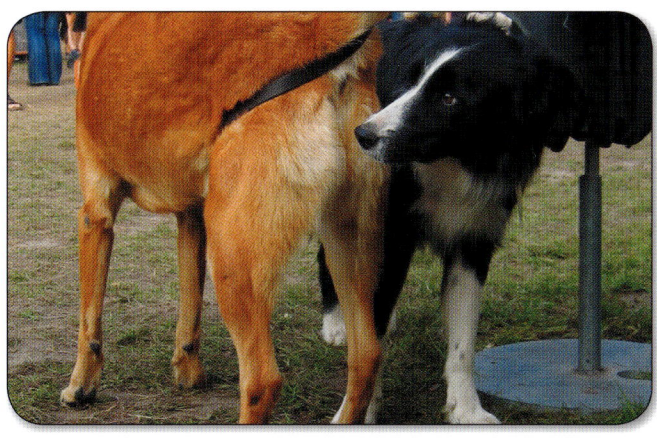

do value
signatures

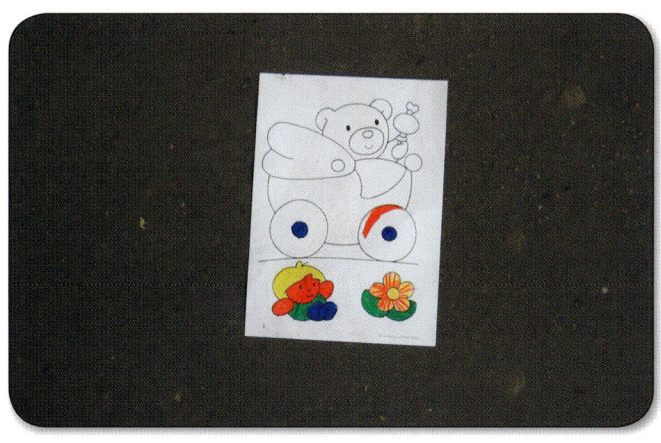

do value
a guy named Mark

"What if Africa were the Ruling Centre of the Wor

Renz
President and Founder

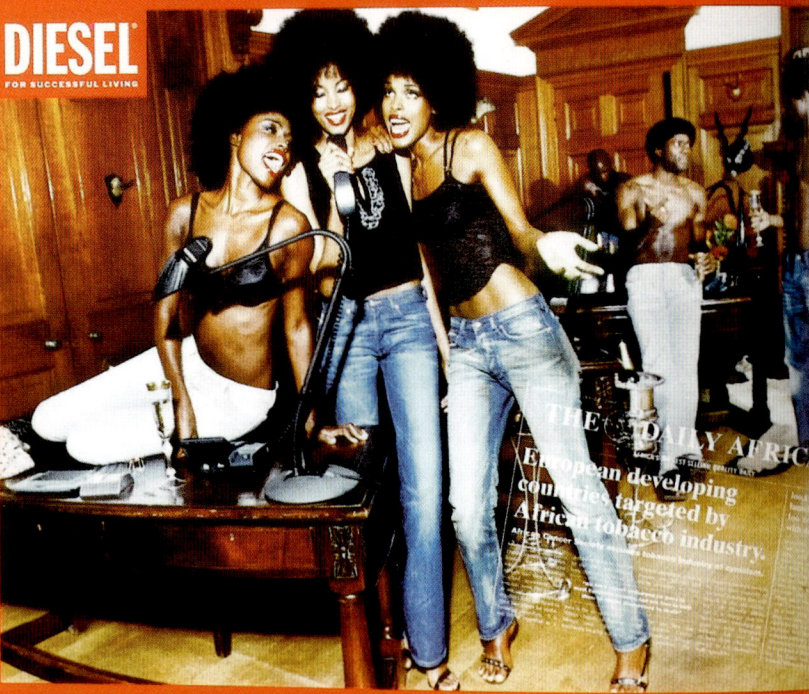

do share

is an experiment from do, an ever-changing brand that depends on what you do. For more, dosurf.com

In 1999, the world gross national product was US$ 29.2 trillion. If we divided that evenly amongst the planet's 6 billion inhabitants, everyone would get US$ 4,890 a year to live on.

We are not taking into consideration the cost of living in each country, the number of children per household, or the problems that would arise in performing such an experiment. We are simply saying, "What if the poor got richer, the rich became poorer, and everyone became more equal?"

How would this change your life? How would it change everyone else's?

By imagining this, perhaps you can see just how good you have it, or how your life could be improved if everyone shared a little bit of the wealth.

To help illustrate this, we found individuals and families from 13 countries who actually make the equivalent of US$ 4,890 a year. In cases where there were more than one member per household, we divided the total yearly income per household by the number of members to equal approximately $4,890, or GNP per do share. We then compared this to the real GNP per capita in each country.

Ethiopia	100 USD / 814.80 ETB
Rwanda	250 USD / 89,757 RWF
Sudan	330 USD / 84,615.38 SDD
India	450 USD / 21,008.40 INR
Egypt	1,400 USD / 5,249.34 EGP
Russia	2,270 USD / 63,129.21 RUR
South Africa	3,160 USD / 23,993.93 ZAR
Mexico	4,400 USD / 42,389.21 MXP
do share	4,890 USD
England	22,640 USD / 15,596.70 GBP
Netherlands	24,320 USD / 63,739.61 NLG
USA	30,600 USD
Japan	32,230 USD / 3,503,401.00 JPY
Switzerland	38,350 USD / 69,237.09 CHF

0   5   10   15   20   25   30   35 $1,000/year

1999 GNP per capita

Sources: All country data courtesy of World Bank national accounts data, and OECD national accounts data files (www.worldbank.org).
Exchange rates courtesy of Xenon Labs (www.xe.net/ucc).

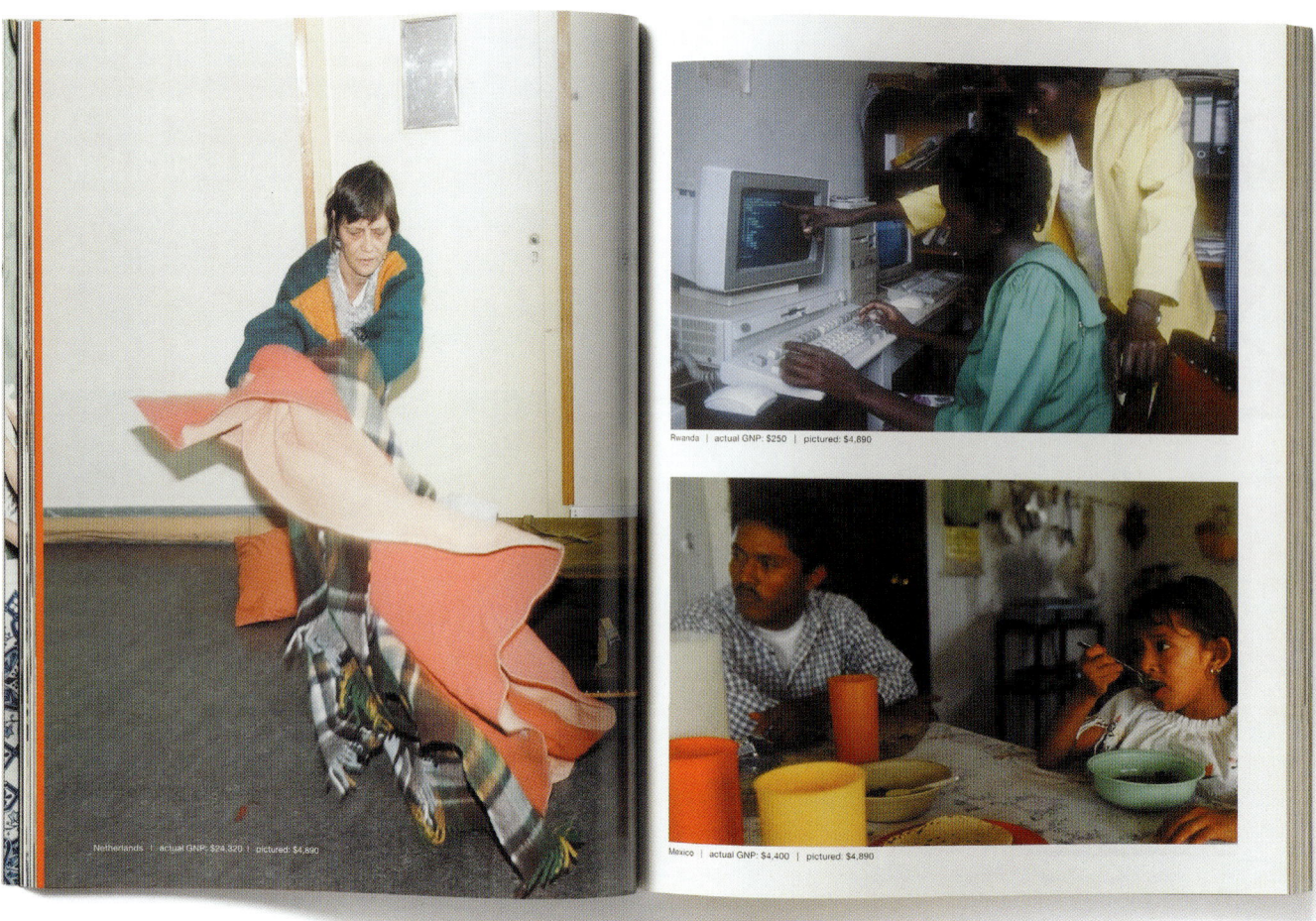

Netherlands | actual GNP: $24,320 | pictured: $4,890

Rwanda | actual GNP: $250 | pictured: $4,890

Mexico | actual GNP: $4,400 | pictured: $4,890

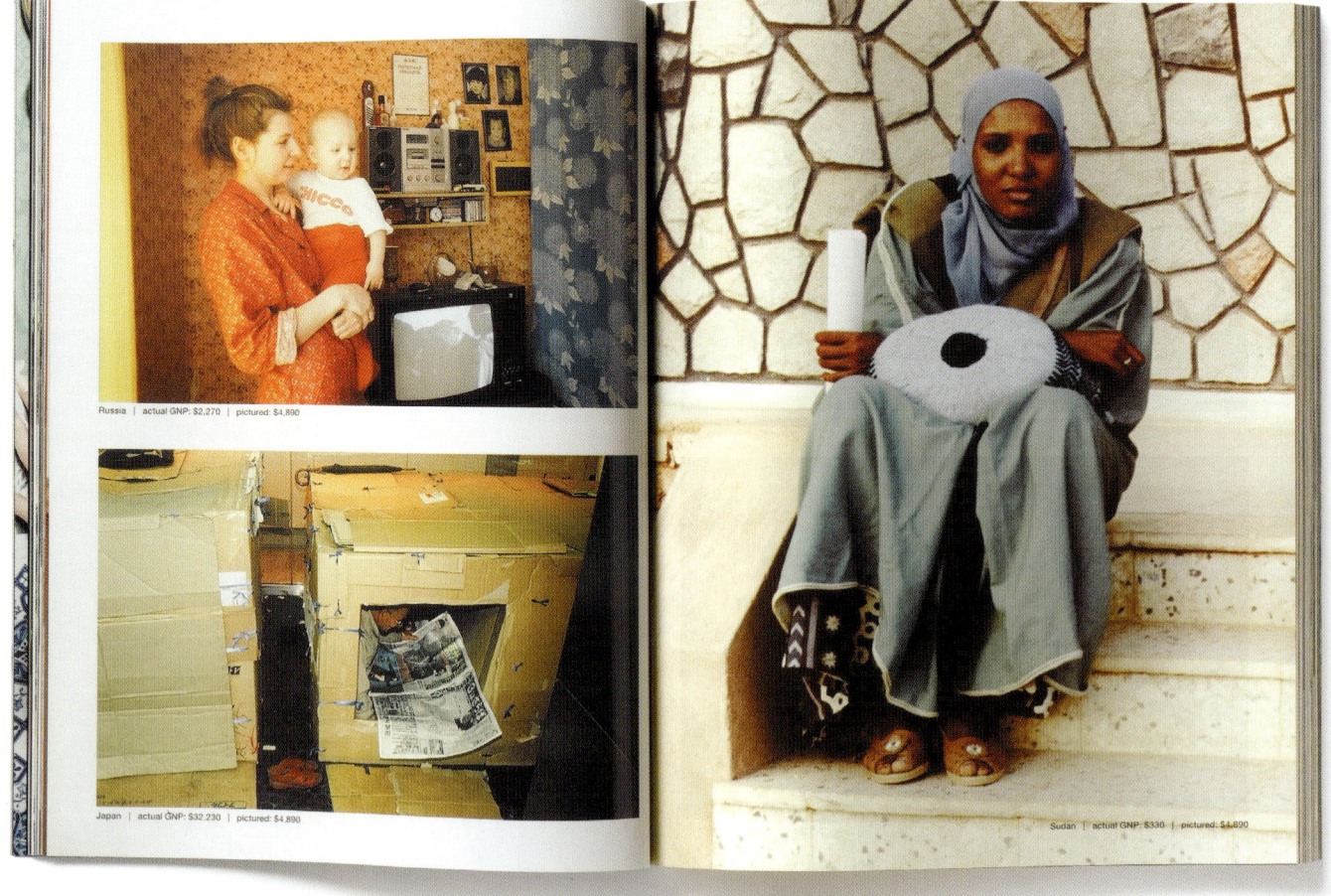

Russia | actual GNP: $2,270 | pictured: $4,890

Japan | actual GNP: $32,230 | pictured: $4,890

Sudan | actual GNP: $330 | pictured: $4,890

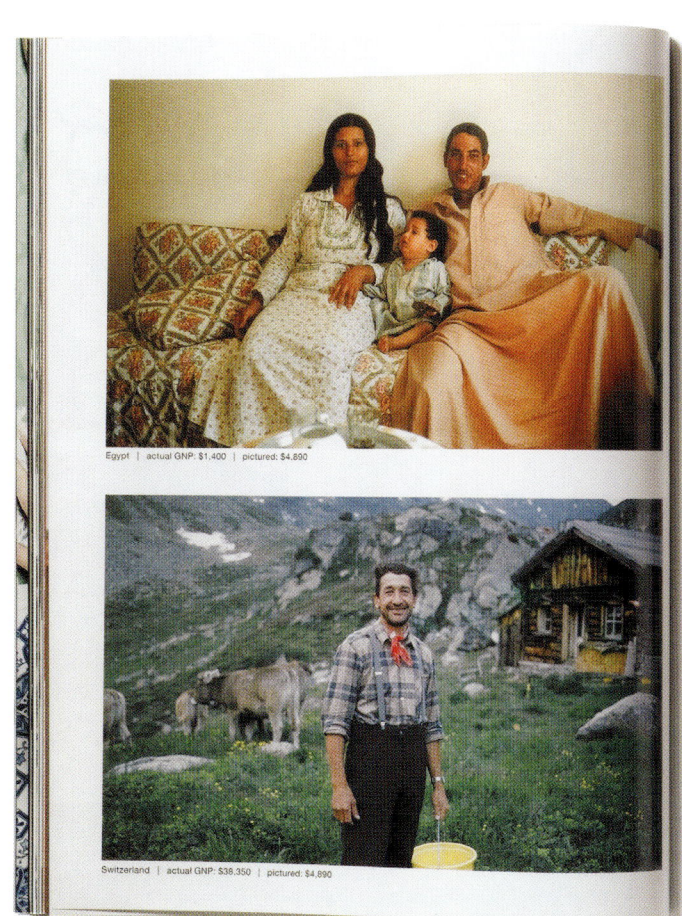

Egypt | actual GNP: $1,400 | pictured: $4,890

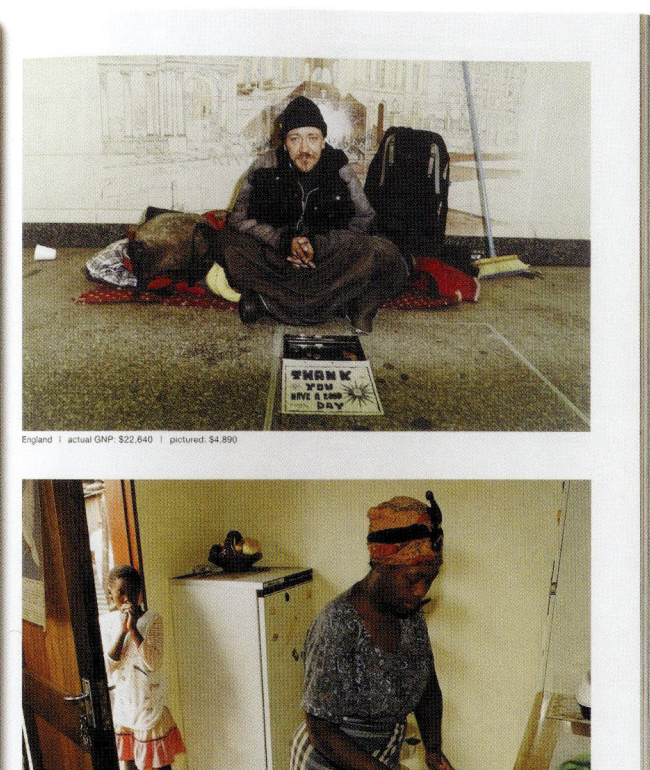

England | actual GNP: $22,640 | pictured: $4,890

Switzerland | actual GNP: $38,350 | pictured: $4,890

South Africa | actual GNP: $3,160 | pictured: $4,890

India | actual GNP: $450 | pictured: $4,890

Ethiopia | actual GNP: $100 | pictured: $4,890

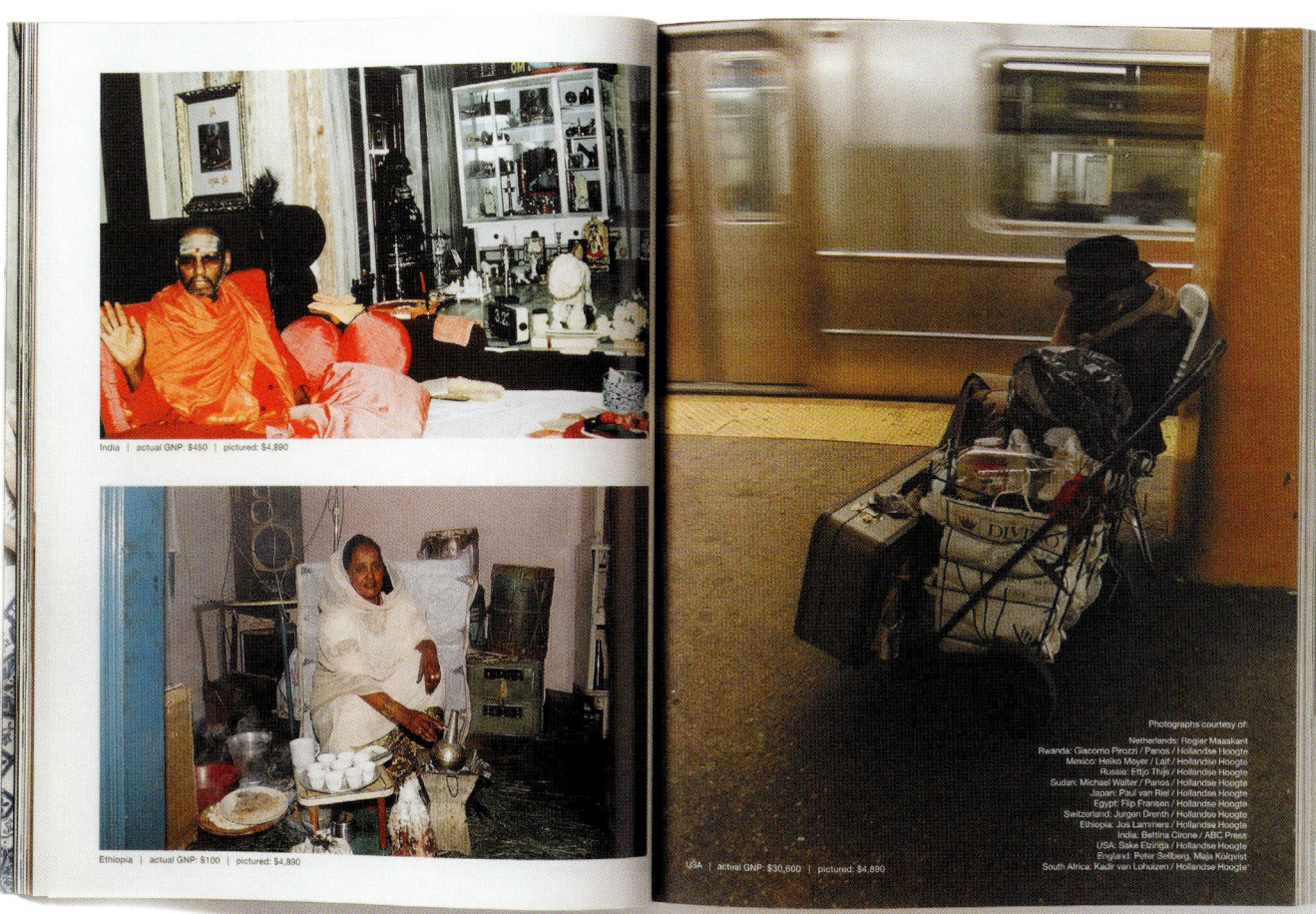

USA | actual GNP: $30,600 | pictured: $4,890

Photographs courtesy of:
Netherlands: Roger Maaskant
Rwanda: Giacomo Pirozzi / Panos / Hollandse Hoogte
Mexico: Heiko Meyer / Laif / Hollandse Hoogte
Russia: Ettjo Thijs / Hollandse Hoogte
Sudan: Michael Walter / Panos / Hollandse Hoogte
Japan: Paul van Riel / Hollandse Hoogte
Egypt: Flip Fransen / Hollandse Hoogte
Switzerland: Jurgen Drenth / Hollandse Hoogte
Ethiopia: Jos Lammers / Hollandse Hoogte
India: Bettina Cirone / ABC Press
USA: Sake Elzinga / Hollandse Hoogte
England: Peter Sellberg, Maja Kristvist
South Africa: Kadir van Lohuizen / Hollandse Hoogte

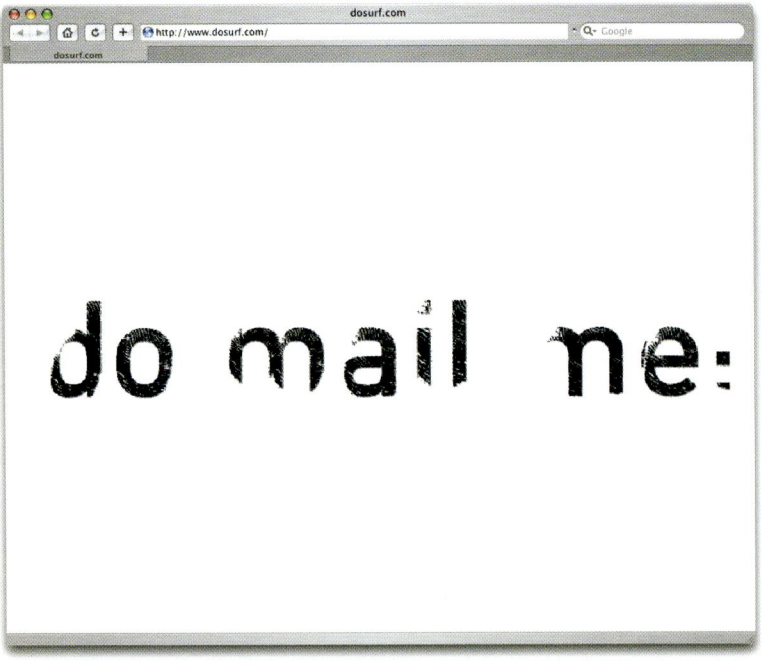

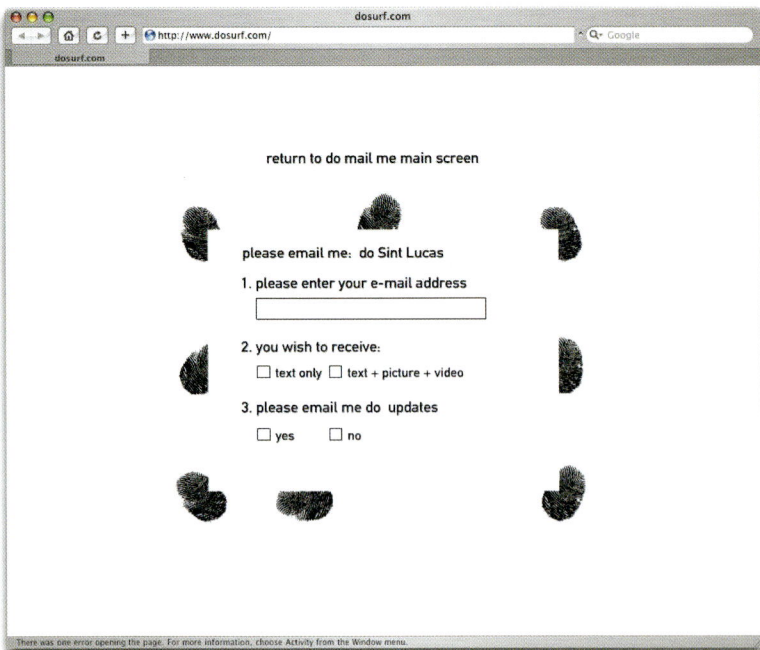

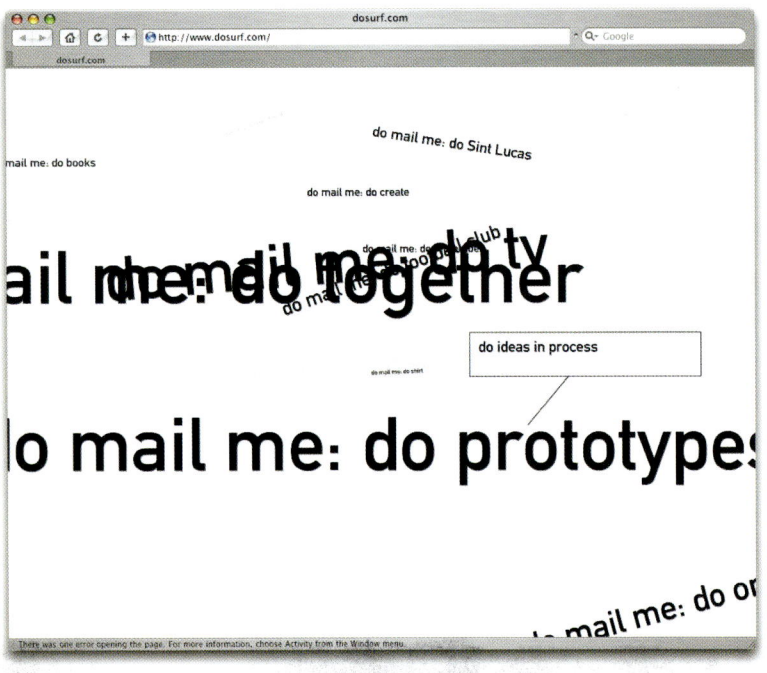

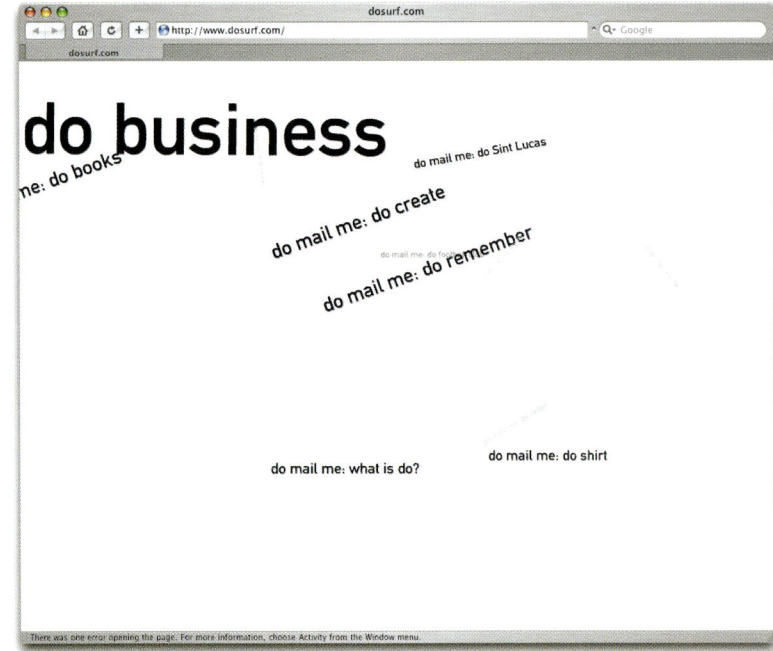

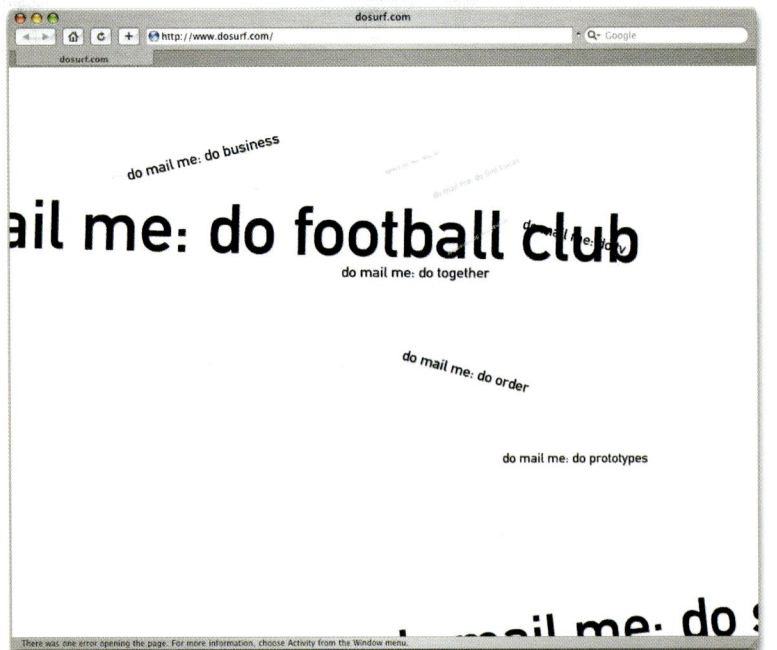

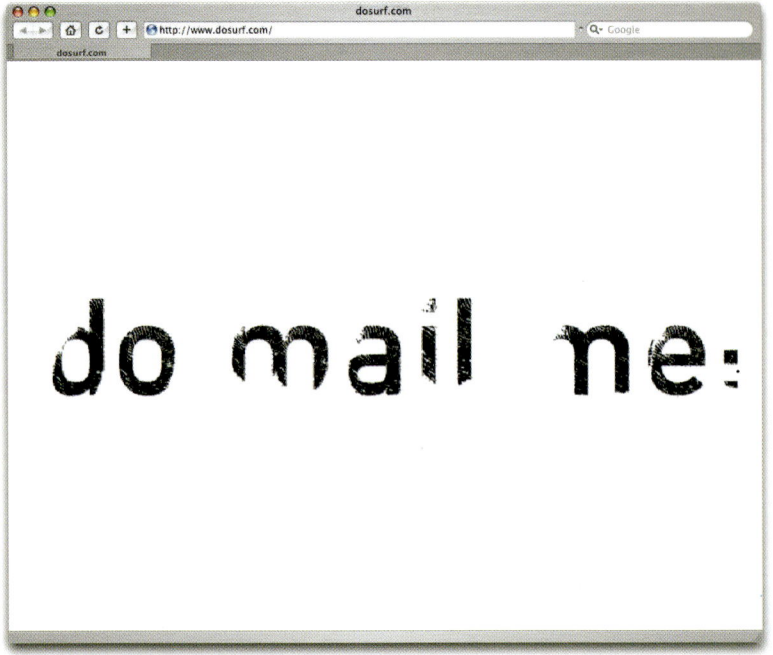

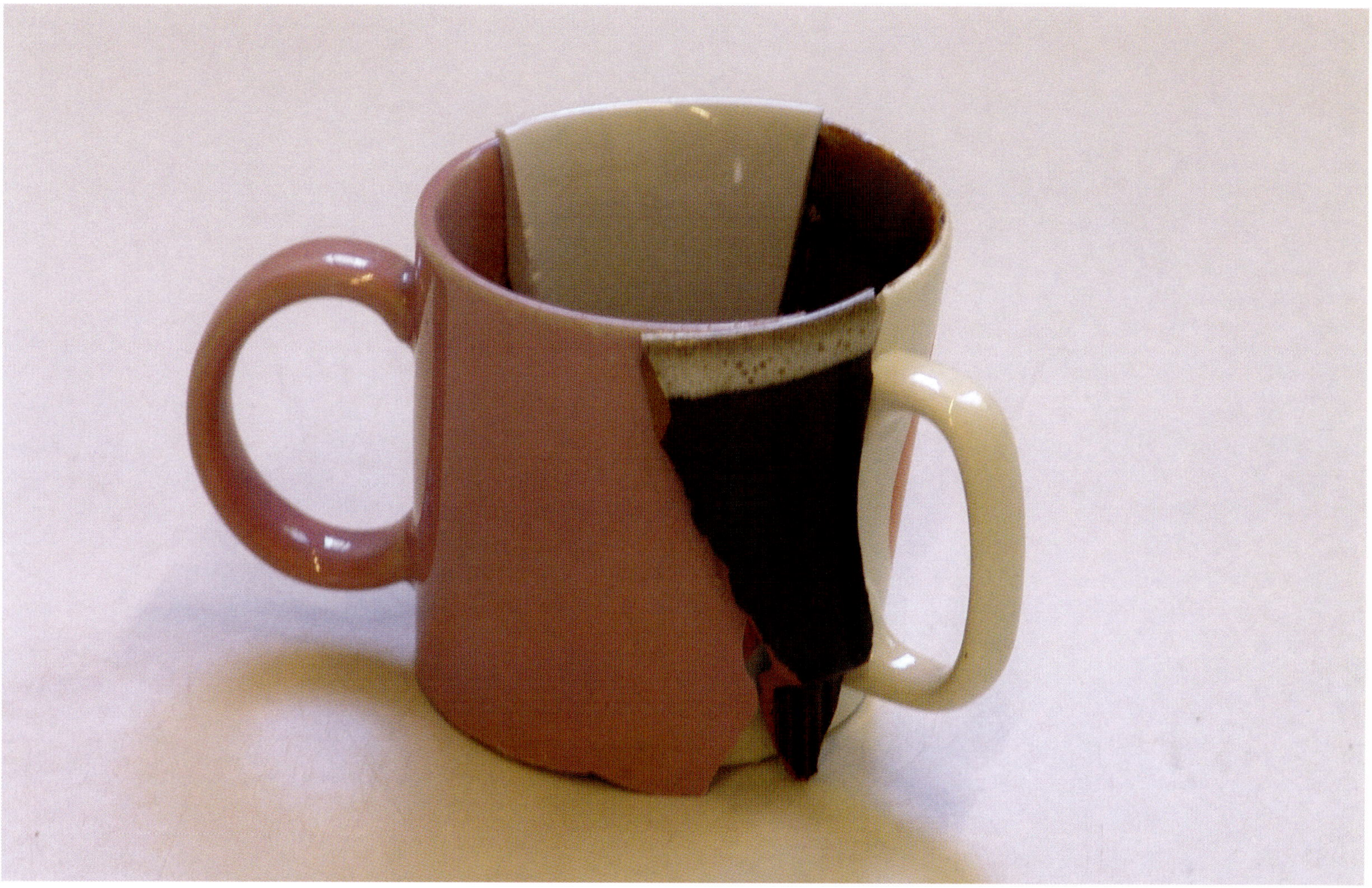

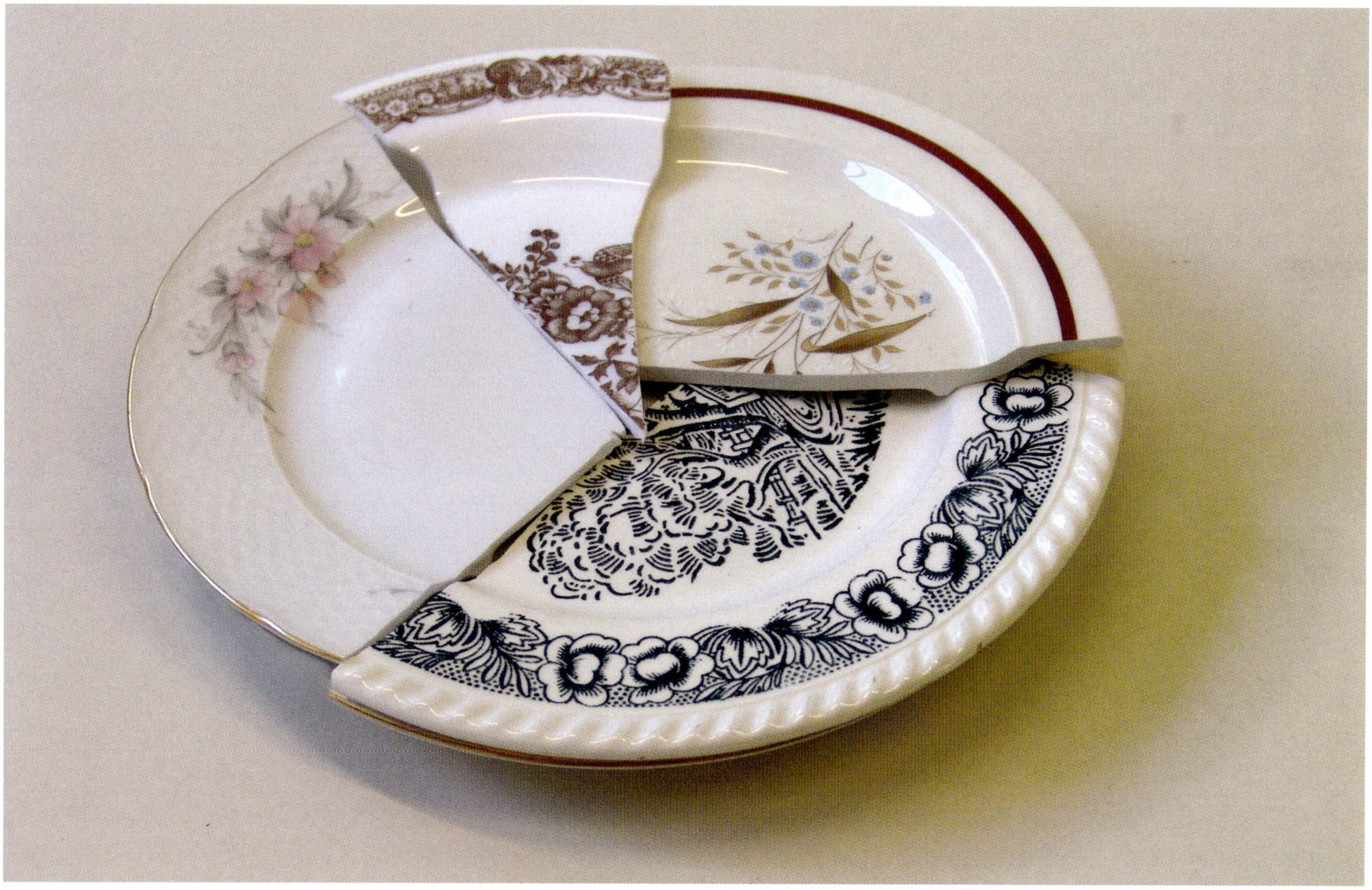

87) do toy

do c

We are all addicts. We all have soul destroying habits. Ones that slowly but surely drag us down, alter our minds and make us do bad, bad things. We're not talking about the obvious ones that destroy our health like smoking or drinking or taking drugs or eating mad beef. We're talking about all these comforting, repetitive, second nature acts we commit every minute of every day. The things we would find most difficult to break if challenged to do so. Habits like tying your shoelaces the same way or walking to work by an identical route as yesterday or the day before that. Habits like that way you always stretch in the morning when you wake up or how you always start reading a magazine from the back page to the front. These are the real killers. These are the real reasons we slowly disintegrate. Without us hardly noticing, we begin to rely, more and more, on our in-built cruise control.

'do change' is here to relieve you, to serve you up a big plate of cold turkey to help kick those habits. And all that is required are a few small shocks to your system.

However, before we start giving you nuggets of advice on how to change your life, we feel it's only polite to introduce ourselves. 'do change' is the name of an experiment from 'do', a new kind of ever-changing brand which, as the name suggests, depends on what you do.

'do' was first set up with only a mentality, offering an antidote to other one-way brands, where you were just the receiver of goods, the end of the production line. 'do' wanted to ask the consumer or other brands to add something of themselves, bringing a unique, personal kind of imagination to products and services of the future. In essence, 'do' survives only when other people want to get involved and do things.

And because 'do' is constantly changing, it has developed projects in a wide arena.

There's the do-tv experiment, a 24-hour worldwide internet conference about the dream demon, television. Over 5,000 people logged on and let themselves be heard - from a viewer in Tonga to TV directors in New York.

Then there's 'do create', doing the rounds in Paris, Rotterdam, London and Tokyo. 'do create' is a series of products that are unfinished, until you do. This includes a chair with one leg shorter than the other three – you need to add something to it, like a pile of magazines, to make it complete. Or there's the ceiling lamp with two handles to allow you to swing to and fro through the air and have some kinky fun in your living room. There's also the do website, dosurf.com which invites together a whole network of interested parties to read and realize do ideas.

ange

And now there's 'do change' which begins with a question: what in the world could be changed for the better? What can 'do' provide to give a solution for the sake of all our tomorrows? The do doctors got to work and constructed some future design prototypes using bits of ordinary household objects, a small toolbox, assorted wires and switches, and a bottle of tequila.

The first idea: something called The Breathing Television, a cure for hopeless TV addicts. The picture on the Breathing-TV screen would get progressively smaller the more you watch it. After some hours of continuous viewing, the picture shrinks to almost nothing. Switch off the TV for a period of time and it will gradually grow back to normal size. Less fat-building hours in front of the box are guaranteed.

Another thought: the 'do watch', where you have to answer 350 questions about yourself before you part with your cash. Questions from 'What is your favourite colour?' to 'Where do you stand on the death penalty?' or the more metaphysical such as 'Is sex the answer?' The watches are programmed with this personal information and allow you to link by infra-red to another person who has a 'do watch' and check your compatibility, or otherwise.

These inventions, or rather positive extensions of existing inventions, fit nicely into the do mentality. They require action and reaction.

Despite this, we felt that we were starting at the wrong place. Rather than giving birth to the latest washing machine, the newest eating utensil, the next revolution in office table lamps, or an updated television or funky watch, 'do' wanted to begin with the most important object. The one that needs constant renovation, the one that we always seem to forget about in our Palm Pilot scheduled lives: ourselves.

A few hundred years ago, being inventive meant simply finding the best methods of survival. It centred on our own immediate needs. Now life is all about the objects around us. We've become so inventive it hurts: we have lotions to cure and pills to kill; electronic products to spend time and win time; machinery of personal instruction and mass destruction. There are inventions so niche most of us will never know they've been invented. Decades of research can be spent revolutionizing the toasting of bread.

It seems that we're running out of things to invent, so we're regurgitating ideas and fantasizing complexities.

What we should really be thinking about is that most of the products we have around us seem to work quite nicely, thanks very much. Effecting any real change and finding the things no one else has thought of before has to come from the everyday.

That means waking up in a different way, doing your job in a way it has never been done before, or with someone you've never considered working with before. Creating real change can mostly involve small measures. What would happen if you decided to eat cereals in the evening instead of at breakfast?

The reason is not to find out just about that specific thing but to explore and look at your normal life in a completely different way. Soon, you might get around to thinking that a table should have more legs or your computer needs a circular keyboard with enough room for five people to allow a more social atmosphere. Maybe it will lead to the one object no one could bear leaving home without three years from now. Maybe it will give us clarity of vision. Maybe it will help provide a solution to something that won't have reference to anything we've ever seen before. Maybe it will help us clear the traffic jams in our heads. At the very least, it will help cure us of our habit addiction.

This is the premise for 'do change'. An experiment in changing the way we do.

You will find here a list of 'do change' ideas designed for the person rather than the machine. These ideas are categorized in the following areas: work / home / anywhere.

do at least one 'do change' experiment from each category, with some offering small changes, others extreme. Feel free to choose your preferred option in this D.I.Y. workshop, then let others know of your successes or otherwise, online. The website address is http://www.dosurf.com/change.

So what can we project will happen? Chaos and anarchy? An outbreak of radical free-thinking? An orgy of free-love? Or will we all just use a different method for spreading jam on our bread? do change, unlike its older cousin, lateral thinking, has no clear problem to solve, so there isn't a logical goal derived from its illogical beginnings.

In the end, these ideas that burst free from the womb of 'do change' are simply about looking at the things we take for granted in a completely different way. They're not about being crazy just for the sake of it, but they can be. Mostly, 'do change' is about changing patterns, about reinventing yourself. That is the way that we'll see real innovations come about in the future.

Ok – enough talk. Let's get to work.

Work–
• Ask some kid on the street for advice instead of your mentor.
• Swap workspace with your boss/employee.
• Leave your phone, diary, wallet and other pocket-bulgers at home.
• Walk to work with a limp in your left leg.
• Open your shop/business when everyone else closes theirs.
• Sing your national anthem in a crowded elevator.
• Talk to the shoes of colleagues.

Home–
• The next time the doorbell rings, answer it naked.
• Have your evening meal on the stairs.
• Don't leave the house for a week.
• Turn off all electricity.
• Avoid using cutlery, glasses, cups or plates.
• Sleep upside down.
• Use your living room window instead of the front door.

Anywhere–
• Dress up as a magician for the day.
• Write notes instead of speaking.
• Leave strange Post-It note messages on the street / subway / supermarket.
• Open your windows in a car wash.
• Don't avoid obstacles, walk into them.
• Repeat everyone's words.
• Change your name for different occasions.

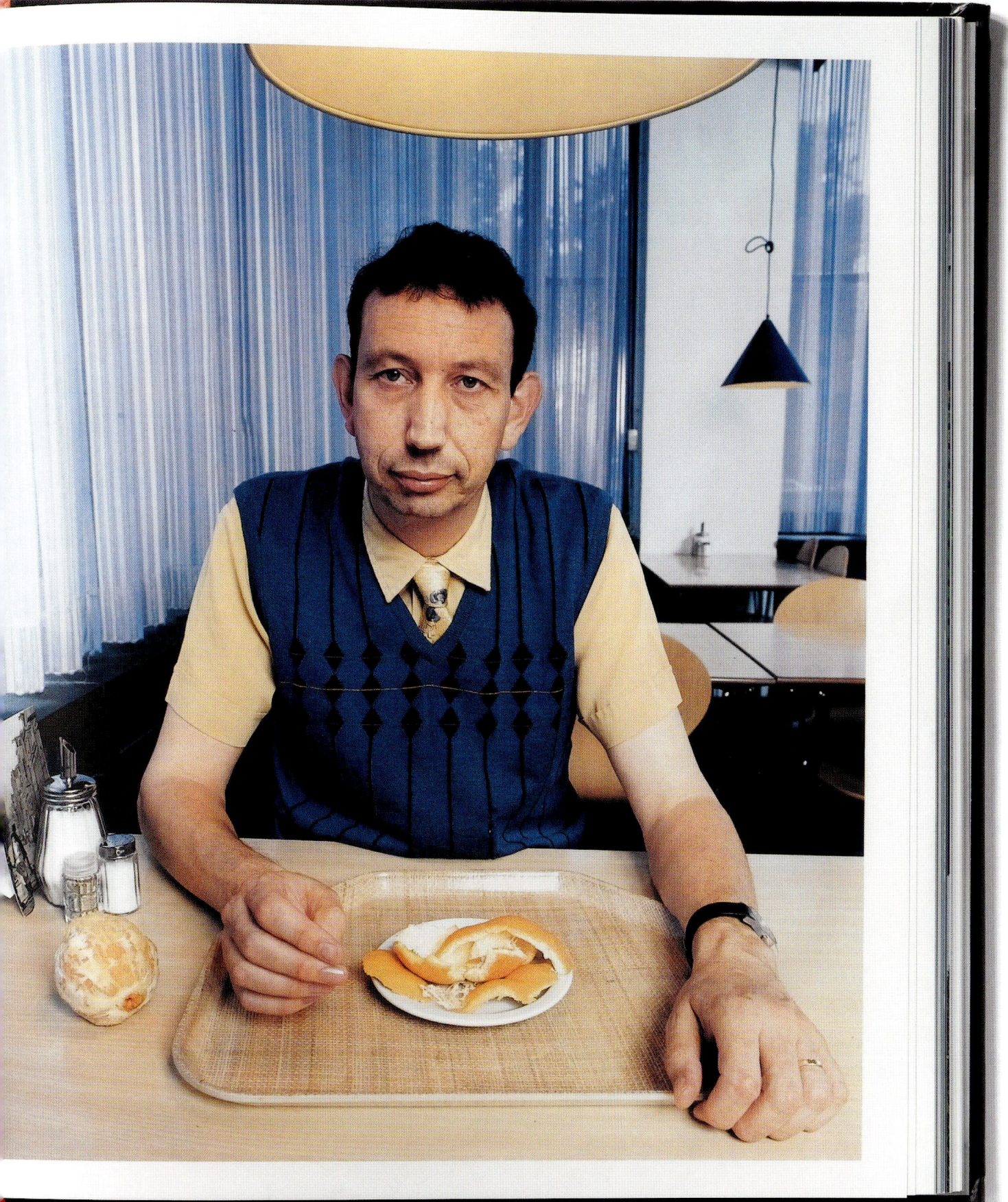

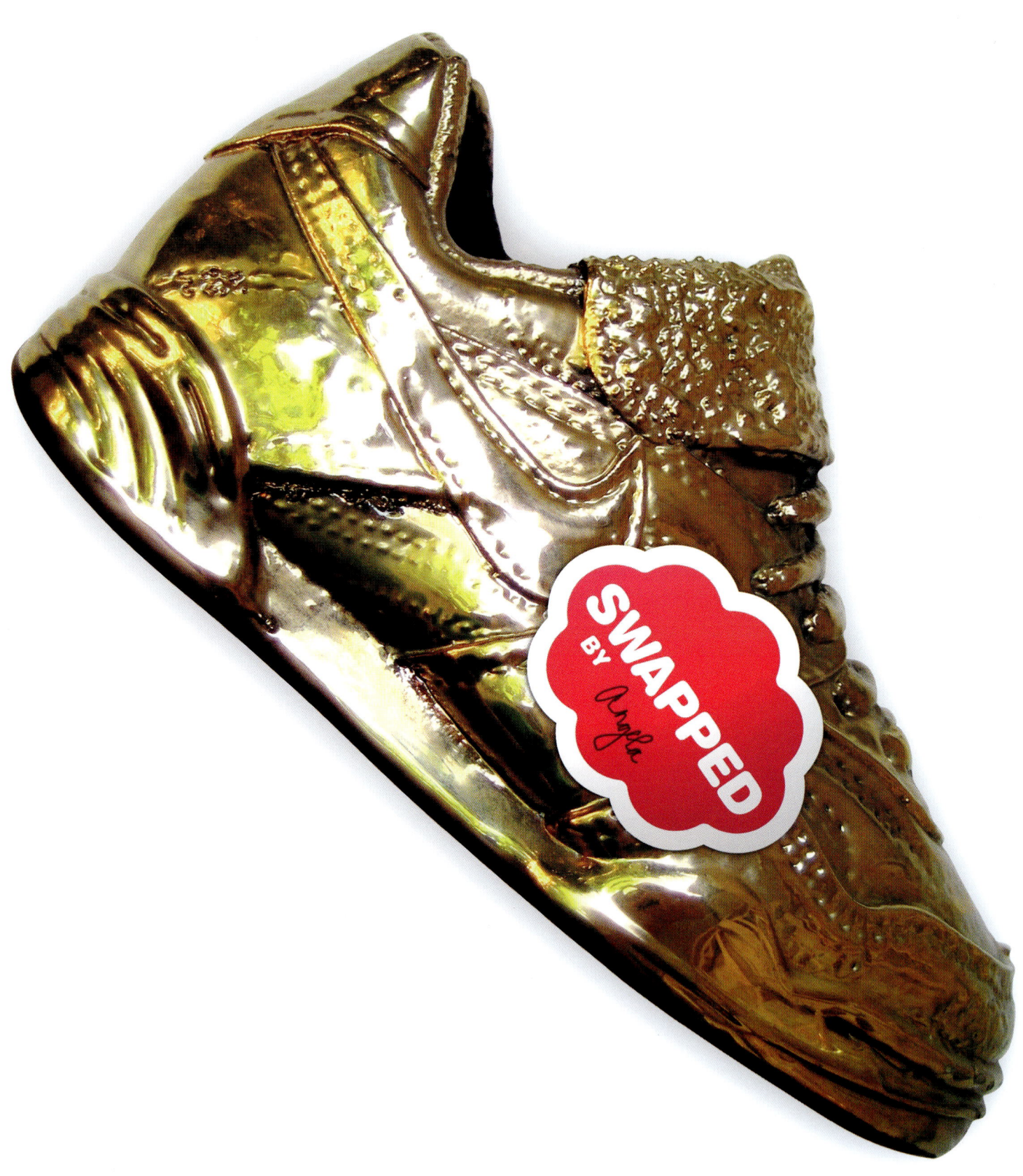

SWAPPED BY

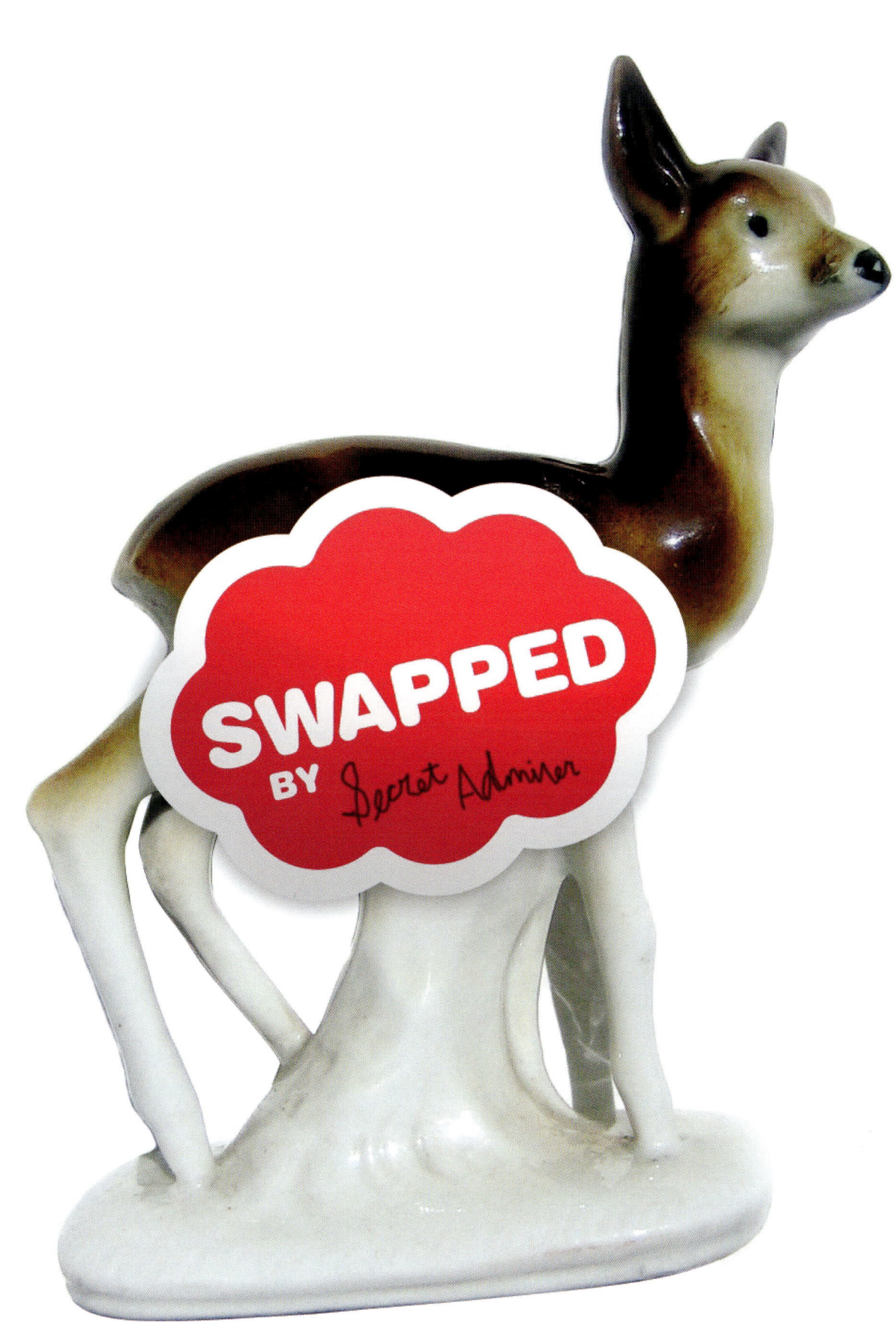

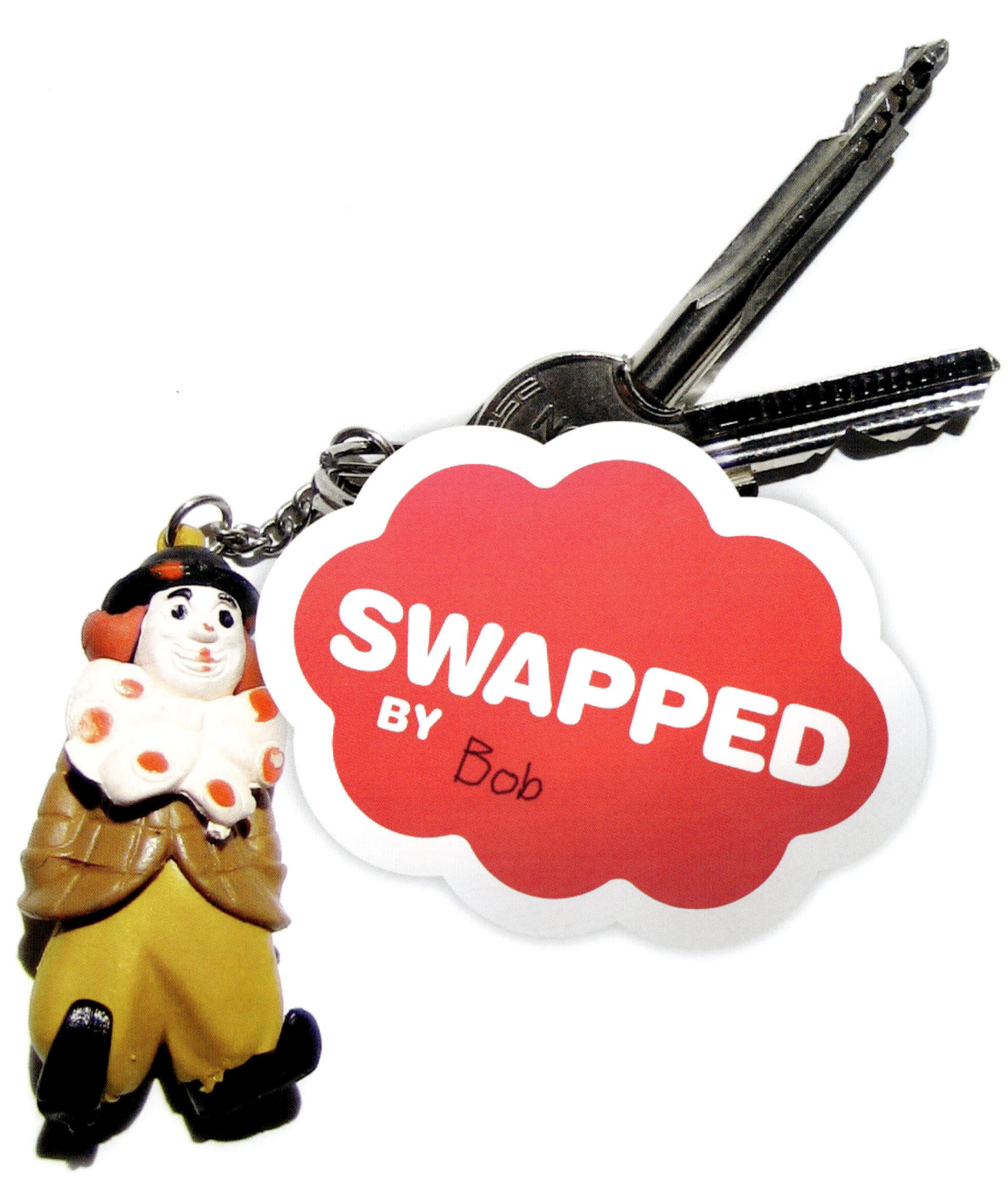

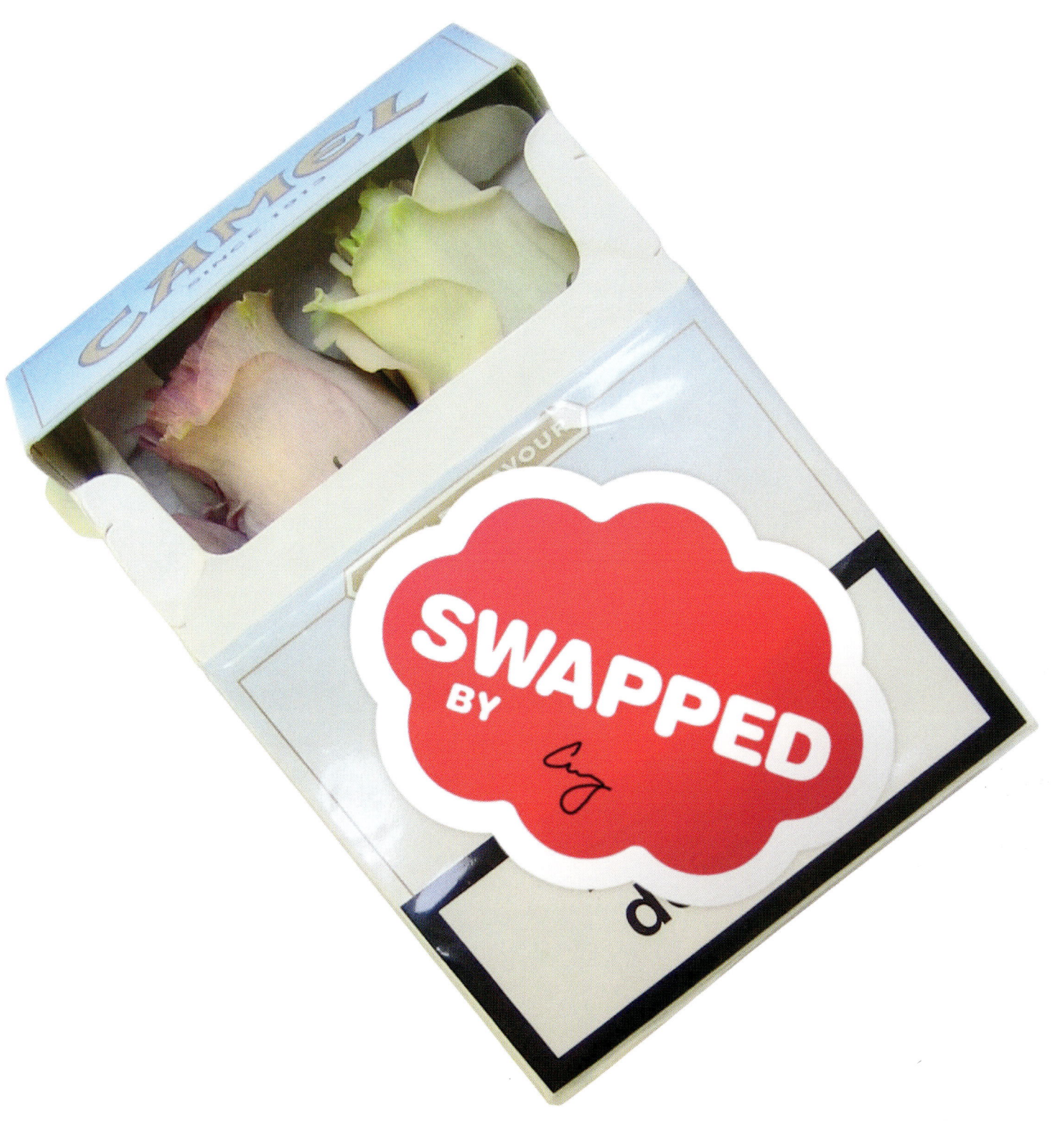

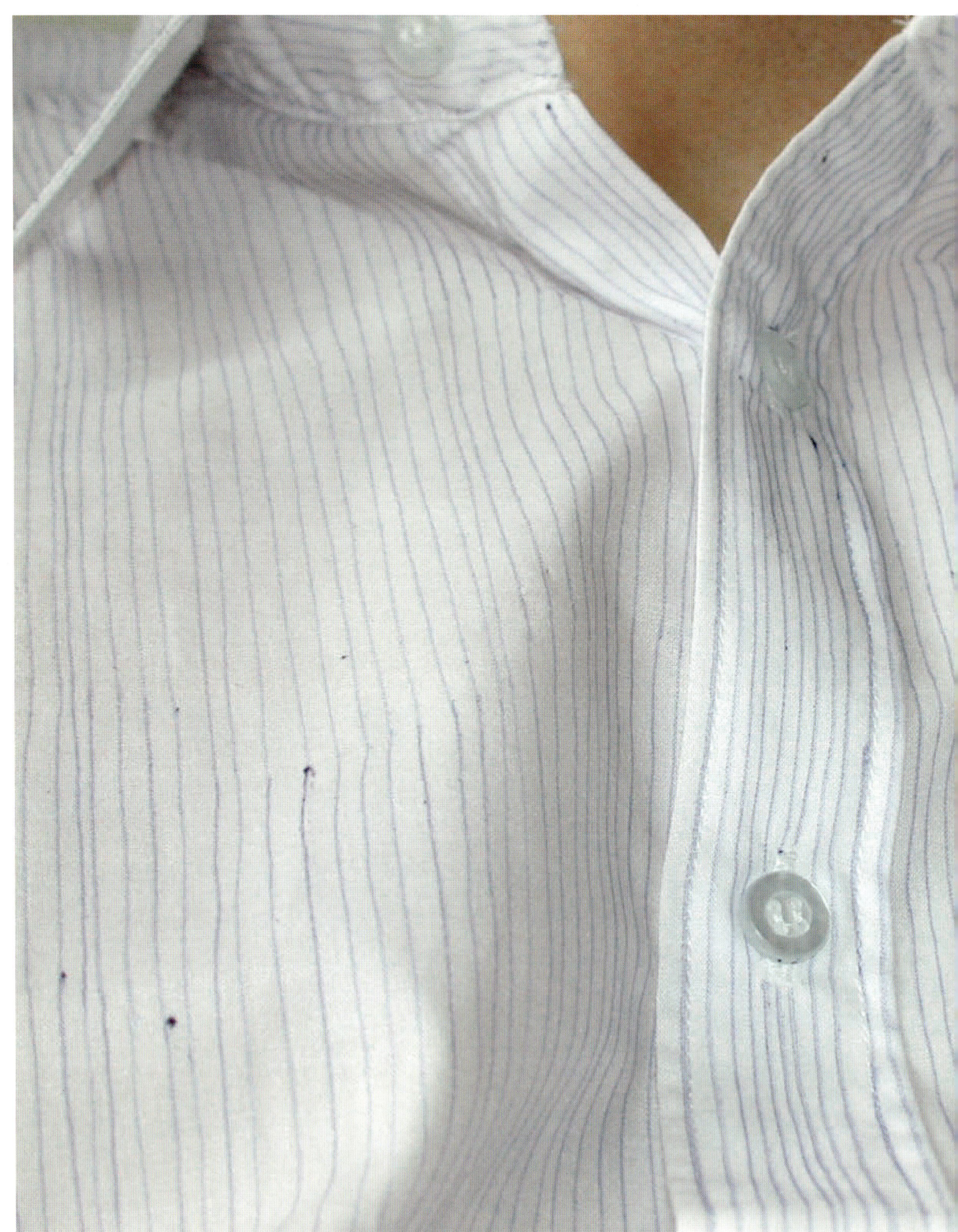

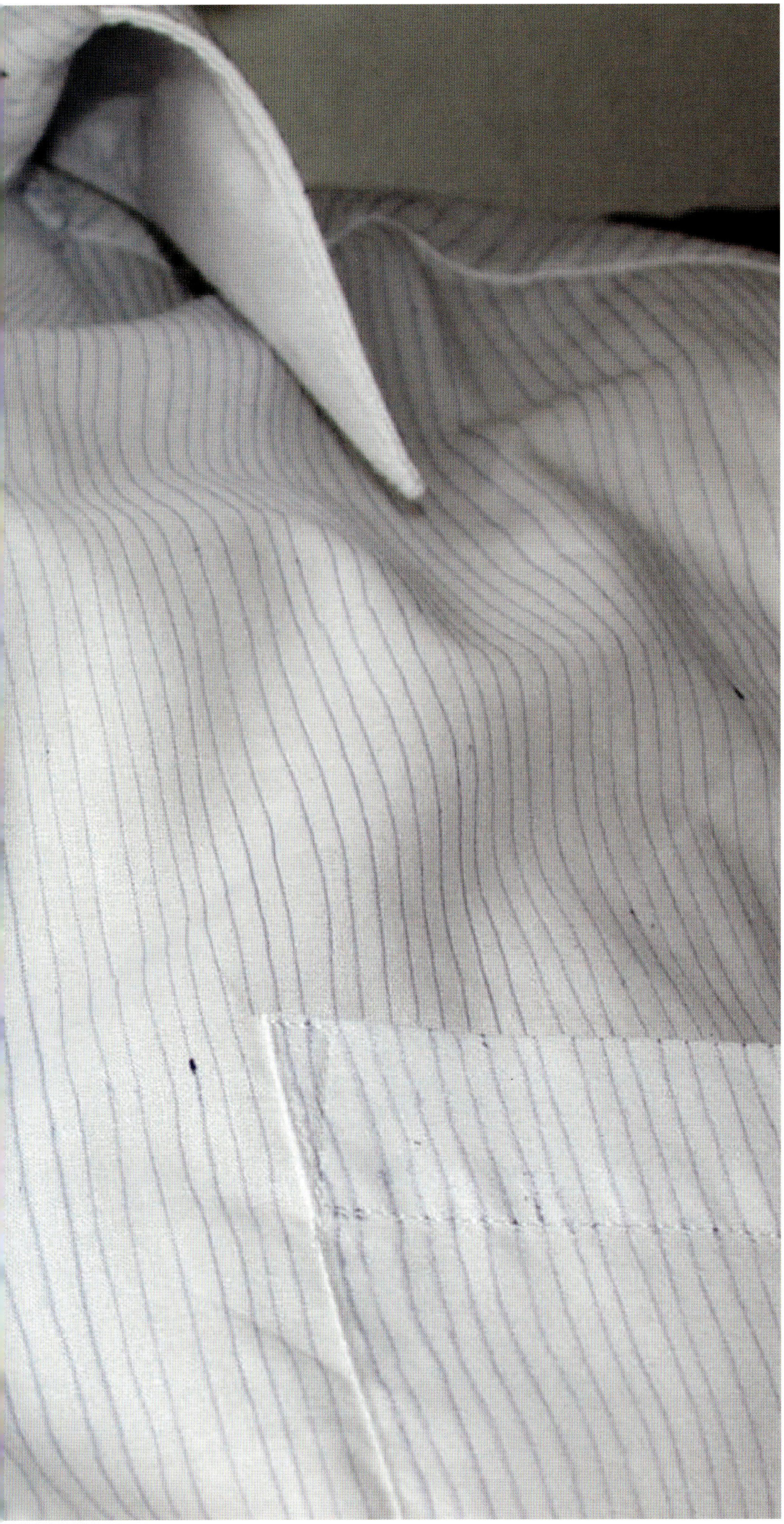

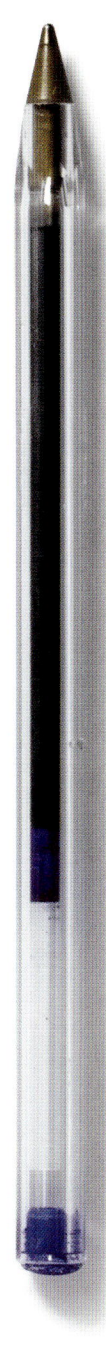

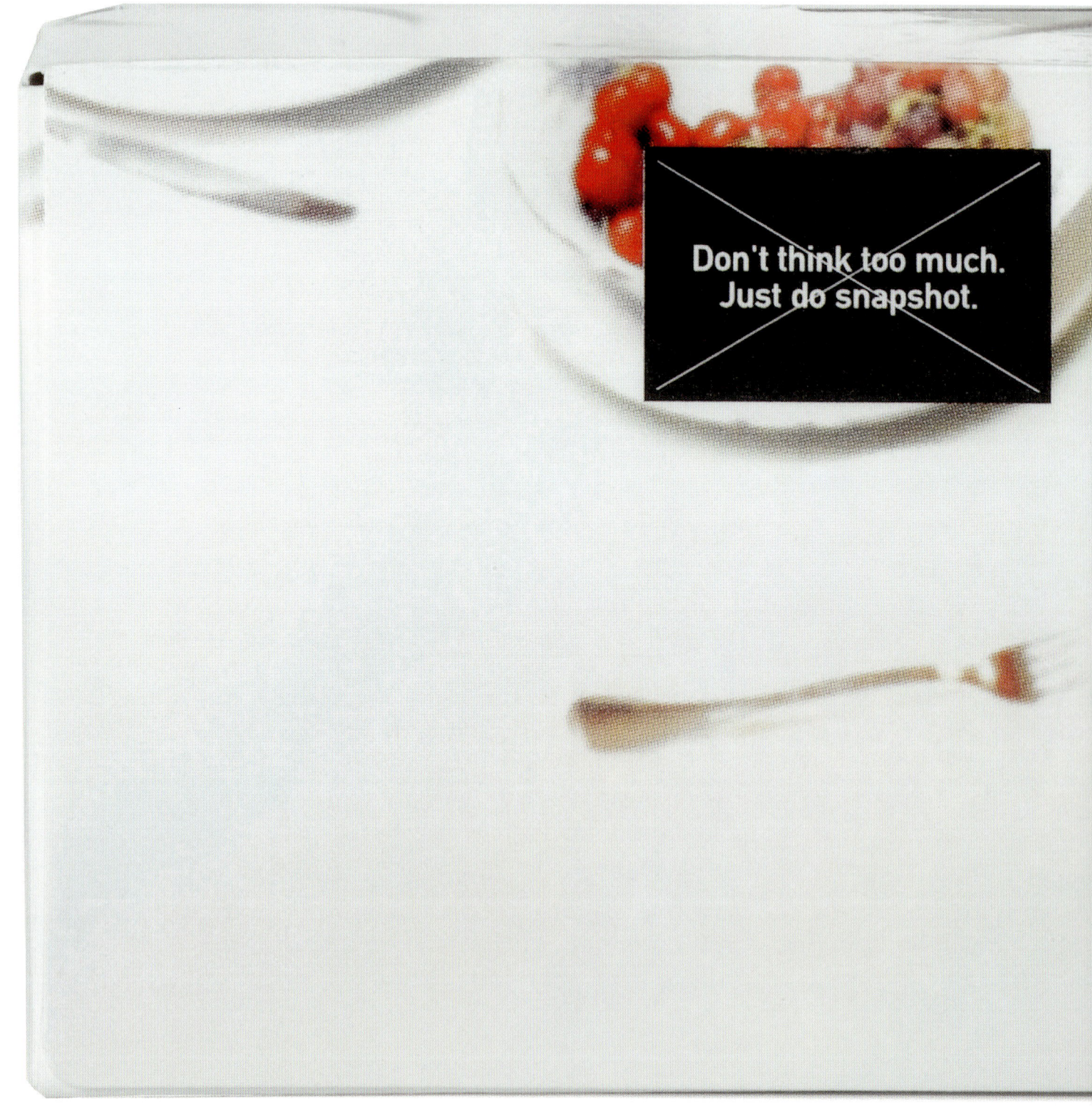

Don't think too much.
Just do snapshot.

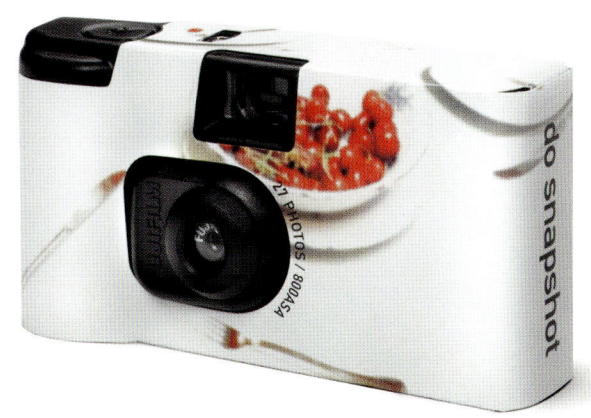

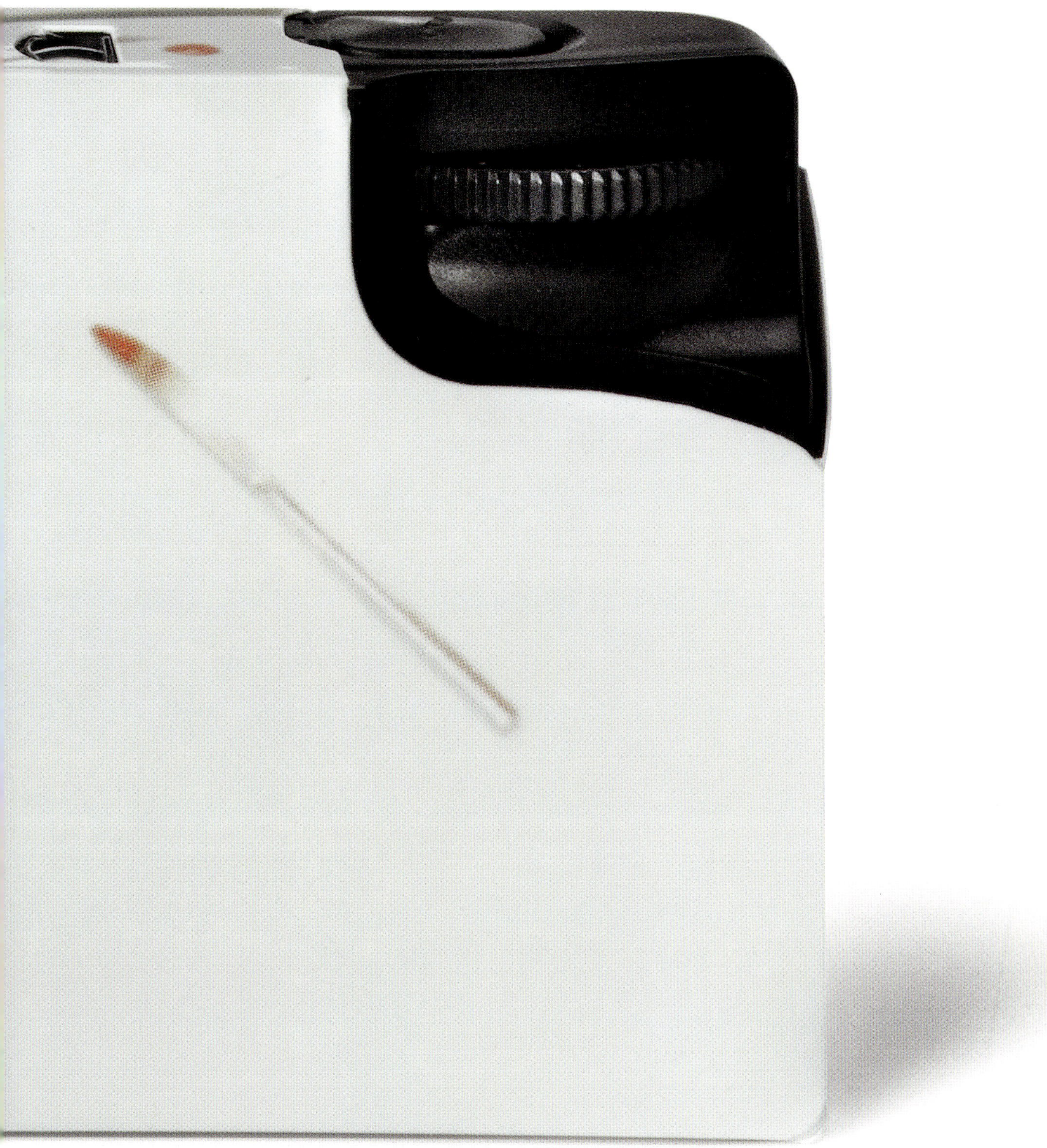

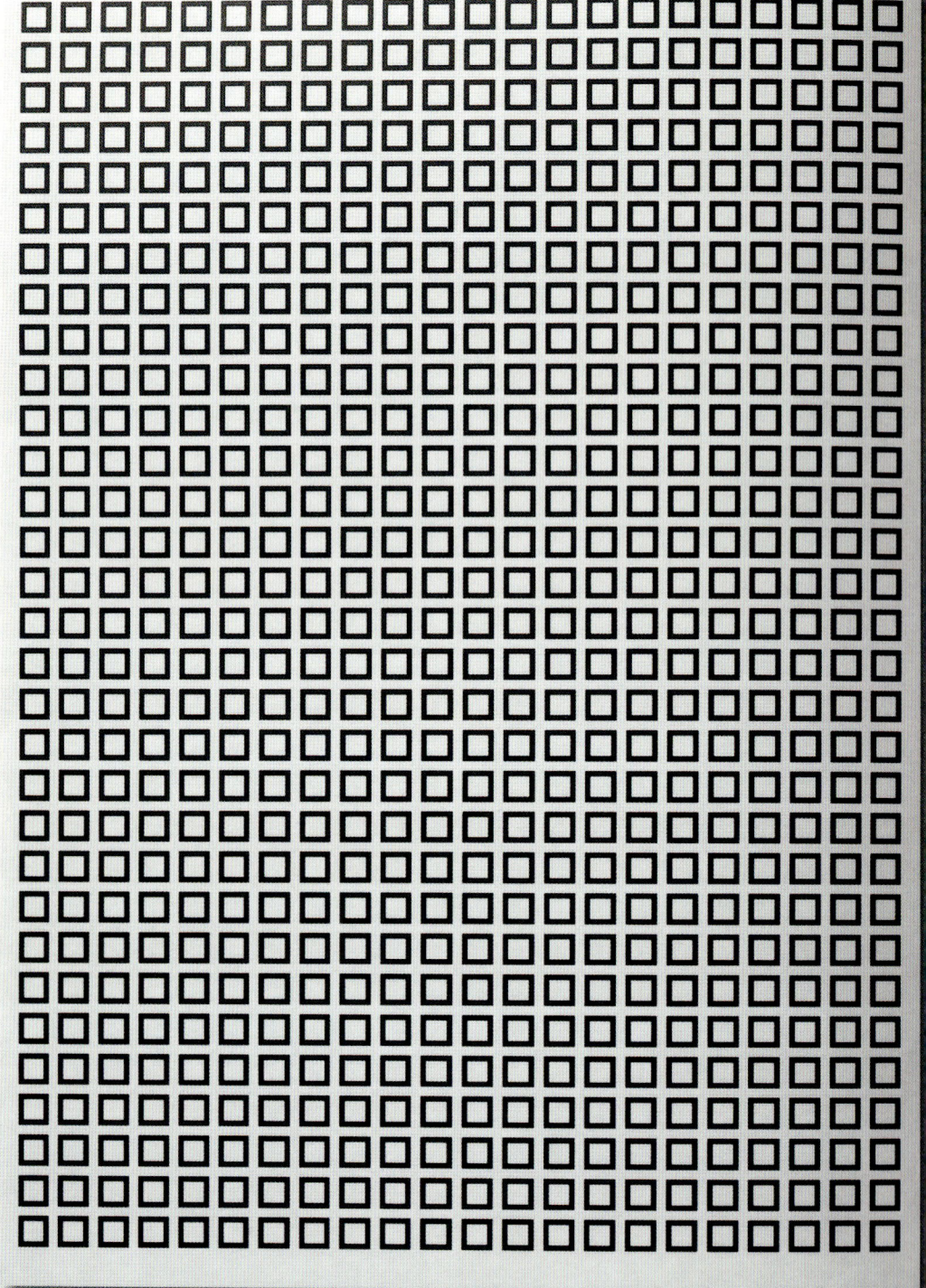

d● Vote.

do is an ever-changing brand.
What do is, and does, depends on you. Sometimes it is a furniture collection, a book, a twenty-fo[...]
hour website, or a performance. This time do is political. do is an interactive voting poster. Take th[...]
crayon, make your cross, and make your own political statement! do politics now! www.dosurf.co[...]

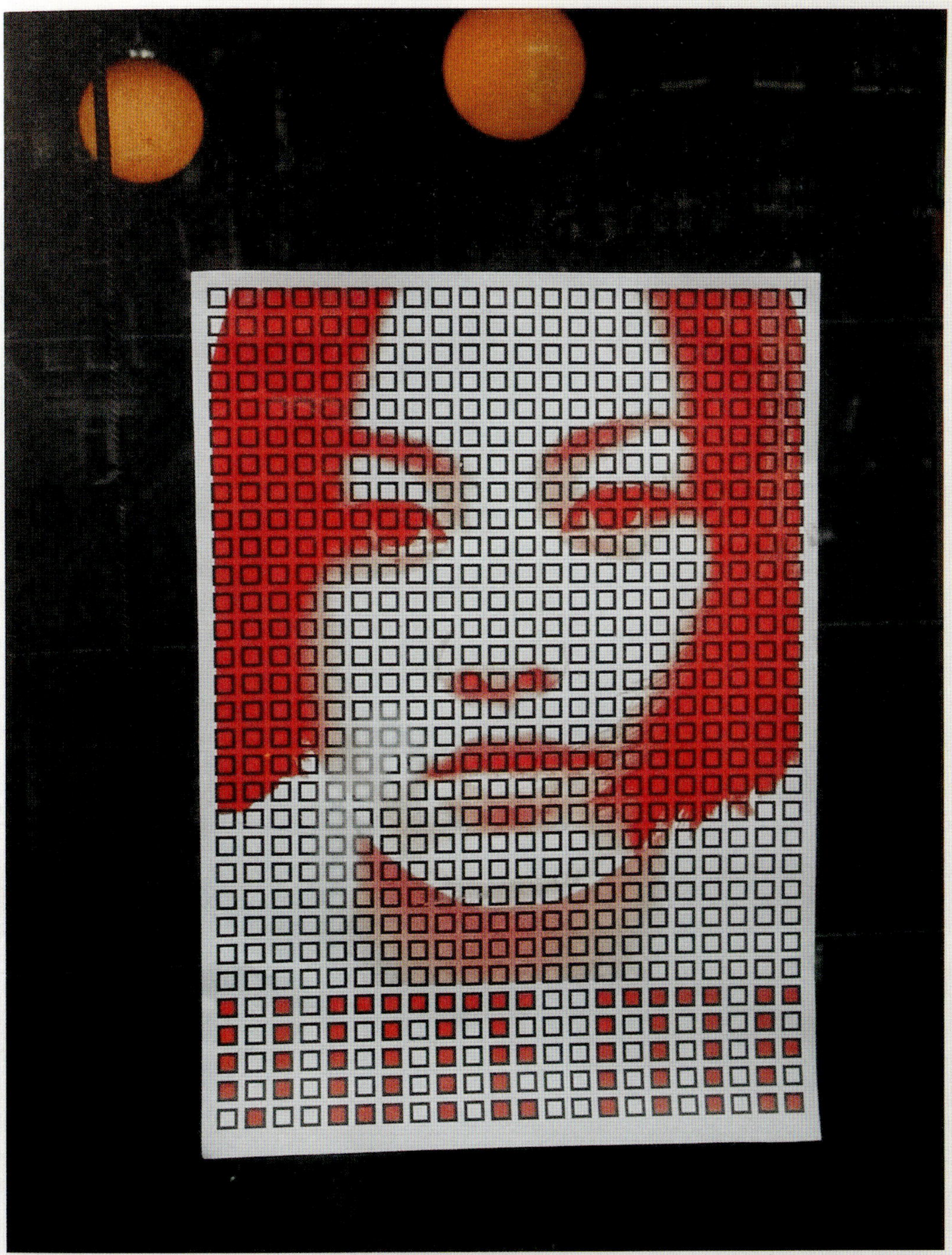

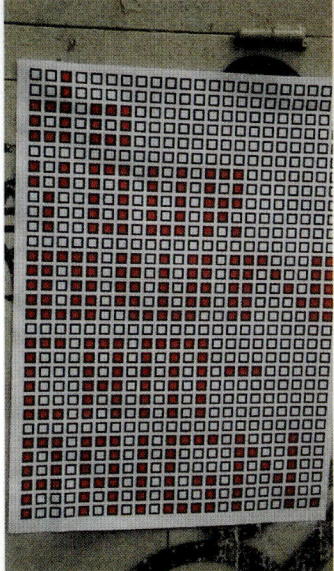
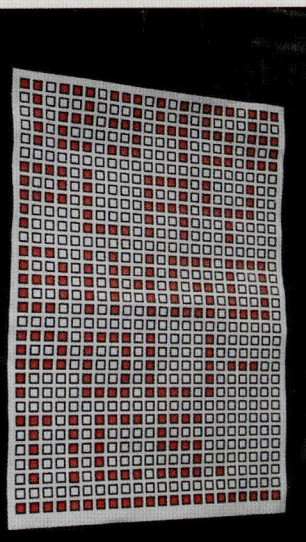
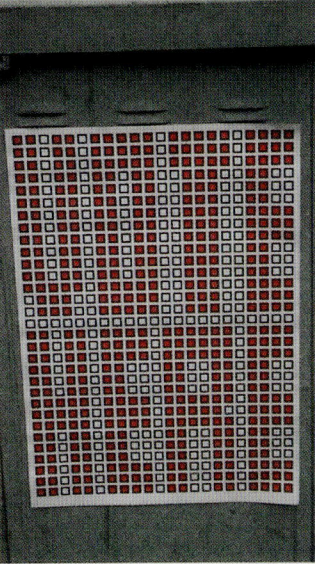

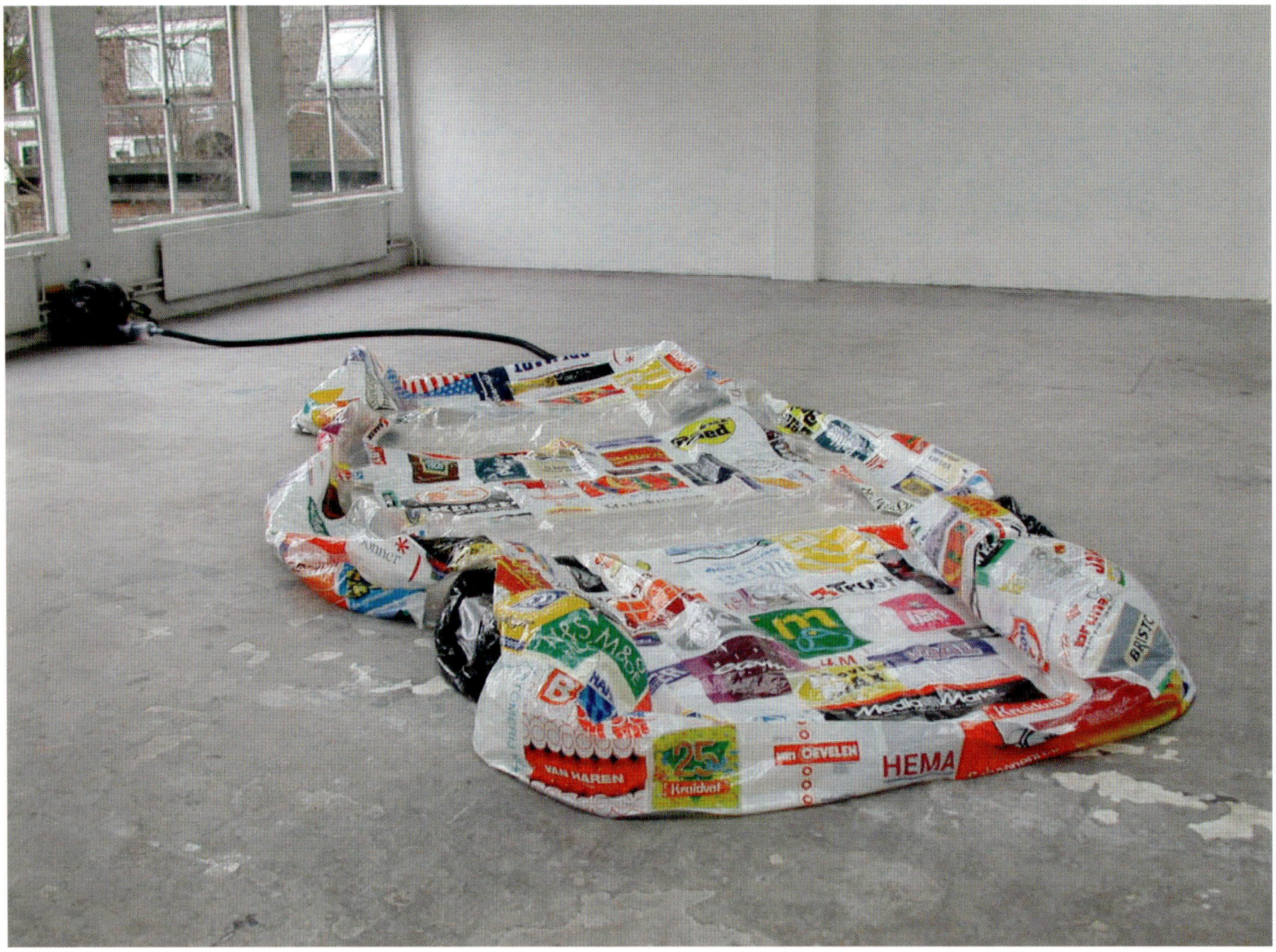
HEMA
VAN HAREN
Kruidvat
van OEVELEN

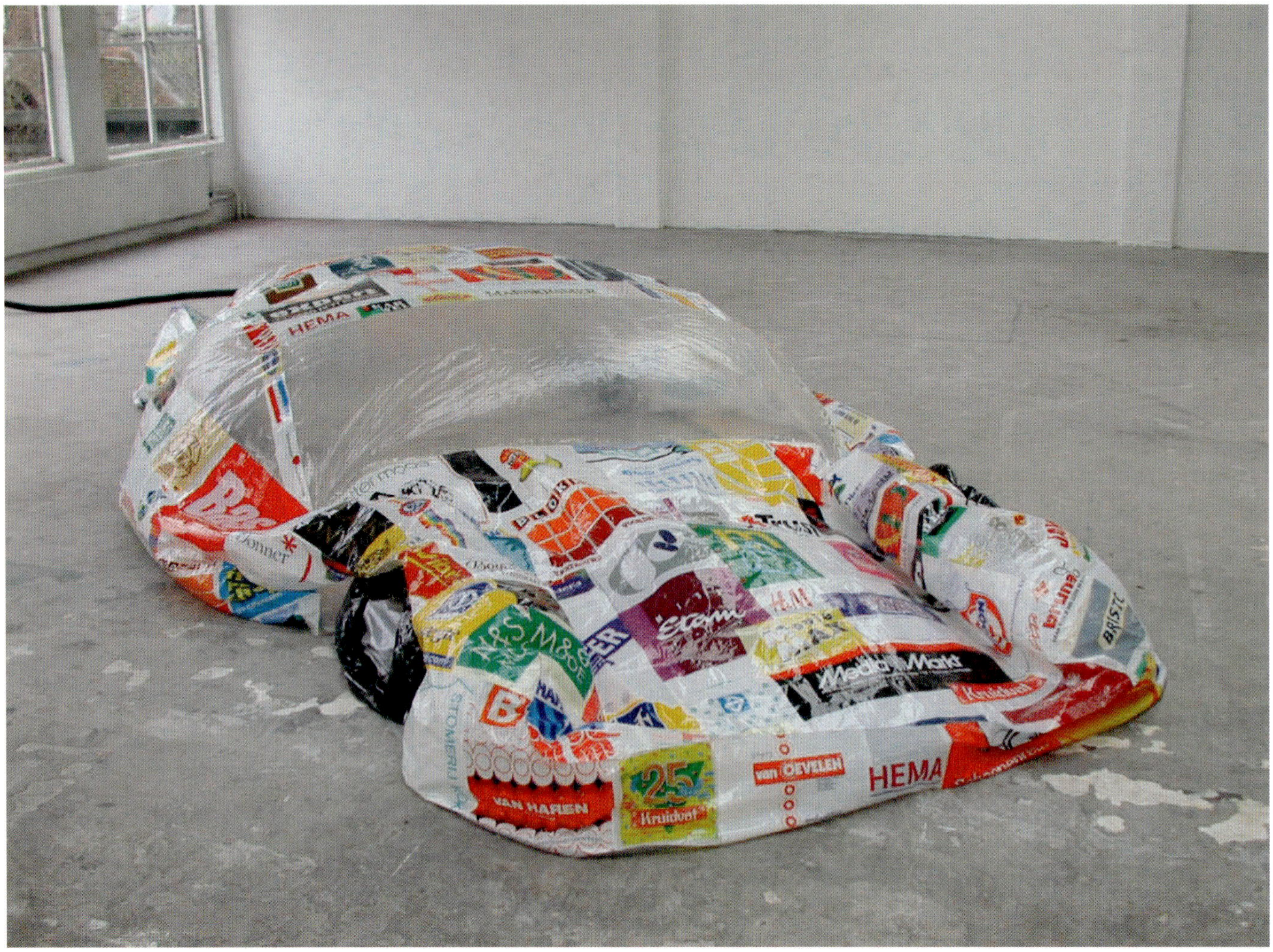
HEMA
VAN HAREN
Kruidvat
van OEVELEN
Media Markt

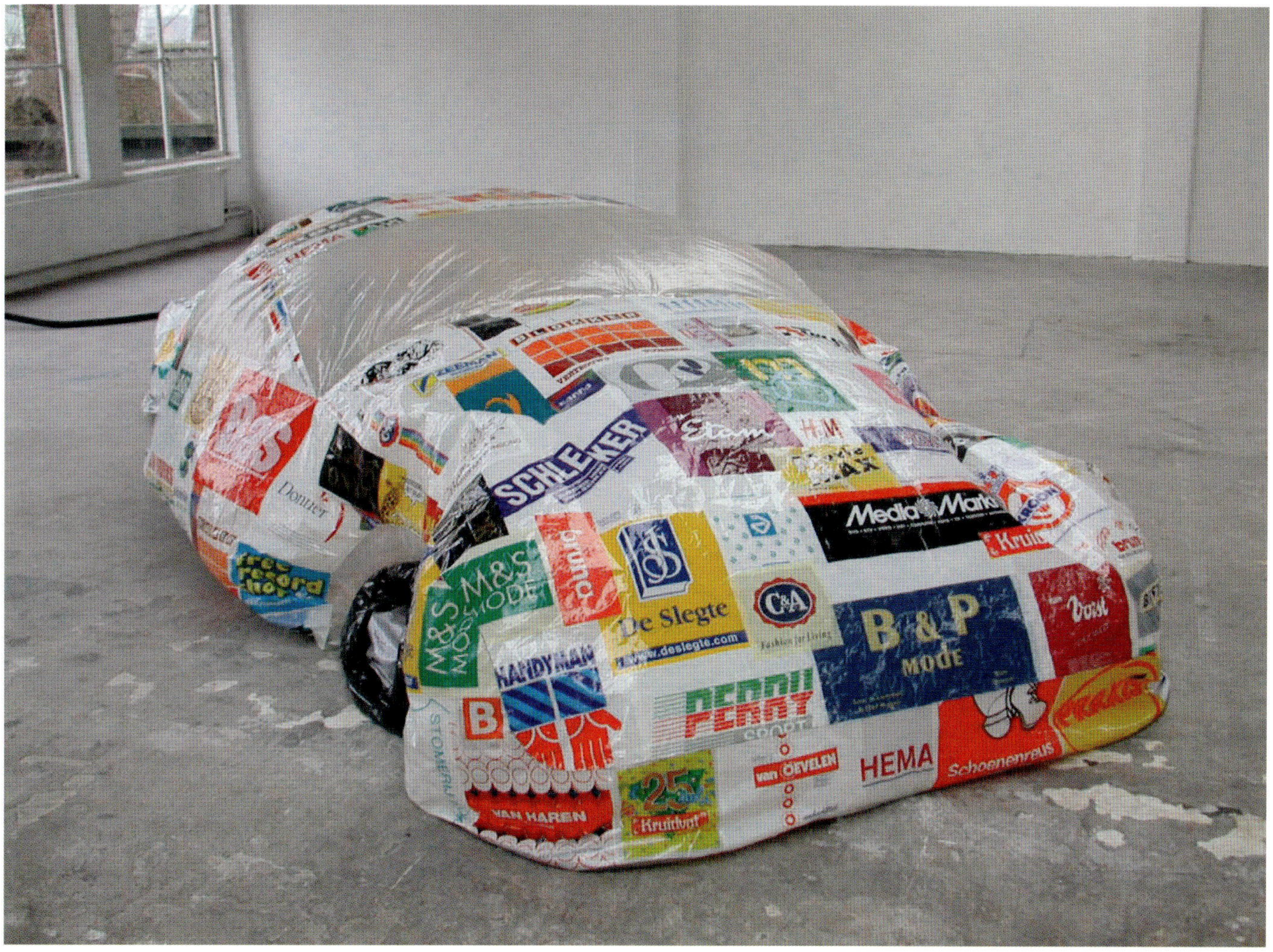
SCHLECKER
Etam
Media Markt
Kruidvat
M&S MODE
De Slegte
www.deslegte.com
C&A
B&P
MODE
HANDYMAN
PERRY
VAN HAREN
HEMA
Schoenenreus
PRAXIS
Donner

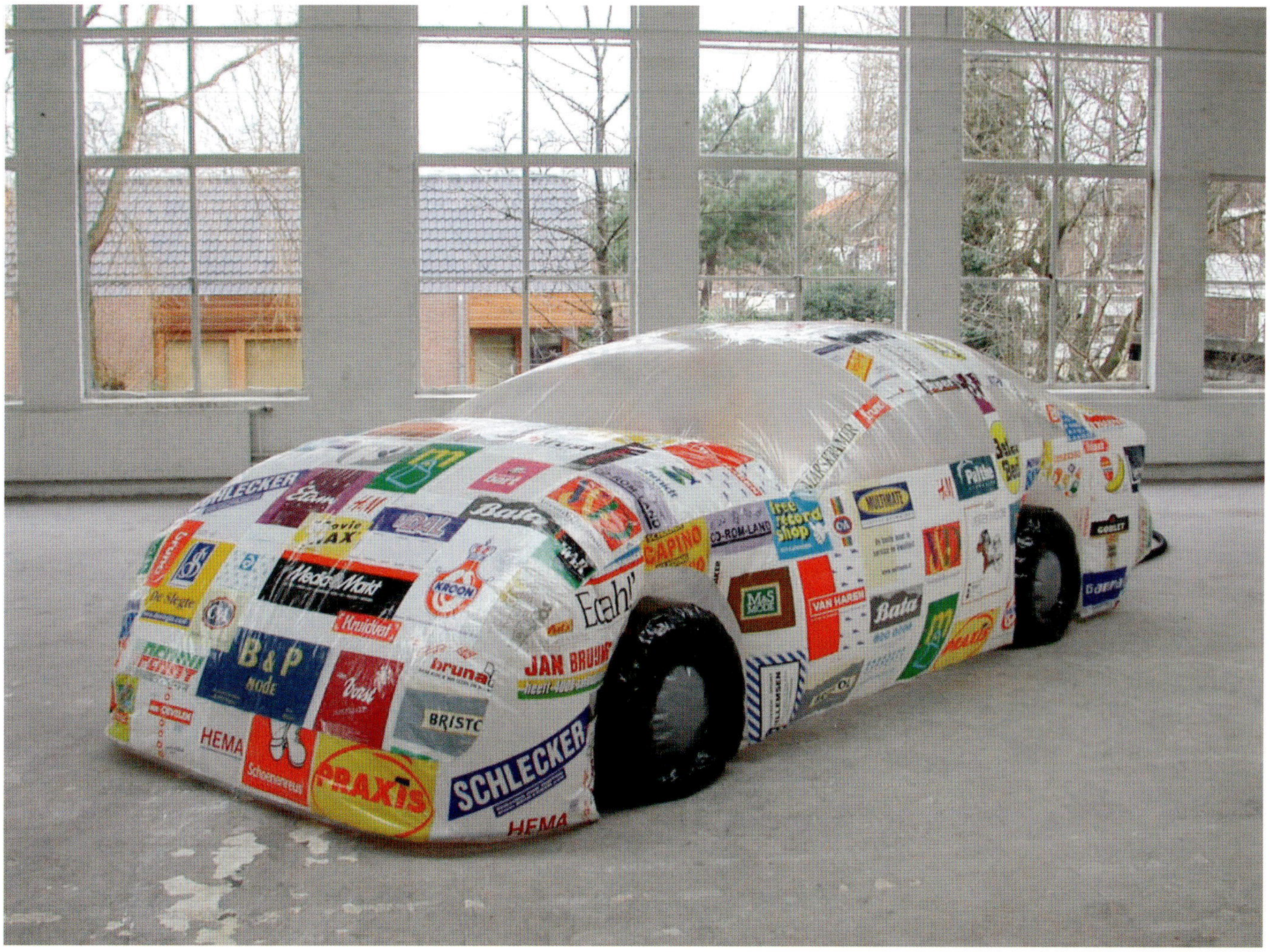
SCHLECKER
Etam
H&M
Media Markt
KROON
Kruidvat
B&P
MODE
PERRY
HEMA
Schoenenreus
PRAXIS
BRISTOL
JAN BRUNA
brunal
Bata
VAN HAREN
M&S MODE
CD-ROM-LAND
CAPINO

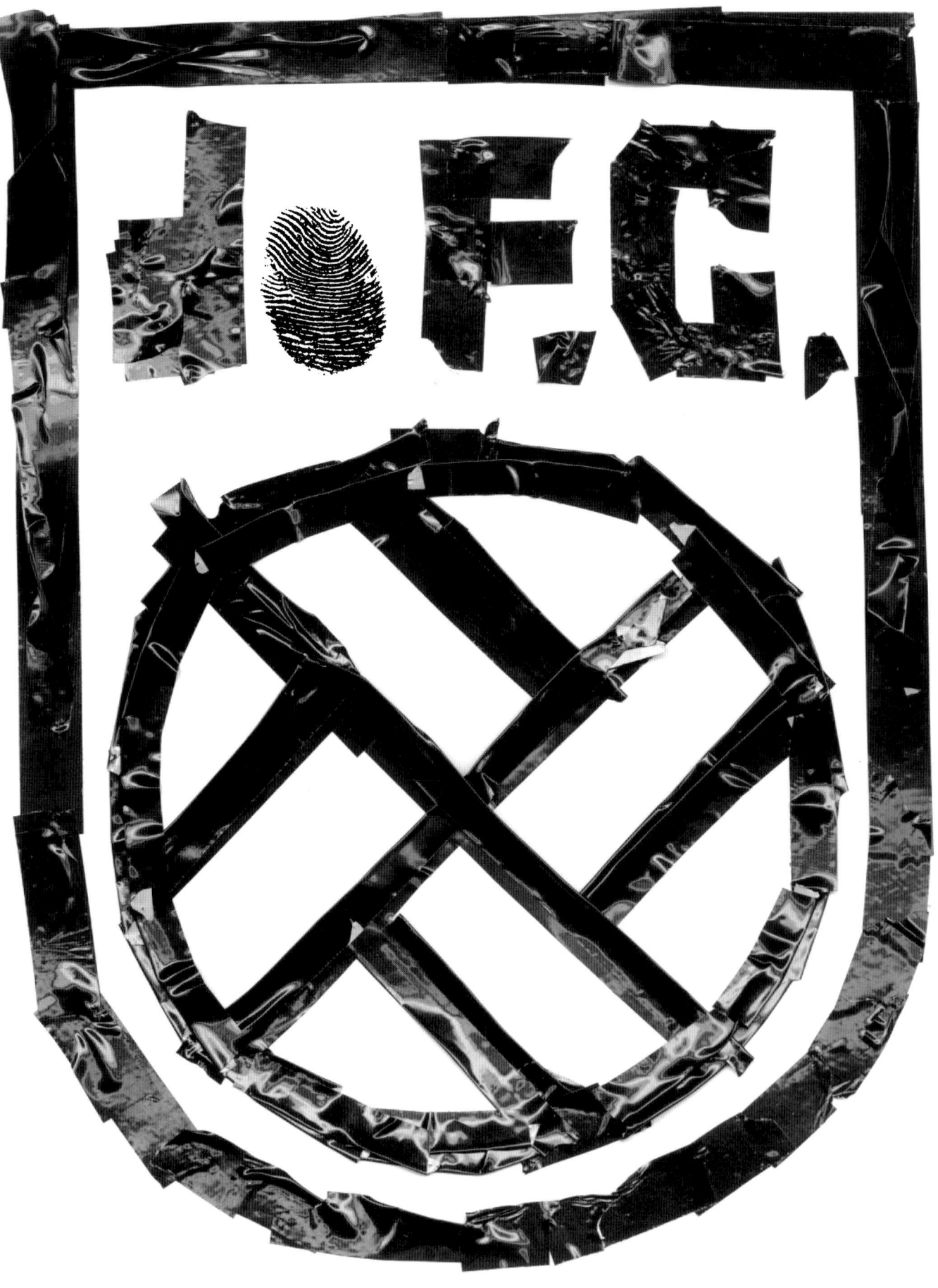

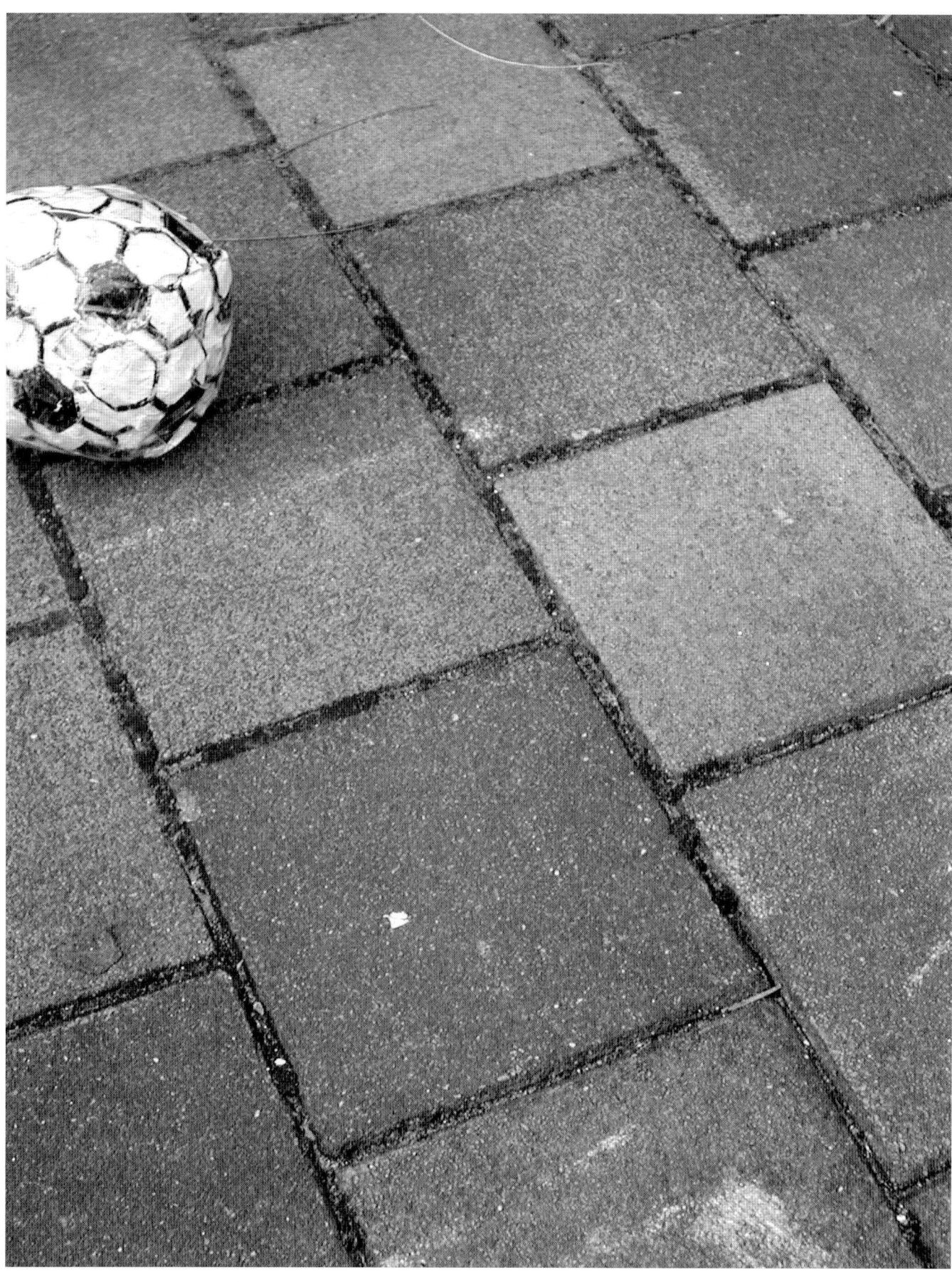

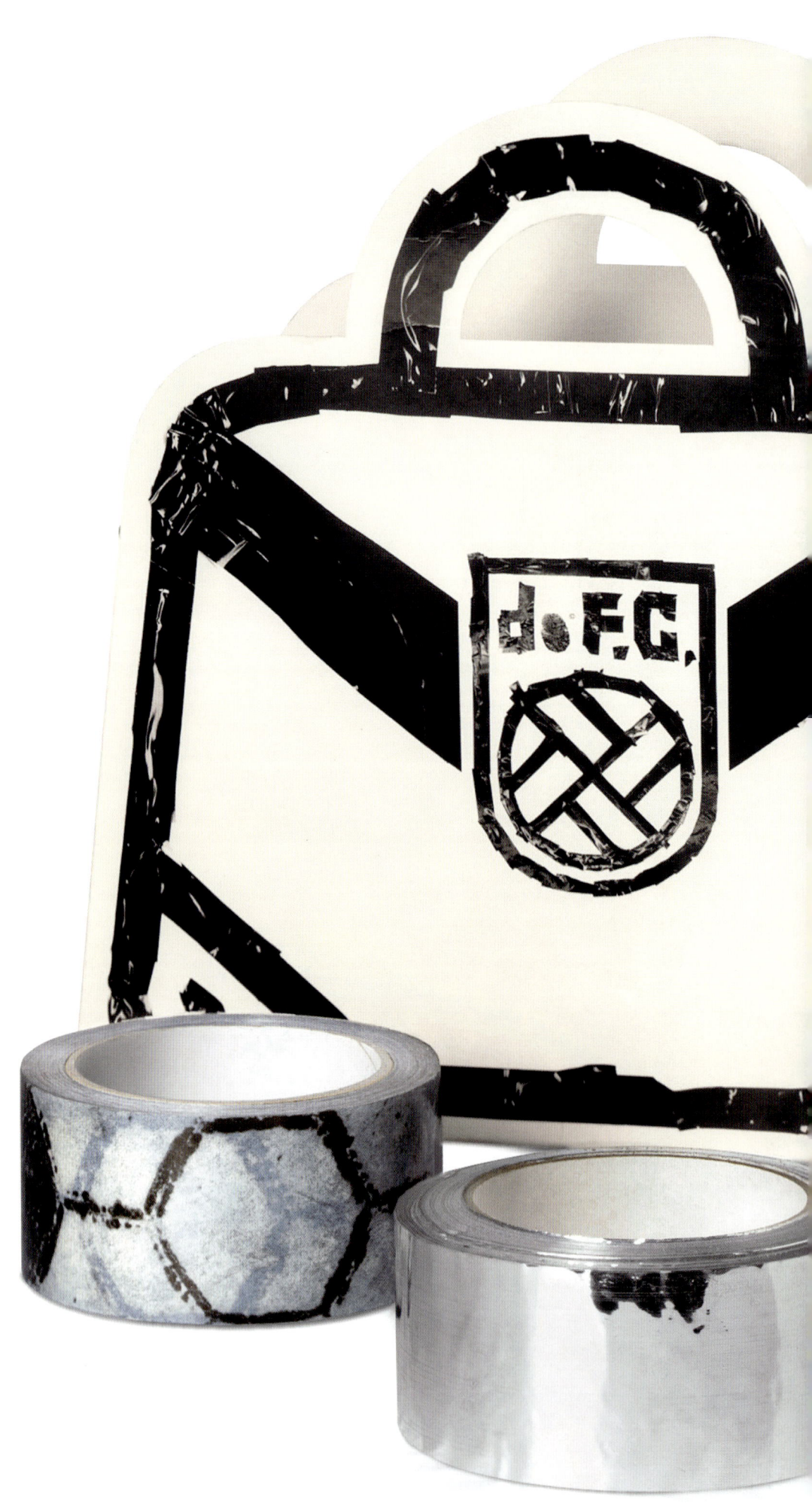

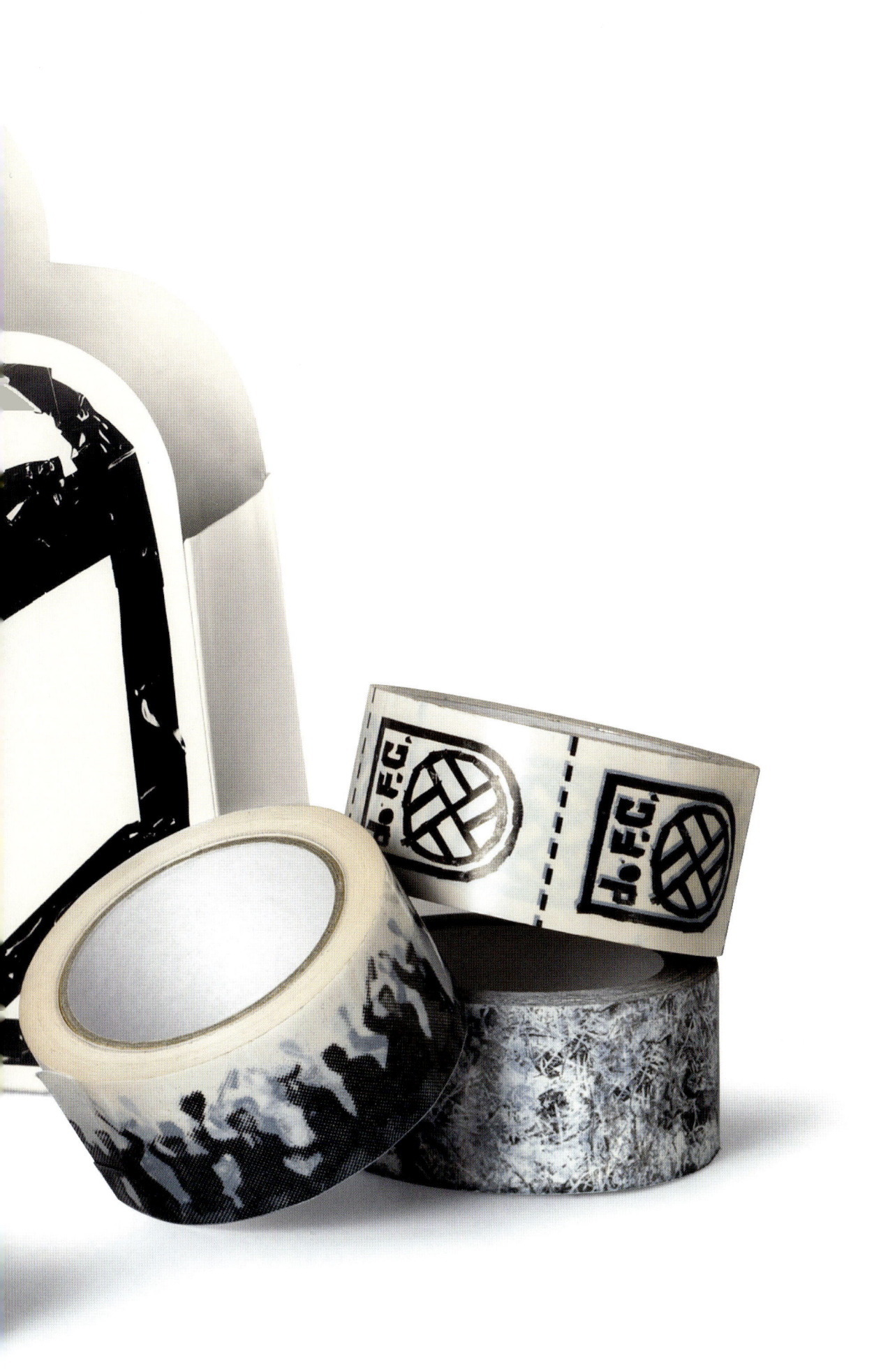

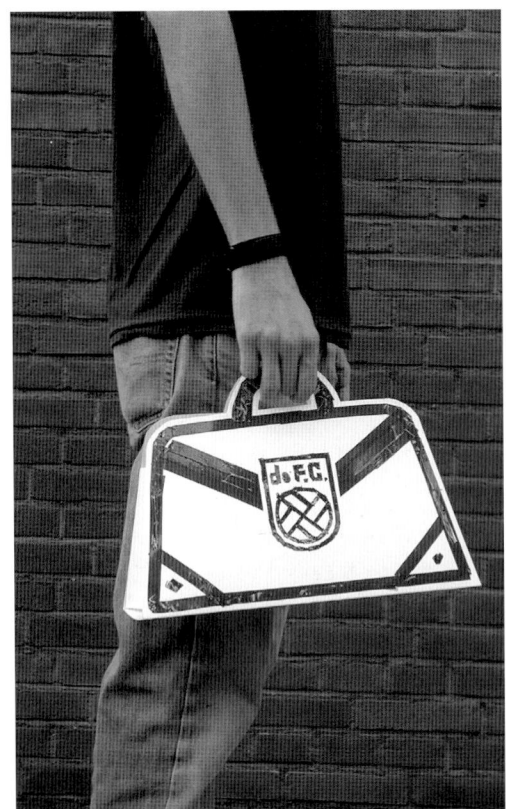
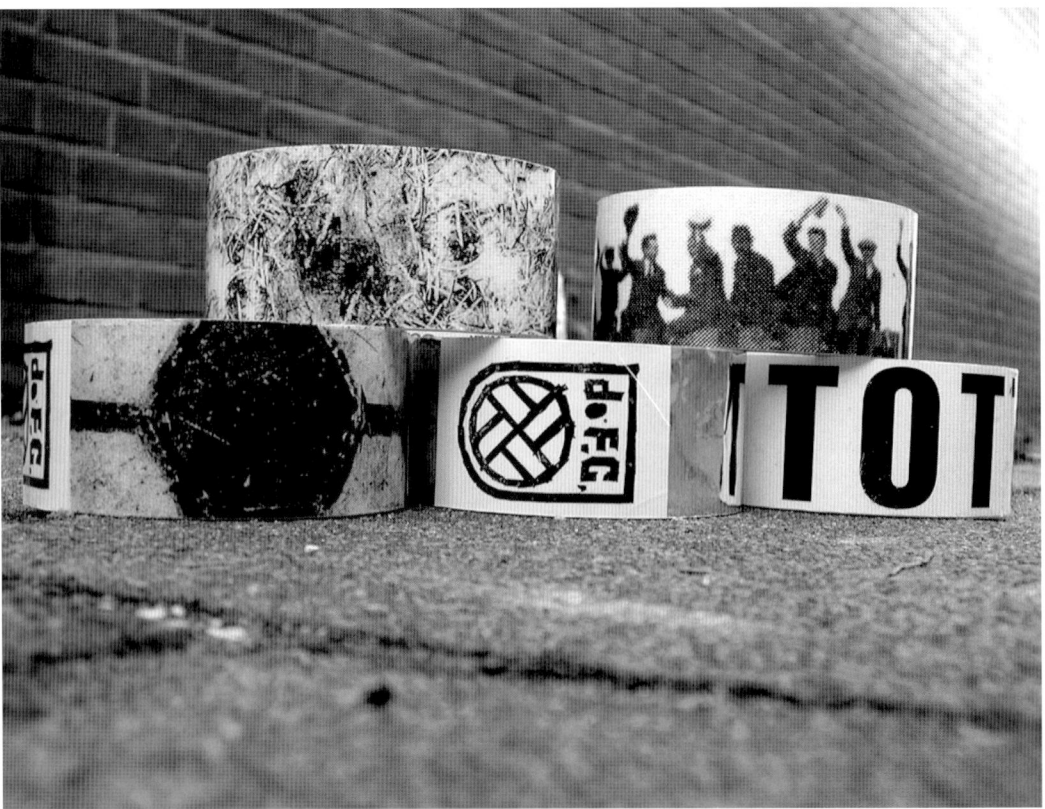
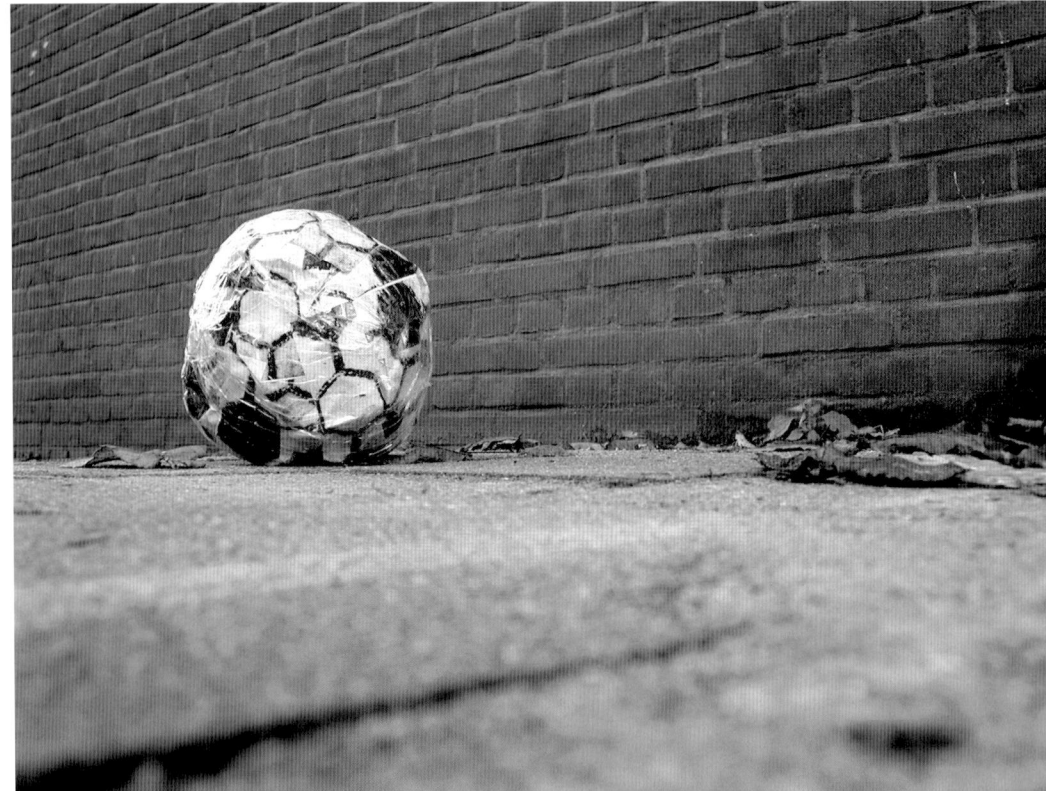
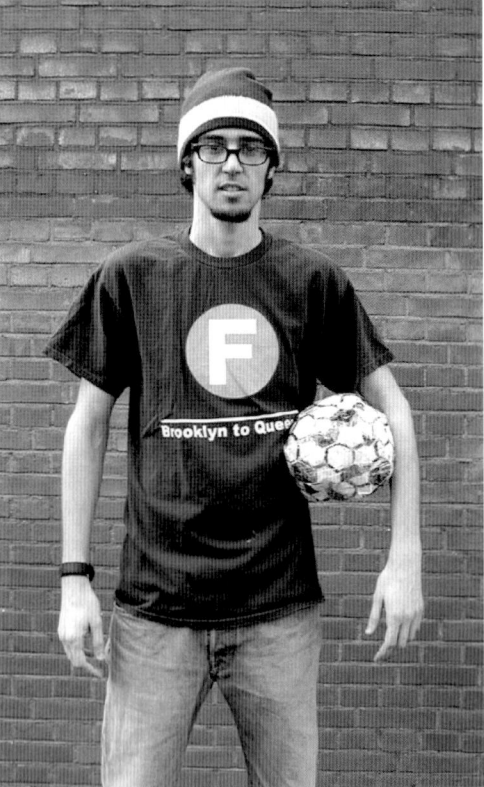

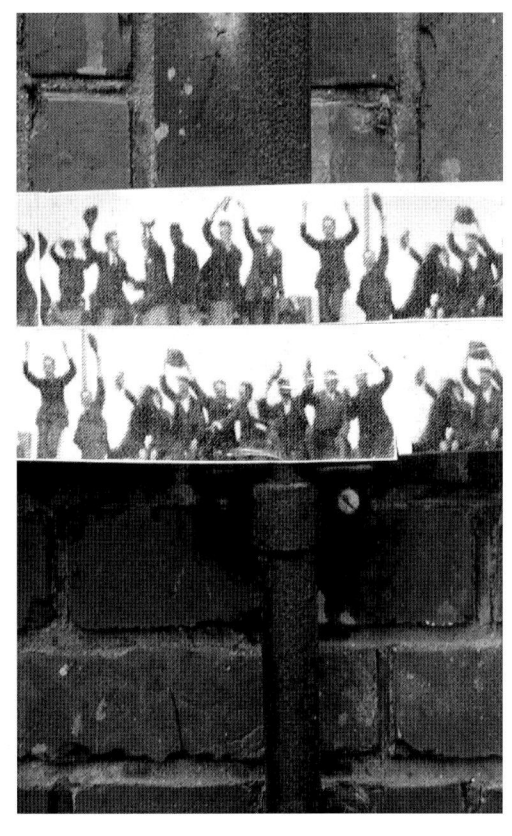

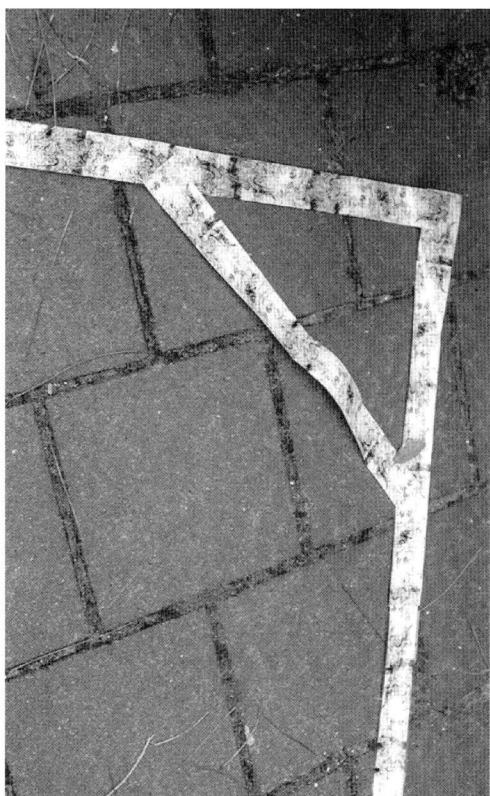

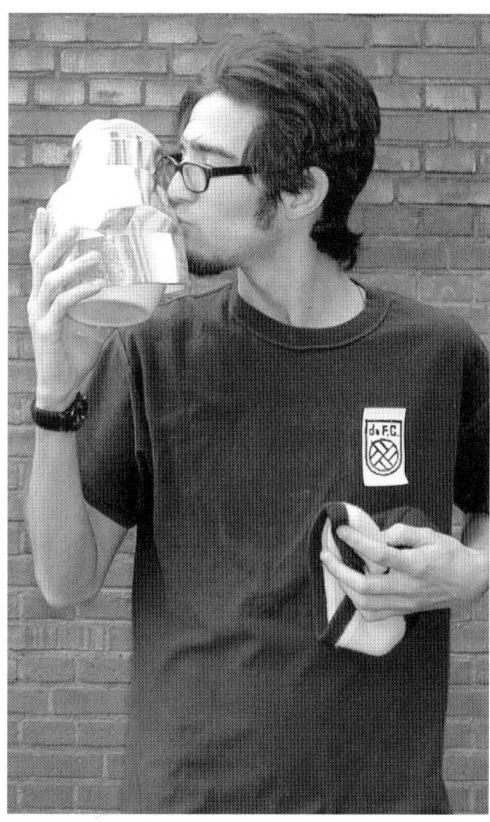

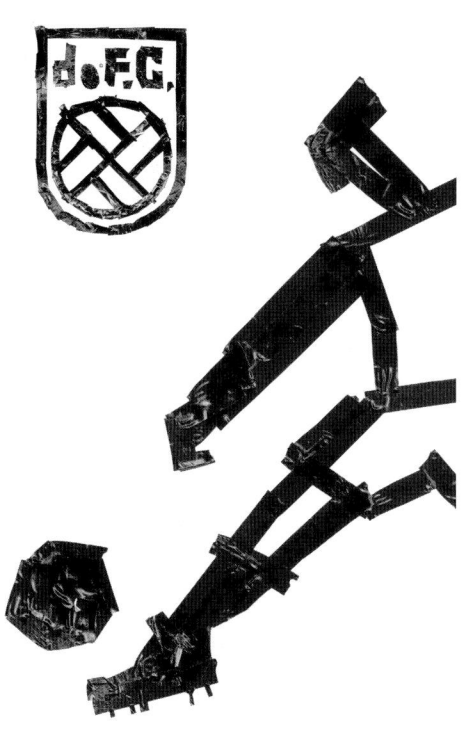

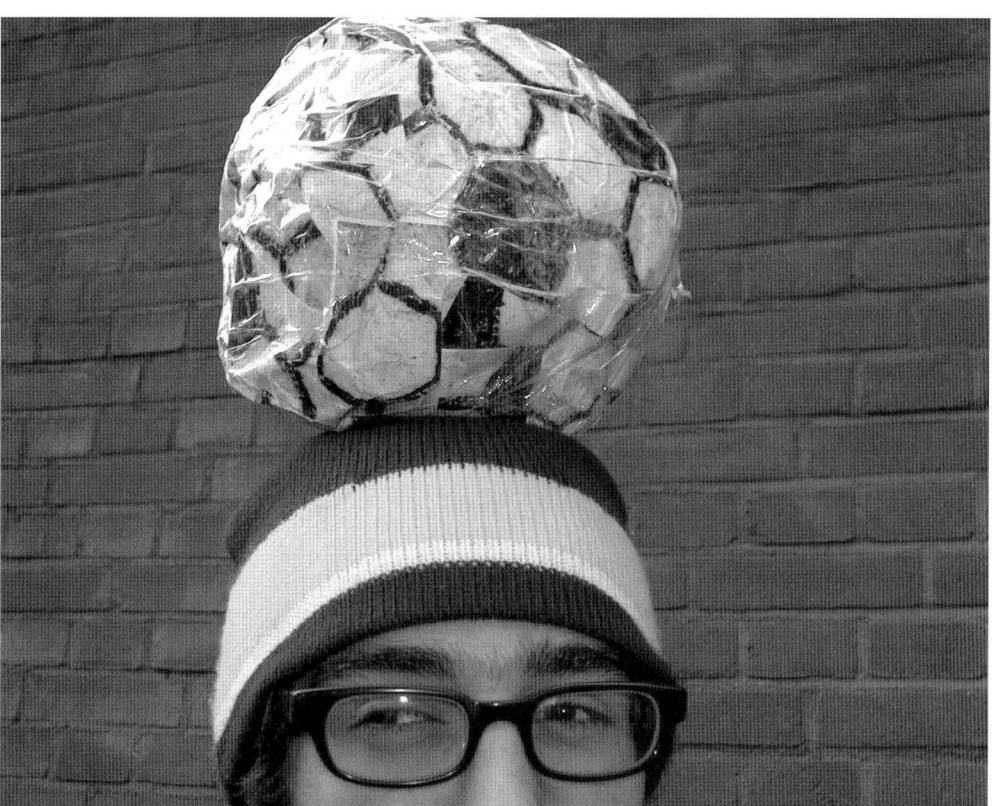

94) do fc

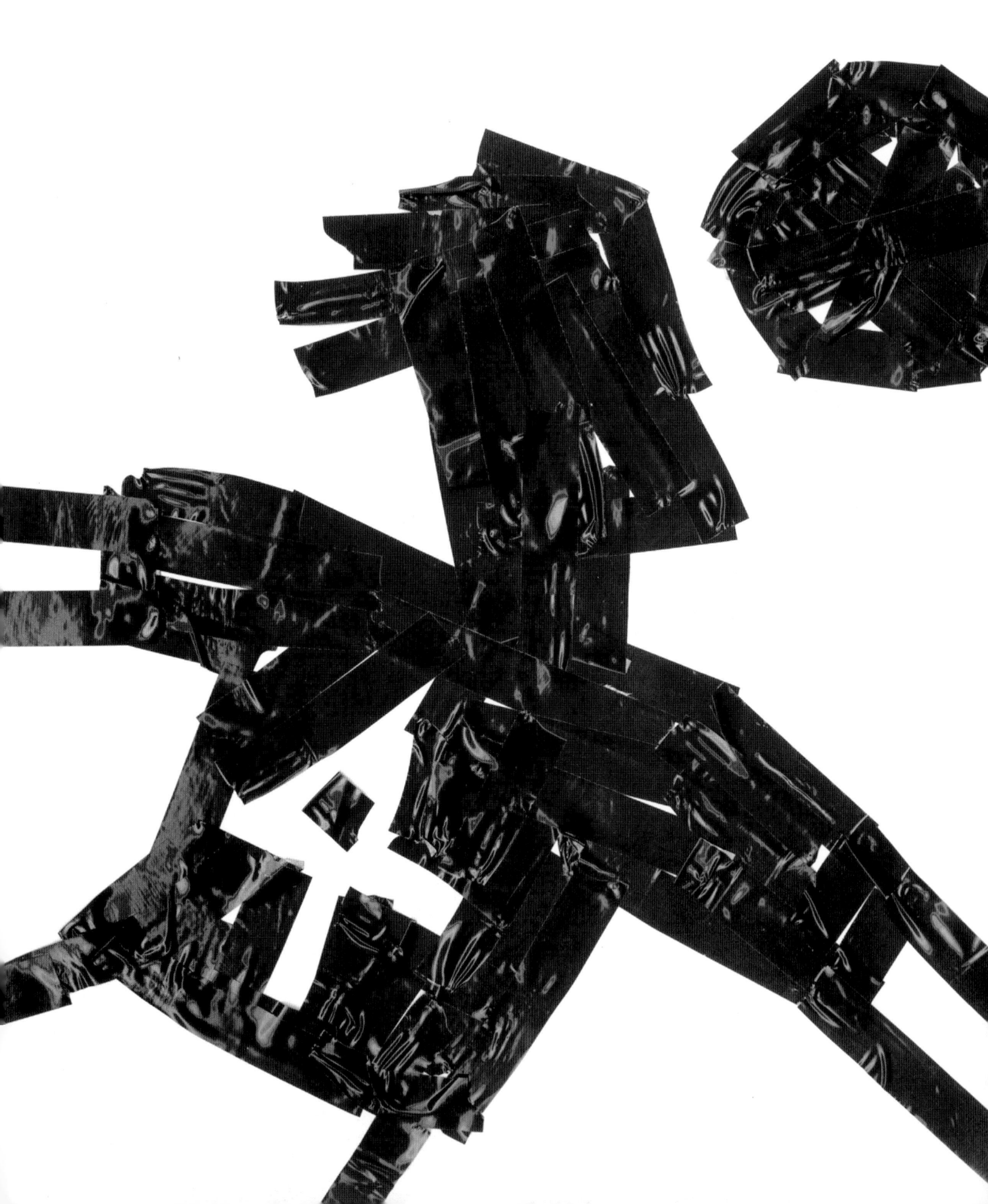

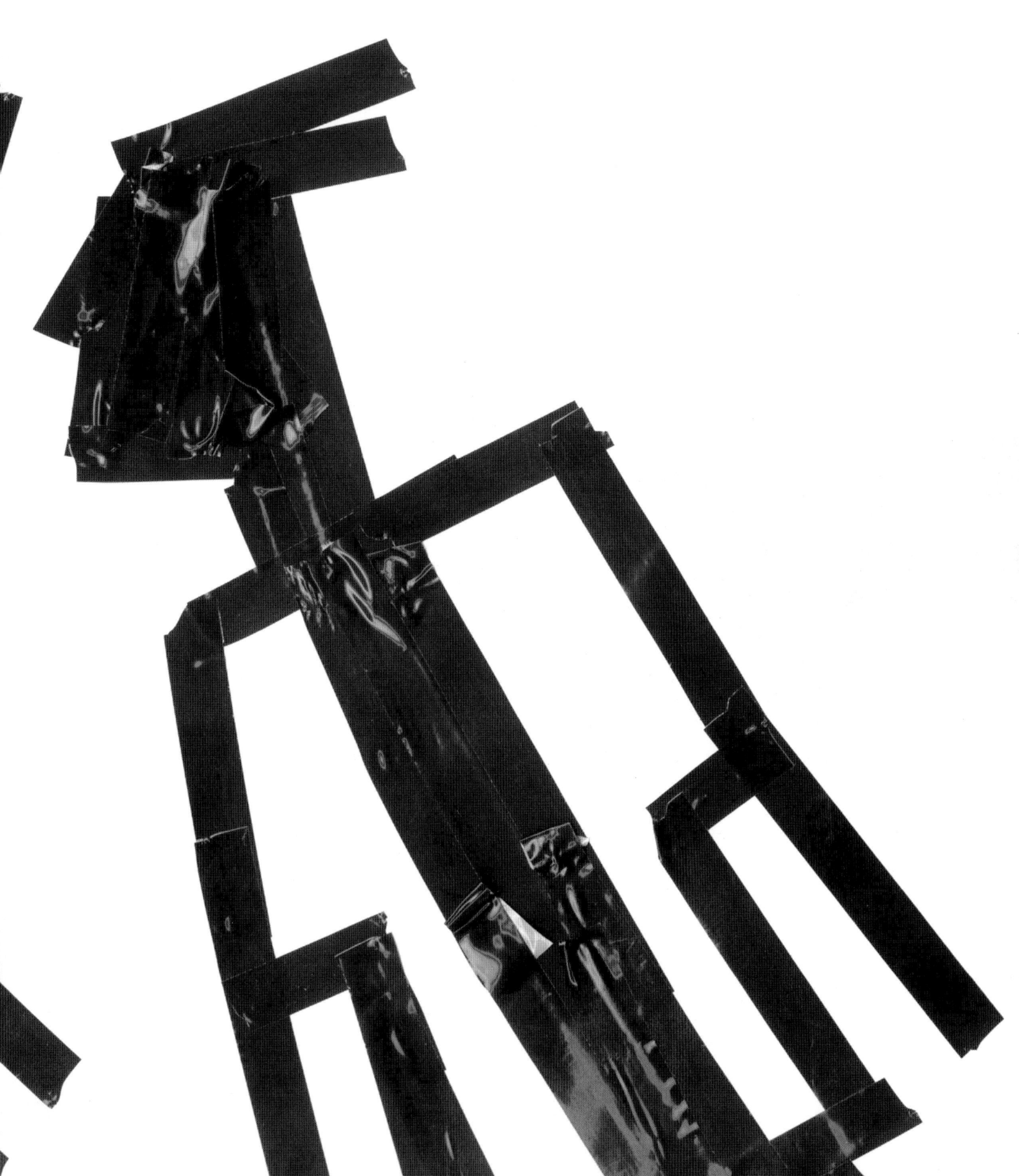

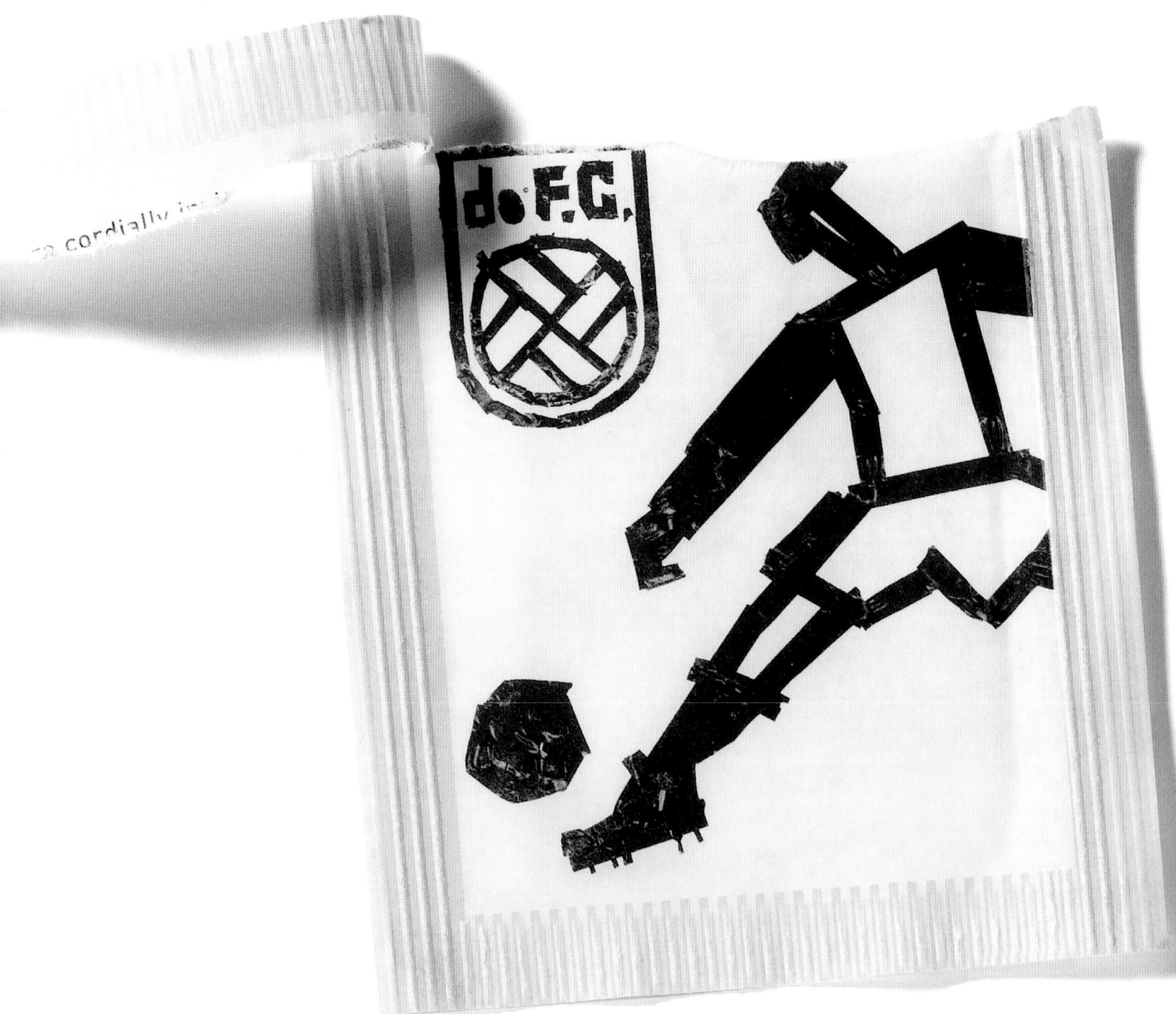

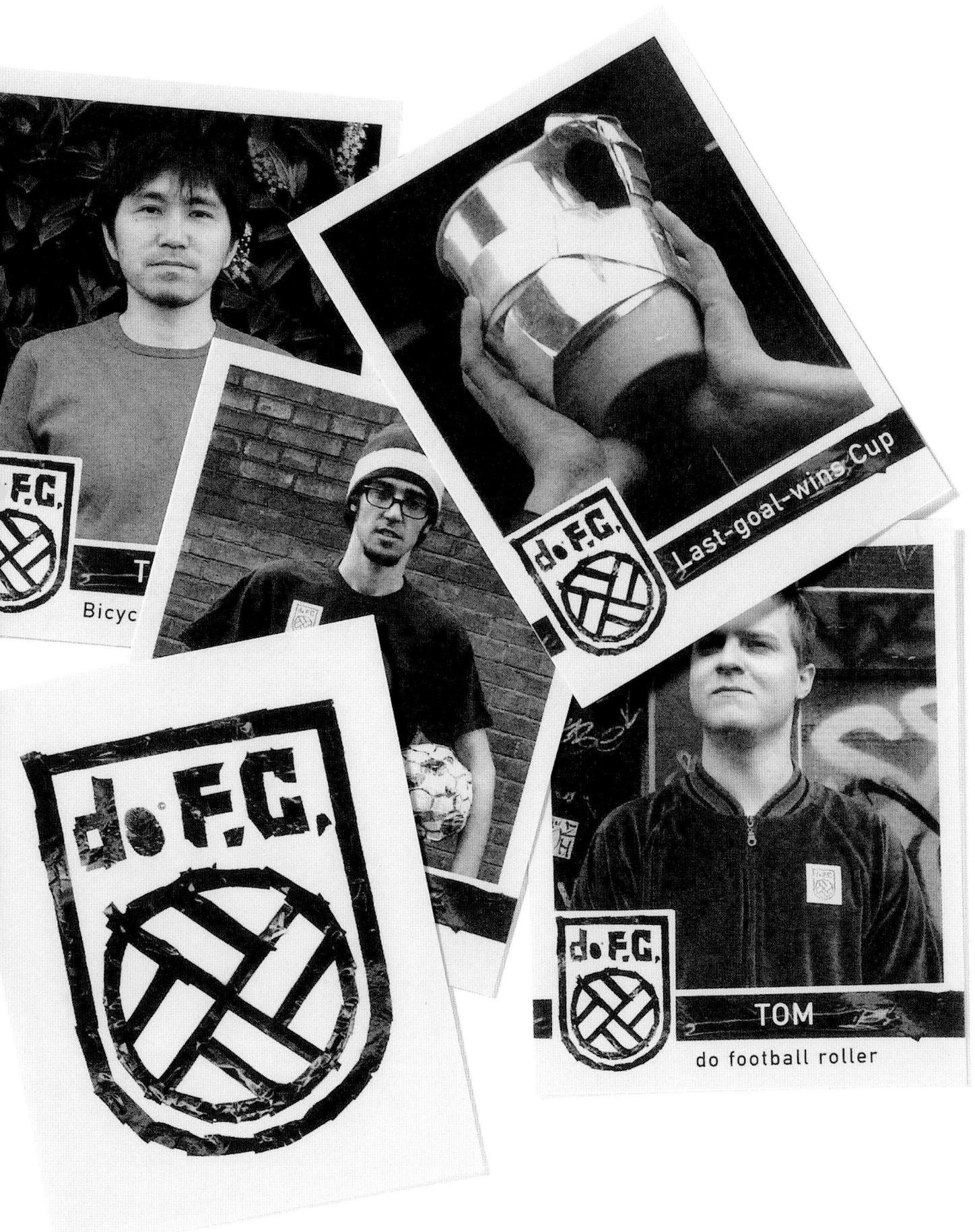

do F.C.

Last-goal-wins Cup

Bicyc...

T...

TOM

do football roller

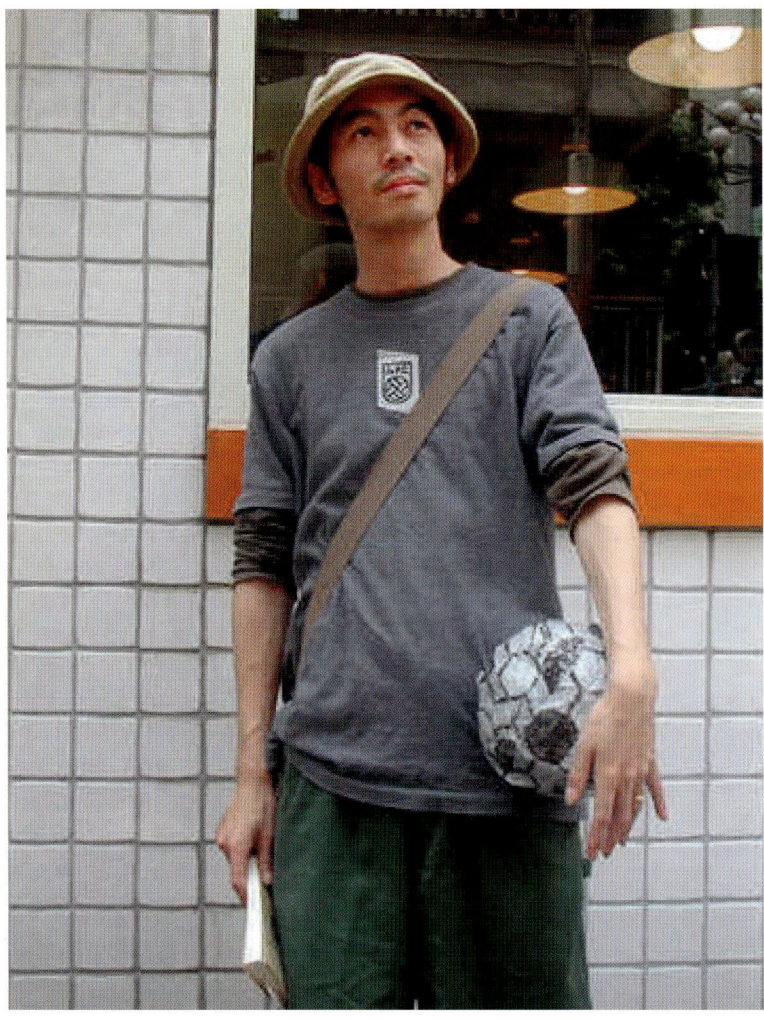

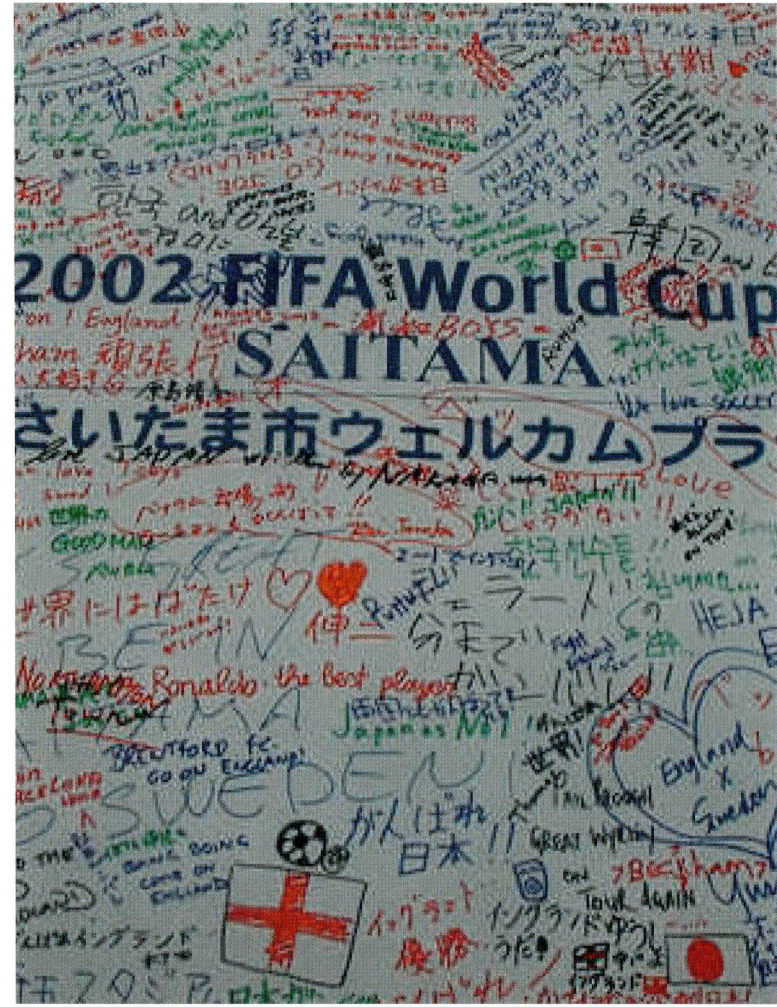

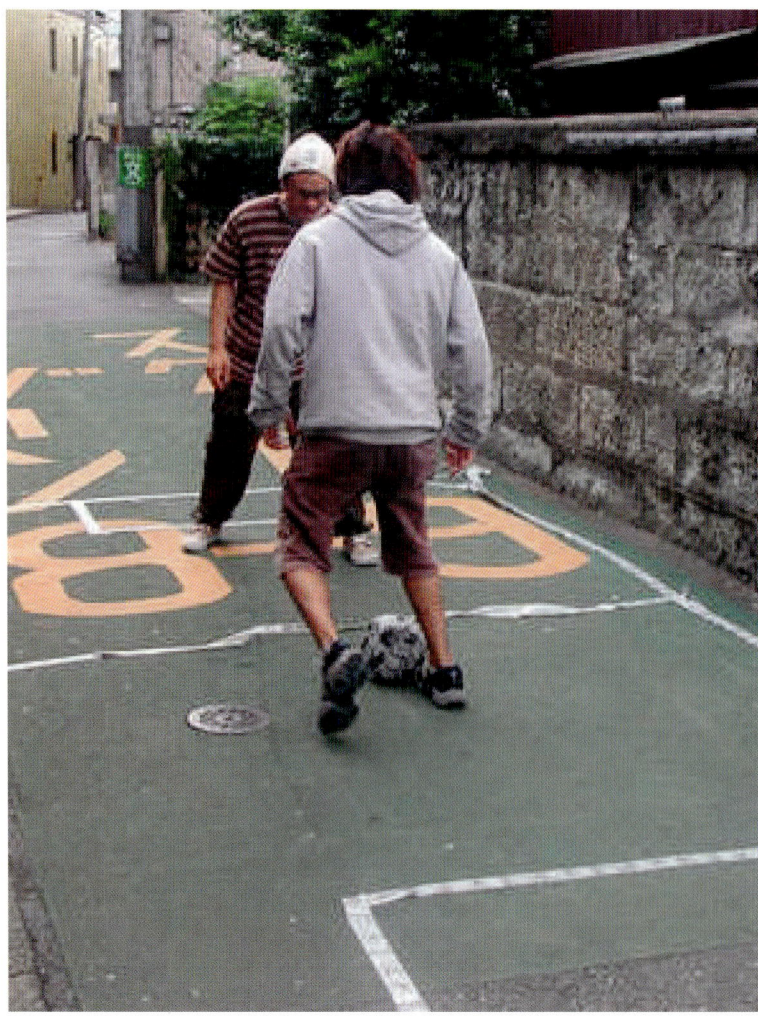

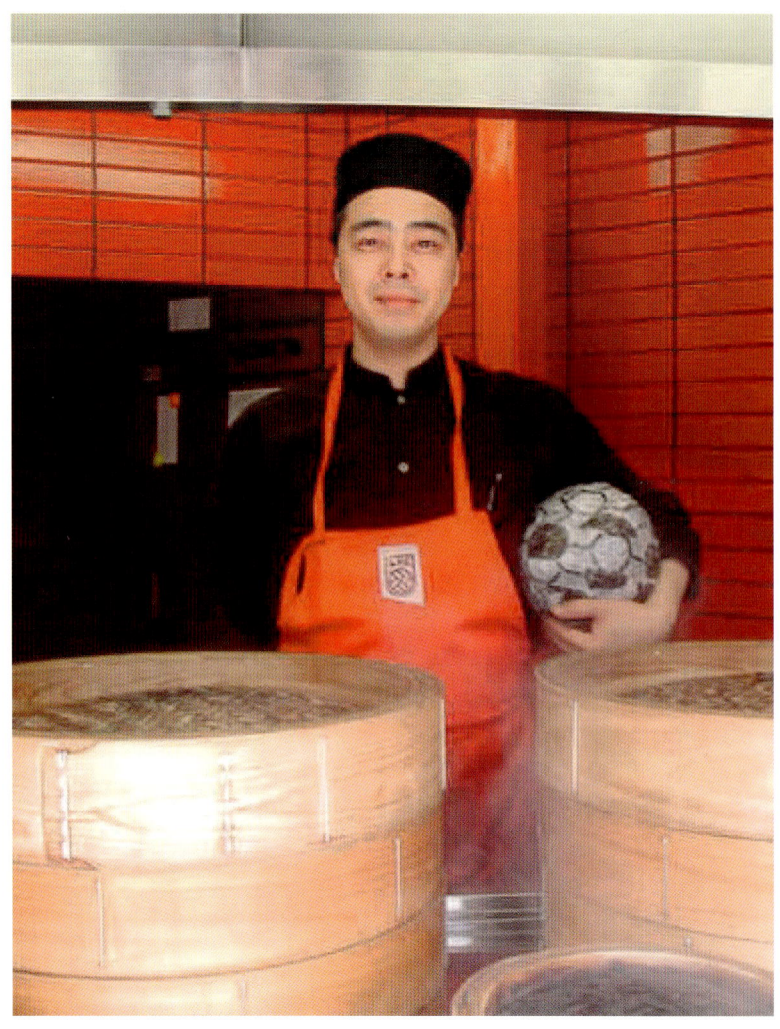

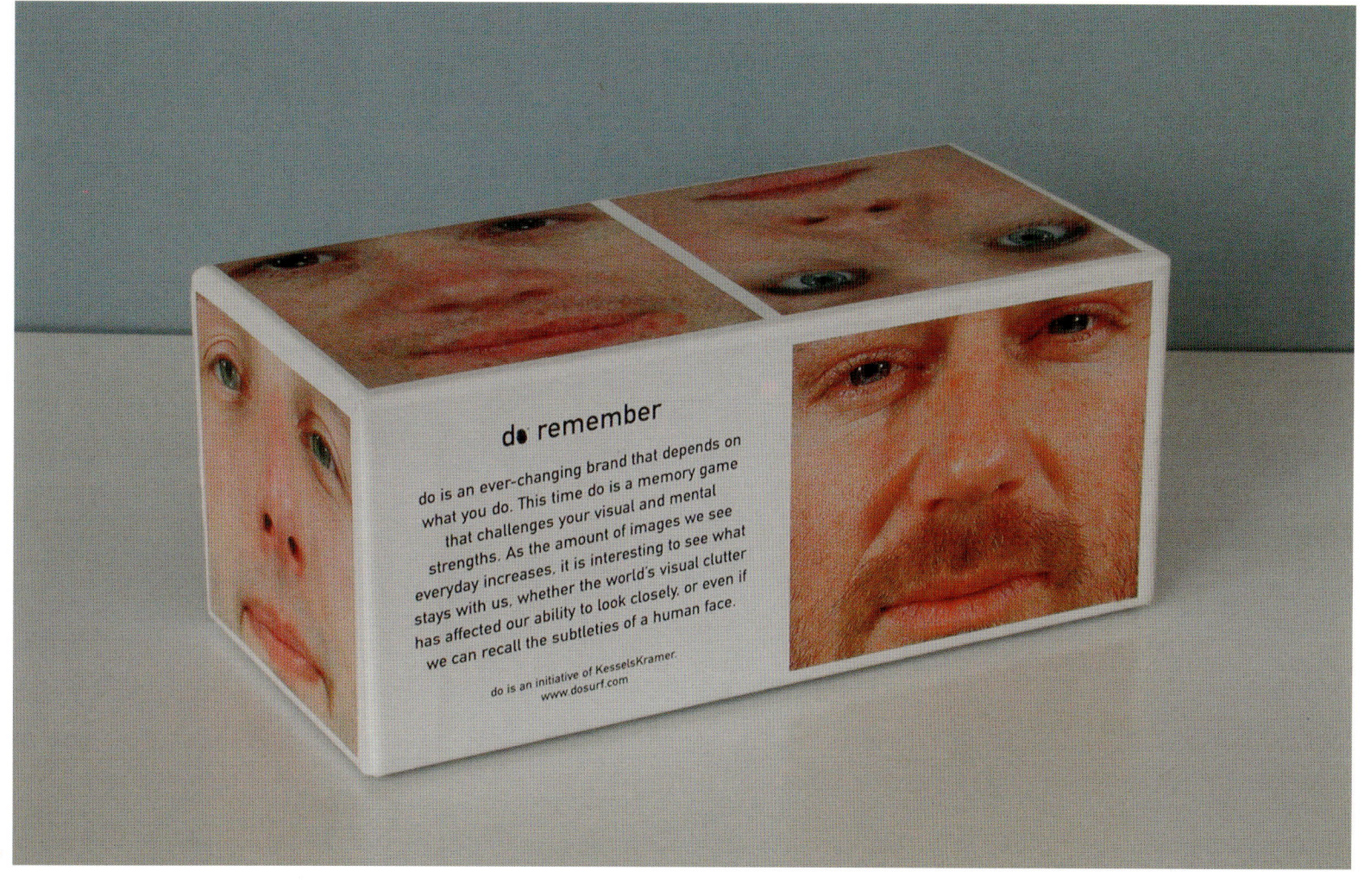

do remember

do is an ever-changing brand that depends on what you do. This time do is a memory game that challenges your visual and mental strengths. As the amount of images we see everyday increases, it is interesting to see what stays with us, whether the world's visual clutter has affected our ability to look closely, or even if we can recall the subtleties of a human face.

do is an initiative of KesselsKramer.
www.dosurf.com

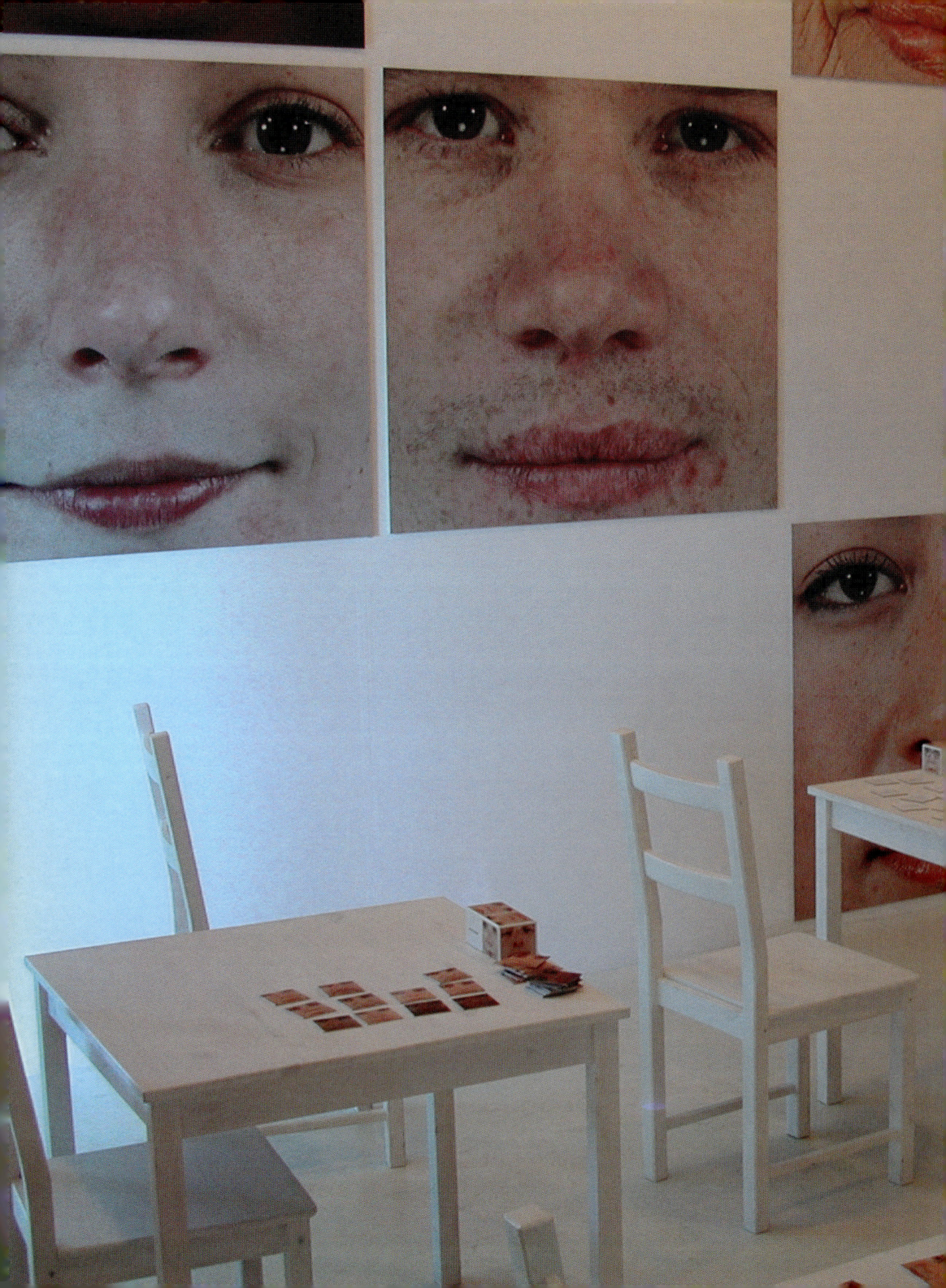

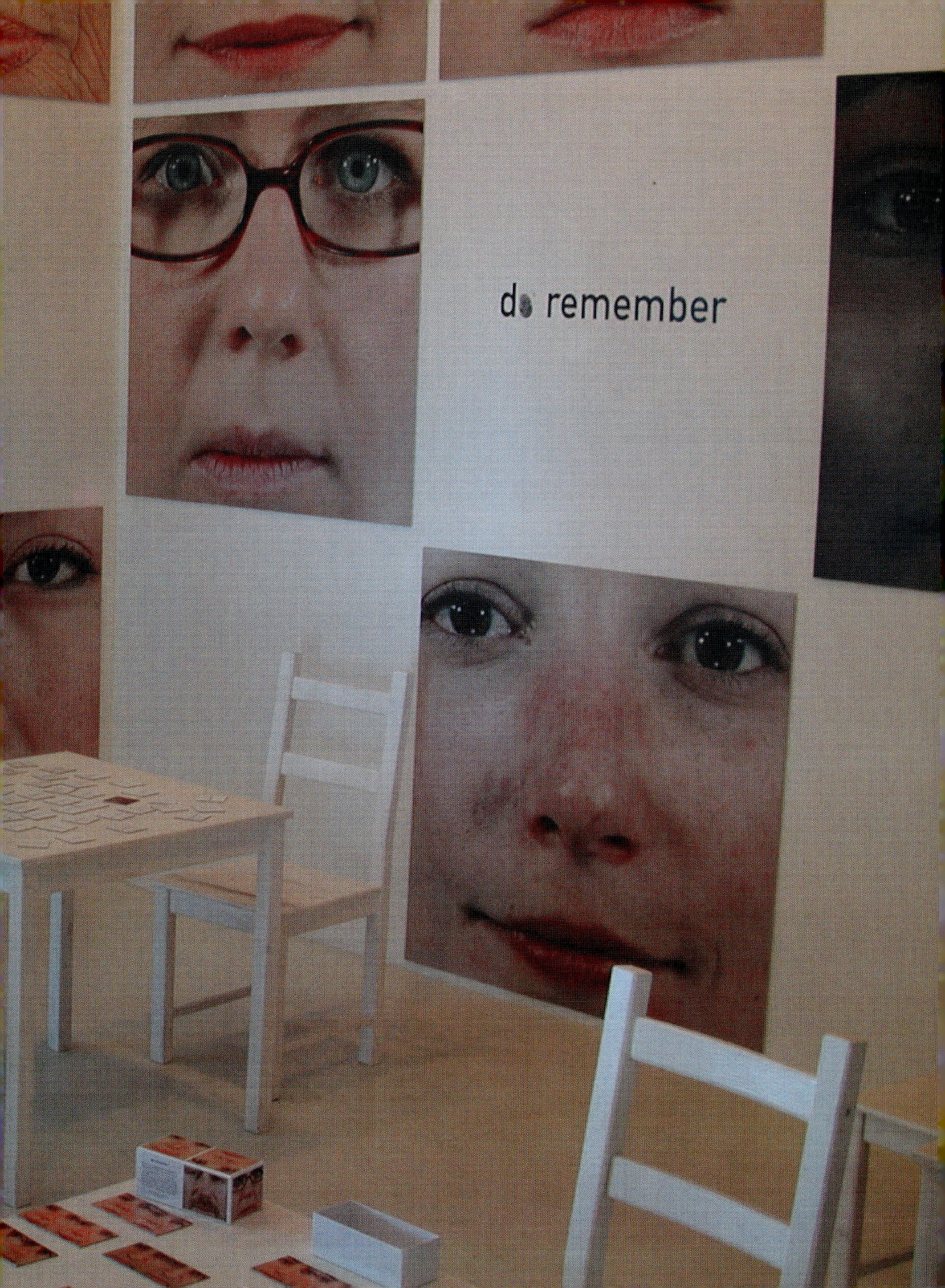

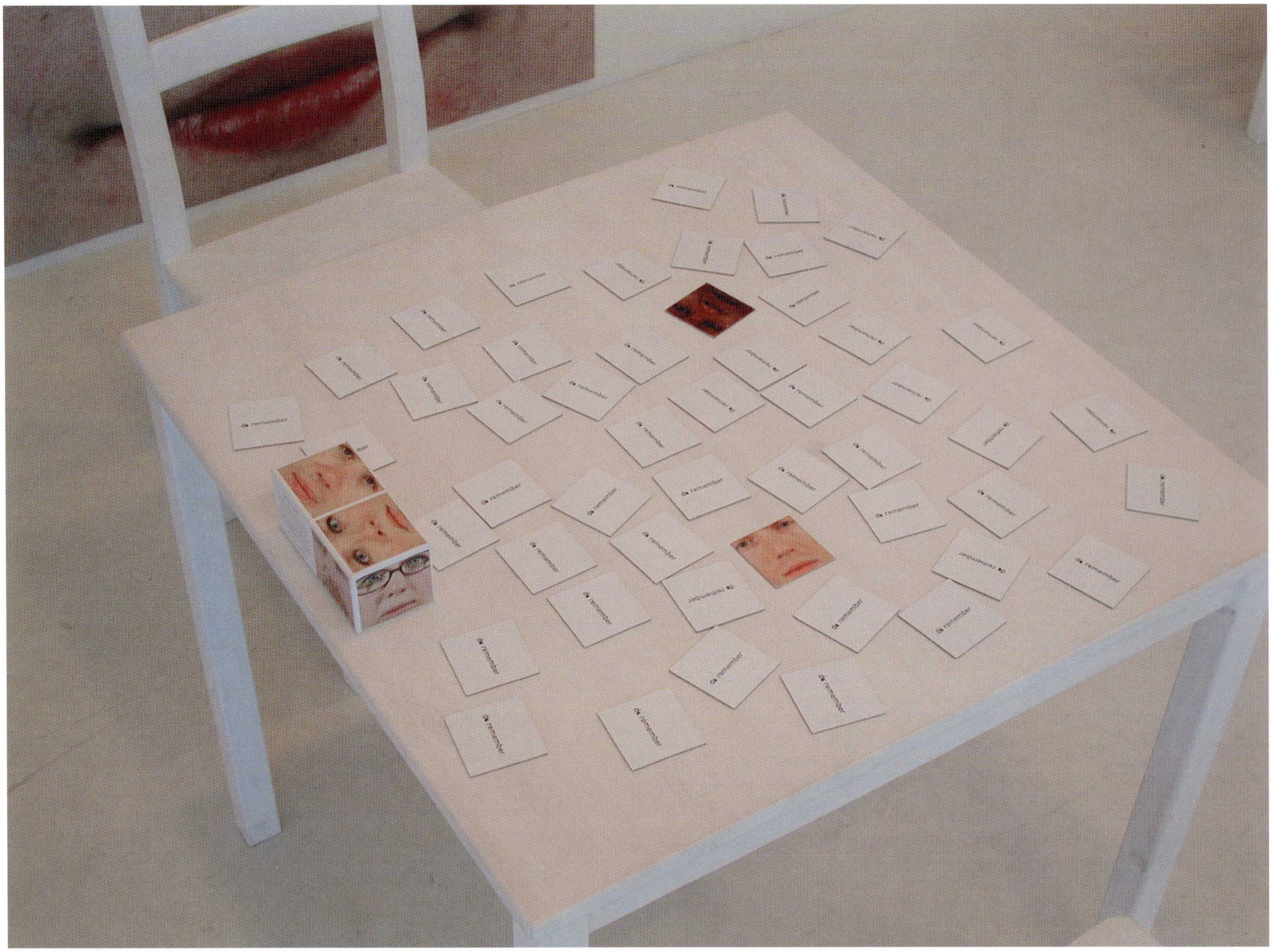

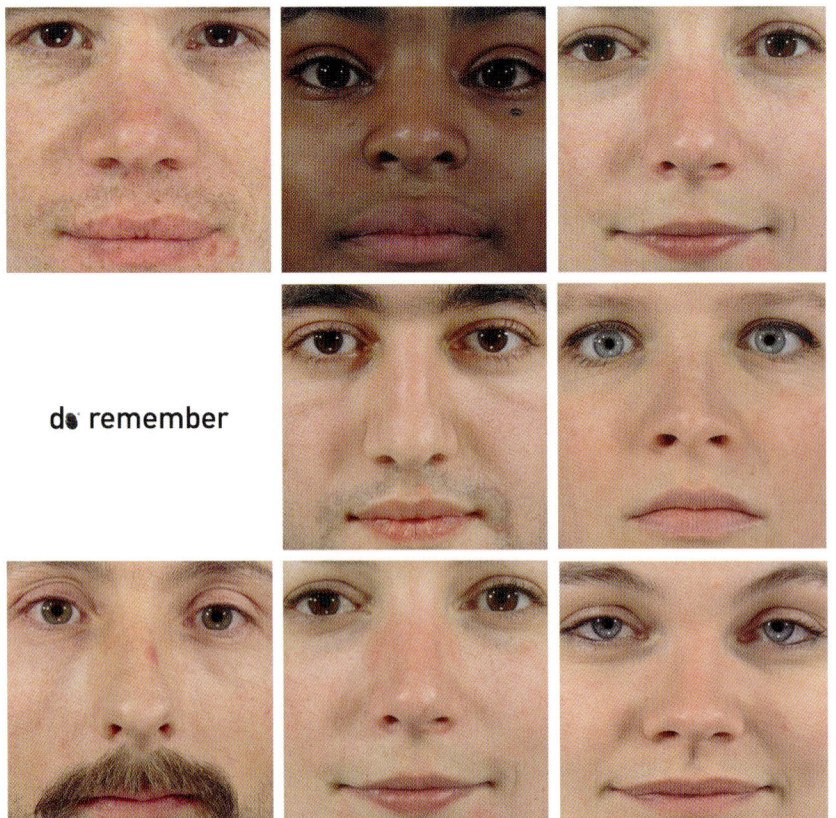

do remember

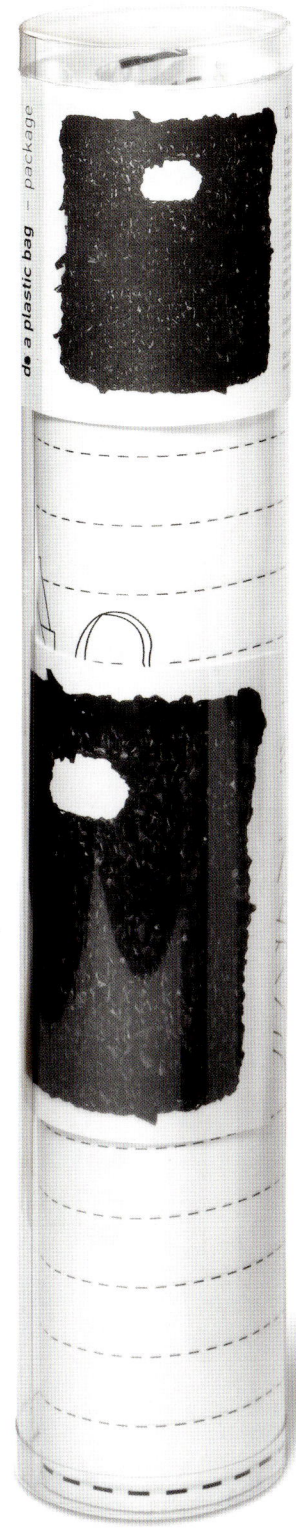
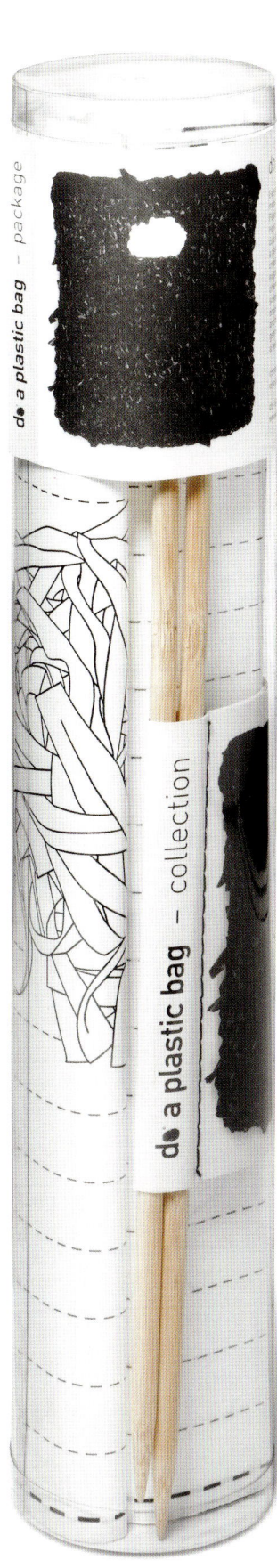
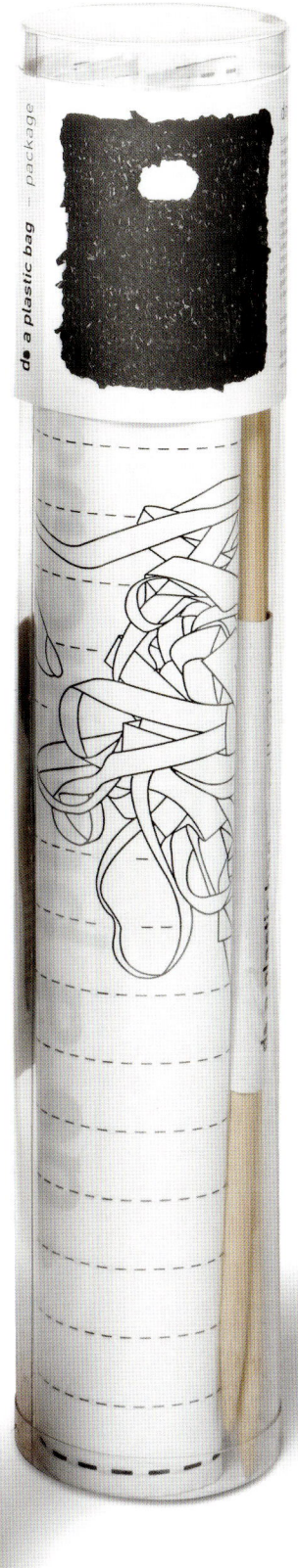

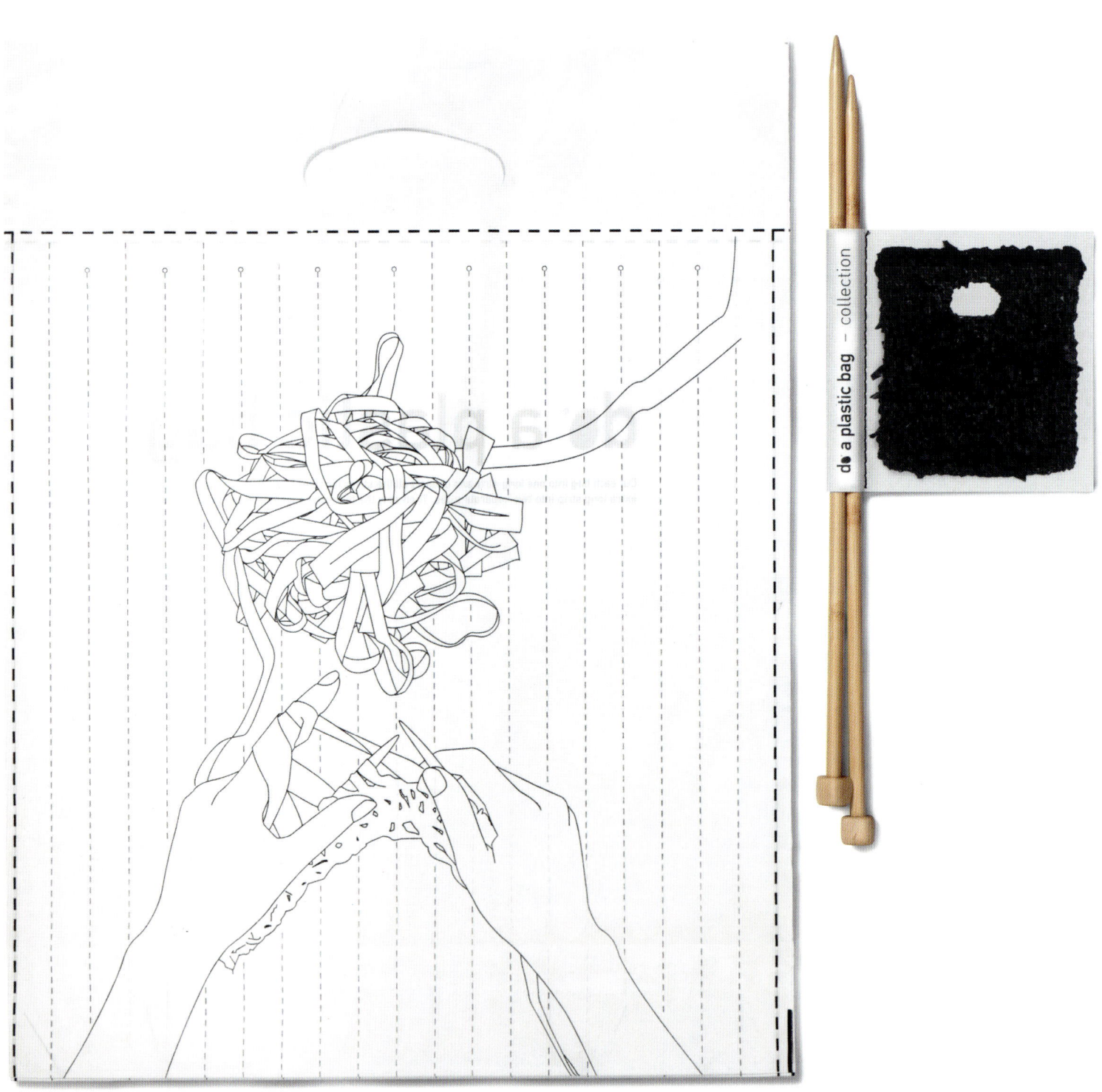

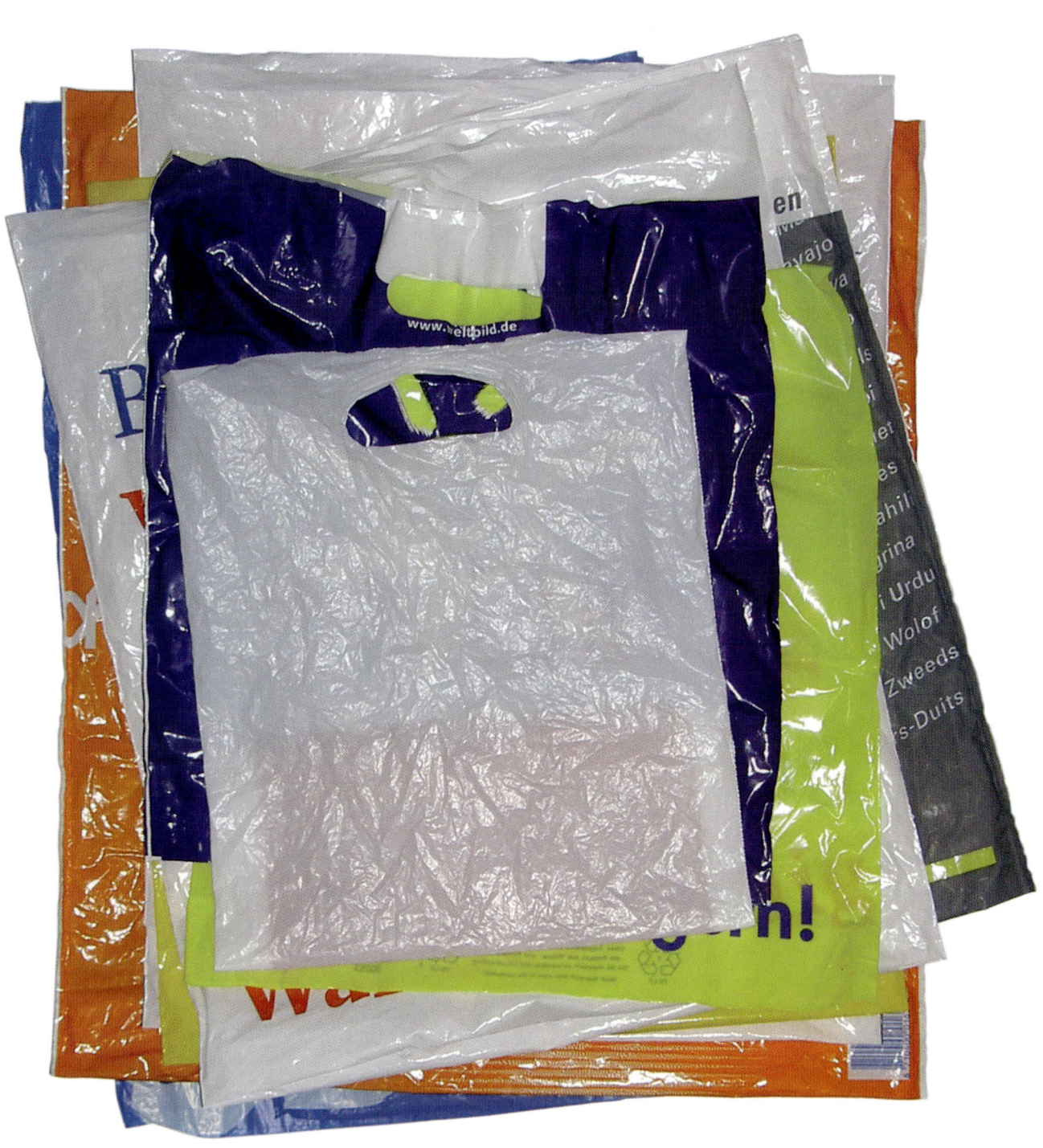

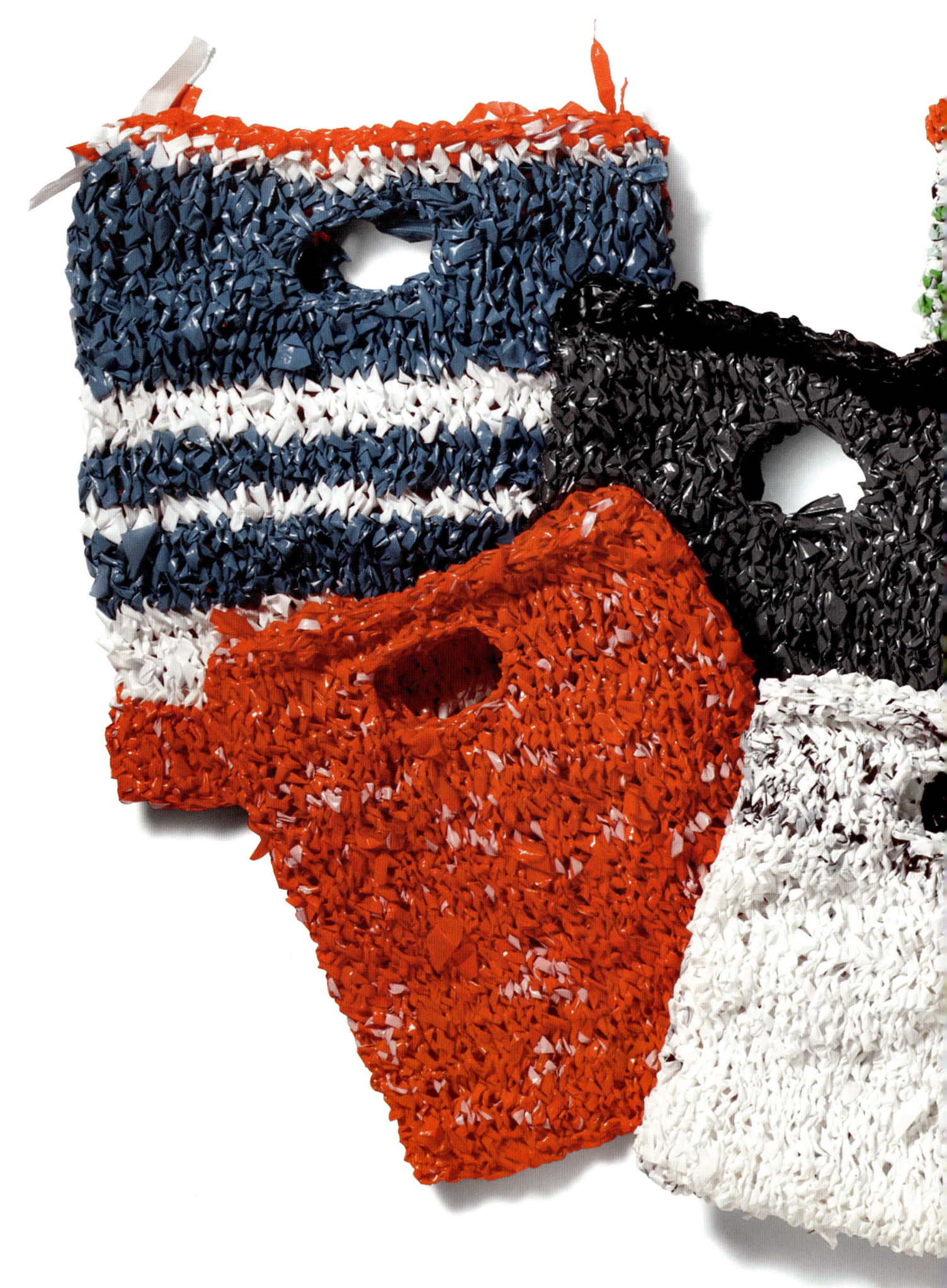

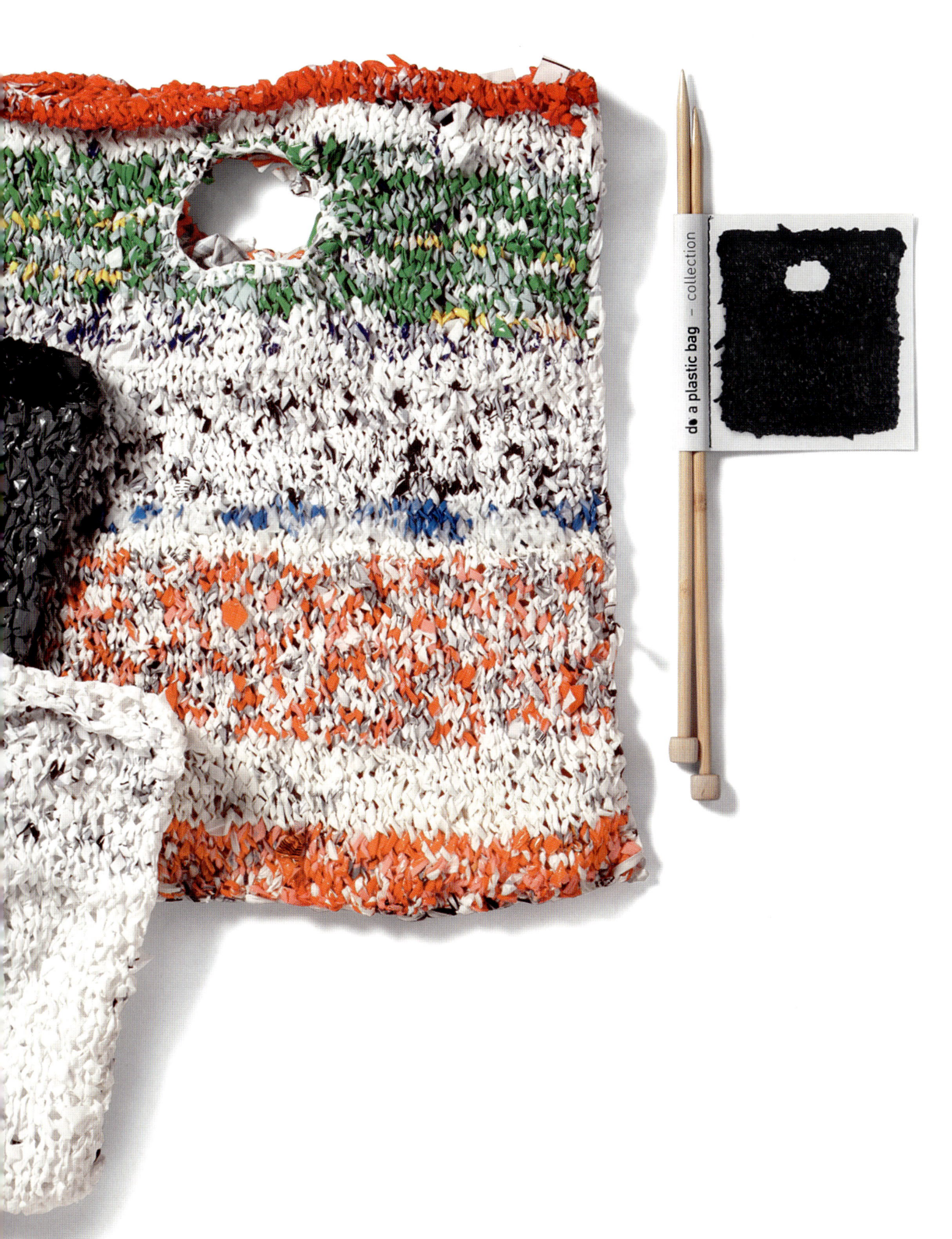

do a plastic bag – collection

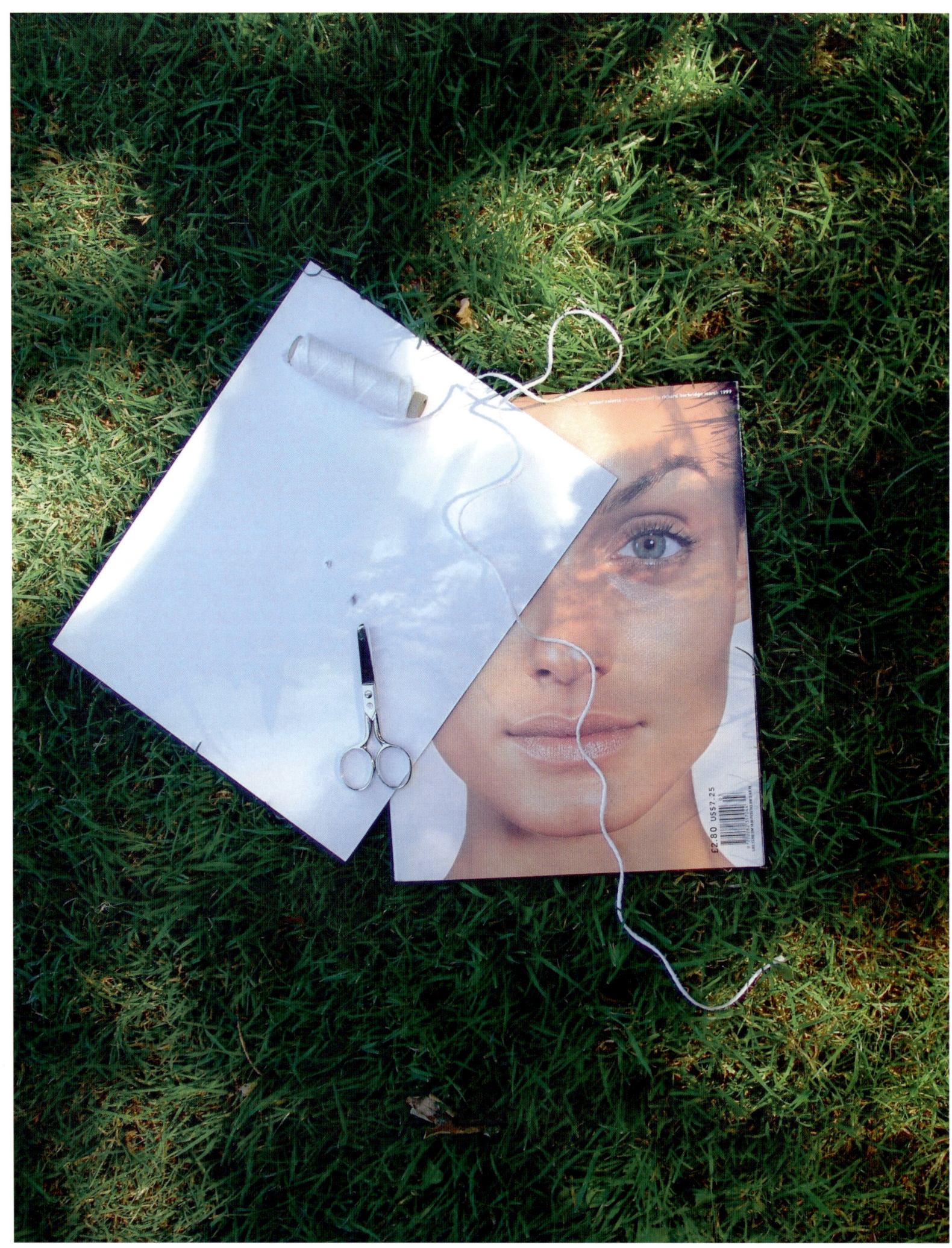

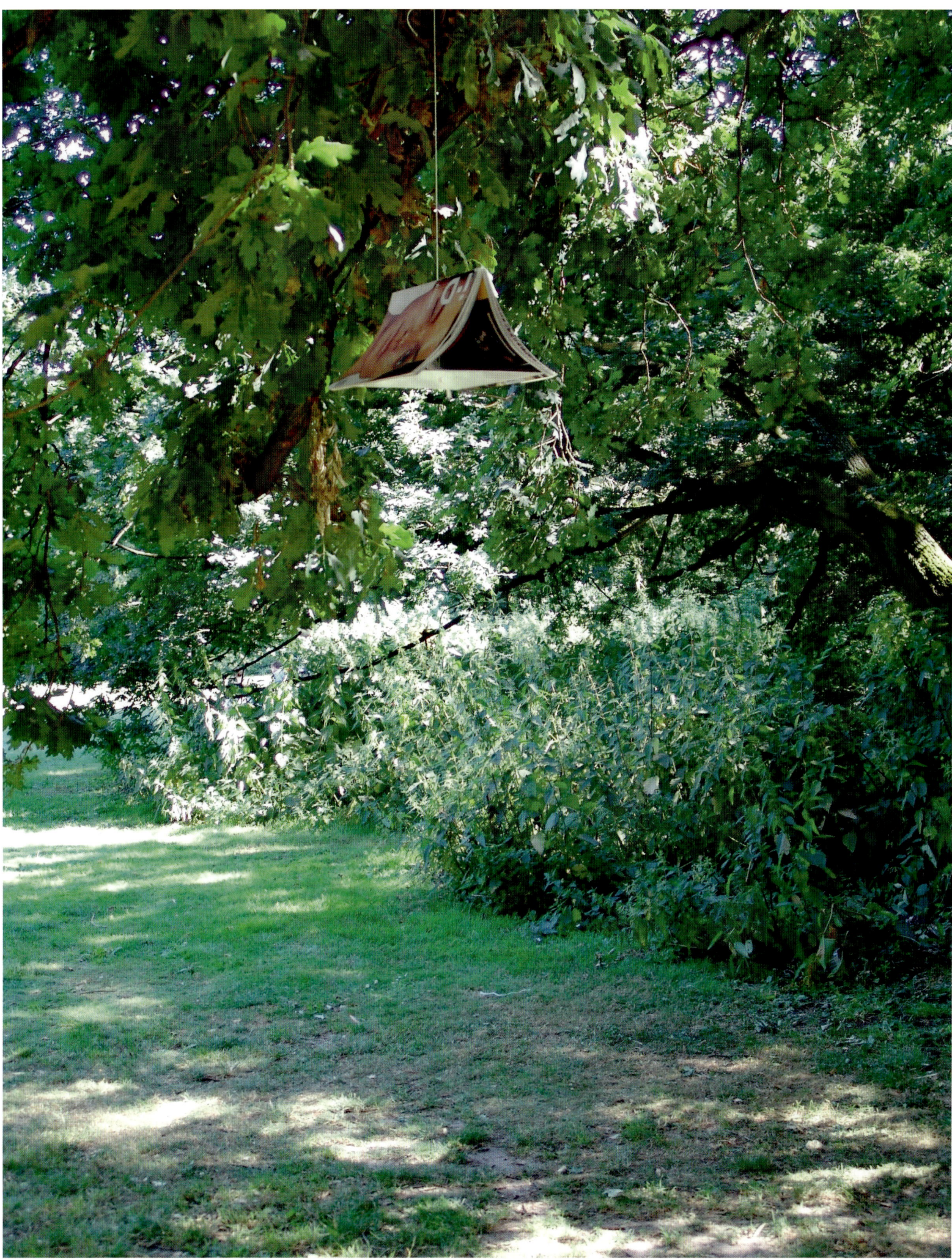

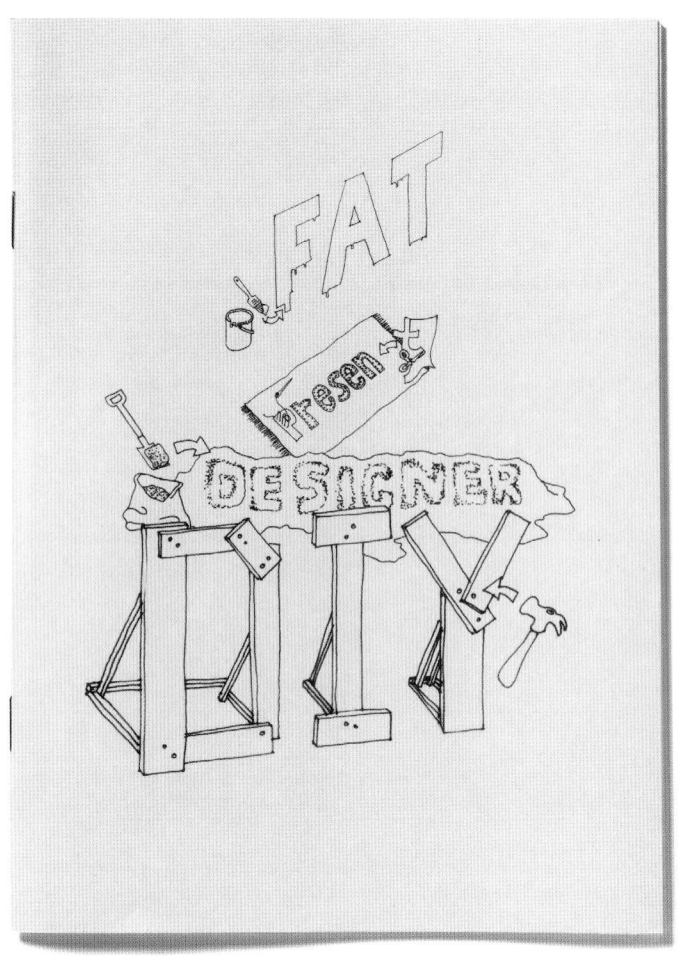

do climb

do / KesselsKramer

As waistlines surge in developed countries, do has an inspiring project for your home or office. Simply choose a preferred course to climb on a wall or ceiling and see life in a different way whilst burning off a few calories.

1. Buy climbing grips from your local climbing shop.

2. Choose a climbing route that will push your physical and mental boundaries. Where you go is up to you.

3. Install climbing grips according to manufacturers instructions.

4. View your world from another perspective.

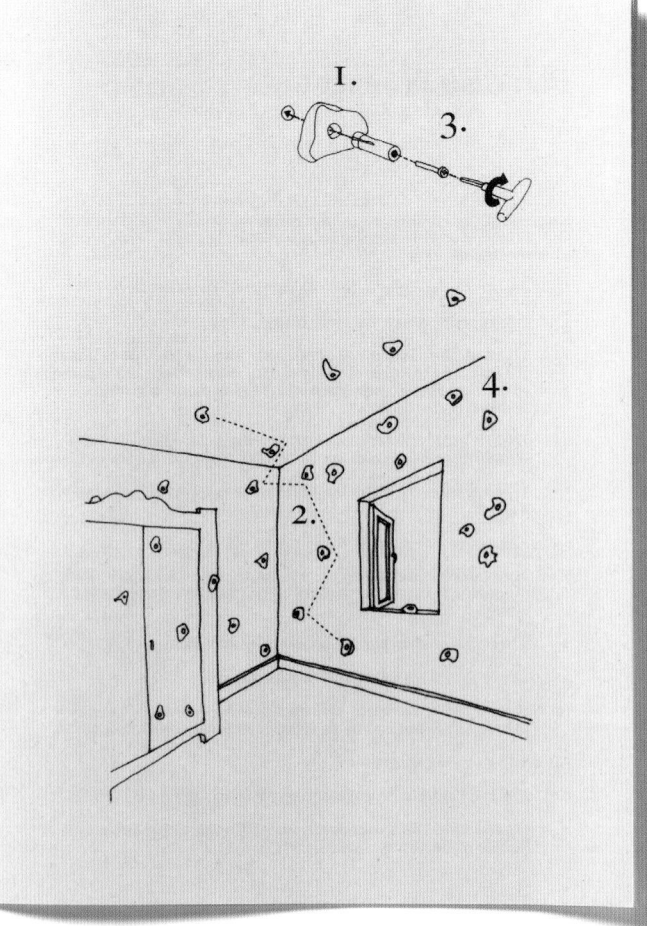

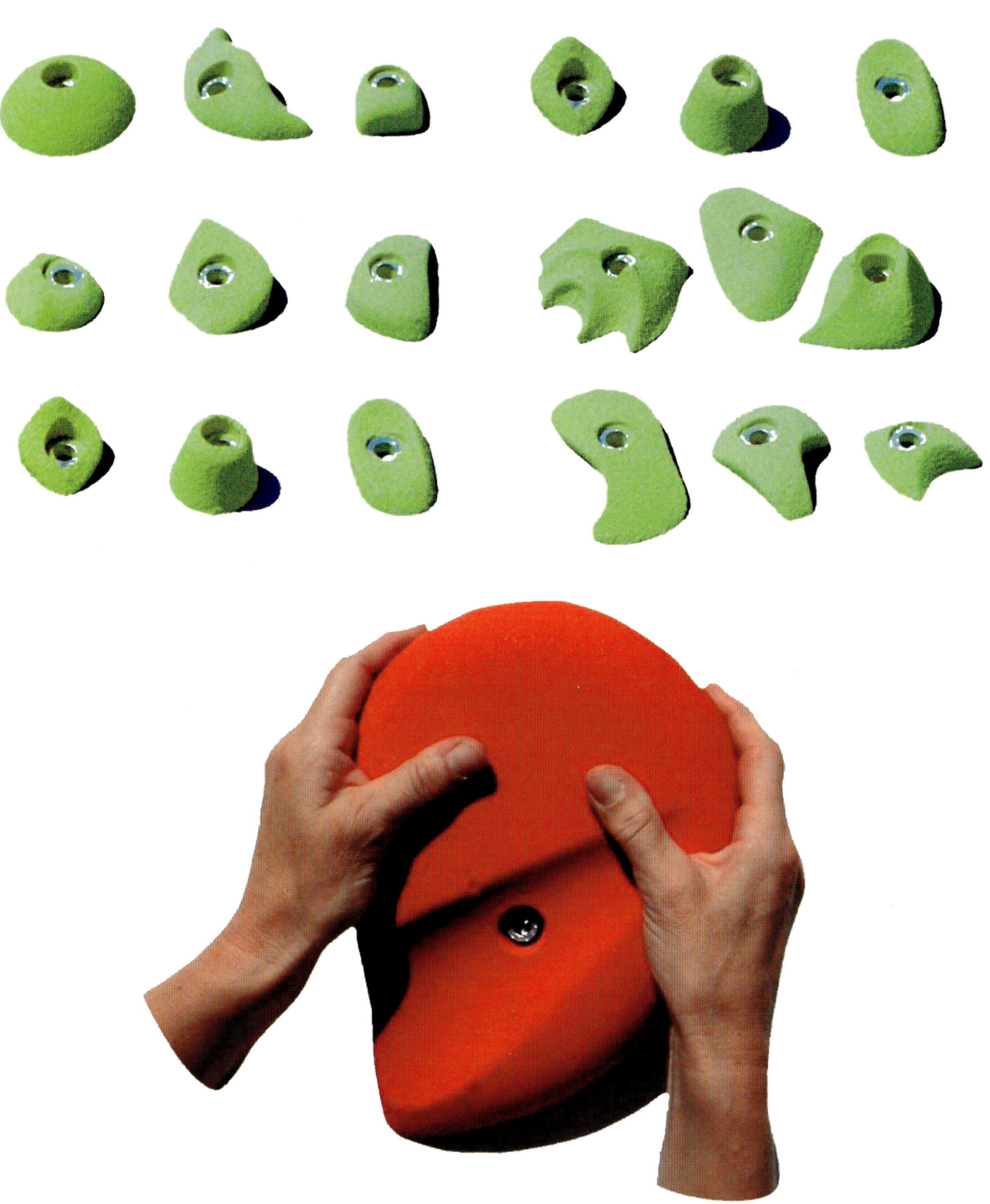

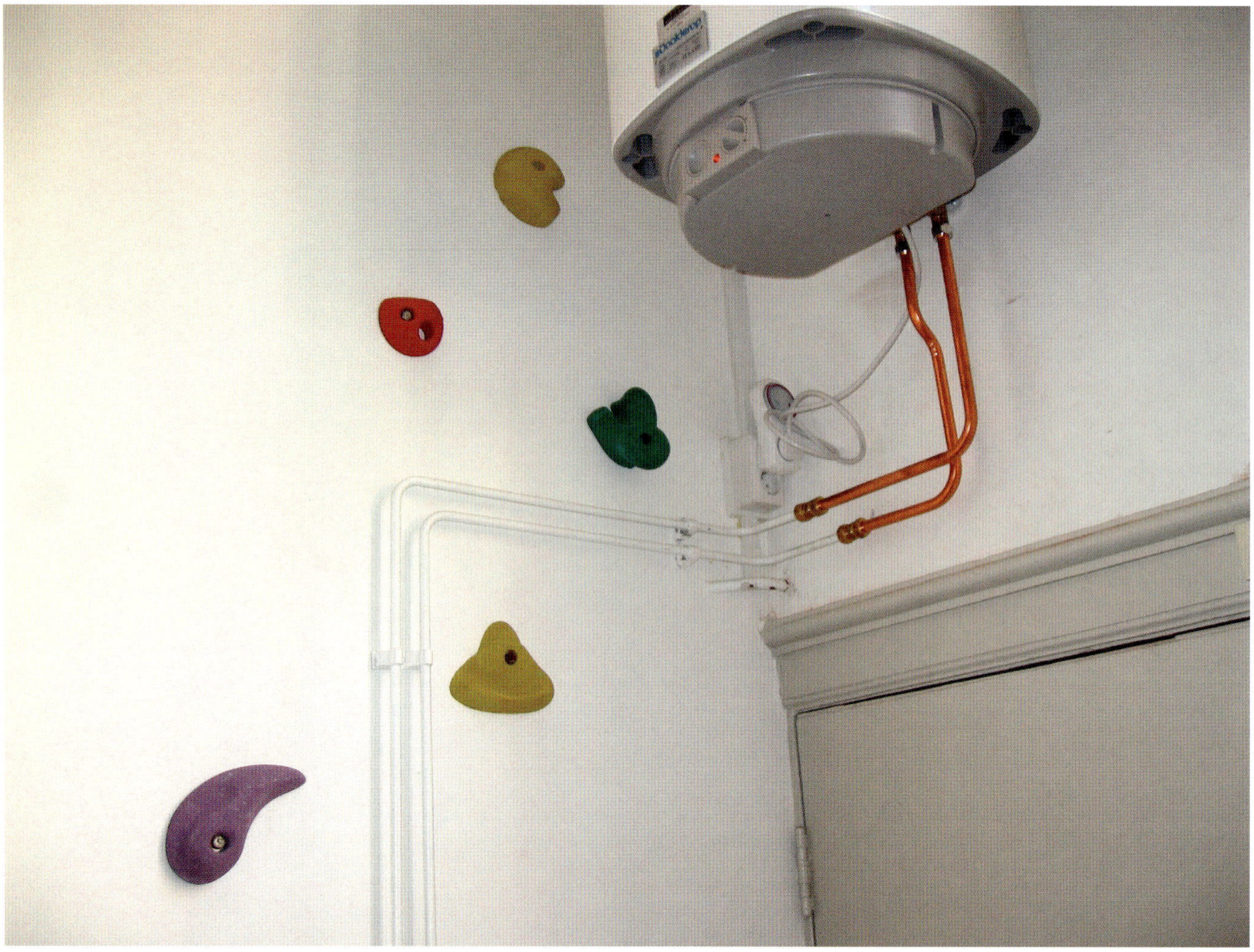

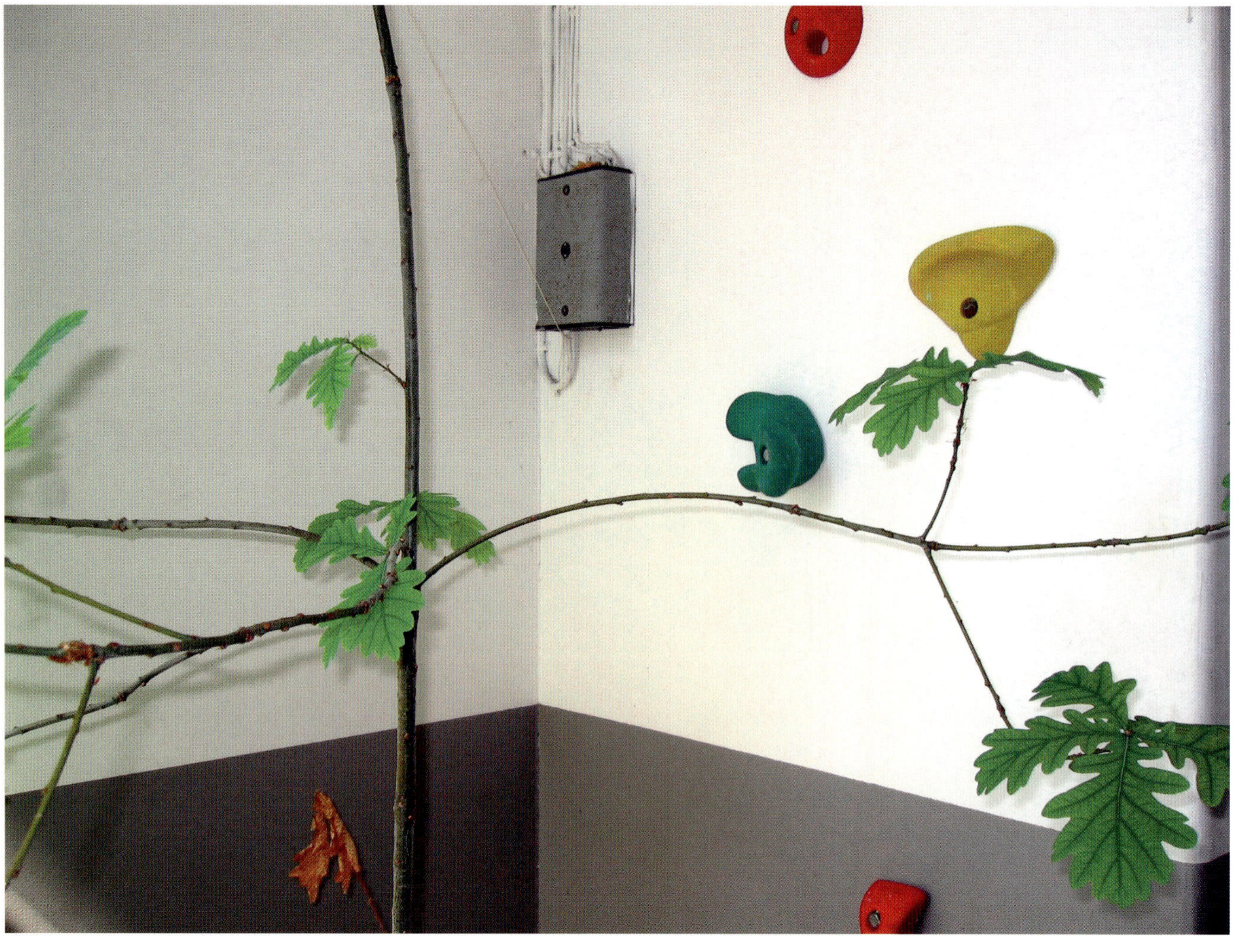

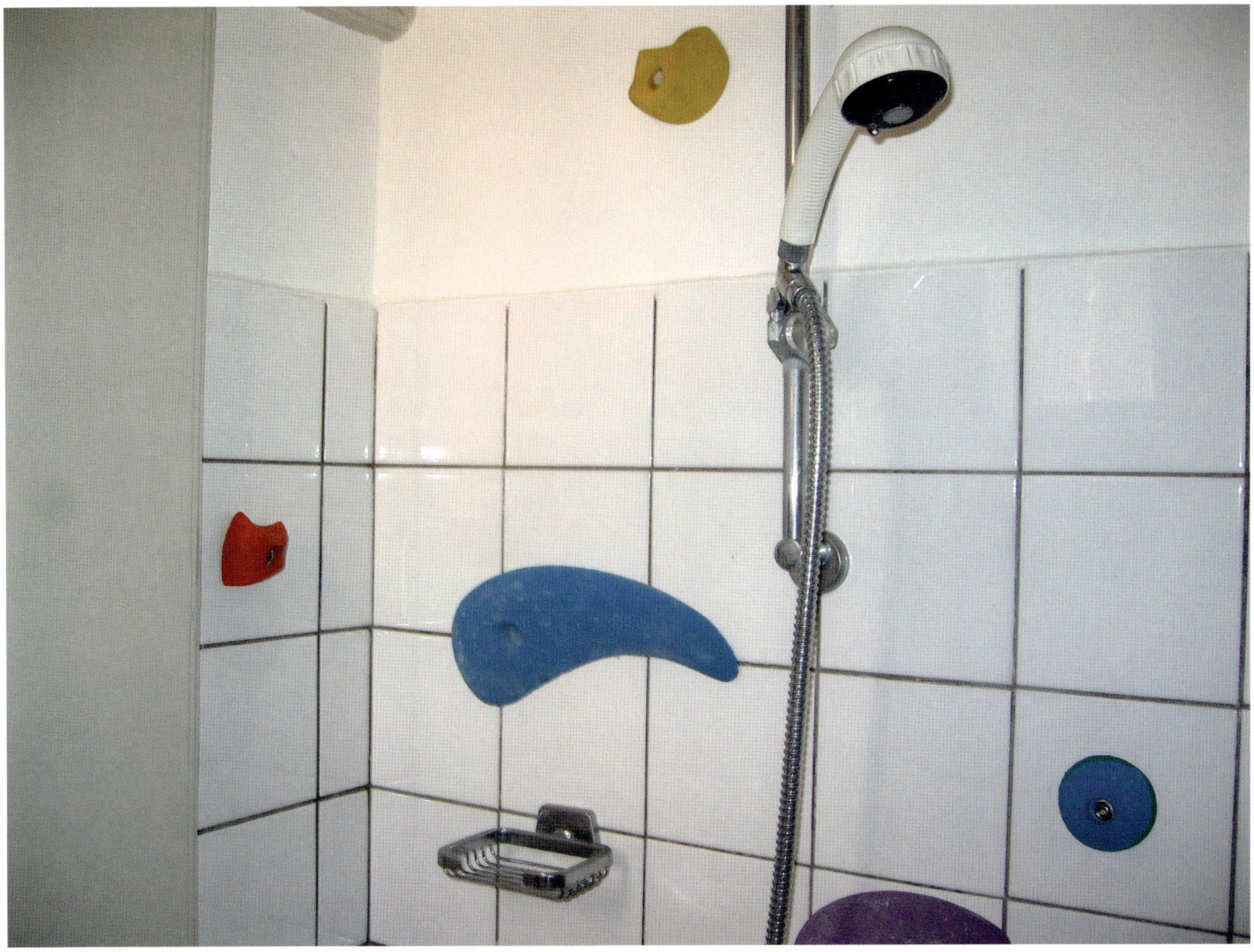

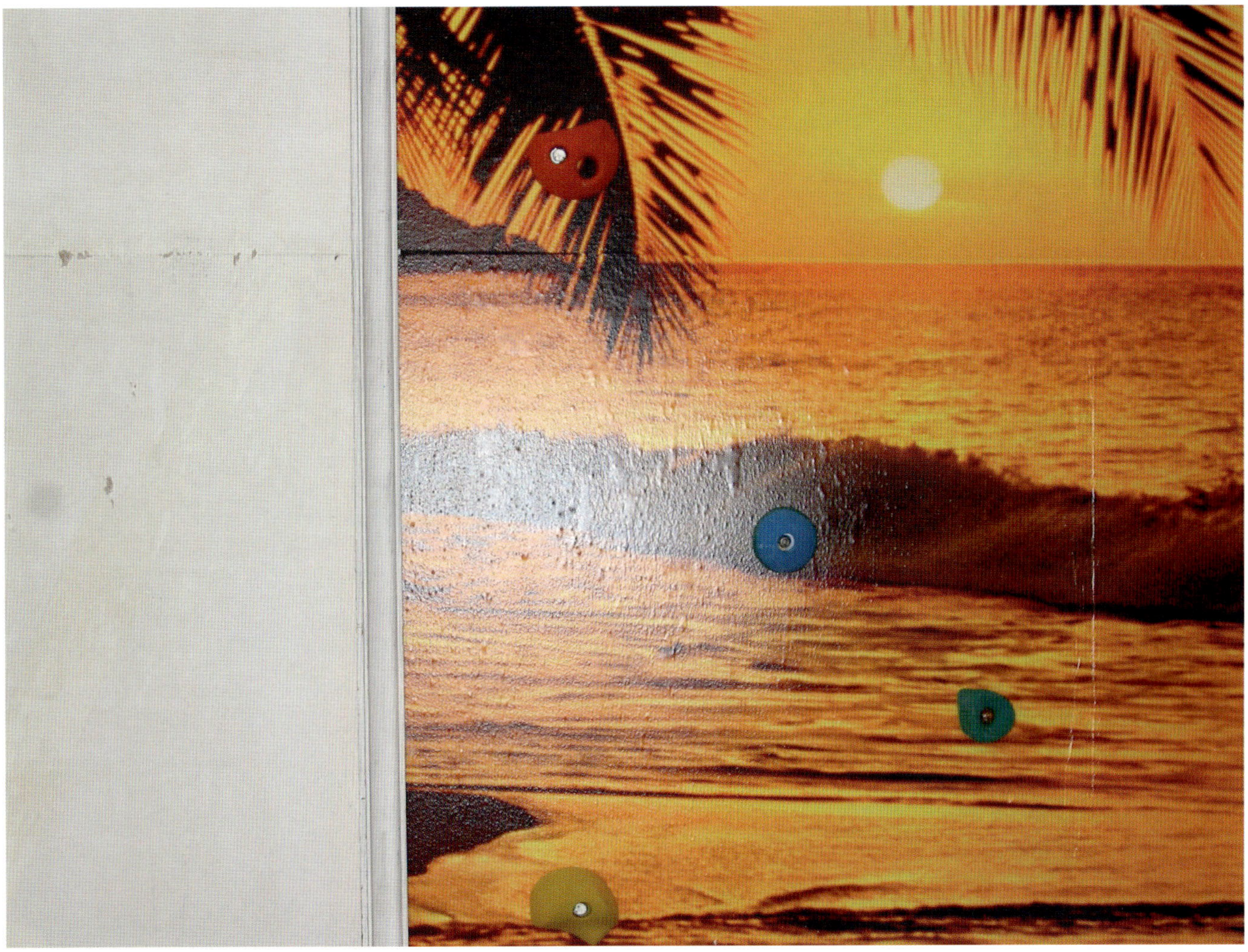

1

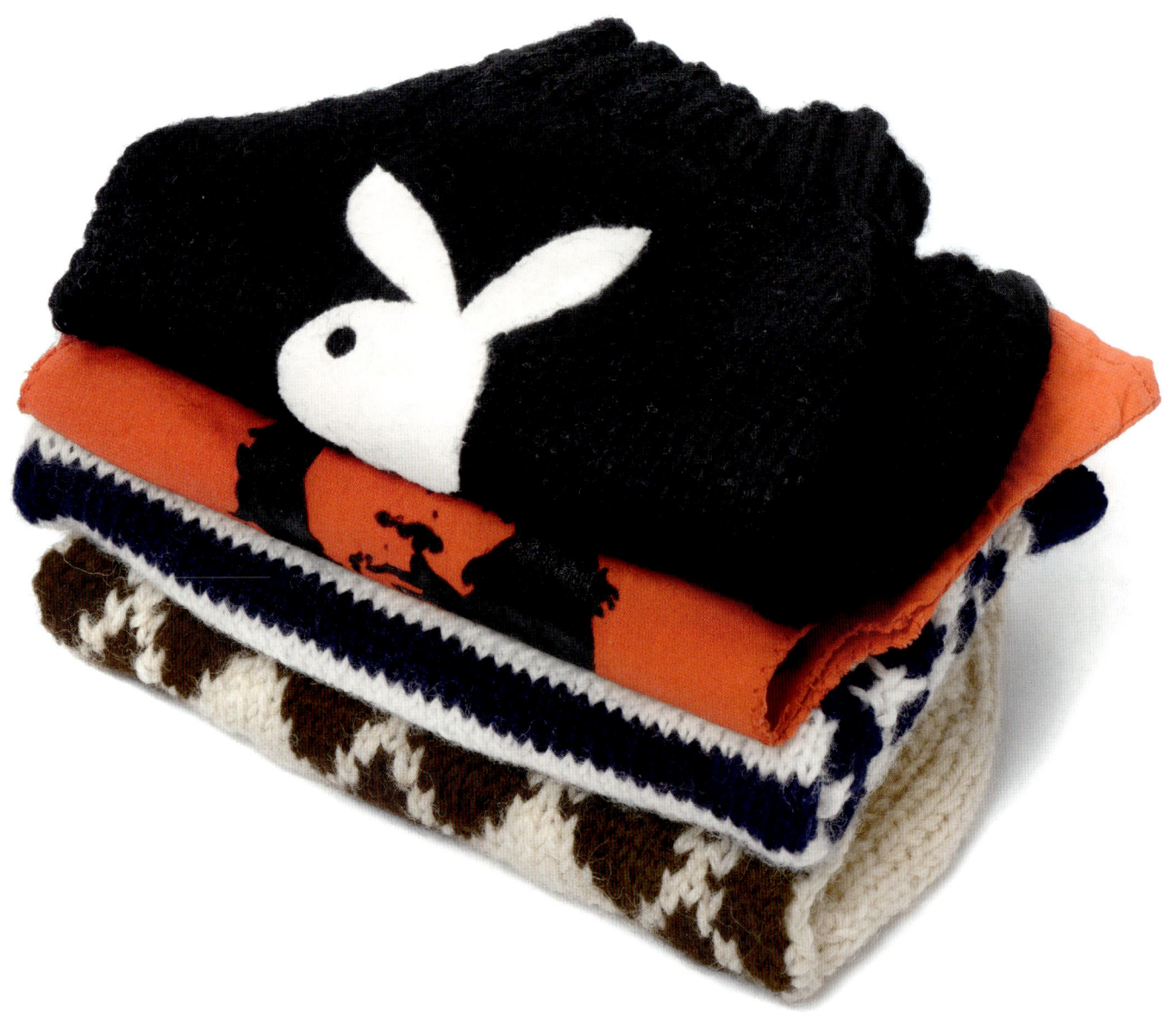

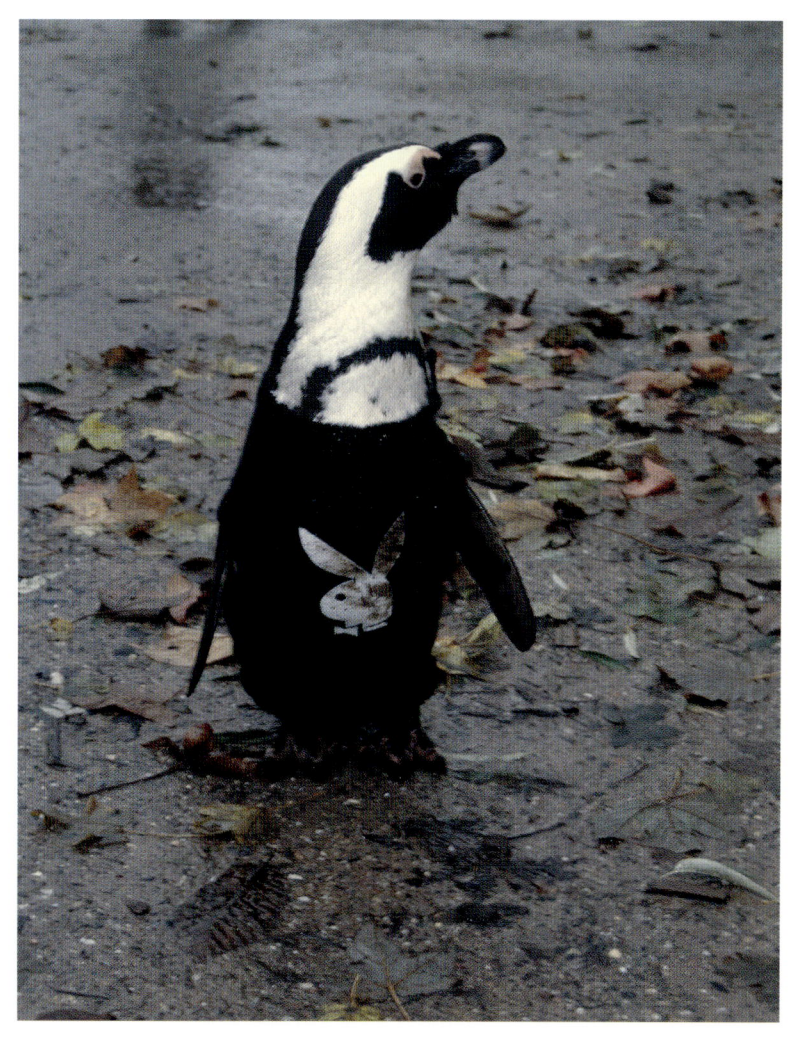
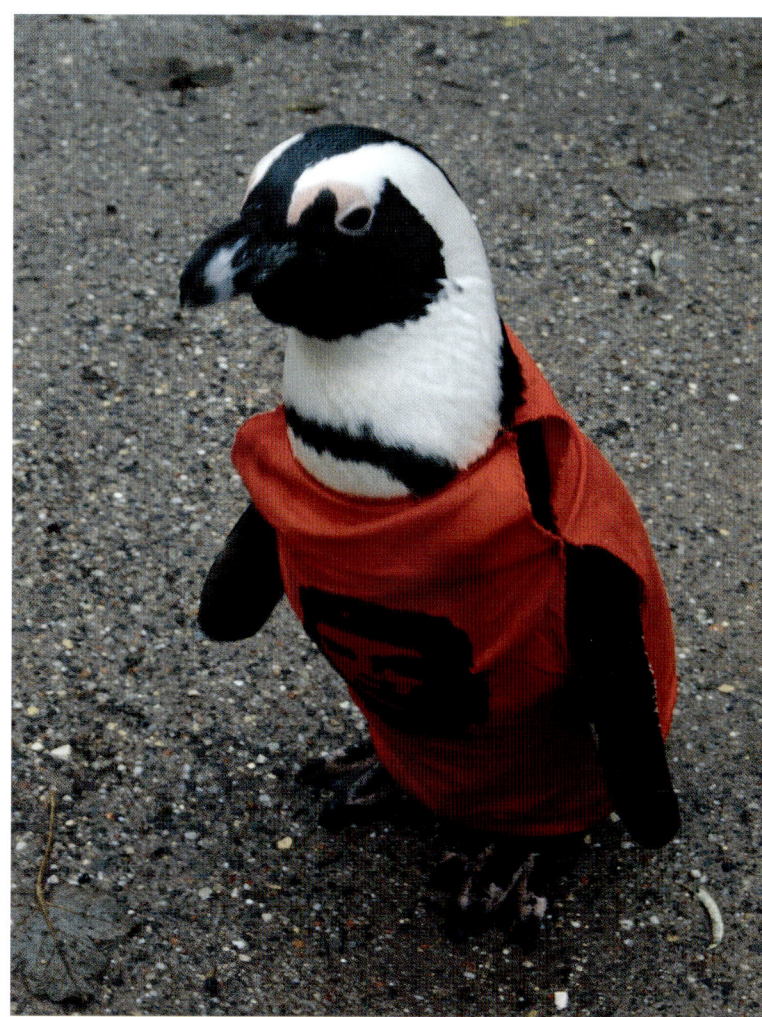
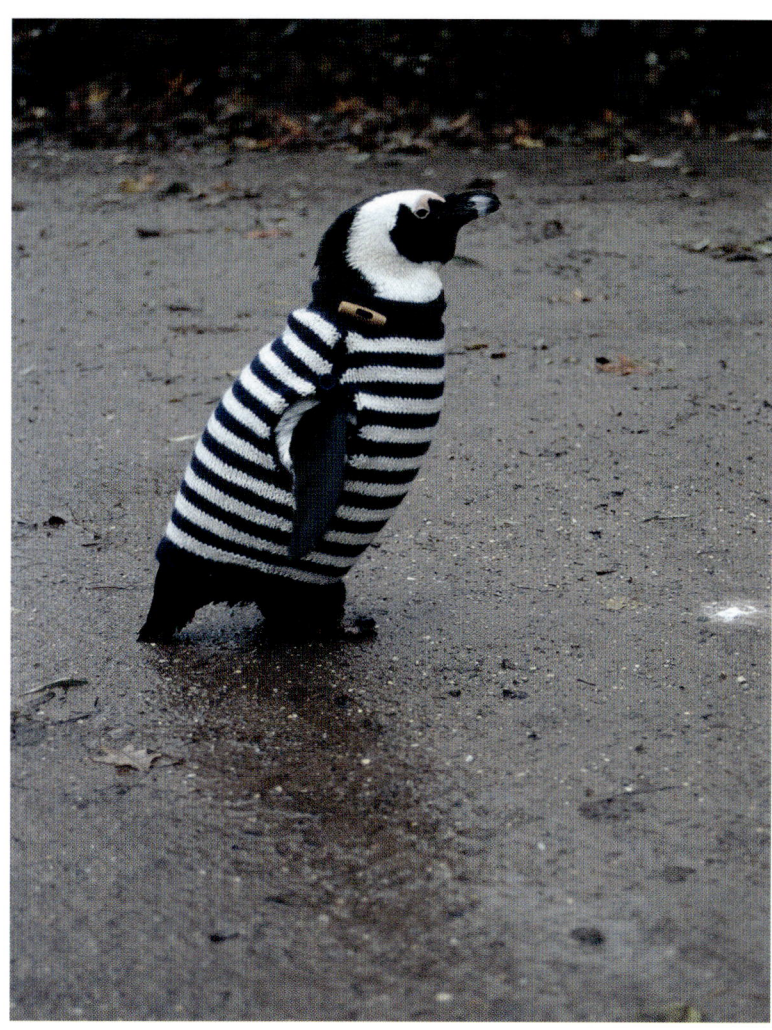
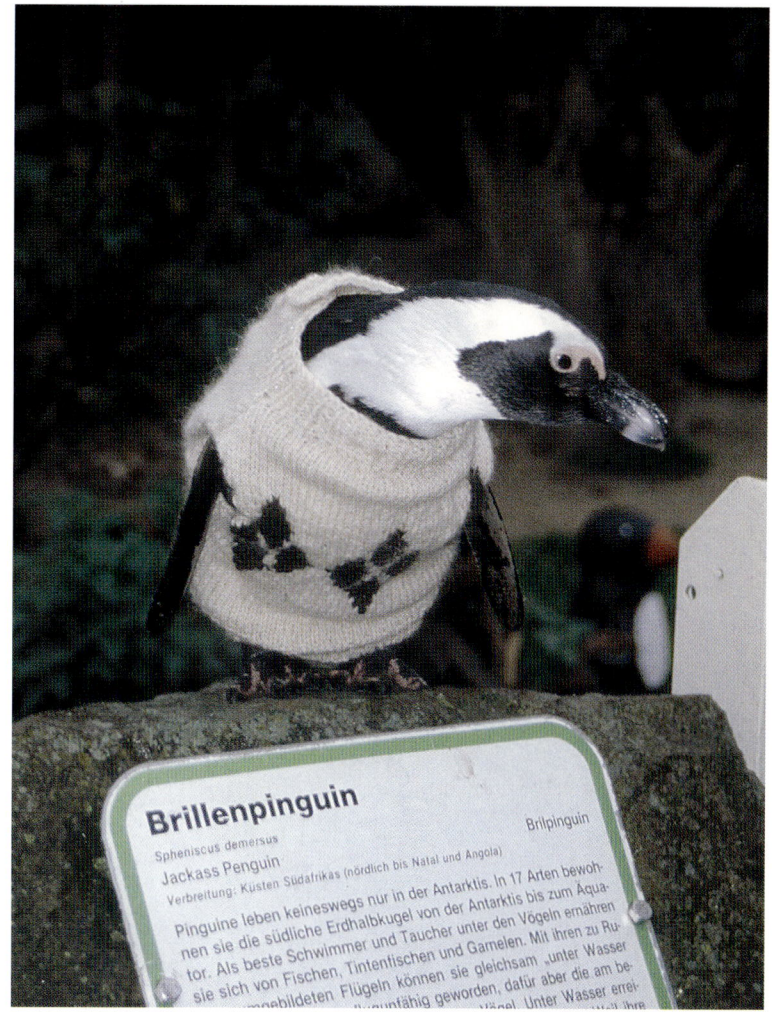

Brillenpinguin

Spheniscus demersus   Britpinguin

Jackass Penguin

Verbreitung: Küsten Südafrikas (nördlich bis Natal und Angola)

Pinguine leben keineswegs nur in der Antarktis. In 17 Arten bewoh-
nen sie die südliche Erdhalbkugel von der Antarktis bis zum Äqua-
tor. Als beste Schwimmer und Taucher unter den Vögeln ernähren
sie sich von Fischen, Tintenfischen und Garnelen. Mit ihren zu Ru-
... moebildeten Flügeln können sie gleichsam »unter Wasser
...unfähig geworden, dafür aber die am be-
... Vögel. Unter Wasser errei-

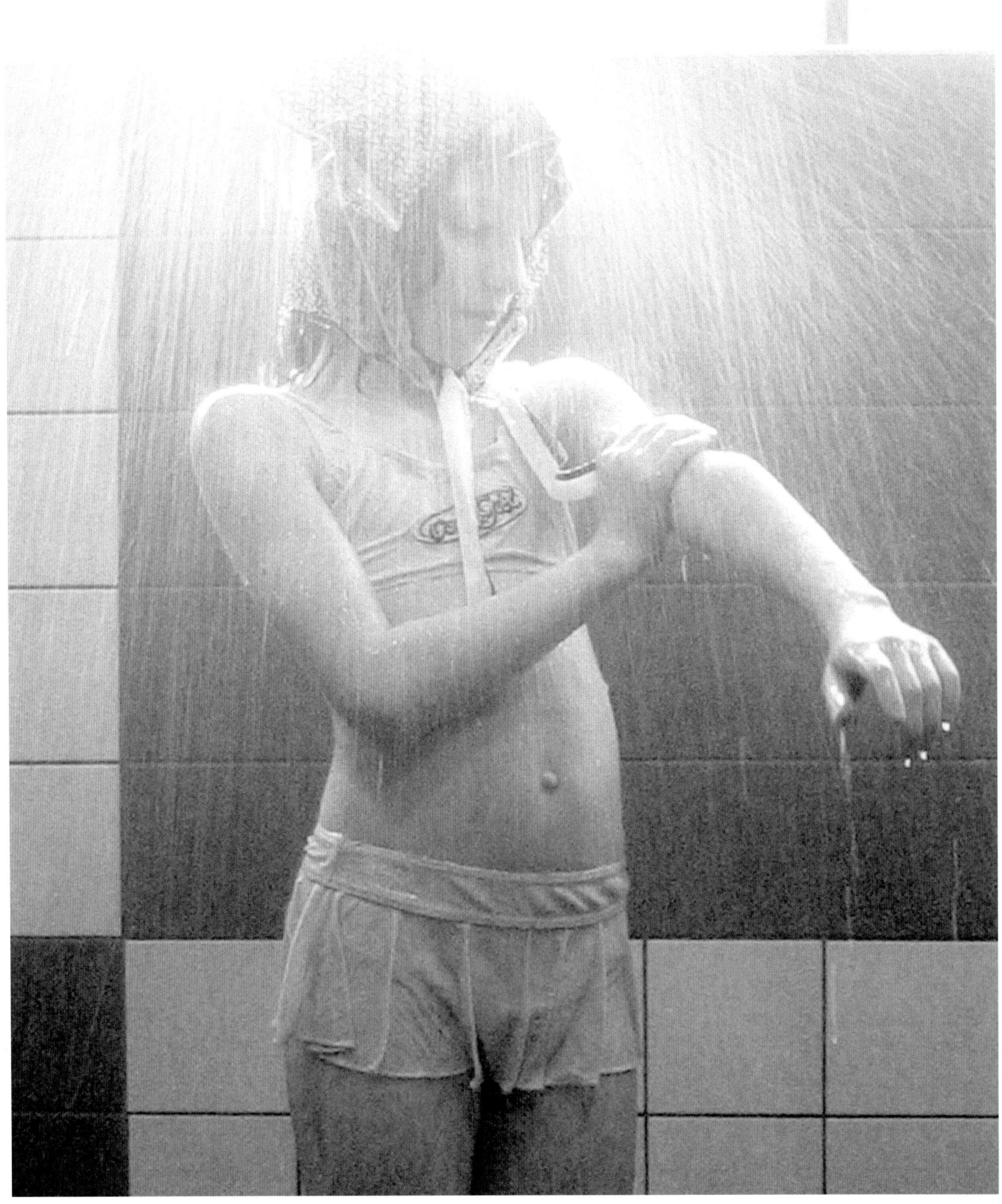

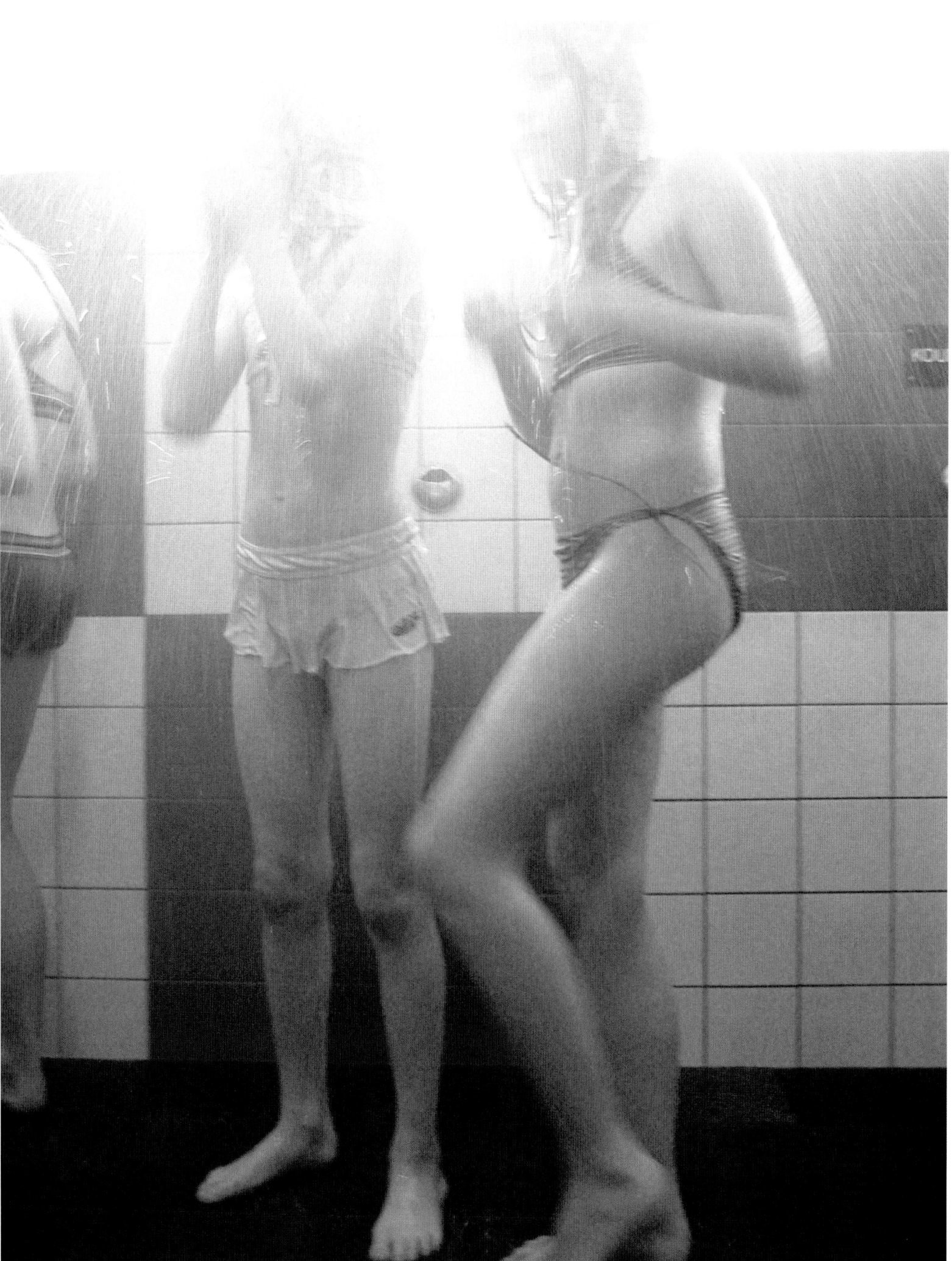

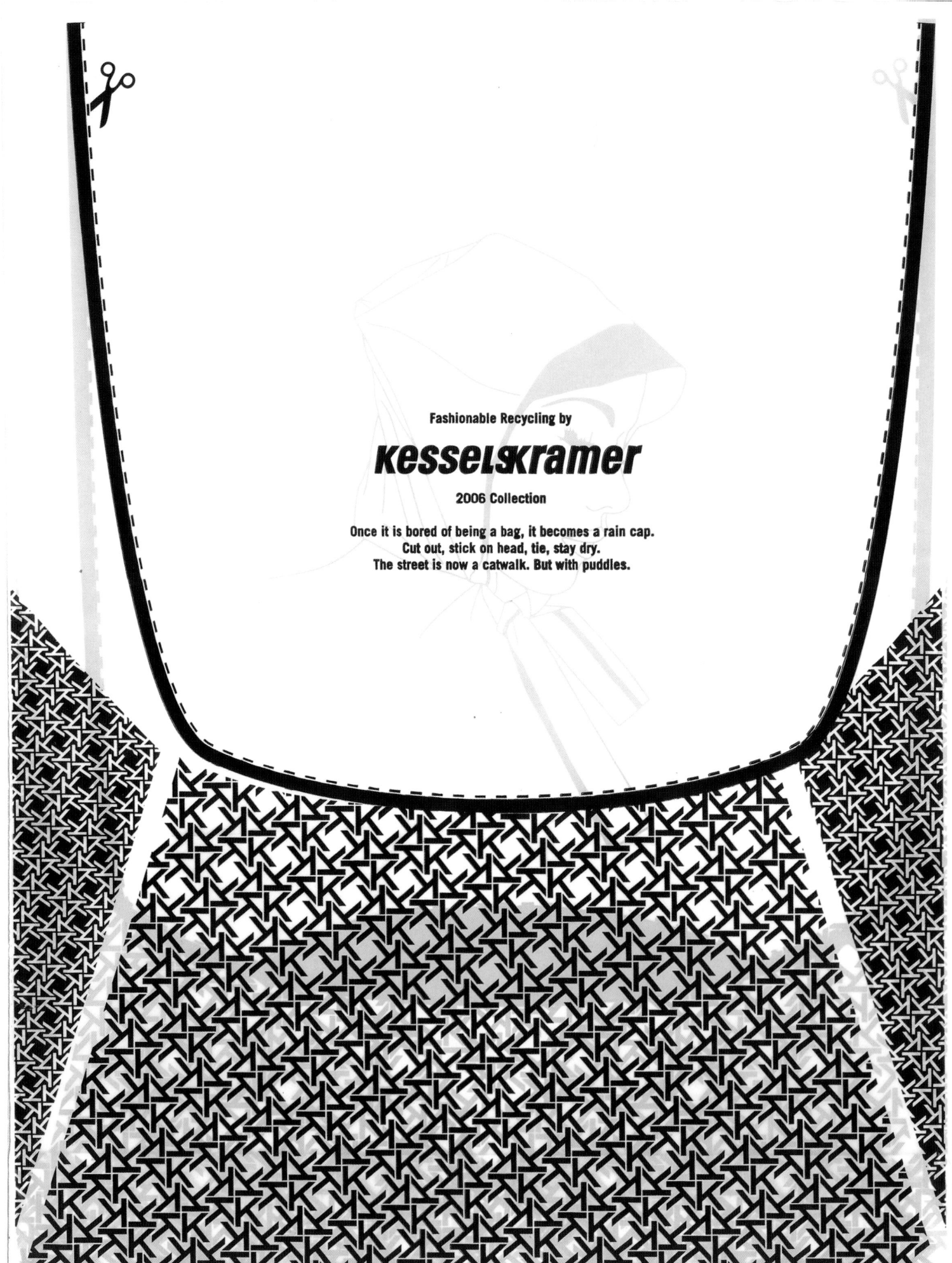

Fashionable Recycling by

kesselskramer

2006 Collection

Once it is bored of being a bag, it becomes a rain cap.
Cut out, stick on head, tie, stay dry.
The street is now a catwalk. But with puddles.

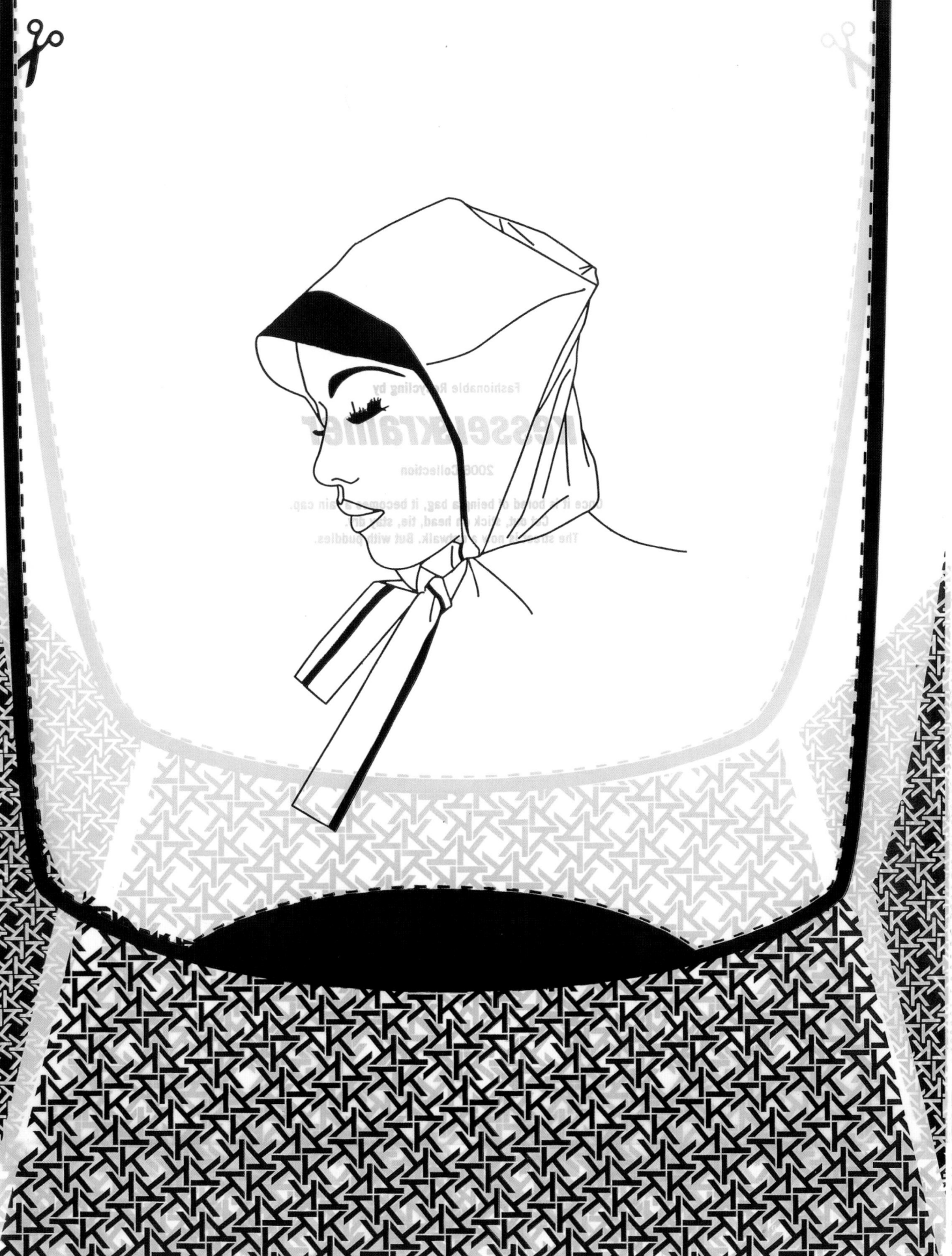

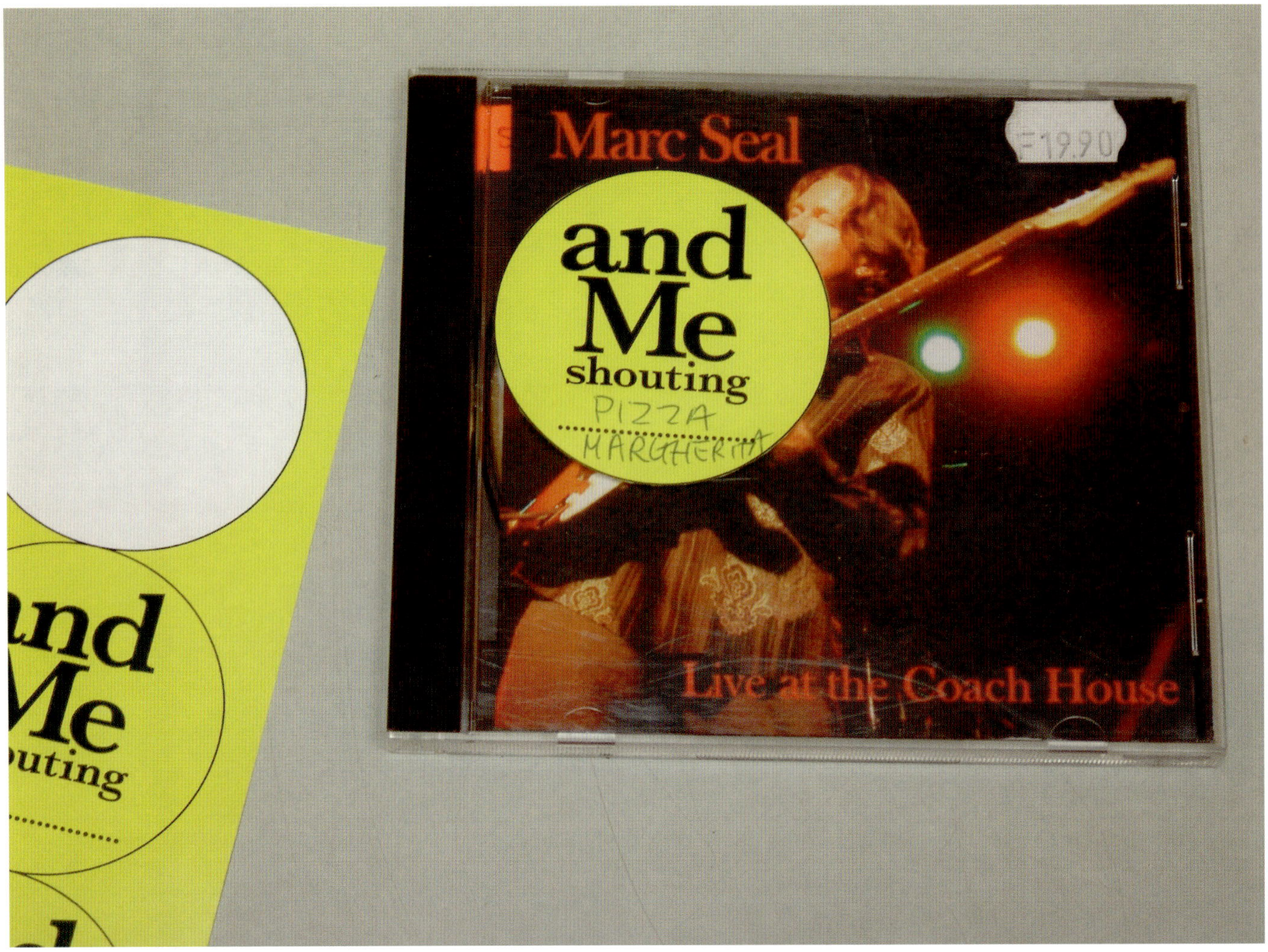
Marc Seal
F19,90
and
Me
shouting
PIZZA
MARGHERITA
Live at the Coach House

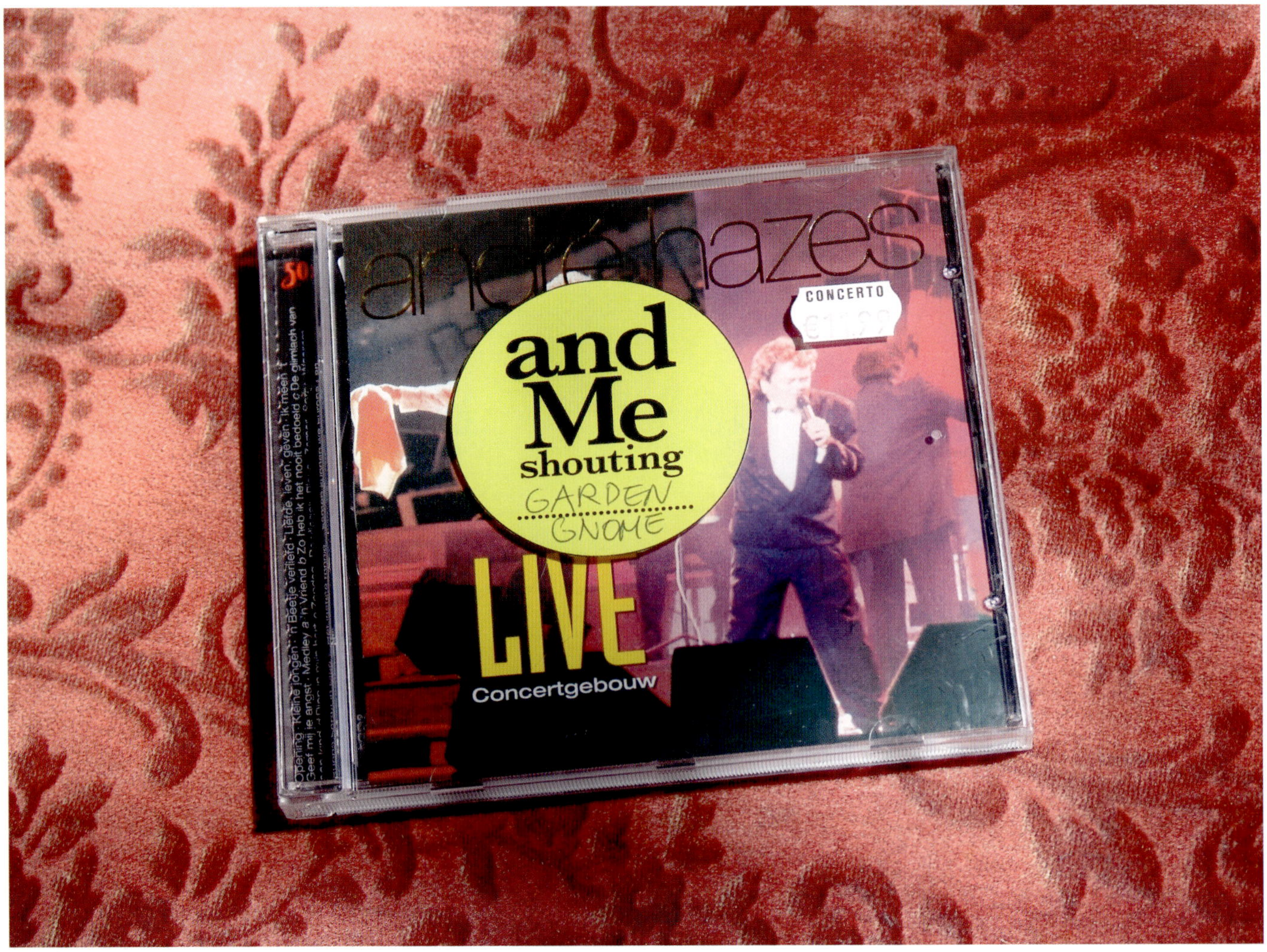
andré hazes
CONCERTO
and
Me
shouting
GARDEN
GNOME
LIVE
Concertgebouw

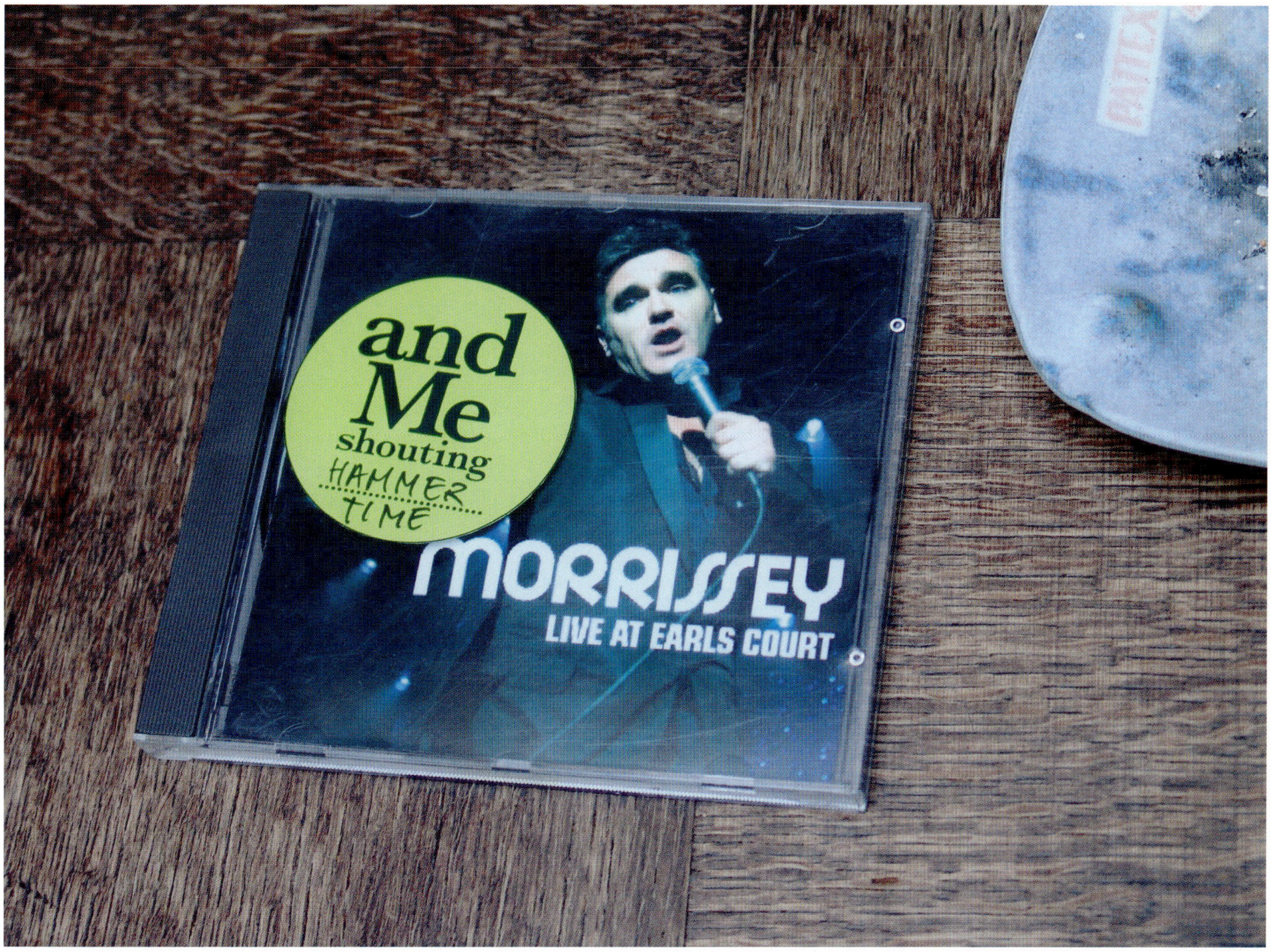
and Me shouting
HAMMER TIME
MORRISSEY
LIVE AT EARLS COURT

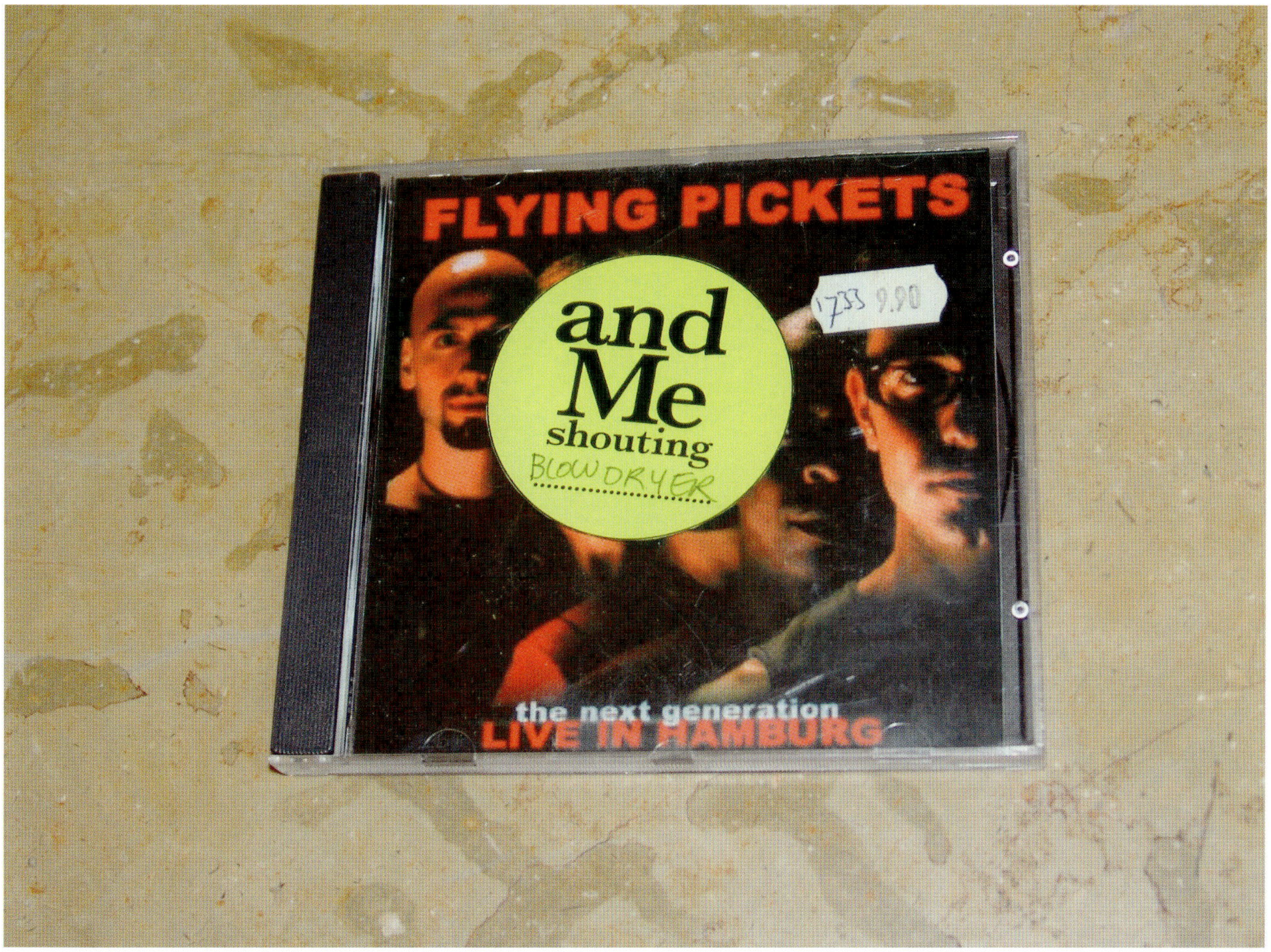
FLYING PICKETS
and Me shouting
BLOWDRYER
9.90
the next generation
LIVE IN HAMBURG

do is an initiative of:

KesselsKramer
Lauriergracht 39
1016 RG Amsterdam
The Netherlands
T +31 (0)20 5301060
F +31 (0)20 5301061
domail@dosurf.com
www.dosurf.com

Special thanks to Joanna van der Zanden for her tireless energy
and to all the people who have done and continue to do all over the planet.